THE NATIONAL
GEOGRAPHIC TRAVELER
JAPAN

THE NATIONAL GEOGRAPHIC TRAVELER

JAPAN

Nicholas Bornoff

Contents

How to use this guide 6–7 About the author 8
The regions 59–348 Travelwise 349–88
Index 389–97 Credits 398–99

Page 1: Child dressed for a festival at Meiji-jinju Shrine
Pages 2–3: Garden font and dipper in fall, tea garden in Kyoto
Left: High-rise buildings in Shinjuku, Tokyo

How to use this guide

See back flap for keys to text and map symbols

The *National Geographic Traveler* brings you the best of Japan in text, pictures, and maps. Divided into three main sections, the guide begins with an overview of history and culture. Following are ten regional chapters with featured sites selected by the author for their particular interest. Each chapter opens with its own contents list.

The regions and sites within the regions are arranged geographically. Some regions are further divided into smaller areas. A map introduces each region, highlighting the featured sites. Walks, plotted on their own maps, suggest routes for discovering an area. Features and sidebars give intriguing detail on history, culture, or contemporary life.

The final section, Travelwise, lists essential information for the traveler—pre-trip planning, getting around, emergencies, and a language guide—plus a selection of hotels, restaurants, shops, entertainment, and festivals.

To the best of our knowledge, all information is accurate as of the press date. However, it's always advisable to call ahead when possible.

Color coding

Each region is color coded for easy reference. Find the region you want on the map on the front flap, and look for the color flash at the top of the pages of the relevant chapter. Information in **Travelwise** is also color coded to each region.

Matsushima
- 153 B3

Visitor information
- Outside Matsushima-Kaigan Station
- 022/354-2263

Zuigan-ji Temple
- 91 Aza-chonai (7 mins. walk from Matsushima-Kaigan Station
- 022/354-2023
- $$

Visitor information

Practical information for most sites is given in the side column (see key to symbols on back flap). The map reference gives the page number of the map and grid reference. Other details are address, telephone number, days closed, entrance charge in a range from $ (under $4) to $$$$$ (over $25), and public transportation. Other sites have information in italics and parentheses in the text.

TRAVELWISE

Color-coded region name — **NORTHERN HONSHU (TOHOKU)**

Town name — **AOMORI**

Hotel name & price range — **AOMORI GRAND HOTEL $$$**

Address, telephone, & fax numbers — 1-1-23 SHIN-MACHI / TEL 0177/23-1011 / FAX 0177/34-0505

Brief description of hotel — Though somewhat old-fashioned, has good standards of service and comfort. Some rooms have sea views.

Hotel facilities & credit card details — 140 All major cards

Restaurant name & price range — **YAMAUTA $$**

Address & telephone number — 1-2-7 O-MACHI, HIROSAKI-SHI / TEL 0172/36-1835

Brief description of restaurant — The fare is *izakaya* style and the entertainment is provided by the owner, a famous *samisen* virtuoso.

Restaurant closures & credit card details — No credit cards

Hotel & restaurant prices

An explanation of the price bands used in entries is given in the Hotels & Restaurants section (on p. 360).

REGIONAL MAPS

Point of interest

Road number

Featured prefecture

Adjoining chapter

Prefecture

Important point of interest

Important featured town

- A locator map accompanies each regional map and shows the location of that region in the country.
- Adjacent regions are shown, each with a page reference.

WALKING TOURS

Featured site (in bold) on walk route

Direction of walk route

Red numbered bullets link site on map to descriptions in the text

Point of interest not on walk route

Start point

Building outline

Walk route

- An information box gives the starting and ending points, time and length of walk, and places not to be missed along the route.
- Where two walks are marked on the map, the second route is shown in orange.

METROPOLITAN MAPS

Map reference

Site of interest

Ward name

Place of interest

Walk start point

Point of interest

Featured site (in bold)

Neighborhood

- An overview of the metropolitan area of major cities.

THE NATIONAL GEOGRAPHIC TRAVELER

JAPAN

About the author

Born in London of Anglo-French parentage, Nicholas Bornoff was educated in both France and the United Kingdom. Fresh out of a Parisian film school in 1974, he worked as an assistant director on documentary movies for UNESCO in Indonesia, sparking his lasting fascination with the Far East. Five years later he moved to Japan and a job in a Tokyo advertising agency. Branching out into journalism, he worked as film critic for the *Japan Times* for nine years, during which he also contributed articles about contemporary Japanese arts and society to the *Far Eastern Economic Review, Asian Advertising & Marketing,* the *Tokyo Journal,* and other English-language magazines in the Asian region.

Bornoff's nonfiction survey, *Pink Samurai: Love, Marriage & Sex in Contemporary Japan,* was published to critical acclaim in 1991, the year he returned to Europe. Now making his home in London with his Japanese wife and young son, Bornoff still focuses mainly on Japan. He has written a book introducing Japan to schoolchildren, and his articles appear in *The Guardian* newspaper and many other publications in Europe and the United Kingdom.

History & culture

Ukiyo-e print depicting a warrior (Osaka school, 18th century)

Japan today

FIRST THERE IS JAPAN THE ARCHIPELAGO. IT'S A NARROW CHAIN ALONG THE Asian mainland stretching some 1,860 miles (2,994 km) from eastern Siberia down almost to Taiwan. North to south, Hokkaido, Honshu, Shikoku, and Kyushu are the four largest islands; the whole is administratively divided into 47 prefectures. Then there is Japan the concept. Chances are you're already familiar with the traditional icons—Buddhist temples, flower arrangements and gardens, the kimono, and martial arts. You've probably eaten sushi, played computer games, and either used or endured karaoke; you know that many of the products and components involved in your daily communication, entertainment, and transport are made in Japan. So most visitors pose themselves the question long before they get there: Which is the real Japan?

Everyone knows the hackneyed calendar image of snowcapped Fuji-san at cherry blossom time with the sleek bullet-train streaking past—perhaps with a kimono girl in the foreground. A Japanese invention, the image symbolizes how the Japanese see themselves. As they never tire of pointing out (along with the fact that they have four seasons), ancient arts, crafts, and traditions coexist in harmony with the cutting edge of modern technological civilization. As different as the composite parts may seem, they're *all* the real Japan. Quite happy with the coexistence of old, new, East, West, tradition, and change, the Japanese take for granted the contradictions and paradoxes that so often leave visitors bewildered. No country wears the old tourist brochure cliché "land of contrasts" at once quite so naturally and with so much style.

Perhaps it's not so surprising. Emerging during the 1860s from the isolation its rulers had enforced for 300 years, the Japanese made as much effort to modernize as they did to retain their cultural identity.

So the real Japan can be made a matter of personal preference; you can devise your itinerary accordingly. Multicultural Tokyo or bastions of culture and traditions like Kyoto; the older, quieter Japan off the beaten track in Northern and Western Honshu or Shikoku. Seventy-five percent of the land area is mountainous, much of it forested and volcanic; depending on the season you can hike, ski, enjoy the great outdoors, or the purely Japanese pleasure of the hot spring. Explore the rugged coast of the far north or the tropical islands of Okinawa-ken—nowhere is

very far from the sea. Whichever way you go, it will always be an encounter with one of the most fascinating countries and cultures in the world.

ECONOMY

Japan's economic miracle, emerging from the advantages of cheap labor and a low yen during the postwar period, saw exports increasing rapidly from inexpensive tin toys to quality goods. Transistor radios (a Japanese first) paved the way for cameras, electrical appliances, ships, steel, color televisions, and cars. With a phenomenal growth rate of 11 percent, Japan was already the world's second largest economy outside the Iron Curtain by 1967.

By devaluing the yen, accepting wage cuts, and redoubling their effort, the Japanese softened the impact of the oil crisis of 1973. Exports soared, pushing up a trade surplus that had started five years before. In 1979 the second oil crisis was dealt with in a similar way.

During the 1980s Japan's economy surpassed even that of the United States. Its formidable wealth was sustained by booming domestic financial and consumer markets, low interest rates, and soaring real estate values. Japanese fortunes swelled in what was called the "bubble economy." A huge overseas trade imbalance, however, prompted international currency markets to force up the yen/dollar exchange rate in 1985. *Endaka*—the high value yen—slowed exports and economic

Harmony between tradition and high-tech: a Japanese ideal

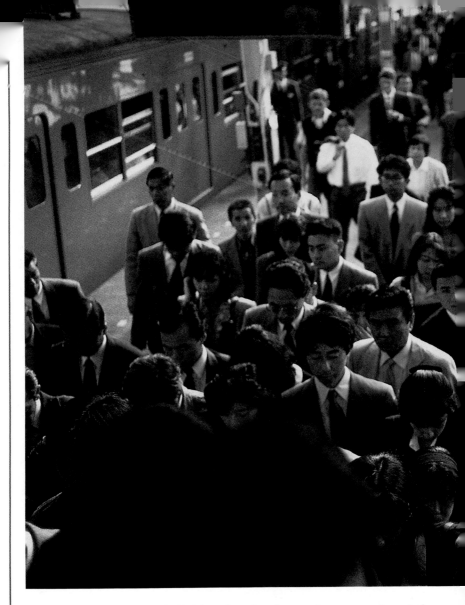

performance at home, but it also doubled the value of national savings and generated a spending spree on overseas property markets. The bubble continued to inflate.

In 1990, the value of Japan's overseas holdings plummeted; its stock market had lost almost half its value by the end of the year. In 1991 beleaguered Japanese banks raised interest rates to cover the loss—only exacerbating the growing problem of bad loans. The bubble burst.

Japan's economic recovery was increasingly hampered by recession in the Asia-Pacific region because of enormous investments in the area. As bad loans accumulated, bankruptcy became rife among the largest financial institutions during the 1990s.

The country's faltering economy has brought changes. During the 1980s the complex, tiered distribution system continued to fatten middlemen, keeping the benefits of cheaper imports from consumers. The 1990s saw direct imports becoming common practice, with the middlemen circumvented and retailers turning to discount marketing.

Japanese consumers are tightening their belts, but the country is only marginally cheaper for foreign visitors. Life insurance savings are astronomical, but no decisive measures have been taken to tap these formidable funds, suggesting that Japan's economy is likely to remain comparatively sluggish for the foreseeable future.

Tokyo's train and subway stations have the world's highest levels of commuter traffic.

THE WORLD OF WORK
The Japanese work ethic is legendary. According to the traditional pattern, the salaryman (male office worker) commutes for an average of two hours and spends up to ten hours in the office, six days a week. O.L.s (Office Ladies—female employees) work eight hours a day. When the office closes, the

salaryman is expected to join co-workers for a drink. His children will be asleep when he gets home; he spends only Sunday with them—if he can stay awake. He is entitled to two weeks' paid holiday a year; his sense of corporate loyalty will reduce this to around four days.

Until about ten years ago, the salaryman was employed for life; he ascended the corporate hierarchy according to age rather than ability. When he reached middle management in his 40s, his workload increased with

responsibilities toward both his seniors and his juniors. If he did not succumb first to *karoshi* —dropping dead from overwork—he went on to senior management and retirement at 60.

Although still typical, this scenario is currently being redefined. Recession has greatly changed working patterns in Japan. Promotion is based increasingly on ability; headhunting and job-changing are becoming much more common. Japan's targeted 40-hour work week remains some way off, though larger corporations and factories adopted the five-day week in the late 1980s, and most six-day firms concede a half-day on Saturday or work six days on alternate weeks.

The smaller the company, the greater the likelihood of a 48-hour week. The backbone of the economy, many small businesses are subcontractors manufacturing parts for larger ones. Competition remains sharp even during recession: If one firm cannot meet low prices and hard deadlines, another is ready and will-

Neon lights up evenings in the main drag of Shinjuku in Tokyo.

ing. Many such companies are sweatshops employing foreign labor, much of it illegal.

Unemployment, which still stood at 2.5 percent in 1991 as it had for decades, shot up in early 1998. Even at the start of the 21st century, the life employment system—though declining—keeps Japan's unemployment down to an enviably low 4.1 percent.

Changing fashions reflect greater independence for women.

MEN & WOMEN

Brought up to prefer the company of their own sex and frequently marrying by arrangement, men and women spend little time together. Outings in mixed company are increasing among the young, but restricted social life arising from work can reduce opportunities to meet members of the opposite sex.

Japan remains preponderantly male dominated. Only about a third of university students are women, and female postgraduates are few. Half the workforce is female, but only around 8 percent reach executive levels. The Equal Employment Opportunity Law, introduced in 1979 to encourage equality in the workplace for women, provides no sanctions for violations. Irrespective of qualifications, the work of female employees tends to be menial and subservient: They often wear uniforms while men do not, answer phones, and serve tea to male colleagues. They are hired at the age of 20 on lower pay than male counterparts and are expected to quit when they marry. Some conservative companies routinely hire only young women living with their parents and fire them after the age of 26, combining prim Confucian ideals with the excuse to pay their female employees less. Women have long rejoined the workforce after raising their family, but the number marrying later in order to pursue careers is still rising.

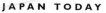

HOME & FAMILY

The old *ie* (household) system, male-dominated and based on seniority, was banned by the constitution in 1946—a factor contributing to the mass urban migration prompted by job opportunities. Traditionally, three generations lived under one roof, an extended family pattern now typical only in rural areas; more than

Couples now wed later, though the social pressure to marry remains strong.

77 percent of the population lives in towns, where the nuclear family is the norm. However, a falling birthrate poses the growing problem of a graying society. With care for the elderly woefully inadequate, extended households are slightly increasing again, but, thanks to generations living in separate apartments in the same building, with much greater independence and privacy for the occupants.

Home for the average one-child urban family is 2LDK (two bedrooms, living/dining/kitchen in one). Because of the lack of living space, the majority of Japanese—especially men—seek entertainment outside the home.

Male domination appears to survive in the modern home, where the oldest male takes his bath first and the youngest female last. When entertaining guests, a wife often serves food to them and her husband first, eating hers later.

Americans and Europeans are often shocked by the status of women in Japan. But if opposition to greater equality comes from male politicians, it also comes, paradoxically, from legions of women content to wield domestic power and unworried by the issue of image. The male TV show host's pretty female sidekick, nodding like an awed schoolgirl and agreeing with what he says, has more to do with public "face" than reality. In a country in which the toughness of women is proverbial, the fondly imagined Western icon of the meek and acquiescent Japanese woman is only a matter of manners. Japanese men, subjected to a routine placing greater pressure on them to conform, can sometimes seem more reserved and hidebound than women.

Inception day in kindergarten—the education rat-race starts early.

On the other hand, a Japanese woman's home is her castle. She manages household finances and makes decisions concerning children and their education, as well as about moving house. A husband brings his wages to her, and she gives him his pocket money: *kotozuke.*

Families living under the *ie* system often lived in extended families, making it convenient for family businesses. A woman used to become the property of her husband's family upon marriage, often severing ties with her own. Yet from feudal times, if his wife's family had no male heir, a husband occasionally entered her family and took its name. Blood has never been considered the quintessence of kinship in Japan, and even today men are "adopted" by families wanting a male heir.

Upbringing & education

Westerners are often said to grow out of the strictures of childhood into the relative freedom of adulthood, while in Japan the reverse is the case. Japanese children are generally indulged to a greater degree than Western counterparts. Spanking is frowned upon; a naughty child is usually threatened with either maternal abandonment or ridicule by others.

The vise starts tightening outside the home. During six years of elementary school

and three of high school, the pressures to conform to rules and group restraints tend to override individual aspirations. The high school workload before university entrance examinations is notorious; the *jiken jigoku* (examination hell) period leaves many children with about five hours' sleep a night. With at least double the homework of U.S. counterparts, children enroll in *juku* (cram schools) for up to three hours after school.

People in many Western countries look at Japanese education with misconceived awe, assuming that it underlies economic success. In fact, although the form was made to follow American patterns during the Occupation (1945–1952), little was done to alter the traditional content. Set out like questionnaires, Japanese exams dictate the rote learning of facts and figures, with neither essays nor anything else to encourage individual thinking. Failure to be admitted to the desired university causes great anguish in parents and pupils alike; those redoubling their efforts to succeed by studying at full-time cram schools outside the state education system are known as *ronin* (masterless samurai). The system is widely considered to be in dire need of an overhaul.

University—four halcyon years of comparative freedom before mounting the corporate

Though small, the average Japanese home boasts a wide array of audiovisual equipment.

treadmill—is widely regarded as a sinecure. Japanese companies train new recruits on the job and will often employ graduates on the strength of the prestige of the university they attended rather than their academic achievements. With mounting competition in the marketplace, however, the need for specialization is placing emphasis on university degrees.

LANGUAGE & WRITING

The origin of the Japanese language is unknown. Possibly related to the Ural-Altaic group, which includes Finnish, Mongolian, Turkish, and Korean, it is grammatically similar to Korean but shares almost no words. Despite Japan's adoption of many aspects of Chinese culture, including writing, the language is unrelated to Chinese. It may go back to the early inhabitants of Japan, such as the Ainu, but beyond a few words and place-names, the Ainu language appears unconnected to Japanese. There is some evidence of a distant relationship with Austronesian languages, such as those of Malaysia, Indonesia, and the Philippines, mainly through similarities in vowel sounds. The mystery continues to inspire theories.

A Latin-sounding A-E-I-O-U syllabary makes picking up a few words of Japanese easy, but learning to speak well is another matter. Instead of the subject-verb-object sentence order of most European languages, Japanese places the object first and the verb, which incorporates the subject, last. Speech is divided into familiar, informal, formal, and humble forms; men and women express themselves using different personal pronouns and synonyms appropriate to the context.

Japanese uses three alphabets—simultaneously. *Kanji,* or Chinese characters, were imported during the fifth century A.D.; of purely Japanese origin, the phonetic *hiragana* and *katakana* alphabets were adopted during the eighth century. Very simply, kanji characters are used for nouns, hiragana for turning them into adjectives and verbs, and katakana for rendering words of foreign origin. Widely used in contexts such as advertising, *romaji* (Roman characters) is virtually a fourth character set. There are too many homophones to make a single phonetic script viable (for instance, unless shown as a kanji character, *seki* could mean a dam, a cough, or a seat).

JAPANESE HOMES

When entering a Japanese home, the first-time visitor may be surprised at the indicators of a different lifestyle beginning in the entrance

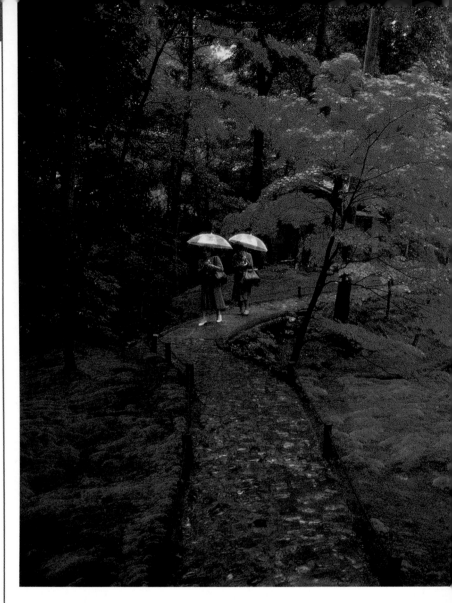

hall with rows of shoes on the floor, which is where you must leave yours. Shoes would quickly destroy the *tatami*—thick, densely woven rush mats found on at least one floor, even in modern apartments. For hygienic and practical reasons, no one enters a Japanese home in footwear—not even on carpets. You are usually provided with slippers; including ones specially for the toilet.

If the home is traditional, it will have *fusuma*, sliding room-dividers made of thick paper stretched on a wooden frame. It will also have *shoji*, wooden grids covered in thin white paper, that slide open and shut behind the windows.

A lot of homes have Western beds, but the traditional bedroom contains nothing at all. Stored away in a cupboard during the day-time, the futon mattresses and bedding are laid out on the floor at night. Chairs are now common in the dining area, but especially in a tatami room you will be entertained at a low

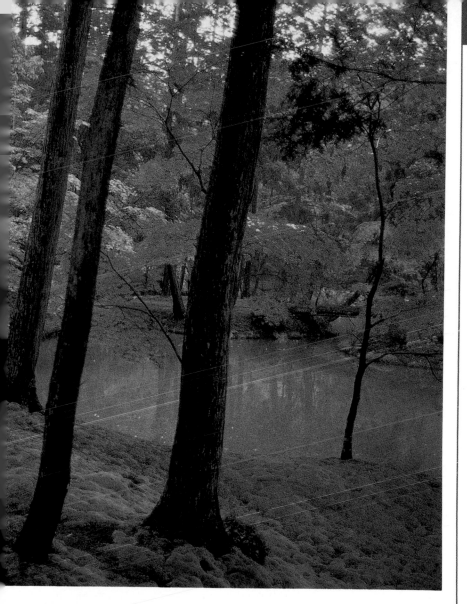

table while seated on cushions on the floor. In winter you will probably sit snugly at the *kotatsu*—a low table with a heater underneath and quilting around the sides.

The bath *(ofuro)* is usually a deep cube in which you sit and soak, but only once you are squeaky clean. You soap yourself first and rinse off using a tap, a shower, or water drawn from the bath in a bucket or bowl. You must never wash in the bath; others will use the water after you.

Visiting gardens is a favorite Japanese pastime whatever the weather.

Western toilets are common, as are astonishing high-tech variants such as the "Washlet," with heated seats and a jet of warm water providing fundamental cleaning at the press of a button. Equally common is the squat-toilet. The Japanese variety has a hood at one end and that is the way you face when you use it.

Boisterous and colorful, Shinto festivals are vital events on each community calendar.

RELIGION

It is facetiously said that the Japanese are born Shintoist, marry Christian, and are buried Buddhist. Although Buddhism and Shinto have countless devotees, Japan is increasingly materialistic and, for many, observances are a matter of form. Over 90 percent of the Japanese practice both Shinto (for the rites of baptism and marriage) and Buddhism, mainly reserved for funeral ceremonies. Christianity is practiced by a minority, but a Christian wedding presents a novel alternative to the standard Shinto ceremony.

Shinto

Shinto (the Way of the Gods) is the name given to various animistic belief systems of prehistoric origin that worship *kami*, the deities in all things. According to Shinto creation myths, the Japanese and their emperor descended from the gods. Many Shinto variants are based on the belief that all people become kami after death and that ancestors should be revered as such. The most sacred Shinto shrine is Ise-jingu (see pp. 259–60).

Very few entertain truly animist beliefs today, but Shinto thrives as a matter of ceremony. Colorful *matsuri* festivals are popular events, throughout the year, and some 70 million people visit shrines during celebrations at New Year. (See also pp. 244–45.)

Confucianism

The code of ethics based on the teachings of the Chinese sage Confucius (551–479 B.C.) preaches humility, frugality, generosity, and temperance. Founded on filial piety, respect for the aged, and the observance of tradition, it was applied to governmental principles in Japan from around the seventh century, but had little direct influence until after 1333, when new Chinese forms were adopted and adapted by the samurai. Confucianism served to reinforce social hierarchy and loyalty to these feudal lords and/or the emperor, according to the swing of the pendulum of power. It also dictated the *ie* system, a patriarchal hierarchy in the household (see p. 17).

Confucianism, with its emphasis on conformity, bolstered strict government control between 1603 and 1868, and was more recently exploited by nationalists. It is still taught in a diluted form in schools. Conformity remains a virtue, corporate loyalty overrides family life, and society remains deeply hierarchical. The Japanese love of social harmony and avoidance of confrontation are also legacies of Confucianism.

Zazen meditation demands composure, not dozing. Awakenings come from a monk's stick.

Buddhism

Holding that the remedy for the pain of existence lies in meditation, the elimination of desire, and awareness of the transience of life, the teachings of the Buddha (Enlightened One) made their way from India to Japan via China and Korea. Brought by Korean emissaries in the mid-sixth century A.D., Mahayana Buddhism was decreed a state religion by Prince Shotoku in 593. During ensuing centuries the Buddhist influence increased as various sects evolved.

Zen Buddhism was introduced from China during the Kamakura period (1185–1333). It discards scriptures and doctrine, believing that enlightenment is attainable only through individual effort, special meditation (*zazen*), and abstinence. Zen was greatly favored by the samurai and, like all other forms of Buddhism, has had a profound and permanent influence on the architecture, arts, and culture of Japan.

Christianity

Christianity was brought to Japan by Portuguese and Spanish friars, notably the Jesuit St. Francis Xavier, in the mid-16th century. It made much headway, especially in Kyushu, but its spread posed a political threat to the shoguns (military governors) who, fearful of European colonial objectives, repressed it with ruthless cruelty. With the closure of the country to outsiders in 1635, Christianity went underground; sects of secret Christians emerged from hiding when the shogunate fell in 1868. Persecution resumed but was stopped due to international pressure.

Although the faith remains largely alien, missionary work in the development of hospitals, in schools, and among the poor has earned Christianity respect. Today there are approximately 6,000 Christian churches in Japan and about one million Christians.

MANNERS & BEHAVIOR

In Japan harmony, achieved through conformity and consensus, is of utmost importance; it dictates masking private cares with public smiles, along with the individual's obligation to conform with the group. People abhor being conspicuous and are reluctant to air personal opinions. Japanese prefer the vague and understated to the forthright. Outspokenness is bad manners, and conversations find participants doing their utmost to agree with each other. Decisions are reached through consensus; in corporate contexts the process can take quite some time.

This underlies the difficulties sometimes encountered by foreigners doing business in Japan, as well as why Japanese politicians seem inarticulate abroad. (See also Travelwise, pp. 354–55.)

Below: Stand-up noodle stalls proliferate near most train stations in busy Japan.

FOOD & DRINK

Visitors will marvel at the gastronomic cornucopia awaiting them in Japan. Eating out ranks highest of all leisure activities among the Japanese—there are over 80,000 restaurants in Tokyo alone.

The great food staple is rice—so sacrosanct that the words for it when cooked, *gohan* and *meshi,* have simply come to mean a meal. Buckwheat noodles—*soba* and *udon*—are very popular. Necessity has led to many delicious discoveries in Japan, notably several different kinds of seaweed and vegetables that, formerly growing wild, include roots and ferns.

Meat-eating, forbidden by Buddhist law from the 10th century, became widespread with the introduction of beef from abroad during the late 19th century. Although most people eat meat today, a marked preference for fish prevails. Ubiquitous and a great source of protein, tofu (soybean curd) is prepared in so many different ways that some restaurants have made it a specialty.

Japanese cuisine is a feast for the eyes; presentation is its quintessence. Food is beautifully served on lacquered trays and attractive ceramics. The importance attached to freshness in Japan is akin to religious ritual. The Japanese consider that between the sea and your palate there should be only the chef's expertise with a knife. Despite the marvelous texture and delicate flavor of sashimi (raw fish), some non-Japanese find it a taste difficult to acquire. Meat too is sometimes thinly sliced and eaten raw.

Thirty years ago the Japanese consumed almost no milk or cheese, but today supermarket shelves sag beneath the weight of milk products and frozen pizza. Fast-food chains, both American (McDonald's, Pizza Hut, KFC) and domestic clones, proliferate. Quality Western cuisine, especially Italian and French, has many devotees and, after training in

Europe, many Japanese cooks, even in rural areas, produce high-quality Western food.

Mentioned as the standard tipple among the gods in Shinto myths, *sake* (rice wine) entered Japan along with rice culture in prehistoric times. "Sake" has come to mean alcoholic beverages in general; the specific Japanese word for rice wine is *nihonshu*. Good sake is as easy to drink as wine, but beware: The higher alcohol content packs a wicked hangover. This may explain why Japan's most popular beverage is beer. Several brands started brewing in the 1870s, among them Asahi, Kirin, and Ebisu. Hokkaido's Sapporo beer followed in the 1900s, though connoisseurs prefer the island's microbreweries. Pioneered in Japan by Suntory, whiskey remains a favorite after-work drink. Several prefectures

A *robatayaki* restaurant: Of all leisure activities in Japan, eating out tops the list.

produce wine; whites from Yamanashi are the most commendable, though the price of a really good bottle is exorbitant. As a domestic content of five percent is sufficient for qualification as "Japanese wine," local vin ordinaires consist mainly of imported bulk wines. Selling at the same price or less than a Japanese bottle, foreign wines are a better buy.

Shochu is a cheap grain distillate akin to vodka. Once the preferred liquor of hard-drinking laborers, it has become fashionable in recent years. It can be drunk hot *(oyuwari)* but is popular cold as *chu-hai* (shochu highball), mixed with ice, water, and lemon. It is often marketed in fruit-flavored cocktails.

THE LAND

Vegetation found in North America, Europe, and all but the tropical regions of Asia grows in Japan. Japanese cedar (cryptomeria) and species of maple, beech, and magnolia are cultivated over most of the country. Forests cover nearly 60 percent of the land. Chinquapin (chestnut), oak, and beech occur mainly in the forests of Honshu, and fir and silver fir in the subarctic climate of Hokkaido.

The vegetation in Kyushu and Okinawa takes a more tropical turn, with several varieties of palm, and flowers that north of Tokyo could bloom only in a hothouse. Trees admired for their spring blossoms, especially plum and cherry, are found over most of the country. Azaleas, hydrangeas, and irises are widespread during early summer, and chrysanthemums and red maples in the fall.

Many animals found in Honshu, Shikoku, and Kyushu reflect those of other areas in the temperate Northern Hemisphere. They include black bears, ferrets, wild boars, and birds such as pheasants, hawks, and cranes. Unique to Japan are the Japanese macaque, the giant salamander, and the *tanuki,* or raccoon dog, a small carnivorous mammal. Up in snowy Tohoku (Northern Honshu), the adaptable macaque has not only acquired a taste for wallowing in hot springs but has also developed thicker fur. Animals in subarctic Hokkaido include sables and red foxes, as well as the brown bear. Standing some 6 feet (2 m) and weighing 880 pounds (400 kg), it is about twice the size of its temperate Honshu counterpart. Okinawa has, in addition to animals commonly found in East Asia, unique species of its own: the Iriomote wildcat, Amami hare, and habu viper.

Frequently hunted or forced out of their natural habitats through urbanization, Japan's animal and bird populations have been steadily declining. Conservation measures adopted by the Environment Ministry during the 1980s protect 136 endangered species, but for the rare Iriomote wildcat (regarded by zoologists as a living fossil), it may already be too late.

RESOURCES

Up to the mid-20th century Japan was mainly agricultural, but after World War II farming declined dramatically with the mass migration from the countryside. Since the war, manufacturing, mining, and construction have continuously accounted for about a third of national industry. And booming retail and service industries account for some three-fifths of the total national industry.

Today, with their livelihoods increasingly threatened by imports, farmers are major recipients of government subsidies. Rice, the national staple for centuries, is overproduced (there are paddies even in suburban Tokyo). A traditional fondness for soybean products means that Japan imports more than 15 times the soybeans it produces. Eggs, poultry, and most vegetables are domestically produced, but half the country's fruit is imported. Dairy products, hardly consumed at all 50 years ago, are gaining ground; three-quarters are produced in Hokkaido, the rest imported. Hokkaido also produces a substantial amount of wheat, feeding a growing appetite for bread, but its crop represents only about one-seventh of the total consumed. The world's largest per capita consumer of fish and seafood supplies half of its demand with imports; Japan also imports half its meat, especially beef. Increases in imports generally may indicate change in consumer tastes but are mainly the result of economics: Many domestic products are more expensive than imported counterparts.

Japan's per capita consumption of wood is only 17 percent of the level in the United States—from its own forests, that is. Its notorious extravagance with wood and pulp products for everything ranging from houses to books—and a tendency to wrap almost everything in shops—is fueled by imports, notably from nations little concerned with the impact of deforestation on the global environment.

A major steel producer, Japan has to import iron. Having very few energy resources, its industry is highly dependent on overseas sources, especially for oil. Some headway is being made with research into greener, cleaner alternative-energy sources, but nuclear energy is a strong competitor—albeit with fairly widespread and vociferous public opposition. ■

Rice paddies form hillside terraces on the island of Shikoku.

History of Japan

STONE IMPLEMENTS FOUND IN JAPAN SHOW THAT PEOPLE WERE LIVING there before the Ice Age, when the islands were linked to the Asian mainland. However, the earliest recognizable culture is known as Jomon, after the method used for decorating pottery and figurines.

PREHISTORY

Jomon means "straw rope," and the era, which lasted from 10,000 B.C. to 300 B.C., gets its name from the use of rope to imprint wet clay. The Jomon people's origins are disputed, but it is known they were hunter-gatherers and fishermen; among them were the ancestors of the Ainu, a people of prehistoric Siberian origin now living on Hokkaido. During the millennium after 500 B.C., mainland migrants gradually pushed these tribes to the far north and came to outnumber them ten to one.

Meaning "early spring," the Yayoi period (300 B.C.–A.D. 300) is the era of the most important mass migrations, mainly of Koreans arriving in northern Kyushu. They brought iron and bronze and, most important, the cultivation of rice. The arrival of agriculture early during the Yayoi was the great determinant in shaping Japan. As farming spread, land ownership became the basis for the pecking order in the community; these changes in social structure paved the way for the feudal systems that would dominate in the future.

EARLY JAPAN
KOFUN (300–552)

During the Kofun (old tomb) period, rice cultivation was concentrated in the region that is now Kansai—probably the country described in fourth-century Chinese records as Yamato, ruled by Queen Himiko, a female shaman. The numerous burial mounds, some of enormous size, found on Honshu and Kyushu indicate that the Kofun era saw tribal headmen replaced by powerful chieftains ruling substantial areas.

Some of the larger burial mounds, typically shaped like a keyhole and surrounded by a moat, have yielded sophisticated artifacts, including *haniwa* (clay representations of animals, objects, and humans), bronze mirrors, armor, swords, and jewelry. The largest of all Kofun tombs, near Osaka, is thought to contain the remains of the fifth-century emperor Nintoku. To this day, however, the excavation of imperial tombs is forbidden.

ASUKA (552–710)

Named after Yamato's first capital, thought to be in the area of present-day Osaka and Nara, the Asuka period saw the accelerated adoption of Chinese culture. Introduced by visiting Korean statesmen during the mid-sixth century, Buddhism brought with it a cultural package including administration and bureaucracy, medicine, geomancy (like the Chinese *feng shui*, a belief in lucky and unlucky cardinal points), Confucianism, and writing.

The process intensified under the scholarly and devout Shotoku Taishi (574–622), prince regent of the ruling Soga family. His active exchanges with China prompted major political, educational, and ethical reforms—including Japan's first constitution, based on Confucian principles—and also brought more sophisticated architecture, sculpture, painting, music, and poetry. Shotoku sponsored the building of many temples in the Asuka area, including Horyu-ji (see p. 247).

Fierce rivalries followed Shotoku's death; his son was assassinated in 643, and the Soga rulers were ousted. Japan lost its foothold in Korea following a sea battle in 663, but exchanges with China continued. The new capital, Fujiwara (see p. 31), the first of three emulations of the great Chinese city of Ch'ang-an, was built south of Asuka in 694.

The Taika (Great Change) Reform, which followed the demise of the Soga, introduced the first legal and penal codes and implemented a system of regional governments. The emperor was established as the sacred figurehead he still remains.

The greatest example of a 4th-century "keyhole" tumulus—said to be the tomb of Emperor Nintoku near Mozu, Osaka-ken

The great hall of Todai-ji Temple houses a colossal statue of the Buddha.

NARA (710–794)

Heijo, a new, larger capital, was established just west of what is now Nara in 710 (see pp. 237–48). In the eighth century greater unification was achieved through a new network of main roads connecting provincial capitals, thus consolidating central government power. Buddhism made substantial headway under the pious Emperor Shomu (R.724–749), who built temples and monasteries—among them Nara's great Todai-ji Temple—in each province of his realm.

Centralized government came under threat from both the Buddhist clergy and clans controlling outlying districts. Prominent in the labyrinth of intrigue was the Fujiwara family, which rose through the astute marriages it arranged for its daughters. Koken, daughter of Shomu by a Fujiwara consort, succeeded him as empress in 749. Koken fostered Buddhism at the expense of temporal government, a failing that is thought to have prompted the banning of women from imperial succession for almost a thousand years. To sever the influence of the Buddhist priesthood over the state, the capital was moved again in 784 to Nagaoka, southwest of what is now Kyoto.

HEIAN (794–1185)

Conspiracies and assassinations spurred the emperor Kammu to move the capital again in 794, to a site 10 miles (16 km) northeast of Nagaoka. Heian-kyo—the capital of peace and

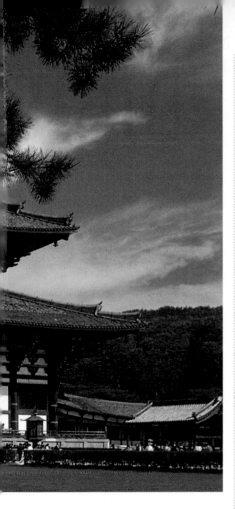

Genji. Splendidly dressed courtiers enlivened their languid existences with lavish ceremonies and the avid pursuit of the arts.

The ruling Fujiwara excelled more as aesthetes than politicians, and there was in fact much unrest. By the late tenth century the Buddhist monks on Mount Hiei (see p. 235) had degenerated into bandits sporadically staging devastating raids on the city. Fonder of dancing than defense, the army was notoriously ineffectual.

In the 12th century, provincial clans increasingly broke away from the Fujiwara. Threatened by the Taira (or Heike) clan during a dispute over imperial succession, the Fujiwara sought protection from the Minamoto (or Genji clan), but the latter was defeated when an army led by Taira Kiyomori (1118–1181) invaded Heian-kyo in 1156. Meting out executions for the first time in centuries, the Taira disposed of the Fujiwara courtiers and put emperors of their own on the throne.

The Minamoto took their revenge during the ensuing Heike War. The army raised by Minamoto Yoritomo (1147–1199), with his half-brother Yoshitsune (1159–1189) among its commanders (see p. 32), drove the Taira from the capital in 1180 and crushed them at the sea battle of Dannaura in 1185. Many survivors leaped into the water and drowned; among them perished the seven-year-old emperor Antoku.

tranquillity (later to become Kyoto)—was the grandest of all the copies of Ch'ang-an. The era was dominated by the Fujiwara family, which reached its zenith with Michinaga (966–1028), who married four daughters into the imperial line and successively placed two nephews and three grandsons on the throne.

Buddhism made great progress with new sects, notably the Tendai, which had greater appeal to commoners and became the state religion.

Exchanges with China ceased with the collapse of the T'ang dynasty in 907. Japanese culture now developed on its own. The arts and culture reached their apogee during Heian; literature flourished with diaries and the earliest novels in the world, notably the female courtier Murasaki Shikibu's *Tale of*

MEDIEVAL PERIOD
SAMURAI

In ancient Japan clan chieftains kept a tenuous hold on territories fraught with brigands, bands of warrior monks, and desperadoes of every description. Having had to raise armies to protect themselves (often from each other), some chieftains became immensely powerful—the forerunners of the great feudal lords. During the peaceful Heian era (794–1185) conflicts dwindled, but in the 12th century the fierce Heike wars broke out between the Taira and Minamoto clans. These inevitably favored the glorification of the warrior, and the protagonists have been enshrined ever since as the first manifestations of the samurai.

The great hero Minamoto Yoshitsune, who finally crushed the Taira in 1185, became a samurai paragon, but it was his brother Yoritomo who established the samurai as the ruling caste for the next 700 years.

The Kamakura period (this page) saw the establishment of *bushido* (the way of the warrior)—the samurai code of ethics, conduct, and strategy. Bushido dictated upholding the clan's honor even at the cost of individual annihilation, figuratively and literally. Glorifying self-sacrifice, it decreed absolute loyalty to the feudal lord. Atonement for any misconduct shaming the clan, which included defeat, demanded *seppuku* (or *hara-kiri*—belly slitting), a gruesome ritual involving self-disembowelment.

The ultimate goal of the warlords was national unification, achieved by the shoguns Oda Nobunaga (1534–1582), Toyotomi Hideyoshi (1536–1598), and Tokugawa Ieyasu (1542–1616). Although Nobunaga's adoption of firearms introduced by the Portuguese changed the style of warfare forever, the samurai never lost their reverence for the sword—which, like armor, displayed exquisite craftsmanship. During the 15th century, samurai attracted to Zen Buddhism for its austerity and self-discipline founded the principles of swordsmanship, archery, and martial arts on its concepts.

In the 17th century Confucian-inspired revisions of samurai codes permeated society with the introduction of a caste system headed by a military aristocracy (see p. 34). Provincial governors became the *daimyo* (great names), and to make sure they remained loyal, they were obliged to divide their time between Edo and their fiefdoms on alternate years, leaving their families behind in the capital as virtual hostages. Although there were no longer any wars to fight, the samurai held power until they were ousted in 1867 (see p. 36).

As with the Crusaders from Europe, the samurai evinced a brutality that has faded in the light of popular culture. Although they were certainly experts in martial arts, the *ninja*—mainly spies skilled at scaling castle walls during sieges—have been idealized out of all proportion. The samurai were often great knights, but unlike their medieval European counterparts, their regard for their womenfolk was nil. Confined to the inner recesses of the home, women were even forbidden to eat at the same table as men.

The samurai era saw the creation of magnificent castles and thriving castle cities, of the Noh theater (see pp. 46–47), the Zen garden (see p. 42 and 220–221), and the tea ceremony (see p. 42 and 225). Many a shogun, such as Ashikaga Yoshimitsu and Toyotomi Hideyoshi, was also a great patron of the arts. The master 17th-century swordsman Miyamoto Musashi (died 1645) was also a philosopher, writer, and master painter. Underlying some of the fanatical excesses of the Japanese army in World War II, the samurai legacy finds echoes in the national characteristics of forbearance and stoicism.

KAMAKURA (1185–1333)

Minamoto Yoshitsune, hounded by his brother Yoritomo, who had turned against him, committed suicide in 1189. Three years later Yoritomo established a new military capital in Kamakura, southwest of present-day Tokyo. The object was to keep the emperor apart from the affairs of state as a divine figurehead in Kyoto—a pattern that was to prevail for some 700 years. As self-appointed shogun (generalissimo), Yoritomo headed a military government known as the *bakufu*. Consisting of provincial governors served by *bushi* (warriors), it was a military dictatorship. When Yoritomo died in 1199, power was taken by his wife's family—the equally ruthless Hojo.

The Hojo established a branch of the bakufu in Kyoto, tightening their grip on the imperial court. Resistance from the court and its provincial allies was crushed during the Jokyu War of 1221, and the Hojo gained direct control over the imperial line.

Later in the 13th century the Mongol emperor Kublai Khan, whose empire embraced all Asia, turned his attentions to Japan. He reached Hakata, Kyushu (see p. 318), in 1274, but his fleet was repelled, thanks largely to a storm at sea. In 1281 Kublai Khan redoubled his efforts with a massive armada of over a thousand ships and 140,000 men. As he neared the Kyushu coast, nature intervened again: A raging typhoon destroyed Kublai Khan's fleet. The Japanese called these fortuitous storms *kamikaze*—the wind of the gods—the name adopted by suicide pilots during World War II.

The Hojo, bankrupted by the preparations for the Mongol Wars, lost popular support. They were driven from Kyoto in 1333 by an army raised by the exiled emperor Godaigo, who exploited growing discontent to restore his power.

Although it was intensely militaristic, the Kamakura era produced many beautiful temples and outstanding works of art. Great castles such as those of Osaka and Himeji were built; swords and armor were exquisitely fashioned and decorated. The age saw the establishment of further Buddhist sects—especially Zen, which was to become a permanent influence on culture and the arts.

MUROMACHI—ASHIKAGA SHOGUNATE (1333–1573)

A poor politician, Emperor Godaigo levied unpopular taxes to support his lavish lifestyle; his brief reign ended when the shogun Ashikaga Takauji (1305–1358) sent him back into exile. The military government moved to the Muromachi district of Kyoto. When Godaigo set up a rival government, known as the Southern Court, in the mountains of Yoshino, south of Nara, Takauji founded the Northern Court in 1336 with handpicked emperors of his own. The rival imperial courts continued for more than 50 years until reunited by the shogun Ashikaga Yoshimitsu (1358–1408) in 1392.

Probably the greatest of the Ashikaga shoguns, Yoshimitsu substantially increased both financial and cultural assets in Japan by accelerating trade with China. He is renowned for nurturing the Noh theater (see pp. 46–47), which reached its apogee under his patronage.

Culture flourished during the Muromachi period. Chinese art, especially ceramics and painting, was widely collected and influenced Japanese culture. The greatest cultural innovations emerged from Zen Buddhism, which was increasingly adopted by the samurai. For all its strife, the Muromachi was an era of great progress. Ports and castle towns thrived; farming and industry prospered.

By the reign of the decadent Yoshimasa (1436–1490), the eighth Ashikaga shogun, the country was falling apart. Provincial warlords came to the fore, and feudal clans such as the Hosokawa undermined the government; many

regions became virtually autonomous. Fanned by a dispute over Yoshimasa's succession, conflict culminated in the Onin War (1467–1477), during which Kyoto was burned to the ground. The war was inconclusive and merely heralded the Sengoku Jidai—the century-long era of Warring States. The enfeebled Ashikaga shoguns remained in Kyoto despite their

A suit of samurai armor

successive domination by other clans, a situation remedied only with the arrival of Oda Nobunaga (1534–1582), a unifying leader.

Nobunaga began his sudden rise to power by crushing the Inagawa clan's bid to invade Kyoto in 1560. Eight years later he invaded the city himself, temporarily restoring power to the Ashikaga shogun Yoshiaki before removing him and closing down the dynasty in 1573.

The Christian century

Three Portuguese sailors from a vessel run aground on Tanegashima, Kyushu, in 1543 were the first Europeans to land in Japan. They brought muskets, which were copied by Japanese swordsmiths within months; in 1549 Nobunaga ordered 500 for his army.

Merchants paved the way for Portuguese and Spanish missionaries, notably St. Francis Xavier, who landed in Kyushu in 1549. By the end of the century missionaries had converted 150,000 Japanese. Initially welcome as a buffer between a shaky state and militarizing Buddhist sects, Japanese Christians were soon seen as a threat. Over the next century, clampdowns on Christianity escalated, with vicious persecution culminating in a total ban and the expulsion of missionaries. During the Shimbara Rebellion (1637–1638), 37,000 people, mainly Christians, were massacred.

AZUCHI-MOMOYAMA (1573–1603)

Nobunaga incorporated 3,000 musketeers into his army to wipe out the troops of warlord Takeda Yoshiaki at Nagashino in 1575. After building a colossal castle at Azuchi, Nobunaga controlled most of the country until 1582, when, betrayed by one of his own generals and ambushed in Kyoto, he committed seppuku.

Nobunaga's avenger, Toyotomi Hideyoshi (1536–1598), conquered eastern Japan in 1590. To secure dominion over the entire country, he conducted a land survey to streamline taxation and forbade peasants to carry arms. Hideyoshi was fond of the arts. The Kano school of painting (see p. 51) burgeoned under his patronage, and the aesthetic pursuit of the tea ceremony flourished during his reign—but he was as ruthless as any military despot.

In 1592 Hideyoshi rashly staged an invasion of Korea. Undaunted by its disastrous failure, he launched a second attempt in 1598; interrupted by his death, it was abandoned. Before he died, Hideyoshi entrusted guardianship of his son, Hideyori, to Tokugawa Ieyasu (1543–1616), a trusted ally.

Territorial rivalry raged again after Hideyoshi's death. Wanting unified Japan for himself, Ieyasu crushed all his opponents, including Hideyori's followers. Raising a formidable army with four leading provincial warlords, he won the decisive Battle of Sekigahara on October 20, 1600, and founded the military dynasty that was to rule the country for 268 years.

EDO PERIOD (1603–1868)

Ieyasu considered Kyoto to be a powerless imperial realm and sought a spot for a new, unassailable military capital. He chose the old

outpost of Edo, near Kamakura; it was a strategic base with access to the rest of the country and had the right topography for developing a port. Having proclaimed himself shogun of all Japan, in 1603 he founded Edo (later to be renamed Tokyo) as the new capital city.

The last of the regime's opponents, Toyotomi Hideyoshi's son Hideyori, committed seppuku after the year-long siege of Osaka castle in 1615. Ieyasu died the following year. His legacy of laws governing society and national administration secured unprecedented national stability.

A social hierarchy placed samurai at the top, followed by farmers, artisans, and merchants. Actors, artists, entertainers, and licensed prostitutes were classless. Beneath them were social outcasts and criminals.

From Edo the shogun ruled over a country of fiefdoms governed by the daimyo in his service.

In 1635 the country's doors were officially closed. No citizen was allowed out of or back into Japan—on pain of death. The only visitors were the Chinese; the only Europeans allowed to trade were the Dutch, from the tiny island of Dejima in Nagasaki Bay.

The rise of the townsman

With a population of over a million by the middle of the 18th century, Edo was the largest city on Earth. Commerce, considered beneath the dignity of the ruling caste, was the preserve of merchants, and merchant princes came to outnumber ten to one samurai with comparable wealth. As money

Sparkling Himeji-jo Castle is the grandest and most beautiful of the handful of authentic samurai castles still standing.

swung the balance of power, the bakufu hit back at intervals with Confucian reforms decreeing sumptuary laws. Ostentatious trappings of wealth were forbidden or confiscated, but to little avail.

Edo's famous Yoshiwara (red light district) moved east after the great Meireki fire of 1657. By the prosperous Genroku era (1688–1704), the heyday of Edo, the pleasure quarters in major cities were flourishing as the *ukiyo*—the Floating World. The home of geisha and courtesans, it formed the hub of an entire popular culture, including fashion, literature, Kabuki theater (see pp. 47–49), and graphic art.

During the Edo period, the arts flourished, boosted by extensive patronage and the mass production of books and woodblock prints. With widespread education, some 40 percent of the population was literate.

"The black ships"

A four-year famine culminated in insurrection in Osaka in 1837. Similar rioting had once been easily quashed, but the bakufu, by now impoverished and politically diminished, barely won the day.

During the 1840s the United States had twice made vain requests for a Japanese port of call on the long trade route between Shanghai and California. In 1853 Commodore Matthew Perry steamed into Edo Bay with his three vessels, which the Japanese refer to as "the black ships." The visitors' tone was cordial but the message clear: Swords and rusty muskets would be no match for modern weapons. After the signature of the Kanagawa Treaty between the United States and Japan when Perry returned a year later, treaty ports (open to foreign trade) were established in 1859 and the doors of the country creaked open.

The balance of provincial power was shifting between the daimyo and away from the ruling bakufu. The great southwestern clans of Satsuma, Tosa, and Choshu rose to prominence; the armies sent by the enfeebled shogunate to repress them in 1866 were defeated. As civil unrest escalated all over Japan, the clans united to overthrow the old samurai regime and restore the emperor to power. Following a coup d'état with comparatively little bloodshed, the Tokugawa shogunate fell in 1867. The last shogun, Yoshinobu, staged a futile attempt to attack Kyoto, but following the defeat of his samurai troops, Edo was captured by the armies of the clan alliance.

MEIJI (1868–1912)
Enlightenment

In April 1868 the 16-year-old emperor Mutsuhito moved from Kyoto to Edo, which was renamed Tokyo—the Eastern Capital. The new era was called the Meiji (Enlightenment), and the return of imperial rule is known as the Meiji Restoration.

The new Meiji rulers, mainly Satsuma and Choshu clansmen, instituted rapid and radical changes. Abolishing the old samurai caste system and prohibiting the carrying of swords, they adopted the solar calendar and introduced compulsory education and military service. As American and European merchants, missionaries, and advisers flocked into Japan, legions of young Japanese went abroad to learn about Western civilization.

Following construction of a railroad between Tokyo and Yokohama in 1872, Tokyo and other cities began sprouting Western-style buildings. Modernization hurtled ahead with mining operations, heavy industry, and factories; mass production turned textiles into a major export. In 1873 a criminal code of French origin was adopted, along with German systems of administration. Western dress became usual working-day attire for men in corporate and government offices.

Satsuma clansman Saigo Takamori, one of the architects of the Meiji Restoration, feared that Westernization was undermining Japan. This last samurai headed 40,000 insurgents in Kyushu during the Satsuma Rebellion in 1877; when defeated, he committed suicide.

Rifts within the government led to the establishment of party politics. Government leader Okubo Toshimichi was assassinated in 1881, and Ito Hirobumi became Japan's first prime minister in 1885. The Meiji Constitution he drafted was approved by the emperor in 1889, setting up a system of government that survived until 1945.

The Emperor was revered as the paramount figure of the era, although his real power was debatable. A legacy from the Edo period, nationalist ideology was revived and became a basis for emperor-worship. The introduction of Shinto as the official national religion was designed to eliminate Buddhist political influence, and succeeded in severely curtailing Buddhism after 1870. Affirming the divine lineage of the emperor and the Japanese, seventh-century Shinto myths were taught as historical truth in schools—with dire consequences in the next century.

Expansion

Colonial expansion was one of the hallmarks of industrialized nations in the late 19th

U.S. ships escorted from Edo Bay in 1846, several years before Commodore Perry's intervention.

century; Japan turned to empire-building to join their ranks. China eyed Korea, but the Japanese invaded it first in 1894. Losing the ensuing Sino-Japanese War, China was forced to cede Taiwan and the Liaodang Peninsula on the mainland to Japan. Germany, France, and Russia, however, prevented Japan from claiming its gains on the Chinese mainland.

In 1900 Japan's key role in releasing thousands of foreign hostages in Peking (Beijing) during the Boxer Rebellion enhanced its status in the West. Wary of Germany's colonial maneuvers, the British sought a strong Pacific ally; the Anglo-Japanese Alliance was signed in 1902. In 1904 Japan astonished the world when its British-trained navy annihilated the Russian fleet. Deadlocked on land, the Russo-Japanese War ended with the intervention of Theodore Roosevelt and the signing of the Portsmouth Treaty in 1905.

The Japanese tightened their grip on Korea, forcing the king's abdication and installing Ito Hirobumi as governor. Following the latter's assassination by a Korean patriot in 1909, Japan annexed the country in 1910, triggering resentment that is only gradually abating today.

With the death of the emperor in 1912, a momentous era came to an end. During Meiji, Western culture had a deep impact on Japanese artistic and literary trends, sometimes to the detriment of traditional arts. The zeal for modernism caused many samurai buildings, notably castles, to be destroyed. Endorsed by imperial approval, the Kabuki (see pp. 47–49) became respectable and Western-style drama took root. By the end of the era Japan was producing its own movies.

TAISHO (1912–1926)

Taisho means "Great Righteousness" but, being mentally impaired, its emperor was unable to make public appearances. Crown Prince Hirohito (1901–1989) became regent in 1921.

Japan sided with the Allies in World War I and seized East Asian and Pacific territories from Germany, including Changdong in China. In 1920 Japan joined the League of Nations and in 1922 the Washington Naval Conference accorded greater power to the Japanese in the Pacific, against British objections. The Anglo-Japanese Alliance was dissolved, but friendship between the two nations was undented.

Democratic aspirations colored Japanese politics during the 1920s. It was a time of socio-political ferment, when Japan saw the introduction of a wealth of concepts and ideologies from overseas, including socialism, communism, labor unions, campaigns for women's suffrage, and student movements. Despite the woeful gap between urban rich and rural poor, the early Taisho period is still regarded as a golden age of emerging democracy—until tolerance was swamped by rising nationalism.

Emperor Hirohito (1901–1989) reigned for 63 eventful years.

World War I triggered an industrial boom, but recession and inflation followed. Cheaper rice was imported, sparking anger among farmers and leading to civil unrest, which culminated in the Rice Riots of 1918.

The Taisho governments never lived up to their liberal ideals. Those calling the tune belonged to the same oligarchy that had ruled during Meiji: a conservative aristocracy, nationalistic politicians, and big business; the huge corporations thrived on militarization.

Calamity struck in 1923: The Great Kanto Earthquake reduced Tokyo and Yokohama to rubble, killing 140,000 and destroying some three million homes. The impact on the economy was equally catastrophic.

The Taisho emperor died in 1925. The year brought good news with the right to vote for all men over 25, and bad news with

the imposition by nationalists of the Peace Preservation Law. This spawned the increasingly virulent repression of communists and dissidents and a special police division to deal with "dangerous thoughts."

Taisho was at the same time an age of intense intellectual activity, producing legions of new writers and thinkers. *Moga* (modern girl) and *mobo* (modern boy) reveled in the Roaring Twenties. Western trends and fashions made deeper inroads—but not for long. Much as in Weimar Germany, the party was to end with the rise of ultranationalism.

SHOWA (1926–1989)
The dark valley

Crown Prince Hirohito became emperor in 1926. The era name was Showa, meaning "Enlightened Harmony," something that was to be a long time coming. The country was sinking rapidly into what the Japanese now call *kurai tanima*—the dark valley.

The economic afflictions of the Taisho era worsened with the Wall Street Crash of 1929. Japanese exports plummeted; unemployment soared. A growing number of nationalists advocated exerting greater control in Asia. Now that the voices of liberals had been silenced in crackdowns, the notion met with little opposition. Out in the hungry countryside, rightist societies, militaristic youth groups, and patriotic farmers' associations proliferated as ultranationalism rapidly gained ground.

During an international conference in London in 1930, Japanese government representatives signed a treaty reducing Japan's armaments, but it infuriated army chiefs of staff and was nullified in Japan. The prime minister was assassinated by a right-wing fanatic the same year.

In 1931 the Japanese army staged the sabotage of a railroad under its protection in Guangdong, China. The fabrication provided a pretext to attack Chinese troops and overrun Manchuria, which fell under Japanese rule as Manchukuo. Condemned by all world powers, the action was also opposed by Japanese Prime Minister Inukai Tsuyoshi, who was murdered in 1932.

Faced with international opprobrium, Japan withdrew from the League of Nations in 1933. Ultranationalism, resentful in its isolation, became more focused. Efforts were made to purge Japan of foreign concepts and words; regressing to nationalistic Meiji-era emperor worship, education promulgated historical disinformation (mythical emperors and warriors were presented as fact) and the glorification of the Japanese race.

By 1942 Japan had invaded almost the whole of Southeast Asia. The same year its navy was drastically battered during the Battle of Midway, which turned the tide. Fanaticism sent young men on mainly futile suicide missions as human bombs. Civilians and soldiers were soon almost starving, but the war effort pressed on relentlessly. Taken by U.S. forces in

The Pacific War

In 1936 Japan signed the Anti-Comintern Pact, allying it to fascist Italy and Nazi Germany. Its aggression in China reached a climax in 1937 with the taking of Nanking, during which some 200,000 civilians were savagely massacred. The military forced the government to pass the National Mobilization Law, placing Japan on a war alert.

Prince Konoe and his cabinet were ousted in 1941. The government was taken over by the military, with Gen. Tojo Hideki as prime minister. The United States reacted to Japan's aggression in China by ceasing to supply raw materials, freezing Japanese assets in U.S. territory, and imposing an oil embargo. Retaliating with a surprise attack on Pearl Harbor on December 7, 1941, Japan plunged blindly into war. The ferocity of its expansionism, nobly dressed up as the foundation of an Asian Co-Prosperity Sphere, wrought some of the worst atrocities in the history of world colonialism.

Schoolchildren on a visit to Hiroshima's Peace Museum

1944, the Pacific island of Saipan became a base for bombing the whole of Japan.

In March 1945 the three-day incendiary bombing of Tokyo left over 100,000 dead and 700,000 homes destroyed; the attack was repeated on key sites around Japan. In April the Allies invaded Okinawa, where more than 200,000 died, half of them civilians. The Potsdam Declaration in July, calling for Japan's unconditional surrender, was ignored. On August 6 the U.S. dropped an atomic bomb on Hiroshima, obliterating the city and killing 150,000 people—over half of them instantaneously. Three days later another atomic bomb was dropped on Nagasaki.

A week later the emperor, apparently taking his own initiative against hard-line opposition, stunned Japan by announcing the inevitability of capitulation. In September he

During the 1980s, Japanese automotive firms came to dominate the world car market.

signed the official surrender before Gen. Douglas MacArthur, who headed the U.S. Occupation forces landing in Japan. With over 2 million dead and 13 million homeless, Japan was broken; having lost all its overseas territories, it would have to feed some 6 million extra mouths when its soldiers and expatriates returned.

The Occupation

Tokyo citizens came out of hiding when they realized that the carnage predicted by militarists was not going to happen. MacArthur was widely respected as Supreme Commander of the Allied Powers (SCAP), even by the Japanese. In 1946 the International Military Tribunal for the Far East (IMTFE) jailed 25 former militarists for war crimes; seven were executed two years later, including Tojo Hideki. Some 4,000 war criminals were simultaneously tried by IMTFE tribunals around the Pacific. It was suggested that the emperor should have been among them, but MacArthur wisely retained him as a figurehead vital to the peaceful restructuring of Japan.

With the exception of Okinawa (which reverted to Japan by popular vote in 1972), the U.S. Occupation forces left Japan to the Japanese. Having abolished the armed forces and purged the government of militarists, the Occupation authorities administered on the basis of mutual cooperation. In 1946 they drafted a new American-style democratic constitution that remains in force today. Emphasizing individual fulfillment and egalitarianism, it announced land reforms, the emancipation of women, and a new education system.

Special procurements for the Korean War in 1950 substantially helped to relaunch Japanese industry, but caused a shift from left to right in U.S. Occupation policy. America needed a strong anti-Communist ally in East Asia; though democracy had been firmly established, Japanese politics were pushed right of center.

In 1951 Prime Minister Yoshida Shigeru (1878–1967) signed a treaty with 48 nations at the San Francisco Peace Conference. The Occupation ended the next year. At the end of the Korean War in 1953, Japan signed the U.S. Security Treaty, allowing substantial American bases to remain on its soil. In 1955 Yoshida lost the vote to the new Liberal Democratic Party, which has remained in power ever since (except for a brief flirtation with coalitions in 1993).

Earthquake-ready Japan was shocked by the destruction of the Kobe Earthquake in 1995.

MODERN JAPAN (1989–PRESENT)

When Japan joined the United Nations in 1956, the economy was growing at twice the predicted rate. Thanks to soaring industry, exports, and good living standards, the country's recovery was declared complete by 1958.

With the renunciation of war written into the constitution, Japan is theoretically forbidden an army, but its SDF (self-defense force) ranks sixth in the world in terms of military strength. Widespread rioting erupted in 1960 with the renewal of the U.S. Security Treaty, but Japan's darkest clouds come mainly from pollution—the price paid for rapid industrialization.

1964 was a landmark year for Japan, when it hosted the Tokyo Olympic Games and launched the *shinkansen*—then the fastest train service in the world. Come 1970 and the International Exposition in Osaka, Japan had a formidable world-class economy based on a widening spectrum of quality industrial products.

Weathering oil shocks in both 1973 and 1979, Japan's spectacular growth prevailed but drew international flak in the 1980s for huge trade surpluses; fraught with tariff barriers, its markets were virtually closed to the outside world. Prizing them open had little effect on the balance of trade. Japan's wealth swelled throughout the 1980s.

In 1972 the Lockheed bribery scandal forced the resignation of Prime Minister Tanaka Kakuei and exposed the corruption endemic in the ruling Liberal Democratic Party. Scandals continued to taint the party through the 1990s.

The death of the Showa emperor in 1989 marked the end of an extraordinary era. Beginning with the accession of his son Akihito in 1990, the Heisei era finds Japan less certain about its future. The miracle ended with the collapse of the bubble economy in 1991, bringing recession and widespread social malaise. A chasm exists between Japanese of the pre- and postwar periods. In a country of enviably low crime, juvenile offenses are increasing. Many Japanese believe that the loss of traditional values to materialism has created a spiritual and moral vacuum.

Attempts to fill that gap include a proliferation of religious cults, among them the demented Aum that launched a deadly sarin gas attack in the Tokyo subway in 1994. The Kobe Earthquake of 1995, which killed more than 5,000 people, underscored the vulnerability of even the most modern cities. Tokyo nervously waits its turn. ■

The arts

SYMMETRY PLAYS NO PART IN JAPANESE AESTHETICS. A MILLENNIUM OR SO ago, Japanese temple complexes abandoned the regular ground plan of the Chinese model they emulated; the most highly regarded ceramic tea bowls are irregularly shaped; flower arrangements evoke the random patterns of nature; and the balance of the composition in prints and paintings is ingeniously off-center. In speech, prose, poetry, and visual arts, the implicit is frequently preferred to the explicit.

During the 13th century Zen Buddhism (see p. 227) inspired radically new forms and concepts, influencing painting, calligraphy, and poetry. Tea drinking, ritualized in China by Zen monks seeking no more than a means of staying awake during meditation, was transformed into a deeply aesthetic and philosophical ceremony in Japan. As developed by, among others, the great tea master Sen-no-Rikyu (1522–1591), *chado* or *chanoyu*—the Way of Tea—spurned ostentation and ushered in a new system of aesthetics.

The tea room is small, spotless, and plain. It contains a *kakemono* (hanging scroll) and a flower arrangement in the *tokonoma* (alcove); plain and rough in appearance, the tea bowls almost belie their master craftsmanship. The kakemono can be a calligraphy (often a poem) or an ink painting; like the flower arrangement, it should reflect the mood and hues of the season. The tea room becomes a space for the appreciation of different art forms working together.

In requiring works created specially for it, chanoyu engendered other forms, notably ikebana—the art of flower arrangement. Zen and the tea ceremony greatly influenced landscape gardening as teahouses had to have the proper surroundings. Kyoto's great Zen gardens of stone and gravel, representing water and mountains and reflecting philosophical ideals, are perhaps the world's earliest examples of conceptual and installation art.

Chanoyu and its correlative arts always reflect *wabi* (quiet taste) and *sabi* (elegant simplicity). These are the criteria for *shibui* (sober refinement), the paramount principle of Japanese taste, whereby less is more. Although not always so refined, aesthetics still preoccupy the Japanese, from the painstaking wrapping of gifts and the elaborate presentation of food to clusters of artificial flowers in toilets.

TRADITIONAL ARCHITECTURE

Japanese architecture is based on wood. The purely Chinese designs of the great Buddhist temples of Horyu-ji (see pp. 247–48), near Nara, set a precedent for religious architecture little altered today. However, some of the oldest and most sacred Shinto shrines, like those at Ise and Izumo, predate the Chinese model and replicate the prehistoric originals.

The raised structure of Ise Jingu is modeled after an ancient granary. Older shrines such as this have thatched roofs, with rafters alternating like crossed fingers placed against the ridge-piece. Others, like the shrine at Izumo, imitate ancient headmen's houses. At the gabled end of Shinto shrines, including many of those in the Chinese style, are the distinctive ornamental *chigi*—large crossed beams protruding from the roof like horns.

Beginning in the 16th century, the heads of the supporting pillars and crossbeams were sometimes carved, often with embellishments in gilded metalwork. Most shrines and all temples stand on foundations of stone and display sweeping roofs tiled in clay or bronze with eaves sloping elegantly upward.

Many temple complexes incorporate a pagoda, typically with five stories according to the Chinese geomantic principle of the five elements: earth, water, sky, wind, and fire. Most castles, regardless of the number of floors inside, also show five roof levels on the exterior. As with most Japanese wooden architecture, these intricate buildings have been constructed without using a single nail.

The traditional Japanese house is raised on low stilts, sometimes above a foundation. The single-story model is said to emulate the

Widely practiced today, ikebana—flower arranging—is an art form rooted in Zen Buddhist culture.

aristocratic dwelling of the 12th century, but between the 17th and mid-19th centuries two and sometimes three stories became common. The walls consist of a bamboo framework set between the support pillars and coated with daub. They are then plastered and often white-washed on the outside, while inside they are either plastered or coated with a smooth daub

and increasingly scarce wood. Many modern homes are prefabricated, incorporating con-crete slabs and plastics—materials also used to build houses in the traditional style.

Originally reserved for official buildings, Western architecture first appeared during the late 19th century. It was typically massive, of red brick and Victorian in style, and was

The International Forum Building in Tokyo designed by U.S. architect Rafael Vinoly

made from paper pulp. Such traditional hous-es are light, airy, and designed to open onto the outside world rather than to seal it off, as in the West. Roofs vary according to place and time. They can be steep and narrow to avert snow or wide and sweeping to provide shade. Thatch was ubiquitous until the 16th century, even on samurai dwellings, but is used today only on a few old farmhouses and some his-toric buildings. Shingled roofs appeared later; they can still be seen on some old mountain farmhouses, especially in Nagano. Clay tiles, first used in towns during the 17th and 18th centuries, became widespread. The roofs of modest homes now commonly display many cheaper alternatives, including metal, corru-gated iron, and plastic.

The cost of building a traditional house is prohibitive today, calling upon vanishing skills

greatly influenced by the British architect Josiah Conder (1852–1920); Tokyo Station was built by one of his pupils in 1914.

Reinforced concrete multistory apartment buildings, built according to utilitarian rather than aesthetic criteria, are becoming domi-nant in cities. But the profile of modern architecture was heightened during the 1960s with many remarkable buildings, notably Tange Kenzo's structures for the 1964 Olympic Games. Highly regarded internationally, architects such as Tange and Ando Tadao often incorporate traditional concepts into modern buildings to striking effect.

LITERATURE

The *Kojiki (Record of Ancient Matters)* and the *Nihon Shoki (Chronicles of Japan),* eighth-century history books that meld creation myths and fact, held sway over Shinto belief and national thinking for more than a millennium. The eighth-century *Man'yoshu*

(Collection for Ten Thousand Generations) is a compilation of 4,500 poems by emperors and aristocrats as well as ordinary people. Many are in the brief, evocative tanka style—a forerunner of the better known haiku (see below) and a poetry form still in fashion.

The great advances in literature during the Heian period (see pp. 30–31) were mainly due to female writers of *nikki* (diaries) and *monogatari* (tales)—the world's oldest true novels. Most prominent were the courtiers Sei Shonagon and Murasaki Shikibu, who created literary milestones around the year 1000. Sei Shonagon's candid *Makura Soshi (The Pillow Book)* is a compilation of vivid (and often unabashedly bitchy) observations of life at court. Murasaki's 54-chapter *Genji Monogatari (The Tale of Genji),* tracing the rise and fall of a philandering prince, is one of the classics of world literature.

After the 13th century, literature was eclipsed for almost 400 years by war—though war itself was the source of inspiration for the great classic *Heike Monogatari (The Tales of Heike),* an epic prose poem recounting the wars between the Taira and Minamoto clans. Often recited or sung, Heike-style epics were adapted for the theater; the melancholy and richly evocative Noh plays of Zeami Motokiyo (1363–1444) are outstanding for their poetic sensitivity.

During the Edo period (see pp. 34–36), plays were written interchangeably for the Bunraku puppet theater and Kabuki drama, notably by Chikamatsu Monzaemon (1653–1725), often regarded as a Japanese Shakespeare. His plays were mainly historical, but the most popular were contemporary tragedies about doomed lovers running afoul of the rules of caste and society. Social and dramatic realism came to color both the theater and novels—the latter revived as a genre after 600 years. Many novels, most notably those by Ihara Saikaku (1642–1692), were satires recounting the adventures of profligates and prostitutes in the Floating World (see p. 35).

In poetry the 17-syllable haiku was brought to perfection by Matsuo Basho (1644–1694). A samurai who converted to Zen, the wandering Basho produced haiku anthologies based on his journeys—masterpieces widely revered today.

The Meiji period (see pp. 36–37) brought Western realism to the Japanese novel. Among the first modern novelists were Mori Agai (1862–1922) and Natsume Soseki (1867–1916). The novels of Nagai Kafu (1879–1959) cast a wistful glance at the vanishing Floating World in the 1900s. Women writers emerged for the first time since the Heian

Nobel laureate Kawabata Yasunari (1899–1973), one of Japan's finest novelists

period, among them the tragically short-lived novelist Higuchi Ichiyo (1872–1896) and the poet and scholar Yosano Akiko (1878–1942).

The postwar period was something of a renaissance highlighted by the best work of established writers such as Kawabata Yasunari *(Snow Country,* 1948) and Tanizaki Junichiro (1886–1965), whose masterpiece, *The Makioka Sisters,* was banned by the militarists. A wealth of emerging talent included Yukio Mishima, Abe Kobo, Endo Shusaku, and Oe Kenzaburo, winner of the Nobel Prize for Literature in 1994. Murakami Ryu's *Almost Transparent Blue* reflects youthful nihilism during the 1970s. Among the most popular current authors are Murakami Haruki *(Dance, Dance, Dance)* and the lightweight Banana Yoshimoto *(Kitchen),* deplored by some as an indicator of the growing superficiality of Japanese taste.

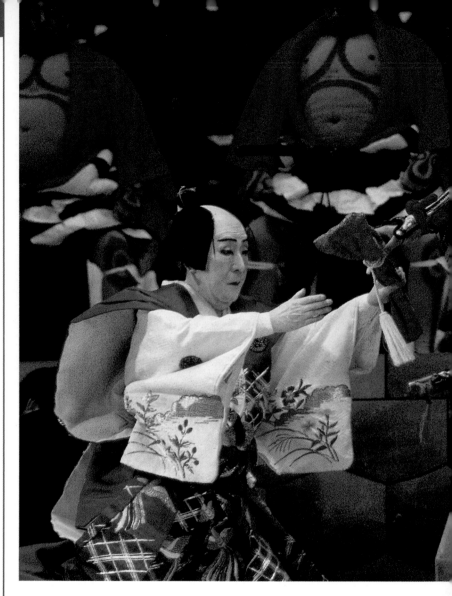

THEATER & DANCE

The sacred masked dance of *kagura,* taking the form of pantomime and featuring musical and vocal accompaniment, goes back to ancient times. Still performed during Shinto festivals, it is the source of inspiration for other forms of dance and drama. *Bugaku,* which survives in imperial ceremonies, and *gagaku* are of Chinese origin. They were forms of music and dance performed at the court in Heian times (see pp. 30–31). More popular types of entertainment were *dengaku* (field music, originating in peasant dances) and *sarugaku* (monkey music), both based on kagura. During the 14th century, sarugaku was refined into Noh, which means "skill." Under the patronage of the shogun Ashikaga Yoshimitsu, the art was perfected by Kan'ami Kiyotsugu (1333–1384) and his son Zeami Motokiyo (see p. 45), who turned Noh into a great classical theater form. Noh has a repertoire of five categories: Using poetic language and an

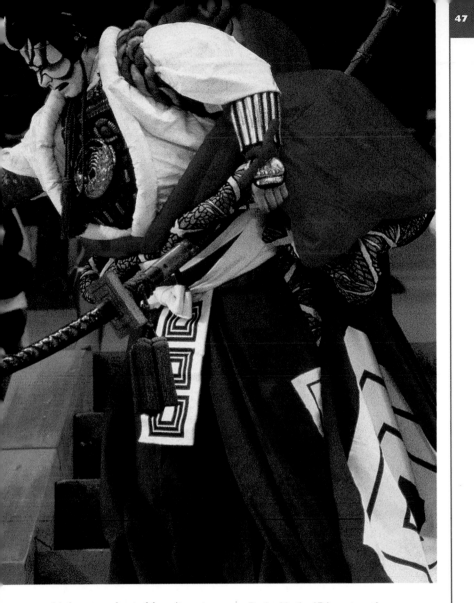

exquisitely costumed cast of three, it enacts tales of gods, ghostly warriors, madness, women, and demons. Noh performances are traditionally accompanied by a *kyogen* (comic interlude), a direct derivative of sarugaku.

Noh became the preserve of the samurai elite; during the Edo period, commoners were forbidden to see it. Early in the 17th century, however, a woman named Okuni presented a new kind of dance drama for the people of Kyoto. Called Kabuki, it went on to take Edo

Devised in the 17th century, the flamboyant Kabuki theater features gorgeous costumes and an all-male cast.

and the rest of the country by storm. It was often a front for prostitution, and the shogunate attempted to kill it by banning actresses from the stage. Kabuki quickly rebounded with an all-male cast; the female roles were portrayed by *onnagata* (woman-forms). Flamboyant and fast-moving in contrast to

Noh, Kabuki featured gaudy costumes, spectacular sets, and special effects. The plays were enacted in contemporary language and embraced modern themes.

The same applies in miniature to the very popular contemporary Bunraku puppet theater; the works of many playwrights, including the great Chikamatsu, are staged in both forms. One-third life size, each stringless marionette is manipulated by as many as three handlers on stage (their presence is soon forgotten). Bunraku remains one of the world's most exquisite forms of puppetry.

Until Western-style alternatives gradually came to eclipse it after the mid-19th century, Kabuki remained synonymous with popular theater in Japan. It retains a wide following and, like Noh, is a revered facet of the national cultural heritage.

Apart from an enduring profile in festivals and drama, dance never evolved much as an independent form until the 19th century.

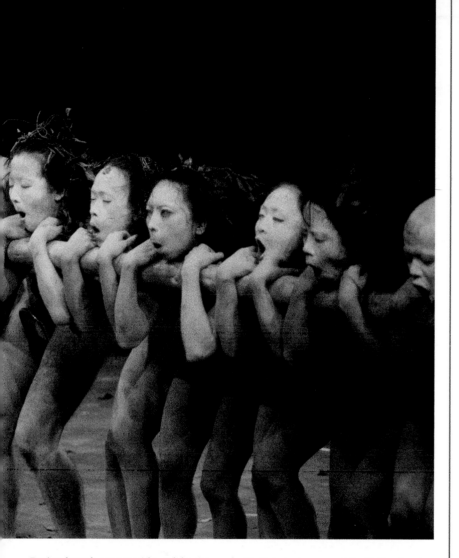

During the 18th century geisha and dancing girls in the entertainment quarters borrowed heavily from Kabuki, and it is in this form that *nihon buyo*—Japanese dancing—is widely practiced today, mostly by women and girls.

Plays have been written and performed in the Western tradition in Japan for over a century. Ballet and modern dance are gaining in popularity and command a wide following. *Angura* (underground) dance and theater made waves in the late 1960s, notably with

Plotless, grotesque, and fascinating, *butoh* dance theater is a blend of traditional Japanese fantasy and Western avant-garde.

butoh (the dance of darkness), introduced by Hijikata Tatsumi (1930–1986). Melding grotesque Western-style imagery with the traditional physicality of Noh and Kabuki, butoh has a global following. Much the same applies to Japan's avant-garde theater; led by Kara Juro and Terayama Shuji during the 1970s, the

Jazz, rock, funk: You name it, someone in Japan plays it.

movement has seen the emergence of several troupes admired overseas. From the dance innovations of Teshigawara Saburo to the stylish theatrical productions of Ninagawa Yukio, Japanese dance and theater come increasingly under the global spotlight.

MUSIC

The grand and sedate *gagaku* (court music) orchestra, using instruments from T'ang dynasty China, has remained in use for imperial, Shinto, and Buddhist ceremonies for more than a thousand years. Its main instruments are the *biwa* (a large teardrop-shape lute), *koto* (a 13-stringed zither), side-blown flutes, and percussion, including the *tsuzumi* shoulder drum and the enormous, vertically played *dadaiko* drum.

Shomyo, chanting of Buddhist ritual, exerted a strong influence on singing styles in Japan, where itinerant monks often gathered alms by singing epic poems to a biwa accompaniment. The epic poem singing style gave rise to *naga-uta* (long songs), influential on the Noh theater in the 15th century, which in turn engendered the *joruri* singing adopted in the 17th century by the Kabuki theater. Joruri was also practiced by geisha in the Floating World as well as by blind minstrels, who had a monopoly on singing epic poems until 1871.

During the Edo period (see pp. 34–36), the *samisen* gradually replaced the biwa. The samisen, introduced from China via Okinawa, is a three-stringed lute with a long, thin neck and a small, round sound box covered in snakeskin (Okinawa) or animal skin (mainland Japan). Adopted in the Kabuki theater, the samisen soon became the instrument of choice for geisha and blind minstrels and for folk music. The Edo period also saw the appearance of the *shakuhachi*, a bamboo flute about 18 inches (45cm) long. It gives the player much scope for expression, and its unique tone makes it a popular instrument today.

The classic singing technique, plaintive and heavily stylized, is an acquired taste for many modern Japanese used to Western harmony. Composed using the pentatonic scale, traditional Japanese music is not always easy listening to the unaccustomed ear—but it is worth the effort.

Western music accompanied the Portuguese in the 16th century but was soon forgotten with the closure of the country. Returning in the form of military bands during the 1860s (most samurai clans wanted one), Western music had a colossal and lasting

Katsushika Hokusai (1760–1849) woodblock print from his "36 Views of Mount Fuji" series

impact. Japanese symphony orchestras, such as the Saito Kinnen and Tokyo Symphony orchestras, are among the world's finest, and the country has produced many outstanding Western-style musicians, among them conductor Ozawa Seiji and pianist Mitsuko Uchida. During the 1960s, composers such as Takemitsu Toru combined gagaku with contemporary Western music to explore new horizons of sound. Japan has many fine jazz musicians, and countless city venues present a broad array of imported and domestic musicians of all types.

VISUAL ARTS
Painting

In early Japan painting was Chinese in form and exclusively Buddhist in content. Among the earliest examples are the murals in the main hall of Horyu-ji Temple near Nara, executed in the seventh century. During the Heian period (794–1185), painting took a more Japanese turn, with landscapes and scenes from court life decorating screens and sliding doors; portraiture and illustrated scrolls became popular.

In the Kamakura period (1185–1333) art of this kind came to be called *yamato-e* (Japanese painting) as distinct from *kara-e* ("outside" paintings in the Chinese tradition). The yamato-e tradition favored fine detail and vivid colors. Focusing on black-and-white, kara-e was characterized by *sumi-e* (ink paintings); the school progressed with the spread of Zen Buddhism and reached its zenith during the 15th century with the monk Sesshu (1420–1506), whose works depicted real (as opposed to the hitherto imaginary) landscapes.

From the late 16th century, wealthy warlords lavished patronage on the rival Kano school, which combined elements of kara-e and yamato-e to embellish the interiors of houses and castles with magnificent works. Motonobu (1476–1559) and Eitoku (1543–1590) were Kano's finest artists. Thanks to the growing patronage of wealthy merchant princes, the established schools flourished alongside growing demand for purely decorative art. This was met notably by the Rimpa school, of which Ogata Korin (1658–1716), famed for his composition of irises on a golden screen door, was a major exponent.

Hishikawa Moronobu (d. 1694), a prominent painter in the Kano style, was the first master—though not the inventor— of *ukiyo-e*, woodblock prints depicting the Floating World. The works of ukiyo-e masters such as Kitagawa Utamaro (1753–1806),

Katsushika Hokusai, and Ando Hiroshige caused a sensation in Europe during the 19th century.

Sculpture

Archaeological excavations have unearthed Jomon-period statuettes, and the Kofun era's more sophisticated *haniwa* clay figures. The

metalwork; many *netsuke*, the wood or ivory toggles used for attaching small medicine cases *(inro)* to kimono sashes, were tiny sculptures of consummate skill. As demand for these declined during the 19th century, former metalworkers and netsuke carvers turned to statuettes and figurines, many destined for export.

Statuette from the Jomon period (10,000 B.C.–300 B.C.)

Sculpture by Mineda Yoshihiro, Makuhari Messe Exhibition Centre, Chiba

latter, representing humans, animals, and buildings, were put in the grave mounds of chieftains, paralleling the Chinese practice.

The first bronze representations of the Buddha (sixth century) were Sino-Korean imports but, styling them after these prototypes, the Japanese soon made their own, following the usual prototypes and with a standard range of symbolic gestures. Styles changed with the introduction of new sects but, although an abundance of magnificent examples reveal the sculptor's individual skill, religious sculpture never displayed the variety of secular art. During the Kamakura period (see pp. 32–33), wooden sculptured portraits became quite common to commemorate both noted priests and secular dignitaries.

Sculpture thrived in miniature. Swords and armor often displayed fine decorative

Modern art

The resounding impact of Western art during the Meiji period (see pp. 36–37) prompted many Japanese artists to study in Paris, among them the influential Kuroda Seiki (1866–1924), founder of the first Western-style art school. Opposition from traditionalists led to the official division of *ninhonga* (Japanese painting) and *yoga* (Western painting), with the latter deprived of government sponsorship. Nevertheless, all significant Western art movements have produced major Japanese representatives from the 1900s to the present day. Although incorporating Western styles, ninhonga painters continue to thrive.

Film

Born with the flickering images of a Kabuki actor in 1896, the Japanese cinema took off during the 1910s with hundreds of one-reelers borrowing themes and actors from Kabuki theater.

Directors perfecting their craft during the 1920s absorbed Russian (Eisenstein), American (D.W. Griffiths), and German (Expressionist) film technique. Among them were Mizoguchi Kenji (1898–1956) and Ozu

but audiences continued to dwindle, declining tenfold between 1958 and 1998. Many film companies had to fight off bankruptcy during the 1970s; the venerable Nikkatsu Company, founded in 1912, launched soft-core *roman poruno* (porno romance), a genre in which many prominent directors and actors cut their teeth until hard-core video killed it overnight.

Yasujiro (1903–1963), whose films progressed from rickety, silent one-reelers to masterpieces of world cinema.

In 1951 Akira Kurosawa's *Rashomon*, a period drama inventively recounted from different viewpoints, won the Venice Film Festival's grand prize. Mizoguchi's *The Life of Oharu*, about a 17th-century noblewoman's descent into prostitution, came second in 1952; his exquisite medieval ghost story, *Ugetsu*, did the same the following year. Ozu's poignant *Tokyo Story* (1953), about a rural family neglected by their urbanized children, is still universally acclaimed. At its zenith, Japanese cinema had a profound influence, particularly on French Nouvelle Vague (New Wave) directors such as Jean-Luc Godard.

Meanwhile at home, major film companies churned out trivial formula flicks, a situation worsened by the onslaught of television. In the 1960s a Japanese Nouvelle Vague, epitomized by Nagisa Oshima, earned critical accolades,

Akira Kurosawa's *Rashomon* (1951) put Japanese cinema on the world map.

Some directors sought financing abroad: Oshima in France (*The Realm of the Senses,* 1976; *Merry Christmas Mr. Lawrence,* 1983); Kurosawa in Russia (*Dersu Uzala,* 1974) and the United States (*Kagemusha,* 1980). Other directors, including Imamura Shohei (top Cannes prizewinner for *Ballad of Narayama* in 1983), found independent financing at home.

During the 1980s independent directors were becoming increasingly successful, especially the late Itami Juzo (*Tampopo, Taxing Woman*). These days the trend still applies; independent production companies, smaller theaters, and lower budgets now give greater scope to original talent. Acclaimed for his idiosyncratic hardboiled-cop movies, Kitano Takeshi won the Cannes prize in 1997 for *Hana-bi*. More than two-thirds of the films currently shown in Japan are foreign.

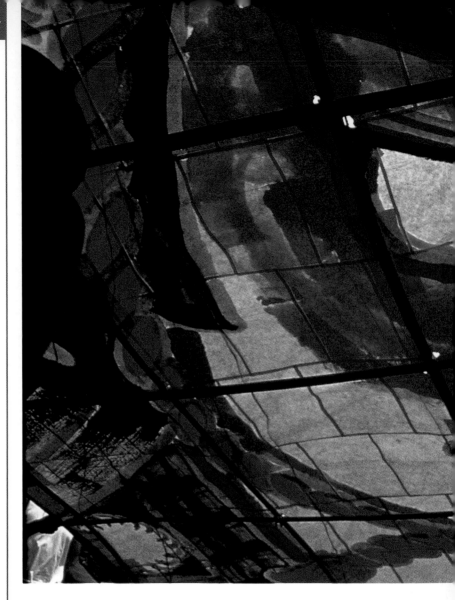

Although the audience for quality domestic films is small, it is nevertheless faithful.

Crafts

The rapid pace of modernization in Japan led inevitably to the loss of countless aspects of its former lifestyle, but the survival of certain traditional crafts is one of the country's marvels. Efforts have been made to preserve them, not least through a system designating older practitioners of traditional arts and crafts as Intangible Cultural Properties or Living National Treasures. The fact that arts and crafts are hereditary businesses has helped to perpetuate them, as has the survival of the traditional ceremonies and pastimes in which they are used. Works by officially treasured craftspeople are rare and revered; even those by lesser masters can be dauntingly expensive. Fortunately a vast range of marvelous handicrafts are still affordable, though unlikely to be really cheap if made in Japan.

Ceramics

Japanese pottery goes back to the ancient Jomon culture but remained rough and practical until techniques from China and Korea became established in the sixth century. Japanese potters continued to make Korean-style ware through the 18th century. Glazed ceramics arrived with the introduction of three-color glazes during the 7th century, but it was not until the 14th century that renewed contacts with China prompted the refine-

Crafts and painterly skills coalesce in an outsize festival kite in Northern Honshu.

ments and sophistication for which Japanese ceramics are renowned. The focus of the industry was Seto in central Honshu, from whence comes the Japanese word for pottery, *seto-mono* (Seto things).

The tea ceremony ushered in stylistic innovations epitomized by the deceptively rough-hewn quality of ware such as Karatsu,

Hagi, and Raku. Introduced during the 17th century, porcelain was first produced in Arita in the Tsushima Islands, especially the blue-and-white ware (and later polychrome too) commonly called Imari. Along with polychrome Satsuma ware, Imari is still seen as most representative of Japanese ceramics today. Mass production caused a decline in traditional ceramics in the late 19th century, but there are still a hundred noted kilns and many master potters active in Japan, especially in Kyushu.

Paper

The surfaces and mats used in pen-and-ink painting and calligraphy are traditionally made from *washi*—paper handmade from wood pulp, especially mulberry bark. Although manufacture dwindled with the

Lacquerware, such as this covered bowl, is immediately identifiable as Japanese.

introduction of Western paper, washi is still in demand for a variety of uses including calligraphy, origami (paper folding), fans, decorations, paper dolls, and traditional stationery. In different thicknesses, plain, dyed, printed and decorated, and sometimes incorporating flecks of gold leaf and colored fragments, washi is sold in stationery and specialty stores.

Lacquerware

Common throughout East Asia, lacquer has long been associated primarily with Japan; in 18th-century England red or black lacquering for furniture was known simply as Japanning. In Japan *nuri* (lacquer) or *urushi-mono* (lacquered things) have barely gone out of fashion since their height from the late 17th to the 19th centuries. *Tansu* (chests), boxes for various uses, tea caddies, combs and hair ornaments, wooden bowls, sake cups, and ceremonial *bento-bako* (packed meal boxes) are still produced by modern craftsmen, notably in Ishikawa, the Kiso Valley, and Okinawa. Authentic urushi-mono is a painstaking process involving three coats of lacquer, and its production commands high prices; plastic imitations, especially tableware, abound today. Often featuring inclusions of gold leaf and mother-of-pearl, beautifully painted designs are enhanced with a deep, glossy finish. Black, red, and occasionally green were once the more common colors, along with rarer *maki-e* (lacquerware with silver and gold leaf), but some of today's craftsmen create striking modern designs in a wider array of subtle (and not so subtle) hues.

Wood and bamboo

The traditional Japanese home has little furniture, low tables and chests (tansu) being the notable exception. Popular overseas, antique tansu command increasingly high prices but remain a good buy in Japan. Although made with considerable skill and still expensive, modern equivalents are often machine finished and tend to have painted gloss where there should be a patina.

Many handcrafted objects are made of wood, notably lacquerware. Trays and bowls, turned on a lathe and hand finished, are often sold polished rather than lacquered.

Bamboo is popular for tea-related utensils and flower holders. It is either sectioned and shaped into a vase or cut into thin strips and woven into a variety of attractive shapes, for displaying on a surface or for hanging.

Textiles

The beauty of Japanese textiles is legendary; the prices of even used silk kimonos and brocade *obi* (kimono sashes) have escalated sharply in recent years. Using hand-cut stencils and rice paste applied to the fabric, *yuzen* is a

Instructors and pupils warm up for a junior high school karate tournament.

skillful dyeing technique that produces patterns of great complexity, especially in Kyoto and Kanazawa. Okinawa, too, produces beautiful textiles; the hand-painted colorful *bingata* designs, often representing stylized flowers and birds, are the most famous.

Rustic *aizome* cotton textiles, mainly dyed with natural indigo, are often exquisitely printed or tie-dyed. Used for garments, bags, and hats commonly sold in gift shops, sophisticated variants of aizome find new applications among fashion designers.

Dolls

Hina-matsuri (March 3) is Girls' Day, celebrated in people's homes with a display of dolls *(ningyo)* representing members of an old imperial court. Not toys but family heirlooms, such dolls are often exquisitely dressed and crafted; fine examples, antique or modern, can be dauntingly expensive. (Boys' Festival on May 5 finds an equivalent in small suits of armor and samurai warrior dolls.) *Hagoita,* the bats used in an ancient shuttlecock game played by girls, are decorated with brocade dolls in bas-relief, mainly representing Kabuki actors. Evolving partly from the *haniwa* figurines of the Kofun period (see p. 28), dolls have long been used as ritual charms in Japan and figure prominently among the folk arts around the country. The most primitive are the cylindrical wooden *kokeshi,* but more refined types are still produced, notably in Kyoto, Hakata, and Saga prefectures.

MARTIAL ARTS

Japan's greatest native sports, apart from sumo wrestling, are its martial arts, which arrived from China along with Buddhism. The core concepts had already been developed by monks as they honed techniques to defend themselves against bandits on their travels.

The oldest Japanese fighting arts are *kenjutsu* (based on the samurai art of swordsmanship), *jujutsu* (unarmed combat of medieval origin), and *kyujutsu* (ancient archery formalized during the Kamakura period). The suffix *-jutsu* means "skill"—especially skills useful to samurai warriors; it was replaced by *-do* (the Way) during the Meiji era.

Although martial arts always involved spiritual as well as physical discipline, the emphasis shifted to the former during the 19th century. *Kendo,* the way of the sword, was introduced into the curriculum during the 19th century and is still widely practiced in schools and universities by girls as well as boys. The same applies to a lesser degree to *kyudo* (archery), which has spiritual principles preponderantly influenced by Zen. Wearing padded armor and helmets to protect the face, kendo protagonists duel with swords of split bamboo; winning is determined according to five principles and the quality of strikes against eight strategic points on the opponent's body armor.

Martial arts are taught by masters in schools known as *dojo.* Most use the *dan* ranking system, whereby proficiency is measured from first to sixth dan, designated with colored belts worn on tunics; black generally denotes the highest level.

Judo, a synthesis of jujutsu, spiritual training, and other old fighting arts, involves grappling and body throws. It was introduced in the 1900s and became a national sport in the 1930s, but like all martial arts it was banned as a feudal remnant by the Occupation authorities. Reinstated in 1950, judo had already found experts around the world before its inclusion in the Tokyo Olympic Games in 1964, when to the disappointment of the Japanese the gold medal went to a Dutchman.

Karate (empty hand), a close relative of kung-fu, was of Chinese origin. It was much practiced in the Ryuku-shoto Islands (Okinawa) following its introduction during the 14th century, but did not reach mainland Japan until the 1900s. Akin to other martial arts in its demands for dedication and spiritual concentration, karate calls upon a variety of blows with the hands, fists, and feet. It differs from other martial arts in its emphasis on attack rather than defense.

Aikido, founded by Ueshiba Morihei during the 1920s and based on ancient arts of self-defense, is the most spiritually oriented of the martial arts. The emphasis is placed entirely on defense; throws are achieved by deftly using the opponent's momentum against him. Borrowing movement from classical Japanese dance, aikido also involves Zen-style meditation to enhance the flow of *ki,* the life-force, through the practitioner's body. ∎

Tokyo means "eastern capital." The name is apt. At once perfectly familiar and totally alien to the foreign visitor, the multifaceted city is so huge, colorful, frenetic, and overwhelming that it seems like a capital for East Asia.

Tokyo

Reflection in a window of Tokyo FM Center

Tokyo

IN 1603 EDO, A FISHING HAMLET clustered around a crumbling castle, became the national capital, replacing Kyoto. By the 18th century it was already the largest city in the world; in the early 21st century Tokyo (its name since 1868) has a population of 11 million.

Edo was built around a colossal castle (the Imperial Palace now stands on the site), with the ruling elite living within the walls; artisans, merchants, and the populace lived in the Low City (shitamachi), which extended eastward to the Sumida-gawa River.

Frequent fires meant that the wooden city had to be rebuilt many times. During the national closure (1637–1868), Edo was the cradle of Japanese urban culture. After 1868 it became the nucleus for Western influences and rapid modernization. It was the city of firsts—railroads, stone buildings, factories, gas, electricity, trams, and telephones.

Almost nothing of Edo remains, and most of older Tokyo was destroyed by the Great Kanto Earthquake in 1923 and incendiary bombs two decades later. Postwar reconstruction transformed Tokyo beyond recognition. As visitors approach the gray urban-industrial sprawl en route from Narita airport to downtown Tokyo, first impressions are grim. Vestiges of the wooden city sit dwarfed beneath towers of steel and glass. Tokyo suffers from a total lack of urban planning. Yet behind busy central thoroughfares and in the suburbs, quieter residential districts have their own temple, shrine, market, and main street, and many retain their old village atmosphere.

Beauty is not confined to the city's hundreds of museums and galleries but lies hidden away from the everyday bustle or comes as an adornment or detail. It is typically Japanese to conceal a hedonistic nature behind a bland, solemn exterior. Epicurean and sensual, Tokyo's amusement districts offer an exhaustive array of pleasures from sunset to dawn.

As echoes of the past resound in traditional neighborhoods such as Ueno and Asakusa, the future looms in the ambitious developments on Tokyo Bay. ■

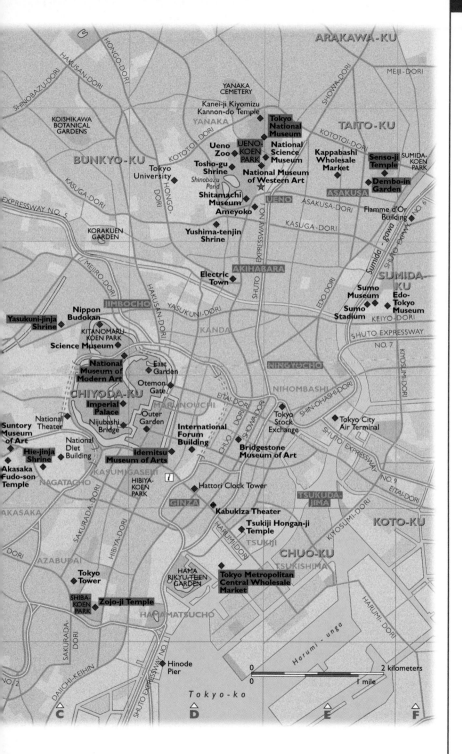

ARAKAWA-KU

MEIJI-DORI

SHINOBAZU-DORI

HAKUSAN-DORI

HONGO-DORI

SHOWA-DORI

YANAKA
CEMETERY

Kanei-ji Kiyomizu
Kannon-do Temple

YANAKA

KOISHIKAWA
BOTANICAL
GARDENS

KOTOTOI-DORI

Tokyo
National
Museum

TAITO-KU

KOTOTOI-DORI

BUNKYO-KU

Tokyo
University

KASUGA-DORI

Ueno
Zoo

UENO-
KOEN
PARK

Tosho-gu
Shrine

Shinobazu
Pond

National
Science
Museum

National Museum
of Western Art

Kappabashi
Wholesale
Market

Senso-ji
Temple

SUMIDA-
KOEN
PARK

ASAKUSA

Dembo-in
Garden

EXPRESSWAY NO. 5

KORAKUEN
GARDEN

HONGO-
DORI

Shitamachi
Museum

Ameyoko

UENO

ASAKUSA-DORI

Flamme d'Or
Building

KASUGA-DORI

Sumida - gawa

SHUTO EXPWY. NO. 61

MEIJIRO-DORI

Yushima-tenjin
Shrine

HAKUSAN-DORI

JIMBOCHO

Electric
Town

AKIHABARA

EXPRESSWAY NO. 1

SHUTO

SUMIDA-
KU

Nippon
Budokan

YASUKUNI-DORI

EDO-DORI

Sumo
Museum

Sumo
Stadium

Edo-
Tokyo
Museum

Yasukuni-jinja
Shrine

KITANOMARU-
KOEN PARK

KANDA

KEIYO-DORI

SHUTO EXPRESSWAY

Science Museum

National
Museum of
Modern Art

East
Garden

Otemon
Gate

NINGYOCHO

NIHOMBASHI

NO. 7

KIYOSUMI-DORI

CHIYODA-KU

Imperial
Palace

Outer
Garden

EITAI-DORI

SHIN-OHASHI-DORI

Suntory
Museum
of Art

National
Theater

Nijubashi
Bridge

National
Diet
Building

Idemitsu
Museum of Arts

MARUNOUCHI

International
Forum
Building

CHUO-DORI

SHOWA-DORI

Tokyo
Stock
Exchange

Tokyo City
Air Terminal

SHUTO EXPRESSWAY

NO. 9

Hie-jinja
Shrine

Akasaka
Fudo-son
Temple

NAGATACHO

KASUMIGASEKI

HIBIYA-
KOEN
PARK

𝒊

Bridgestone
Museum of Art

EITAI-DORI

AKASAKA

DORI

AZABUDAI

SAKURADA-DORI

HIBIYA-DORI

GINZA

Hattori Clock Tower

Kabukiza Theater

TSUKUDA-
JIMA

KOTO-KU

Tsukiji Hongan-ji
Temple

HARUMI-DORI

TSUKIJI

CHUO-KU

TSUKISHIMA

KIYOSUMI-DORI

HARUMI-DORI

Tokyo
Tower

HAMA
RIKYU-TEIEN
GARDEN

Tokyo Metropolitan
Central Wholesale
Market

SHIBA-
KOEN
PARK

Zojo-ji Temple

HAMAMATSUCHO

SAKURADA-
DORI

Harumi - unga

SHUTO EXPRESSWAY NO. 2

DAIICHI-KEIHIN

Hinode
Pier

Tokyo-ko

0   2 kilometers
0   1 mile

C   D   E   F

Central Tokyo, the hub of the Japanese business area, is characterized by office buildings.

Central Tokyo

Comprising Chuo-ku, Chiyoda-ku, and the north of Minato-ku, the center of Tokyo is given over mainly to administration (Kasumigaseki and Hibiya), business and finance (Marunouchi, Otemachi, and Nihombashi), and shopping at various focal points throughout. Aside from the Imperial Palace and some good museums, the tourist sights are few. The sedate streets of towering offices in Marunouchi at least afford a glimpse of the economic engine that drives Japan. At lunchtime Marunouchi business employees work off stress with a stroll in Hibiya-koen Park, near the Imperial Palace, a pleasant but unremarkable oasis of green. Despite wartime bombing and runaway modernism, some prewar Western-style buildings survive in the area, including the Bank of Japan and Tokyo Station.

The **Imperial Palace (Kokyo)** stands on the site of what was Edo-jo Castle, a crumbling 14th-century fortress magnificently restored by the shogun Tokugawa Ieyasu in the 1590s. By the mid-17th century it was the largest castle in the world, almost a walled city. The structures were burned down (notably during the Meireki Fire of 1657) and rebuilt several times. The castle was too dilapidated for Emperor Meiji to live in when he moved to Tokyo in 1868. He inhabited the Akasaka Detached Palace, pending the building of a new palace on the original castle site in 1888.

The new palace was destroyed during the bombing of 1945, and the present building was completed in 1968. The massive walls and surrounding moats are part of the original Edo-jo complex, as is the restored Otemon gate, which stands beyond the famous Nijubashi access bridge and before the East Garden, the actual site of Edo-jo. Elegantly landscaped with ponds and pines, the garden contains the ruins of Edo-jo and the 100 Guard Office, built in 1863—the last remaining original structure.

Within the garden is the Imperial Palace itself. It is open to the public only on January 2 and on

Imperial Palace

🗺 61 C3

✉ Chiyoda, Chiyoda-ku. (follow signs for correct exit)

☎ 03/3213-1111 ext. 485

🕐 Garden only: closed Mon. & Fri., except during national holiday. Imperial Palace only open Dec 23 & Jan 2

💲 Free (plastic token handed to you on entry, returned on leaving)

🚇 Subway: Hibiya, Nijubashimae, Tokyo; JR: Tokyo Station

Echoes of Edo

Edo lingers on in countless place-names. Marunouchi (meaning "inside the walls") was where the samurai elite lived. Ginza (seat of silver) gets its name from a long-vanished coinage mint. Akasaka (red hill) was once used for cultivating plants yielding a red dye. Edo continues too in certain neighborhood characteristics: Nihonbashi was the haunt of high finance in samurai days, and still is; and the site of the Yoshiwara licensed quarter,

banned in 1957, is now the realm of Soapland massage parlors.

Nihonbashi—the Bridge of Japan—was the starting point for measuring distances around the country. Here the main roads to the city converged, notably the old Tokaido road from Kyoto. Built in 1911, the present bridge is eclipsed by a tracery of overhead highways. Regardless of the layers of concrete, history remains almost eerily present in Tokyo. ∎

the emperor's birthday (December 23), but huge crowds make this a grueling experience.

The Outer Palace Garden, within the outer moat to the south of the palace compound, is a public park. Unprepossessing except for an impressive view over Nijubashi bridge and the palace walls, it is popular with joggers, strollers from the nearby business districts, and courting couples.

Kitanomaru-koen Park, on the north side of the Imperial Palace grounds, is notable as the site of **Nippon Budokan** (*Tel 03/3216-5100*), a martial arts stadium now largely used as a venue for rock concerts, and for its museums. The **Science Museum**

(**Kagaku Gijutsukan,** *2-1 Kitanomaru-koen, tel 03/3212-8471*), less than a quarter of a mile (300m) southeast, does not have the reputation of the national equivalent in Ueno, but hands-on exhibits make it a perennial favorite with schoolchildren.

Kitanomaru-koen Park

 61 C4

✉ Just south of Kudanshita subway station, a short walk from northern exit of Imperial Palace East Garden

🚇 Subway: Kudanshita

National Museum of Modern Art

 61 C4

✉ 3 Kitanomaru-koen

☎ 03/3561-1400

🕐 Crafts Gallery closed Mon. Main building under reconstruction until late 2001

💲 $$

🚇 Subway: Takebashi

The long-sleeve fire

Of Edo's many fires, the Great Meireki Fire of 1657 was the worst. The conflagration is also called *Furisode-no-kaji*—the long-sleeve fire. A legend attributed the cause to a *furisode*—a long-sleeve kimono—worn by a girl who pined to death because of unrequited love. According to former Buddhist custom, the kimono was given to a temple after her death. The priests sold it to another girl, who mysteriously sickened and died—a pattern that was repeated three times. The priests finally threw the furisode onto a brazier, but as it caught fire, a gust of wind sent it up to ignite the temple, causing the blaze that killed over 100,000 people and destroyed most of the city. ∎

The **National Museum of Modern Art (Kokuritsu Kindai Bijutsukan)**—closed for reconstruction until late 2001—is to the right of the park entrance. This is one of Japan's finest modern art museums, with a substantial collection focusing on contemporary artists and tracing the major developments in Japanese art since the Meiji era in both traditional and Western styles. The museum is also Tokyo's prime venue for large retrospective exhibitions of such major Western artists as Edvard Munch, Henri Matisse, and Francis Bacon. The **Crafts Gallery (Kogeikan)**, housed in the adjacent old Imperial Guard Headquarters of 1911, presents a fascinating array of exhibits showing the Japanese propensity for turning the most banal everyday objects into art. It includes ceramics, basketware, dolls, lacquerware, and metalwork.

Yasukuni-jinja Shrine, founded in 1869, honors the 2.5 million soldiers who died for their country during and since the Meiji era. The enshrinement of World War II criminals along with them has sparked bitter controversy both in Japan and abroad. However, war criminals are a minority among the soldiers honored and, as a place visited by families paying their respects to lost relatives, the shrine has great poignancy. The adjacent museum, **Yushukan**, contains military memorabilia and hardware, and is of historical interest. Despite its controversial reputation, Yasukuni is a favorite spot for viewing cherry blossoms in April. ∎

A favorite Tokyo view in all seasons: Nijubashi Bridge spanning the Imperial Moat

Yasukuni-jinja Shrine
- 🗺 61 C4
- ✉ 3-1-1 Kudan-kita, Chiyoda-ku. 330 yards (300 m) due east of Ichigaya stations along Yasukuni-dori

Yushukan Museum
- ☎ 03/3261-8326
- 💲 $$
- 🚇 Subway: Kudanshita

A modern look

Japan's architectural transformation from wood to reinforced concrete began in the late 19th century but really took off—and upward—with mass reconstruction during the postwar period. Much of Japan's architecture looks inspired by city-of-the-future features in sci-fi comic books of the 1950s, while the monster *danchi*—state apartment buildings—parallel Soviet architectural brutalism. With little urban planning, the astonishing heterogeneity of the urban environment, though frequently hideous, is enthralling in itself. Rickety wooden houses often stand wedged between structures of reinforced concrete; even Las Vegas could envy the palatial Chinese rococo architecture of the *onsen* (hot spring) resort, the neon-splashed *pachinko* (pinball) parlor, or the outrageous kitsch of the love hotel.

The soaring economy resulted in the *kenchiku bumu* (architecture boom), dragging a ruthless building spree in its wake through the 1980s. Most towns can boast a share of noteworthy modern buildings; Japanese contemporary architecture frequently incorporates traditional aesthetic concepts to great effect.

Foreign architects in Tokyo
The list of works by major architects in the capital reads like an international hall of fame, with Le Corbusier and Frank Lloyd Wright alongside homegrown architectural stars such as Tange Kenzo and Ando Tadao. A notable landmark is New York architect Rafael Vinoly's vast Tokyo International Forum Building in Yurakucho, completed in 1996—a kind of indoor city famous for its colossal glass atrium crossed by walkways (see p. 69). British architect Norman Foster's Century Tower was built in 1991 near Ochanomizu; U.S. architect Peter Eisenman was responsible for the Koizumi Lighting Theater and, out in Koiwa, a suburb of Tokyo, the strange Nunotani (NC) Building that looks as if it's about to fall apart; and Italian architect Renzo Piano designed the Kansai Airport Terminal (1994).

Having designed a number of Tokyo's most surreal recent constructions, some foreign architects are more famous as such in Japan than at home, where they are better known as designers. Britain's Nigel Coates made the arresting Wall Building in Hiro, with its facade curiously festooned with rusting ironmongery, and Frenchman Philippe Starck the eccentric Flamme d'Or Building (1989). Looking like a giant golden chili pepper sitting atop a massive cylinder of shining black granite, the latter houses the Asahi Super Dry Beer Hall and restaurant in Asakusa.

Japanese modernism
The 1980s saw the rise of several important Japanese architects, notably Isozaki Arata (Shukosha Building, Fukuoka, Kyushu, 1974–75; Tokyo Globe Theater, 1988) and Osaka's extraordinary self-taught Ando Tadao (Rokko Housing One project, Kobe, 1983; La Collezione fashion building, Aoyama, Tokyo, 1989). The most universally famous is Tange Kenzo, noted first for his remarkable stadium buildings for the Tokyo Olympics in 1964 and, fronted with blue-tinted mirror glass, the Hanae Mori building (1977) on Tokyo's fashionable Omotesando-dori boulevard. Completed in 1991, Tange's colossal granite-and-glass Tokyo Metropolitan Government Office, a monumental blend of modernism and cathedral Gothic, is probably one of the most visited new buildings in Japan. It soars above western Shinjuku, where skyscrapers first emerged after the Tokyo Olympics. A great area for vertical architecture, Shinjuku is bleak at ground level; most people find the architecturally less remarkable eastern side of the district more colorful and congenial.

Not that all modern buildings in Tokyo are cold. Incorporating one of the city's best exhibition spaces and a restaurant-cum-auditorium, Maki Fumihiko's sweeping Spiral Building on Aoyama-dori is very much alive. With its sci-fi shapes, his extraordinary Tokyo Metropolitan Gymnasium is a 1990s answer to Tange's Olympic architecture of the 1960s. Imaginative, eclectic, and effective, Takahiko Yanagisawa's 1995 Museum of Contemporary Art, in Kiba-koen Park, was designed as an update on the old counterpart in Ueno. ∎

Above: The Flamme d'Or Building, Asakusa, Tokyo. Below: Tokyo Metropolitan Government Office

Above: Fuji Television Building at Odaiba on Tokyo-wan Bay

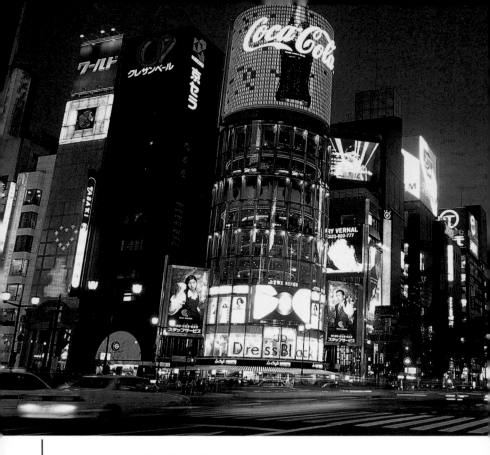

Bright lights, big city—Ginza 4-chome crossing at night

Ginza-Hibiya-Yurakucho

During the late 19th century, Ginza became the showcase for Western-style development, with cafés and restaurants appearing in the wake of shops and department stores. Today Ginza is on a par with New York's Fifth Avenue, with many elegant shops standing on their ancestral sites. Among them is the Wako Building, a prewar landmark with a clock tower on Ginza 4-chome crossing—the heart of the district. Ginza's prosperity after World War II spread to Hibiya and Yurakucho.

New department stores and malls that appeared during the 1980s have given the district an air of mercantile futurism.

Ginza is also an entertainment district. The winking neon of small bars in Ginza backstreets may entice, but many of the exclusive hostess clubs are among the most expensive watering holes in the world. Not all of Ginza's wining and dining options are expensive; you'll find less costly options toward Hibiya and Yurakucho, even little beer-and-yakitori dives under the railroad tracks (see p.70).

The area is a nucleus for art galleries, with dozens between Ginza 1- to 4-chome and Kyobashi, and from Ginza 5- to 8-chome. The accent is on the contemporary—mainly Japanese but including some Western artists. Hibiya and Yurakucho contain scores of movie houses (many showing films in English), as well as other theaters.

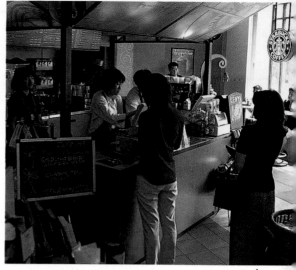

the future, **Tokyo International Forum.** It comprises a colossal atrium with interior walkways beneath a vast glass roof. The building houses corporations, galleries, restaurants, and the **visitor information center** *(3-5-1 Marunouchi, tel 3201-3331, closed Sat p.m. & Sun.).*

You can take a closer look at the frenetic financial activity in the business sector by visiting the **Tokyo Stock Exchange (Tokyo Shoken Torihiki-sho).** From the stock exchange, head

A welcome cup of coffee and a relaxing break from Tokyo's fast pace of life

Sights in Ginza are varied, including museums of Japanese and Western art and a uniquely Japanese theater experience (see p. 70). **Idemitsu Museum of Arts (Idemitsu Bijutsukan),** covering 26,900 square feet (2,500 sq m), houses Tokyo's finest private collection of Japanese art and ceramics. The collection has pottery fragments from archaeological excavations all over Asia, and Chinese ceramics including Song-dynasty and T'ang-dynasty three-color ware, as well as fine antique Japanese pottery—Seto, Oribe, Kutani, Karatsu, and Kakiemon. The museum also features Zen calligraphy and ink painting, notably by the 17th-century monk Sengai.

Near Yurakucho Station is the embodiment of the indoor city of

A Ginza relic

The vast Sapporo Lion Ginza beer hall *(7-9-20 Ginza, Chuo-ku),* founded in 1934, retains its prewar decor down to the furnishings and art deco mosaics—but not its original home. Dismantled some 15 years ago, it was reassembled piece by piece in a modern building. Popular with the local business crowd, it's a great place to slake your thirst. ∎

Idemitsu Museum of Arts

⬛ 61 D3
✉ 9F Teigeki Building, 3-1-1 Marunouchi, Chiyoda-ku
☎ 03/3213-9402
🕐 Closed Mon.
💲 $$
🚇 Subway: Hibiya, Yurakucho

Tokyo Stock Exchange

⬛ 61 D3
✉ 2-1 Nihombashi-kabuto-cho, Chuo-ku
☎ 03/3665-1881
🕐 Closed Sat.–Sun.
🚇 Subway: Hibiya, Yurakucho

A Tokyo landmark, the Kabuki-za is the country's foremost traditional playhouse.

Burijisuton Bijutsukan

🗺 61 D3

✉ 2F Bridgestone Bldg., 1-10-1 Kyobashi, Chuo-ku

☎ 03/3563-0241

🕐 Closed Mon. & Dec. 20–Jan. 6

💲 $$

🚇 Subway: Kyobashi

southeast to Chuo-dori and then go north to the **Bridgestone Museum of Art (Burijisuton Bijutsukan).** This is one of Tokyo's finest private art collections. Owned by Japan's foremost tire manufacturer, it specializes in major French Impressionists but also contains works by Picasso and Modigliani and some important old masters, including Rembrandt. It also focuses on *Yoga* (Japanese art in the Western tradition) and includes works by the Paris-based Tsuguji (or Léonard) Fujita (1886–1968).

Just outside Higashi-Ginza station, five minutes' walk along Harumi-dori from Ginza 4-chome crossing, is a Tokyo landmark that curiously blends Western and Japanese shrine architecture. The 1925 **Kabuki-za Theater** *(4-12-15 Ginza, Chuo-ku, tel 03/3541-3131)* vies with the National Theater in Nagatacho as Tokyo's premier location for Kabuki drama. The performances last about three hours. Drinks and snacks are on sale in the foyer; you can also buy a ticket for a set *bento* (lunch box)—it will be served to you in the dining room downstairs during the interval. The cheapest seats are high up and farthest from the stage, so you might like to rent binoculars in the foyer, along with a taped commentary in English. ∎

Hibiya under the tracks

After the war Hibiya retained some of the only stone buildings left standing in Tokyo, and it was here the Occupation authorities set up their headquarters in 1945. A legacy from black market days now popular with the office crowd, several stalls still do a thriving beer-and-yakitori (grilled chicken) business beneath a cavernous railroad archway just behind the Imperial Hotel (see Travelwise p. 361). ∎

A warren of stores and eateries under the tracks

Dwarfed by towers of concrete, Tsukudajima still reflects its past as a fisherman's islet.

Tsukudajima

On the north end of the islet of Tsukishima, off Tsukiji (now joined to the mainland by bridges), the area called Tsukudajima survived both the 1923 earthquake and World War II bombing. Despite some recent concrete redevelopments, many buildings along the main street and behind it retain an antiquarian charm and flavor. The charm comes notably from a view of the old fishing port from a humpbacked bridge, and the flavor from Tsukudajima's famous *tsukudani* (a popular condiment of fry—small fish—or seaweed preserved in sugar and soy) and its *monja-yaki*. Once fare for the poor, this stir-fried noodle mixture is now a popular dish served in restaurants catering to a growing number of visitors. Nevertheless, little has been done to preserve Tsukudajima. Ten'Yasu, one of the tsukudani manufacturers, has been in the same building for nearly 200 years, but much of the rest may soon be history.

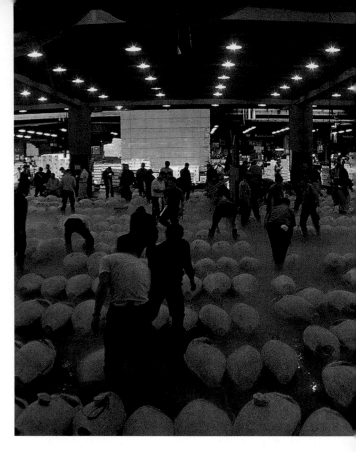

Tuna aligned for early morning auction at the wholesale fish market in Tsukiji—the largest in the world

Tokyo Metropolitan Central Wholesale Market
- 🅰 61 D2
- ✉ 5-2-1 Tsukiji, Chuo-ku
- ☎ 03/3542-1111
- 🕐 Closed Sun. & hols.
- 🚇 Subway: Tsukiji

Hamarikyu-teien Garden
- 🅰 61 D2
- ✉ 1-1 Hamarikyu Teien, Chuo-ku
- ☎ 03/3541-0200
- 🕐 Closed Mon.
- 💲 $

Boat trip to Asakusa
- 💲 $$
- 🚇 Subway & JR: Shimbashi

One mile (2 km) south of the Imperial Palace, **Tokyo Metropolitan Central Wholesale Market (Chuo Oroshi-uri Ichiba)** in Tsukiji handles nearly all the meat and fish sold in the Kanto area (the whole region around Tokyo). This is a fascinating sight (though the professionals turning up for the auction at 5:20 a.m. might not agree). The auction is ostensibly closed to the public, but a discreet glimpse is usually overlooked.

It makes sense to get there early, as most of the action is over by 7 a.m. Next to the main hangar is the Tsukiji Outer Market, a dense cluster of wholesale and retail stores selling fish on ice or dried, as well as a wealth of other food products. Although none of the ramshackle wooden stalls is truly old, they suggest a market from a bygone age. The bustling activity can be a little overwhelming in narrow alleys packed with shoppers, porters, and forklift trucks, but the strong (and pungent) dose of local color is unforgettable. For workers and visitors alike, the highlight of Tsukiji is a superfresh sushi breakfast in one of the market's several small restaurants.

On your way to the Tsukiji market, you will probably pass a curious Buddhist temple. **Tsukiji Hongan-ji Temple** (*3-15-1 Tsukuji, Chuo-ku, outside Tsukiji subway station*) was built in 1935 to replace a 17th-century original destroyed in the 1923 earthquake. It was designed to evoke the classical Indian temple style by the celebrated architect Ito Chuta, It's sheer strangeness makes it a worthy landmark.

South of Ginza, and a ten-minute stroll from the fish market, is **Hamarikyu-teien Garden.** Turned into a landscaped pleasure garden in 1709 from reclaimed land owned by the shoguns, the garden fell into disuse following damage in one of the city's great fires. It passed to the Imperial Household Agency in 1869, and became the Detached Palace Garden. Graced with a lavish Western-style pavilion, it was used for entertaining foreign dignitaries, among them Gen. Ulysses S. Grant.

Today the pavilion is gone, replaced by attractive teahouses. Although Hamarikyu's horizons are walled off by high-rise buildings, it

remains a fine landscape garden and an elegant haven of green in a distinctly ungreen area of Tokyo. Hamarikyu is a stop on the boat trip on the Sumida-gawa between Hinode pier (near Hamamatsucho) and Asakusa. Boats pass roughly every half hour. ∎

Hamarikyu-teien Garden is a landscaped oasis in a highly urban neighborhood.

The water trade—Japan after dark

The origin of the term *mizu shobai* (the water trade) is endlessly debated. The more prosaic interpretation is that the "water" is simply the alcohol upon which the trade floats; the more poetic is that the business reflects the impermanence of life itself. The ancestor of today's mizu shobai was the *ukiyo*—the Floating World, a name ascribed to the pleasure quarters in major towns during the 17th century.

The focus on prostitution in the ukiyo was greater than in the mizu shobai but, like today's amusement districts, the old pleasure quarters boasted a whole gamut of other entertainments—especially of a bibulous kind. The quarters declined during the 19th century with the rise of more general amusement districts elsewhere; the word "ukiyo" simply died with them.

During the postwar period, Tokyo's greatest emerging amusement district was Shinjuku. Although prostitution flourished there, Shinjuku really took off when racketeers erected rows of ramshackle drinking dives in the rubble east of the train station in 1946. Bars, already popular as "cafés" during the 1920s, were all the rage in Japan during the 1950s. The traditional *nomiya* (drinking shop), with its red paper lantern outside, now had a serious rival. The tone was ostensibly American. Sporting Western fashions, the girls enticing customers to drink were hostesses, and the owners of the establishment were *mama-san* and/or *masutaa* (master). These characters, the mainstays of the mizu shobai, signaled the demise of the teahouses and the geisha of prewar times, as their establishments increased in numbers, standing, and price.

Hostess bars are fewer since the recession, especially in Ginza, but remain for the most part exorbitantly expensive. A small minority traffic in prostitution, but not the better clubs. Hostess bars are often luxuriously appointed, but the experience generally holds little appeal for Westerners. A bevy of pretty girls (including exotic and popular Caucasians) in designer dresses cajole and flatter the tired salaryman's ego, pouring drinks and lighting cigarettes. They will also sing karaoke duets with him, often to the strains of the house combo. There may be flirtatious banter, but nothing more. Hostesses are very good at arousing a customer's desire, so that he keeps coming back—mostly in vain. There are exceptions, however, and those—like the geisha—are fishing for a wealthy *danna* (master) to keep them as a *mekake* (mistress) or rarely a wife.

All bars and many nomiya have a system called bottle-keep. On your first visit you buy a bottle of liquor (usually whisky), which is replaced on the shelf with your name on it— yours to drink from when you come back next time. If you are sharing with friends and/or planning to come back, the system can be very economical.

Things are seldom what their English name implies. A hostess bar is usually called a club *(kurabu)*, which it may be, and sometimes supper club, which it is not. Be wary of piano bars, for some keep hostesses. If one sits at your table, you will be charged accordingly.

Another postwar bar legacy is the misnamed *sunakku* (snack), the hostess bar's poorer relative. Most popular in the countryside, sunakku are generally variants of the ubiquitous karaoke bar. The majority are harmless, but some are seriously sleazy; generally sunakku are best avoided unless you are taken by friends. In fact, this is the general rule for smaller bars in the mizu shobai. If a bar is inconspicuously hidden behind a thick door, the chances are that patrons have been introduced; wandering in unaccompanied feels a bit like intruding in a private living room. In a sense, it is. Home is not usually the place for socializing in Japan; the bar, presided over by a mama-san who knows all her customers by name, makes a handy substitute.

Until as recently as 15 years ago, frequenting the mizu shobai was a male preserve, but these days many a woman keeps her own bottle on the shelf. ∎

Left: **Blazing signs in Kabukicho**
Above: *Mama-san:* **the mainstay of the Japanese bar**
Below: **A drink with colleagues after work is the usual conclusion to the working day.**

Hie-jinja Shrine in Akasaka is one of Tokyo's most important Shinto shrines.

Akasaka-Nagatacho

Going southeast from the Imperial Palace, close to Kasumigaseki district and the Diet Building in Nagatacho, Akasaka is devoted to both business and upscale entertainment. Bars and restaurants proliferate along three narrow parallel streets called Tamachi, Hitotsugi, and Mitsuji. The exclusive and astronomically expensive *ryotei* restaurants, identifiable by their traditional wooden architecture, are the haunts of geisha entertainment. Open to patrons only upon introduction, ryotei stand mainly on Mitsuji-dori, one of the only places in Tokyo where you might catch a glimpse of a geisha. Distinctly restrained compared with other entertainment districts, Akasaka is still an attractive place for an evening stroll, especially for those with wining and dining in mind.

Architectural conservation

The Japanese don't wait for only nature or war to demolish buildings. Having survived both, some peripheral wooden neighborhoods and old stone buildings simply vanished under a tide of ferroconcrete.

Beyond designation as an "Important Cultural Property," there is no other system for preserving historic architecture, and only Buddhist temple complexes and prominent Shinto shrines are safe from redevelopment. Conservation is an alien concept, but it is rapidly gaining ground. Now that preservation is proving lucrative for tourism, conservation organizations are gaining clout. ■

The Akasaka district goes uphill to the west behind Misuji-dori; a steep path flanked with glowing stone lanterns leads up to the **Fudo Hall (Akasaka Fudo-san,** *4-1-10 Minato-ku, tel 03/3583-1128),* a tiny curio of a temple dedicated to the fierce Fudo, one of the guardians of the Buddhist hell.

Hie-jinja Shrine, also called Sanno-sama, was the favorite shrine of the Tokugawa shoguns and the focal point of the grandest festival in Edo. Although a Shinto shrine, it owes its existence to Buddhism. When the Tendai sect was founded on Mount Hiei-zan (near Kyoto) during the eighth century, the monks also erected a Shinto shrine to protect the temple from the demonic northeast; the trend spread all over Japan. Such a shrine existed on this spot long before the arrival of the shoguns, who were delighted to have it safeguarding nearby Edo-jo Castle. Today it protects the Imperial Palace.

Hie-jinja was destroyed in the air raids of 1945; the current structures are reproductions built between 1959 and 1967. Accessible via a steep path straddled by rows of small red *torii* (shrine gateways), this is a very pleasant haven. In mid-August, Hie-jinja stages Takigi Noh, outdoor Noh theater performances of some of the most representative plays in the repertoire —an unmissable experience.

Less than 200 yards (150 m) northwest of Akasaka-mitsuke subway station on Aoyama-dori, the beer and liquor company Suntory shows how cultural funding in Japan is best reflected in the private sector. **Suntory Museum of Art (Santori Bijutsukan),** an excellent collection of lacquerware, ceramics, Noh masks, costumes, paintings, and prints, is regularly complemented with special exhibitions (check listings for schedules).

On Aoyama-dori, about half a mile (800 m) west of Akasaka-mitsuke station, the **Sogetsu Art Center (Sogetsu Kaikan)** is the headquarters of the Sogetsu school of flower arranging, which pioneered a modernist approach to traditional ikebana. Low-key floral arrangements enhance the grandeur of the main hall of this architecturally impressive building by Tange Kenzo, in which modern art exhibitions are regularly held. The Sogetsu building also has a museum and a gallery; both frequently host some of the most impressive art exhibitions in town. ■

Hie-jinja Shrine
- 61 C3
- 2-10-5 Nagata-cho, Chiyoda-ku. Entrance in Nagata-cho, next to Capitol Tokyu Hotel
- 03/3581-2471
- Subway: Kokkai Gijido-mae

Suntory Museum of Art
- 61 C3
- 11F Tokyo Suntory Bldg, 1-2-3 Moto Akasaka, Minato-ku
- 03/3470-1073
- Closed Mon.
- Subway: Akasaka-mitsuke

Sogetsu Art Center
- 7-2-21 Akasaka, Minato-ku, Tokyo 107
- Closed Sun
- Subway: Akasaka-mitsuke

Painting of Gion and Sanno festivals, Momoyama period, in the Suntory Museum of Art

Almond is Roppongi's premier meeting spot—not the coffee shop but the corner outside.

Roppongi-Shiba-koen Park

As foreign embassies multiplied in the area during the 1950s, Roppongi developed, along with nearby Azabu and Hiro, as a residential district for expatriates. Renowned then as now for its foreign restaurants, it became a favorite with Japanese as the hub of Western-style entertainment. Today its many restaurants include some of Tokyo's best, offering a staggering array of both world and Japanese cuisine.

Roppongi rivaled Shinjuku for its proliferation of discos in the late 1970s and became one of Tokyo's most fashionable districts during the 1980s. Although still cosmopolitan and sophisticated, in recent years it has exploded as an entertainment district as raucous as any. In the process it has become more tacky here and there, but for the visitor it remains one the best and most accessible options for a fun night out in Tokyo.

Roppongi

Roppongi means "six trees," but the area is hardly renowned for its greenery today. If Roppongi seems too turbulent at night, follow the overhead expressway down to Nishi Azabu Crossing, where the backstreets on the left abound with quieter bars and restaurants. ■

mination technology has turned it into a surprisingly attractive feature of Tokyo's nocturnal skyline. The Grand observation platform is 490 feet (150 m) up; the top observation platform offers a Tokyo panorama. There is a dusty wax museum on the Grand level and an unremarkable aquarium among other uninspiring exhibits on the first floor. This is mainly for lovers of the incongruous and passé.

Zojo-ji Temple was moved to its present location (now Shiba-koen) in 1598, where it was the centerpiece of a temple city of hundreds of buildings. Razed and rebuilt more than once, Zojo-ji has had a tumultuous history. After being torched during the Meiji Restoration, it was burned by a vagrant in 1909 before being destroyed during World War II. The *sanmon* (two-storied) gate, built in 1605, is a miraculous and magnificent survivor. One of the very few buildings of such antiquity in Tokyo, it is designated an Important Cultural Property. The main hall, built in 1974, contains several treasures, including the huge old temple bell.

Another survivor is the Nitenmon gate, which now stands on land belonging to the Tokyo Prince Hotel *(3-3-1 Shiba-koen, Minato-ku, tel 03/3432-1111);* other parts of the compound, including the old Tokugawa burial ground, now find themselves within the confines of a private golf club. ■

A monk rings the huge bell at Zojo-ji Temple.

In the development frenzy of the 1950s, Tokyo set its sights on having its own Eiffel Tower. Radio and TV signal transmission provided the excuse; the 1,092-foot (330 m) **Tokyo Tower** was erected in 1958 on land that was once part of **Shiba-koen Park.** At first it was swamped by Japanese visitors, but now it is regarded as a blight on the cityscape. However, improved illu-

Tokyo Tower
- 61 C2
- 4-2-8 Shiba-koen, Minato-ku. 550 yards (500 m) due south of Kamiya-cho subway station
- 03/3433-5111
- Grand platform $$; top platform $$$; Wax Museum $$; Aquarium $$
- Subway: Kamiya-cho

Zojo-ji Temple
- 61 C2
- 4-7-35 Shiba-koen, Minato-ku. About 550 yards (500 m) from Daimon (east), Shiba-koen (south), & Onarimon (north) subway stations
- 03/0432-1431
- Subway: Daimon, Shiba-koen, Onarimon

Almond

Ｏn the southern corner of Roppongi crossing is the Almond coffee shop. Although it has nothing much to recommend it beyond a rather lurid pink facade, the area outside the coffee shop is one of the main meeting places for Roppongi revelers and is packed tight on weekend evenings.

It can be something of a struggle finding your friends in the scrum outside, but Almond is a good place for touching the pulse of the local fauna. ■

Shibuya, with its amazing array of fashion outlets, is a magnet for the young.

Aoyama-Harajuku-Shibuya

Shibuya-ku (the ward as opposed to its central area described in the walk on pp. 82–83) as a whole covers a wide area embracing Yoyogi-koen Park, the youthful Harajuku district, the Meiji-jingu Shrine, Tokyo's most fashionable shopping precincts, and some notable museums. The Aoyama area has been the home of international chic since the mid-1970s; renowned for its expensive big-name designer boutiques, one street has been facetiously named "Killer dori." The area abounds with interesting galleries and exhibition spaces devoted mainly to modern art, and notable exhibitions are often held in some of Tokyo's finest examples of modern architecture, among them Maki Fumihiko's remarkable Spiral Building on Aoyama-dori. Kotto-dori (Antiques Street) has many outstanding antiques shops, but no bargains.

A broad tree-lined boulevard running from Aoyama-dori to Harajuku, **Omotesando-dori** is one of Tokyo's most pleasant locales. You can sit and watch the world pass by from the Parisian-style cafés, or explore stores and boutiques ranging from the sleek, glass-fronted Hanae Mori Building (which contains many shops) to the lunatic fringe of teen fashion in Harajuku, which reaches its climax in the boutiques along narrow Takeshita-dori. Midway along Omotesando is the Oriental Bazaar (see p. 381), a good place to buy quality souvenirs and moderately priced antiques. Closed to traffic on Sundays, Omotesando finds Tokyo youth thronging to impromptu rock bands up and down the avenue.

The 133 acres (54 ha) of **Yoyogi-koen Park** became a park when the buildings, erected for U.S. Occupation staff, were demolished; it is now a wooded and pleasant place for strolling. It was also the main site of the 1964 Tokyo Olympics, as Tange Kenzo's amazing stadium buildings testify.

Like Tokyo's other major districts, Shibuya grew up around a major railroad terminal. Shibuya station developed rapidly after the
(continued on p. 85)

Yoyogi-koen Park
60 A3

Sundays finds various youthful groups, musical and otherwise, congregating on Omotesando boulevard— including Rockabillies.

Two walks through Shibuya-ku

Sights tend to be scattered in Shibuya but, as a rule of thumb, the southwestern part is mainly concerned with shopping and entertainment and the northwestern sector, though it has no shortage of shops either, focuses on the Meiji-jingu Shrine and surrounding parkland.

WALK 1: SHIBUYA

Start from Hachiko Square. Standing in front of the intersection with your back to the station, you will see 109 Building (a cylinder with 109 emblazoned on the front) standing on a sharp corner to your left. Cross straight over into Koen-dori in front of you and 100 yards (90 m) up on your left is **Seibu** ❶ department store (see p. 381). The store sells everything imaginable but is particularly strong on fashion. Next turn left into the narrow street between Seibu's two buildings on Koen-dori and then take the first right behind the right-hand one.

Next turn left and left again into Koen-dori. Take a break from the stores 220 yards (200 m) up the street in the **Tobacco & Salt Museum (Tabako to Shio no Hakubutsukan)** ❷. Love or hate tobacco, it has a long and colorful history. Exhibiting aspects of world salt and tobacco lore from Mayan times, the museum is also notable for Edo-period woodblock prints on smoking themes.

Retracing your steps along Koen-dori will bring you to Parco 2 on your right on the next corner and the main Parco just across the road from it. Having turned right into this road (Inokashira-dori); keep walking until you reach Tokyu Hands (see p. 382). Turn left into the small street that runs down from Inokashira-dori along the side of the building and keep going straight. The array of shops and boutiques along here is a foretaste of the nucleus of Shibuya's youthful fashion and café culture. Center Gai is a narrow pedestrian street that you reach by crossing over the next intersection.

Turning left along here will bring you back to the station and crossing over it will bring you into Bunkamura-dori, level with **One-Oh-Nine** ❸, a "fashion building." Exit onto Bunkamura-dori and return to 109 Building, notable above all for one of Shibuya's most curious sights: a small wooden traditional restaurant sticking out of the concrete wall. The proprietor stood his ground against the developers, so they built 109 around him.

Turning sharp right here will take you to Dogen-zaka—a sloping street with bars and restaurants proliferating in the alleys on both sides. They constitute Shibuya's main entertainment district—not a bad place to wind up the day. Alternatively, if you're traveling with kids, a final destination for walks or a break between them is the **National Children's Castle (Kodomo no Shiro,** see p. 363) ❹. Easily identifiable by Okamoto Taro's weird, multicolored, totemlike sculpture outside, this is kiddie heaven: a giant activity center on several floors, including play areas and facilities for painting, handicrafts, computer games, and video, as well as a hotel for families.

WALK 2: AOYAMA-HARAJUKU

Start at JR Harajuku Station. Enter the path on your left (signposted in English) leading up to Meiji-jingu Shrine (see p. 85). After 220 yards (200 m) you will come to the entrance to the **Meiji-jingu Inner Gardens** ❶; always a lovely park, it's truly unmissable when the irises bloom in June. Continue along the same path to **Meiji-jingu Shrine** ❷. After your visit, retrace your steps to Harajuku Station. Turn left and after 160 yards (150 m) you'll find, on your right, narrow Takeshita-dori—a famed teenage shopping alley. At the end of the alley you'll reach the intersection with Meiji-dori. Turn right and walk on down the avenue toward the next intersection. The cream-colored building with the cylindrical facade on your right is Laforet Harajuku, with boutiques inside.

Just behind the Laforet building is the **Ota Memorial Museum of Art (Ota Kinen Bijutsukan)** ❸ *(1-10-10 Jingumae, tel 03/3403 0880, closed Mon. and from 25th to end of each month)*. The Ota collection of 12,000 *ukiyo-e* prints is probably the largest privately owned in Japan. The museum is beautifully laid out in Japanese style, with a small rock garden and a tea room downstairs.

Make your way down Meiji-dori again to the intersection and turn left down Omotesando-dori. After a further160 yards (150 m), on the right-hand side of the street you will find several stores for souvenir shopping. Nearly 400 yards (350 m) further on is architect Tange Kenzo's elegant Hanae Mori building, which contains antique stores in the basement, l'Orangerie restaurant, and fashion designer Hanae Mori's flagship store. From here, cross over the intersection with Aoyama-dori and walk some 550 yards (500 m) to the **Nezu Institute of Fine Art (Nezu Bijutsukan)** ④ *(6-5-36 Minami, tel 03/3400 2536, closed Mon.).* Located in a quiet residential district, this notable museum stands in a delightful Japanese garden replete with ponds and tea-houses (still used for tea ceremonies). Despite

☒ **See area map page 60–61**
Walk 1
► Hachiko Square
⬌ 2.5 miles (4 km)
🕐 2 hours
► Dogen-zaka
Walk 2
► Harajuku Station
⬌ 1.7 miles (2.8 km)
🕐 2 hours
► Aoyama-dori

its small size, the museum boasts one of the country's finest collections of Japanese (as well as Chinese and Korean) classical and Buddhist art, including the famed 17th-century screen painting of irises by Ogata Korin. Walk back toward Aoyama-dori. On the way you'll see an elegant building faced with blue and white tiles on your left; it's the Yoku Moku confectionery—a great place to stop for coffee. ■

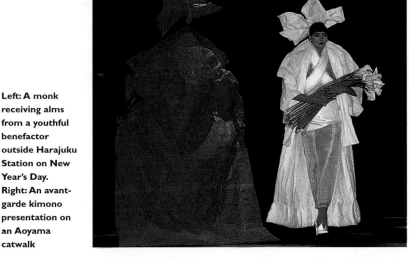

Left: A monk receiving alms from a youthful benefactor outside Harajuku Station on New Year's Day. Right: An avant-garde kimono presentation on an Aoyama catwalk

Meiji-jingu Shrine

🅰 60 A3

✉ 1-1 Kamizono-cho, Yoyogi, Shibuya-ku. Just west of stations

☎ 03/3379-5511

🚇 Subway: Meiji-jingu-mae; JR: Harajuku

TEMPLES & SHRINES

All temples in Japan are Buddhist and all shrines are Shinto. Temples and shrines are usually part of a complex; the area covered by a complex can be extensive (see p. 246).

(continued from p. 81)

1923 earthquake, when many people moved to the area from devastated Asakusa, and it is the commuter gateway between the capital and the western suburbs out to Yokohama. Like other station areas, it has sprouted an amusement quarter.

From the end of the 1970s, Shibuya's Seibu and Parco department stores established themselves as the harbingers of high fashion. When nearby Harajuku became the city's prime teenage hangout, Shibuya took the overflow, especially on the narrow Center Gai street opposite the station. The trendy bars, cafés, and boutiques spread out from here over a decade; often dubbed *yangu taun* (young town) in the 1980s, Shibuya remains the ultimate mecca of fashion and culture for the under-25s.

Among the fashionable department stores is the remarkable Tokyu Hands (see p. 382); several floors are exhaustively devoted to home crafts and do-it-yourself projects. Pioneered by the Seibu conglomerate, the area abounds in theaters, movie houses, and exhibi-

tion spaces. The rival Tokyu corporation's impressive Bunkamura (culture village) presents facets of contemporary culture, including films, theater, and art exhibits, in a single building.

Straddling Aoyama and Harajuku, and just south of Shinjuku, is Tokyo's greatest shrine, **Meiji-jingu Shrine,** which commemorates Emperor Meiji, whose reign saw the momentous passage from feudal to modern Japan. Construction began in 1915, a year after the death of the emperor's wife, Empress Shoken, and was completed in 1920.

The shrine was destroyed during World War II but was rebuilt in 1958, exactly as before, standing in a broad courtyard with characteristically sweeping architecture of unadorned cypress wood beneath a splendid roof of copper tiles. With a fine cloister hung with bronze lanterns adjoining the main hall, this is Tokyo's most impressive shrine. The main approach behind Harajuku, a shaded avenue of majestic camphor trees, features at the entrance a towering *torii*

Above: Like colored streams, iris beds meander through Meiji-jingu Inner Gardens in June. Right: At New Year, thousands buy lucky *hama-ya* ("evil breaking") arrows.

gateway made of gigantic cypress trees from Taiwan.

Noh and kagura (see p. 46) performances are held in the shrine courtyard on Emperor Meiji's birthday (November 3). Meiji-jingu is Tokyo's most popular shrine for observances over the New Year holiday, when its visitors number around a million.

Mainly of interest to history buffs, the **Meiji-jingu Treasure House (Homotsuden)** displays a collection of state costumes and miscellaneous items belonging to Emperor Meiji, including the imperial carriage. *(Follow signs from the shrine's Harajuku entrance, closed 3rd Fri. each month.)*

The beautiful 150-acre (60 ha) **Meiji-jingu Inner Gardens (Meiji-jingu-gyoen,** *entrance on the left, about halfway along main approach to the shrine)* is noted for its lily pond in summer and its 126,000 trees, contributed from all over Japan when the garden was created in 1920.

Much cherished by the Meiji emperor and empress, the iris garden is particularly lovely in June, when displays of hundreds of varieties bloom along a broad serpentine bed. ■

Above right: A Shinto priest at Meiji-jingu Shrine wielding a paper wand protects the faithful from evil.

Shrine and temple merchandise

During festivals, large Shinto shrine and Buddhist temple compounds look like markets. Stalls sell delicacies such as *tako yaki* (barbecued octopus dumplings) and fried noodles, as well as toffee apples, candy, cheap toys, and souvenirs. The main buildings trade briskly in religious trinkets, notably key-ring size *mamori* (talismans) against misfortune, as well as *omikuji* (fortune papers). For around 100 yen you pull a numbered stick out of an oblong box and are given the paper with the corresponding number. Rolled up, the paper is tied to a tree (the right one is the one festooned with fortune papers) to enhance good fortune and, hopefully, avert the bad. ■

Shinjuku & Ikebukuro

Shinjuku means "new inn," after the taverns that sprouted here in the late 17th century, when the area became the post town nearest to Edo along the road out toward the Japan Alps. The township rapidly grew and soon came to include a large unlicensed red-light district—as indeed it still does. Respectability came with the building of Shinjuku Station in 1885, now one of the busiest train terminals on Earth. Less damaged than other areas after the 1923 earthquake, Shinjuku became the hub of Tokyo.

After the Olympics in 1964, Shinjuku took off—mostly upward—as the "new heart of Tokyo." Starting with the Keio Plaza Hotel, completed in 1972, the western side of Shinjuku developed a forest of skyscrapers. Tange Kenzo's new Tokyo Metropolitan Government Office became the colossal centerpiece in 1991. Combining plush hotels, official buildings, shopping areas, a lovely park, and a raucous amusement district, the marvelous eclecticism of Shinjuku is archetypically Japanese.

North of Shinjuku, Ikebukuro is another major station area. Its amusement district, near the station, has long been a shabbier relative of Shinjuku's Kabukicho. Although devoid of sights, Ikebukuro comes into its own as a shopping heaven and, more recently, for its

Hanazono-jinja Shrine

⚠ 60 A4

✉ Meiji-dori

Below: Shinjuku's brash, bright Kabuki-cho amusement district

Right: Ornamental rakes on sale at the Tori-no-Ichi festival at Hanazono-jinja Shrine

EAST SHINJUKU

Make sure you leave plenty of time if you catch a train at Shinjuku Station: Getting lost in the crowded station labyrinth is something that happens even to the locals. Exits from the subway lines lead straight into a gigantic underground shopping mall, and the surges of people in every direction at rush hour merely add to the general confusion above ground.

Anywhere else, **Kabuki-cho** in East Shinjuku would be sin city, but the Japanese do not believe in sin. As in other amusement districts, all the facets of pleasure exist here cheek by jowl: eating, drinking, movies, game arcades, and sex. Out of some 3,000 entertainment outlets, the 500 devoted to sleaze are signaled by tuxedoed touts in doorways or skimpily-clad *kanban gyaru*—signpost girls—enticing customers inside. The streets, a kaleidoscope of electric signs and blazing neon, are lined with speakers blaring recorded come-ons and deafening music. Full of garish *pachinko* (pinball) parlors, this is a capital of kitsch; it even has a reproduction of Rome's Trevi Fountain lit in green neon.

With so many great restaurants and thousands of bars, about 500,000 visitors flock here every night; at the long evening's end pub-crawling salarymen totter through the streets, propping each other up. The party extends beyond Kabuki-cho northward and on to Shin Okubo, a kind of little Southeast Asia renowned for both its superb ethnic restaurants and the loose ladies lurking in the alleyways. Though Kabuki-cho is perfectly safe, some caution is advisable in the backstreets when the crowds thin much later on.

Heading west, **Hanazono-jinja Shrine** provides a pleasant retreat from the sheer lunacy of nearby Kabuki-cho. Dedicated to Inari, the deity of gain and grain, the shrine was moved to its present site during the 17th century. The otherwise rather unprepossessing shrine comes into its own during Tori-no-Ichi—the chicken festival—on November 3 (see p. 38).

Shinjuku National Garden *(11 Naito-cho, Shinjuku-ku, tel 03/3350-0151, closed Mon.)* belonged to the regional governor of Naito during the Edo period, then to the imperial family, before becoming a public park after World War II. Lying to the southeast of Shinjuku, this is not only one of the city's largest parks at about 150 acres (60 ha), but it is also one of

the most beautifully landscaped, with substantial sections devoted to both Japanese- and Western-style gardens. Its 1,900 cherry trees make it a highly popular location for blossom viewing in April. The view of skyscrapers over the greenery is a favorite with amateur painters.

WEST SHINJUKU

Leaving Shinjuku Station by the west exit places you in a very different world from the vibrant east side. Beneath the soaring towers lies a popular warren of cut-price camera stores (as do Shibuya and Ikebukuro). Awe-inspiring as the tall buildings are, they are utterly devoid of anything so prosaic as human warmth. That said, Tange Kenzo's impressive 797-foot (243 m) **Tokyo Metropolitan Government Office,** completed

Pachinko

Ablaze with colored neon, rural pachinko parlors can sometimes be seen for miles over the paddies; in cities their garish architecture can ruin a neighborhood. Pachinko (from *pachin*, slap, and *ko*, a ball) took off during the 1950s. In this vertical pin-

Players in a pachinko parlor

ball game, hundreds of ball bearings clatter along the pins and traps on the machine's gaudy face as, immobile and mesmerized, customers spend hours twiddling a knob with one hand. The knob fires the balls: Success requires skill and luck.

There is a pachinko culture with tales of little old ladies eking out an existence playing the game. There is even a profession of "pin straighteners," whose job consists of straightening the pins on the machine face to prevent bending from ostensible overuse.

Prizes include cookies and cigarettes, often exchanged (but don't tell anyone) for cash through a backstreet pigeonhole. Pachinko profits top the entire service industry in Japan. ■

Tokyo Metropolitan Government Office
- Arrowed from 60 A3
- 2-8-1, Nishi-Shinjuku, Shinjuku-ku
- 03/5321-1111
- Closed Mon.

Ikebukuro
- 60 B6

Sunshine 60 Building
- 60 B6
- 3-1-3 Higachi-Ikebukuro
- 03/3989-3331

in 1991 and inspired by European cathedrals, is a must-see. Like most tall landmarks, it has a number of restaurants in the basement and on the panoramic top floor (with prices escalating accordingly).

However, for panoramic views at night, it is hard to beat the one from the nearby Keio Plaza Hotel's delightful bar, the Little Bear, where the twinkling city lights match the low lighting glinting on the bottles.

IKEBUKURO

Ikebukuro is another major terminal station area, serving commuters to the northwest. Near the station, its amusement district has long been a shabbier relative of Shinjuku's Kabuki-cho. To the east is the colossal **Sunshine 60 Building,** part of the Sunshine City complex; most of its 60 stories are devoted to offices, but several contain restaurants and shopping malls. It stands on the site of Sugamo prison, where war criminals such as Tojo Hideki were executed. Ikebukuro continues to rise as a shopping district: The Seibu and Tobu department stores on the east side are among the world's largest. Not to be outdone, the west side of Ikebukuro has recently risen to prominence with two gigantic malls, the Metropolitan Plaza and Spice 2.

Culture is Ikebukuro's rising star, enhanced recently with the multiple theaters in the **Tokyo Metropolitan Art Space,** the new headquarters of the prestigious Tokyo Metropolitan Orchestra. Despite this and its variety of shopping options, Ikebukuro remains strangely colorless, an also-ran in the race to excel as one of the great Tokyo districts. ■

The towers of Tange Kenzo's impressive new Tokyo Metropolitan Government Office dominate the Shinjuku skyline.

Ueno-koen Park has long been a favored location for *hanami* (flower-viewing) picnics.

Ueno

Ueno Hill (now Ueno-koen Park), scattered with shrines and temples erected by the Tokugawa shoguns and famous for its cherry trees, was the spot favored by aristocrats for *hanami*—blossom viewing. The site of the only significant (and futile) battle resisting the Meiji Restoration, the hill was a stronghold for some 2,000 Tokugawa loyalists trounced by the country's first modern army in 1867. The fleeing survivors torched the buildings of the Tokugawa's Kanei-ji Temple complex in order to deny their use to their conquerors, but they fortunately overlooked Tosho-gu Shrine, dedicated to Tokugawa Ieyasu himself (see below).

The hill area became the city's first public park in 1873 and was used for popular national exhibitions; the art gallery built for the second exhibition in 1892 was the ancestor of the Tokyo National Museum.

Ueno-koen Park contains outstanding museums, Tosho-gu Shrine, temples, Ueno Zoo, and Shinobazu Pond, which is particularly delightful in summer, but the areas of greenery seem fragmented and neglected. All this makes the park a representative centerpiece for the entire district, which presents a curious mixture of things old and venerable and others not quite so old and rather shabby.

With the development of railways, Ueno Station increased in importance after the start of the 20th century as the gateway to northern Japan. Following the devastation of World War II, the station area found many thousands of homeless Tokyoites sheltering under the elevated tracks. Since the 1950s the area has attracted a large number of poor farmers from Northern Honshu (Tohoku); they would leave their snowbound fields in winter to seek employment in Tokyo—often in vain. Although Tohoku's greater prosperity later reduced their number, the Ueno area is still haunted by the homeless.

Hanami

Hanami is flower viewing. It sounds elegant and refined, as indeed it was in Ueno during the Edo period. Dandies and ladies of fashion, who often changed their kimono several times during the event, sat picnicking as flakes of palest pink fell from the resplendent blossoming cherry trees above them.

Today hanami parties are enjoyed all over Japan. After spreading plastic sheeting beneath the trees, flower watchers—often in the thousands—sit down to a substantial sushi picnic washed down with copious sake and beer. Foreign observers will often be entreated to join the fray; afterwards they might feel as the parks look—littered with picnic wreckage and trampled blossoms.

People travel to some 60 prominent hanami sites around Japan from early April in southern Honshu to mid-May in Hokkaido. For springtime travelers to Japan, hanami is a must-see. Torrential rain is no deterrent: Flower-viewing parties simply sit under their umbrellas. ■

Yushima-tenjin Shrine

- 61 D5
- 3-30-1 Yushima, Bunkyo-ku
- 03/3836-0753
- Subway: Yushima

Many visitors to Ueno are northern daytrippers; the area accordingly is filled with department stores and shopping options to suit all budgets. The district includes a rather seedy if spirited entertainment area, but tucked away in the streets just below the park are some vintage restaurants and shops that make Ueno one of Tokyo's most fascinating areas. Less than 20 minutes from Ginza on the Hibiya or Ginza subway lines, Ueno could hardly present a greater contrast to that district's glitz.

Today's colorful **Ameyoko market,** alongside Ueno Station, is a legacy of the black market that thrived in the immediate postwar period. The name is short for Ameya-yokocho (Candy Store Alley), so called after the candy stalls that were often fronts for other goods—especially those made in the United States—sold by black marketeers.

This is Tokyo's liveliest market and the last with something of the flavor of an Asian bazaar. Stalls sell jeans of every known brand and configuration, aloha shirts, leather jackets, bags, and sneakers next door to dried squid and bonito flakes, groceries, and fresh fish. The prices of famous-brand clothing are the same as elsewhere , but bargains and discounts abound on everything else.

Halfway along Candy Store Alley is Tokudai-ji Temple, a little Buddhist temple located on the first floor above a collection of sundry stores.

Yushima-tenjin Shrine, near JR Okachimachi Station, was originally built in the 14th century and restored during the 19th. The shrine is dedicated to Sugawara no Michizane (845–903), a Heian-period statesman and scholar later deified as the patron of learning. Yushima-tenjin is particularly revered by students praying for success in exams, as well as for its garden of plum trees, which attract large crowds when they blossom between mid-February and mid-March.

Yanaka
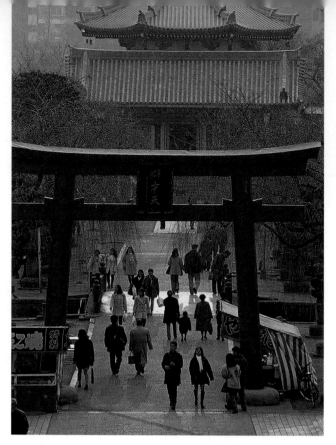

🅐 61 D5

Ueno-koen Park

🅐 61 D5

✉ Ueno-koen, Taito-ku

🚇 Subway: Ueno

National Science Museum

🅐 61 E5

✉ 7-20 Ueno-koen, Taito-ku

☎ 03/3822-0111

🕐 Closed Mon.

💲 $$

🚇 Subway: Ueno

Dedicated to the goddess Benten, Benzaiten Temple (Benten-do) stands in the middle of Ueno's Shinobazu Pond.

National Museum of Western Art

🅐 61 D5

✉ 7-7 Ueno-koen, Taito-ku

☎ 03/3828-5131

🕐 Closed Mon.

💲 $$$

🚇 Subway: Ueno

Shitamachi History Museum

🅐 61 D5

✉ 2-1 Ueno-koen, Taito-ku

☎ 03/3823-7451

🕐 Closed Mon.

💲 $

🚇 Subway: Ueno

To the northwest of Ueno-koen, **Yanaka Hill,** maintained as a temple town during the Tokugawa era (see p. 32), still has more than 80 temples, most managing funeral rites in nearby Yanaka Cemetery. There are so many temples that the streets are scented with incense. A survivor of both the 1923 earthquake and wartime air raids, this is the last bastion of Meiji- and Taisho-era Tokyo. Yanaka is close to Tokyo University (the nation's most prestigious seat of learning) and the University of Fine Arts and has been favored by academics, artists, and intellectuals since Meiji times.

UENO-KOEN PARK

From Ueno Station, take the west gate entrance where you will find an information desk. Walk north to the **National Science Museum (Kokuritsu Kagaku Hakubutsukan).** Presenting all aspects of science and natural history, the museum is a firm favorite with schoolchildren and sometimes holds large-scale special exhibitions. About three minutes' walk south of the science museum, the **National Museum of Western Art (Kokuritsu Seiyo Bijutsukan),** opened in 1959, was designed by Le Corbusier. The museum's impressive collection includes European old master paintings such as El Greco's "Crucifixion," Rodin sculptures ("The Thinker" and "The Burghers of Calais"), French Impressionists, and works by modern artists such as Max Ernst, Fernand Léger, and Jackson Pollock.

At the south end of the park is **Shitamachi History Museum (Shitamachi Fuzoku Shiryokan),** a two-story museum founded in 1980. Upstairs are exhibits and artifacts (many locally contributed) that afford fascinating glimpses into the lives of the *edokko*—the proud but often very poor inhabitants of the "Low City" of Edo and Tokyo (see pp. 100–101). Downstairs, the reconstructed shops, workshops, and homes of the Edo and Meiji periods, brought to life with wax figures, provide a nostalgic picture of a vanished and very different way of life.

Ueno Zoo (Ueno Dobutsuen), which opened in 1882, is particularly popular for its pandas. The grounds contain a pagoda and teahouse of Edo-period vintage, as well as a section of Shinobazu Pond (see p. 98) devoted to cormorants. The animals are well cared for, but space is cramped; if the sight of animals in cages distresses you, bypass this place.

Regrettably eclipsed these days by Ueno Zoo and the monorail connecting its two halves is **Tosho-gu Shrine.** This opulent shrine, noted for its rich Chinese-style carvings and Kano-school (late 16th-century) paintings in the prayer hall, is designated an Important Cultural Property. Among Tokyo's oldest shrines, it remains as it was when completed in 1651. To the south of the shrine approach is its famous peony garden *(mid-April to mid-May)* containing some 200 varieties.

In the north of Ueno Park, Japan's largest museum, **Tokyo National Museum (Tokyo Kokuritsu Hakubutsukan),** houses the best collection of Japanese art in the world. It comprises 86,456 works of art, plus nearly 2,000 on permanent loan; the Japanese collection includes 84 National Treasures and 521 Important Cultural Properties. It is impossible to show everything simultaneously and most exhibits are shown on a rotating basis.

The 25 rooms of the **Main Building (Honkan,** built in 1937) are devoted to Japanese art. On the first floor, sculpture and metalwork are displayed to the right; ceramics, swords and armor, textiles, and applied arts are to the left. The right-hand side of the second floor consists of paintings and lacquerware; the left has mainly calligraphy, ink paintings, and drawings. Despite the splendor of the exhibits, the museum is antiquated and the lighting gloomy; it reflects a concept of art appreciation based on deference to the work rather than pleasure in it.

Left of the main hall, the nine-room 1968 **Gallery of East Asian Art and Antiquities (Toyokan)** exhibits objects from

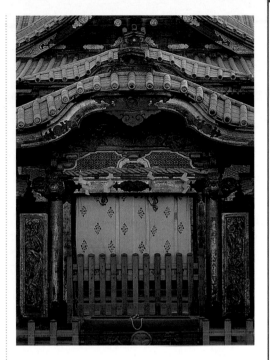

Ornate Chinese-style decoration characterizes Tosho-gu, Tokyo's oldest Shinto shrine.

Ueno Zoo
- 61 D5
- 9-83 Ueno-koen, Taito-ku
- 03/3828-5171
- Closed Mon.
- $
- Subway: Ueno

Tosho-gu Shrine
- 61 D5
- 9-88 Ueno-koen, Taito-ku
- 03/3822-3455
- Shrine $, Peony Garden $$
- Subway: Ueno

Tokyo National Museum

- 🅰 61 D4–D5
- ✉ 13-9 Ueno-koen, Taito-ku
- ☎ 03/3822-1111
- 🕐 Closed Mon.
- 💲 $$$
- 🚇 Subway: Ueno

Tokyo National Museum

- ceramics
- textiles
- arms & armor
- sculpture
- metalwork
- painting
- lacquerware
- calligraphy
- other areas

Gallery of East Asian Art and Antiquities (Toyokan)

■ Korean art
■ Chinese art
■ sculpture
■ Egyptian art
▨ other areas

The Hyokeikan was built in the early 20th century and is a designated Important Cultural Property representing Western-style architecture of that era. The gallery space will be used for special exhibitions.

Haniwa figurine of seated shrine maiden, 6th century

India, West Asia, and Southeast Asia on the first floor, China on the second, and Korea and the Pacific on the third. The 1909 **Heiseikan Gallery,** right of the main hall, is devoted to Japanese archaeology, notably prehistoric pottery and sculpture, and early Buddhist art.

The **Gallery of Horyu-ji Treasures (Horyu-ji Homotsukan,** built in 1964) houses a collection of 318 treasures from the great seventh-century Horyu-ji Temple near Nara, donated to the imperial family in 1878. The displays include sculptures, metalwork, furniture, painted scrolls, masks, and textiles. The building is open only on Thursdays, weather permitting. The age of these objects makes them fragile, so they are not displayed when it rains or on humid days in summer.

Several notable structures that survived the post-battle fires of 1867 (see p. 92) are almost hidden behind the museum. They include the Kanei-ji Temple (rebuilt after World War II), Edo's most important Buddhist temple, the elaborate gates of the old Tokugawa mausoleums, and the attractive Jigendo Hall, with the old Koku-mon gate in front of it. ■

A walking tour of Ueno-Nezu-Yanaka

There is more to see in the Ueno area than anywhere else in Tokyo. This walk takes three to four hours, but leave yourself a full day if you want to see the museums at the same time.

As you leave **Ueno Station** (JR or subway), turn left and walk south down the main road. Entering Ueno-koen Park on your right, you will reach the bronze statue of Saigo Takamori, commemorated (like many Japanese heroes) for his courageous espousal of a lost cause: He was defeated and died in 1877 as leader of the Satsuma Rebellion (see p. 36). Opposite, to the north, is a monument dedicated to the luckless Shogitai, the 2,000 Tokugawa loyalists who similarly opposed the imperial forces in 1867. On your right is **Kanei-ji Kyomizu Kannon-do Temple** ❶ (Tel 03/3821-4749), one of the Kanei-ji Temple buildings to survive burning by samurai loyalists (see p. 92) and war. It was built to house a statue of the Buddhist deity Kannon presented by the abbot of the Kyomizu-dera Temple in 1631 and its design is based on Kyomizu-dera (see pp. 213–14).

From the temple, a short walk west will lead you to the path around **Shinobazu Pond** ❷. The pond was designed in the 17th century and is divided between a boating area and the famous lotus pond.

On an islet connected by a land bridge ahead of you is the **Benten-do Temple** ❸, dedicated to Benten, variously worshiped as a goddess of wealth, muse of the arts, and patron of amorous couples. There are several old teahouses nearby; some serve snacks such as yakisoba—fried noodles. (Ueno-koen has more substantial restaurants too; see p. 365.) During the month from mid-July, the grounds of Benten-do and the path around the pond are used for local evening fairs and festivals. Festival stalls sell plants and insects (crickets, fireflies), as well as antiques and bric-a-brac.

Continue north up the path; take a right at the first fork, then follow the signs for the **Tosho-gu Shrine** (see p. 95). The approach to the shrine, flanked with stone lanterns, is the best place to view the **Kanei-ji Pagoda (Kanei-ji Goju-no-To)** to the left, another 17th-century survivor now within the confines of Ueno Zoo. After visiting Tosho-gu, go back toward the pond, turn right, and head north along Shinobazu-dori. After passing the Ogaiso Hotel on your left, cross over the main intersection with Kototoi-dori. Some 440 yards (400 m) uphill on your left is the entrance to **Nezu-jinja Shrine** ❹ (1-28-9 Nezu, Bunkuo-ku, tel 03/3822-0753), a delightful and elaborately carved shrine built in 1706. Ponds and trees adorn the shrine compound, which is renowned for azaleas. A popular azalea festival is held here between the end of May and the beginning of June.

After the shrine walk down to the southern edge of the shrine compound and turn left. Keep straight on until you reach the **Daimyo Clock Museum** ❺ (2-1-27 Yanaka, Taito-ku, tel 03/3821-6913, closed Mon. & July 1– Sept. 30) on your right. Housed in a very old private house, the museum exhibits a remarkable collection of rare Edo-period clocks.

From here walk northwest until you reach the Yanaka main street. To the left you will find old shops such as Isetatsu, a fancy paper shop established in 1858, and Kikumi Sembei, a rice cracker store of similar vintage. Known locally as "Yanaka Ginza," the local market street resembles a film set for 1920s Tokyo. The wealth of old temples, houses, and shops around here will tempt you to explore the side streets. Don't worry if you get lost: The Yanaka area is small, and local inhabitants are helpful.

Walk north from the main intersection on the Yanaka main street (with Yanaka cemetery on your right) toward the JR Nippori Station and Nishi Nippori (farther northeast) on the Chiyoda subway line. You will come to **Asakura Chosokan** ❻ (7-18-10 Yanaka, Taito-ku, tel 03/3821-4549, closed Mon. & Fri.), the former home and studio of celebrated sculptor Asakura Fumio (1883–1964), now a museum. On your way up to Nishi Nippori there are more temples along the street, as well as the charming **Space Oguraya** ❼. Set in a restored home (once a pawnshop, where the owners lived on the premises) of the late Edo period, this gallery sells works by reputed artists and craftspeople working in traditional styles. Just before you go down toward Nishi Nippori Station you will find **Suwa-jinja Shrine ❽** on your right, a pleasant little shrine with a hilltop view over the city. For something completely different, you could indulge in coffee and homemade cakes at **Swiss Mini Chalet** (a real wooden one), set in a small garden improbably arrayed with Snow White statuary. Go downhill afterward to your right and turn right into the main street at the bottom. Nishi Nippori Station is on your right. ■

See area map pp. 60–61
▶ Ueno station
⟷ 3.3 miles (5.3 km)
⟳ 3–4 hours
▶ Nishi Nippori Station

NOT TO BE MISSED
- Kanei-ji Kyomizu Kannon-do Temple
- Shinobazu Pond
- Nezu-jinja Shrine
- Daimyo Clock Museum

Low City, high times

Extending northeast across the Sumida-gawa River, *shitamachi* comprises Ningyocho and Ueno, with Asakusa as its heart. The world shitamachi (*shita* means "down" and *machi* means "town") harks back to early 17th-century urban planning.

The "down" referred to the lower castes; Edo's samurai class lived sedately behind the castle walls up on the hill. Plebeian shitamachi was the more lively home of commoners, merchants, entertainers, artists, craftsmen, and the demimonde. Then as now, anyone born and raised in shitamachi—the Low City—is an *edokko*, a child of Edo. The Yoshiwara pleasure quarter, the heart of the old Floating World, stood just beyond in Asakusa. Originally near Ginza, shitamachi sprawled as the city grew.

Rivaling the Yoshiwara it embraced, Asakusa rose from the 1880s through the 1930s as the nation's prime entertainment district and a favorite haunt for writers and poets, artists and intellectuals. It was a gaudy merry-go-round whirling millions through a kaleidoscope of fairs and markets, playhouses, movie theaters, music halls, comedy houses, and thousands of bars and restaurants.

Allied fire-bombing devastated the Low City in 1945, but then so had many earlier city conflagrations, notably in 1657, 1872, and 1923 after the earthquake. Destruction is a harbinger of rebirth; taking disaster in their stride, the hardy survivors retain edokko attributes today: nonchalance, facetiousness, pluck, and, despite a certain mistrust of authority, conservatism.

Reaching its height during the building sprees of the 1980s, modernism took care of whatever had not been accomplished by the bombs. No longer fashionable, postwar Asakusa declined with the rise of Shinjuku as the city's main amusement district. Once Asakusa's theater land, Rokku Avenue became the seedy domain of shabby movie houses and dilapidated striptease theaters. Attempts to revive the district during the 1980s failed;

two art deco cinemas (Japan's oldest) were replaced with featureless concrete boxes in 1994. Refusing to concede that Asakusa is visited mainly as a bastion of tradition, developers also erected the gleaming Rox Plaza, a glaring failure in a city with too many shopping alternatives already.

In the streets behind Senso-ji Temple (see p. 103), loud clothes and florid kimono are sold in a flea market setting; small bars look unabashedly Asian, especially where Korean stores stock garishly colored fabrics and fiery *kimchee* pickles.

Asakusa retains its atmosphere. Scores of shops sell sweet *dango* rice dumplings and *sembei* biscuits; you can often watch them made on the premises. In the shopping arcades northwest of Senso-ji, behind the Nakamise, or even along the main avenue, you can still find such Japanese arcana as firemen's lanterns, *happi* coats, traditional ironmongery, combs and hair ornaments, fans, wooden footwear, high-quality kimono fabrics, festival paraphernalia, and musical instruments.

The area is still full of bars and restaurants, but the grandest, boasting geisha entertainment, are almost gone; from more than a thousand before the war, the Asakusa geisha now number about 40. You are more likely to see them in the woodblock prints on the walls of several more sophisticated *nomiya* (bars) boasting an antiquarian decor. To modern Tokyo, shitamachi is exotic.

Asakusa is the heartland, but parts of Ningyocho and Ueno are contenders. Although originally created as a Buddhist temple enclave and thus not strictly speaking shitamachi, Yanaka is architecturally the last area affording a glimpse of the Meiji and Taisho plebeian neighborhood.

Every May the edokko put heart and soul into the celebration of the Sanja Matsuri in Asakusa (see p. 386). Some 800,000 people leave technopolitan Tokyo behind and for two frantic days bring shitamachi alive with the last remnants of the frenzies of Edo. ∎

Above: Female shrine bearers—a popular
recent addition to the Sanja festival
Left: A fan shop in Asakusa
Below: Cycling along Yanaka Ginza

Bearers strain beneath the weight of portable shrines during Asakusa's Sanja festival.

Asakusa

The very heart of the old city, Asakusa remains Tokyo's most colorful and traditional district. Combining old-fashioned Japanese refinement with the brash and lively aspects of a working-class neighborhood, Asakusa has a wonderful atmosphere. Moreover, with some of the city's most important attractions, it is understandably a premium stop for visitors.

The Yoshiwara

The Tokugawa shogunate believed in confining social evils (including Kabuki theater) in one place. Licensed quarters opened in Japanese cities, starting with the Yoshiwara in Edo in 1617. Moved to Asakusa following the disastrous Meireki Fire in 1657, it was the most dazzling pleasure quarter on Earth. The brothel inmates were slaves, but some rose to become great courtesans; like geisha and Kabuki actors, they were the celebrities of the "Floating World." Decline started in the 1870s, due both to Western opprobrium and to the departure of Kabuki theaters for sites elsewhere. Destroyed by fires and war, the Yoshiwara always rose again until Japan outlawed prostitution in 1957. ■

The sights here are mainly in the area around **Senso-ji Temple,** probably the only Buddhist temple in Japan to constitute such a strong focus for a neighborhood—a privilege normally reserved for Shinto shrines. Senso-ji is approached from Kaminarimon, the Thunder Gate, renowned for its colossal central red paper lantern and the fierce guardian deities on either side. Beyond it is the Nakamise, an avenue of souvenir and specialty stores leading to the temple itself.

Senso-ji (also called Kannon-sama) has been standing on the same spot for more than a millennium; legend has it that the temple was built by three fishermen in the seventh century. After finding a statuette of Kannon, goddess of mercy, in their nets, each dreamed

that the deity told him to build the shrine. It was restructured several times from the ninth century, and took its final form early in the 17th. This version survived the earthquake in 1923, but vanished completely during World War II. The gigantic concrete replacement, built in 1958 with a sweeping roof of 70,000 bronze tiles, is sufficiently imposing to do justice to the original; the same applies to the great five-storied pagoda to the west of the temple. Paintings on the ceiling of the main hall are originals saved from the bombing. In the temple courtyard stands a huge bronze caldron full of burning incense; it is considered auspicious to spread the smoke over your head.

West of the temple compound is the tranquil **Dembo-in Garden,**

Visitors to Senso-ji Temple congregate around a roofed caldron of incense—the smoke is thought to ward off misfortune and disease.

Senso-ji Temple
🗺 61 E5
✉ 2-3-1 Asakusa, Taito-ku
☎ 03/3842-0181
🚇 Subway: Asakusa

Sumotori battle it out at Sumo Stadium in Tokyo, where good seats sell out a year ahead.

Dembo-in Garden
- 🅰 61 E5
- ✉ Dembo-in-dori, Taito-ku
- 🚇 Subway: Asakusa

Edo-Tokyo Museum
- 🅰 61 E4
- ✉ 1-4-1 Yokoami, Sumida-ku
- ☎ 03/3626-9974
- 🕐 Closed Mon.
- 💲 $$
- 🚉 Rail: JR Sobu line, Ryogoku Station,

Sumo Museum
- 🅰 61 E4
- ✉ 1-3-28 Yokoami, Sumida-ku
- ☎ 03/3622-0366
- 🚉 Train: JR Sobu line, Ryogoku Station

which is not only an original surviving from the 19th century but probably Tokyo's most beautiful garden. Although not officially open to the public, tickets for Dembo-in can be obtained from the Senso-ji office at the foot of the pagoda. As you go through from Senso-ji, turn left at the intersection on Nakamise into Demboin-dori. The garden is about 55 yards (50 m) along on the right side of the road. Look for the sign indicating it in English. Collect pieces of dried bread on the way in to feed the turtles and rapacious carp in this unmissable garden.

On the banks of the Sumida-gawa River, **Sumida-koen Park** has long been a favorite place for cherry blossom viewing despite its unattractive concrete embankment. *Yakatabune* pleasure boats are hired for private parties, especially for the Sumida fireworks display (see p. 387). A cheaper option is to take the Sumida-gawa cruise from Azumabashi Bridge to Hamarikyu-teien (see p. 73). The trip is not especially scenic but offers a welcome sit-down after sightseeing.

The Azumabashi skyline is dominated by French designer Philippe Starck's eccentric Flamme d'Or building (see pp. 66–67).

You may be coveting those amazing plastic food displays you see in restaurant windows; one stop south from Asakusa (Tawaramachi Station) is **Kappabashi wholesale market (Kappabashi Dogugai).** Here you can buy such gastronomic emblems as a forkful of spaghetti suspended above a plate, plastic sushi, and all kinds of kitchen paraphernalia.

Across Sumida-gawa from Asakusabashi is an astounding building, seemingly from the realm of science fiction, that houses **Edo-Tokyo Museum (Edo-Tokyo Hakubutsukan).** With a fascinating array of exhibits evoking the Tokyo of the past, this facility has a reputation as the premier city history museum. It lies east of the the main national **Sumo Stadium (Kokugikan).** While you are in the area, you could visit the **Sumo Museum (Sumo Hakubutsukan),** near the stadium entrance. ∎

More places to visit in central Tokyo

AKIHABARA

Under the train tracks, south of Ueno, is what would be a bustling Asian-style bazaar if it were not for the fact that the only goods sold are electrical and electronic. Beyond the station the broad main avenue of **Electric Town (Denki Gai)** presents a cacophony of sounds and flashing lights from discount stores selling audio and video equipment, electrical appliances, lighting, and computers. In some you can haggle over the price, but take note: Temptingly cheap though a computer may be, Japanese hardware and software are incompatible with non-Japanese systems. Electronics superstores such as Laox or Rocket do sell export versions, but computer prices will be higher than in the U. S. Before buying electrical goods, always check on the voltage.
61 D4   Subway: Akihabara or Suehirochoo. Walk 5 minutes down Chuo-dori and turn right

NINGYOCHO

Farther south, near the Tokyo City Air Terminal, is Ningyocho, one of Tokyo's oldest neighborhoods. Site of the original Yoshiwara pleasure quarter built in 1617, it remained a major theater district until Asakusa took over in the 1870s. Ningyocho (Doll Town) was named for the many workshops making and repairing puppets for the Bunraku theater. Leveled by the 1923 earthquake but unscarred by wartime bombing, the neighborhood has many buildings dating from the 1920s. The traditional shops selling *wagashi* candy, green tea, and *sembei* crackers are among Tokyo's most venerable.
61 E4   Subway: Ningyocho

JIMBOCHO

The focus for antiquarian booksellers since the 1880s, this is Tokyo's main center for books new and used. Its stores yield used books in many languages, as well as woodblock prints and delightful Edo-period illustrated paper books. The Tuttle bookstore is a gold mine for books in English about Japan. The bookstores extend from Jimbocho subway station, going left toward Kanda along Yasukuni-dori.
61 C4   Subway: Jimbocho ■

In Akihabara's Electric Town, bargains are hawked by a garish hubbub of loud signs.

Outlying districts of Tokyo

HORIKIRI SHOBUEN IRIS GARDEN

Every June Horikiri Shobuen provides a spectacular note of color in the drab northeastern urban-industrial sprawl. The garden, already popular in the 1800s, was celebrated by artists in woodblock prints. Uprooted during World War II to make paddies, it was restored in 1960 and contains more than 6,000 iris plants of 130 varieties.

⛰ 109 C3 ☎ 03/3697-5237 🚇 Rail: Horikiri Shobuen stop on Keisei main line from Ueno, then 15 minutes' walk southwest

KAWAGOE

This castle town was of particular strategic importance to the Tokugawa shoguns because of its proximity to Edo. It is now home to some 300,000 people living an hour from Tokyo on the northwestern commuter belt. Following a massive conflagration in 1893, cautious local merchants built new houses

Buddhist pilgrims walk over burning coals on Mount Takao-san.

called *dozozukuri,* combining home and warehouse in a solid structure faced with fireproof clay. Several of these picturesque houses have been preserved as national cultural assets, some as museums. The Kita-in Temple, whose buildings (including a pagoda) have survived since the early 17th century, is another good reason to visit Kawagoe.

⛰ 109 B3 🚇 Train: Hon-Kawagoe (Seibu Shinjuku line) from Tokyo's Seibu Shinjuku station. Journey time 60 minutes

MOUNT TAKAO-SAN

To the west of Tokyo, the urban sprawl vanishes into hills and deciduous forest in the vicinity of Takao-san, 1,968 feet (600 m) high, a delightful day trip from Tokyo—but crowded on weekends. There are numerous signposted hiking trails to and from the summit, as well as a cable car. Yakuo-in, a notable temple near the summit, is famous for its curious Hiwatari festival (second Sunday in March), in which devotees walk unharmed over red-hot embers. Down in the valley are the outstanding Ukai Tori-Yama *(3426 Minami, Asakawa-machi, Hachioji-shicho, tel 0426/61-0739)* and Chikutei *(2850 Minami Asakawa-machi, Hachioji-shi, tel 0426/61-8419)* restaurants, where you can dine in private rooms in authentic traditional buildings (mainly teahouses) in a beautiful garden setting.

⛰ 109 B2 🚇 Train: Takaosan-guchi Station from Shinjuku (Keio line or Chuo line, changing for the Keio line at Takao Station). Journey time 50 minutes

OGASAWARA-SHOTO ISLANDS

A quirk of national administration officially designates Ogasawara-shoto as a part of Tokyo prefecture, but at some 1,200 miles (1,930 km) out in the Pacific, they are about as "outlying" as a district can get.

The majority of the population (fewer than 2,000) lives on Chichi-jima (Father Island), and the remainder on Haha-jima (Mother Island) and even tinier Ani-jima (Brother Island). A less hospitable relative, Iwo-jima, was the scene of one of the fiercest battles of World War II; still strewn with live ammunition, it remains off-limits to visitors.

The Ogasawaras are blessed with a pleasant subtropical climate and offer excellent scuba diving but few beaches. Despite only once-weekly ferry service to Tokyo, some 30 *minshuku* (bed- and-breakfast accommodations) cater to vacationers on Chichi-jima.

⛰ See map on inside front cover ⛴ Journey time 28–30 hours ■

Soaring above the Kanto plain is Fuji-san, probably the world's most beautiful conical volcano. Tokyo is a base for visiting Fuji-san, as well as Yokohama and Kamakura. Slightly farther afield is historic Nikko.

Excursions from Tokyo

Nio guardian deity, main gate Sugimoto-dera Temple, Kamakura

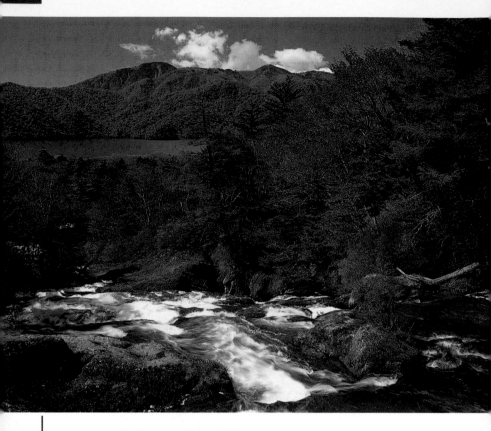

A picturesque image of Lake Chuzenji-ko and Kyusu Falls, Nikko

Excursions from Tokyo

TOKYO MAKES AN EXCELLENT BASE FOR A NUMBER OF EXCURSIONS INTO the surrounding areas. The most popular day trips are to Yokohama, Kamakura, Fuji-Hakone, and farther afield to Nikko. Yokohama is the closest to Tokyo, but a trip to Nikko will introduce you to some of the region's best-known historic sights.

From Tokyo, there are several ways to get to Yokohama, Japan's most important 19th-century doorway to the outside world. From Shibuya Station, take the Toyoko line to Sakuragicho and Yokohama Stations. The trip takes around 45 minutes by ordinary train (*kakueki teisha*) or 35 minutes by limited express (*kyuko*). From Shinagawa, Shimbashi, or Tokyo Stations, either the JR Keihin Tohoku or JR Yokosuka lines stop at Yokohama (35-minute journey). The shinkansen stops at

Shin-Yokohama Station; you need to change to the Yokohama line.

Kamakura, capital of medieval Japan, is slightly farther on the JR Yokosuka line from Shimbashi or Shinagawa Stations in central Tokyo. The journey to Kita Kamakura takes 60 minutes, and to Kamakura it takes 63 minutes.

The fastest way to reach the Fuji-Hakone area is to take the JR Tokaido Shinkansen from JR Tokyo Station to Odawara, which takes just over 40 minutes. Note that whether you are

NORTHERN HONSHU (TOHOKU)

NIKKO NAT. PARK p 151

JO-SHIN-ETSU KOGEN NATIONAL PARK

Nakano

Suzaka

Numata

Shibukawa

GUMMA-KEN

50

Ueda

Saku

Maebashi

Takasaki

Kumagaya

17

NAGANO-KEN

p 171

3192m

Nirasaki

Kofu

YAMANASHI-KEN

Fujiyoshida

FUJI-HAKONE-IZU NAT. PARK

3776m Fuji-san

Fujinomiya

Shimizu

Shizuoka

Yaizu

Suruga-wan

CENTRAL HONSHU (CHUBU)

20

600m Takao-san

20

CHICHIBU-TAMA NATIONAL PARK

TOKYO-KEN

SAITAMA-KEN

Kawagoe

Kawaguchi

Hachioji

Horikiri Shobuen

TOKYO

Kawasaki

Gotemba

Gora

Ashino-ko

Mishima

Atami

Odawara

Hakone

Owakudani

Miura

Numazu

Fuji

SHIZUOKA-KEN

Izu-hanto

Ito

Shimoda

Sagami-nada

O-shima

KANAGAWA-KEN

Kamakura

Yokosuka

YOKOHAMA

Tokyo-wan

Futtsu

Boso-hanto

Chuzenji-ko

Nikko

Imaichi

TOCHIGI-KEN

Utsunomiya

Oyama

Shimodate

Koga

50

Kiryu

IBARAKI-KEN

Kasukabe

Urawa

Toride

Kasumiga-ura

Tsuchiura

Hitachi

Katsuta

Nakaminato

Mito

Narita

Choshi

Ichikawa

Funabashi

Chiba

Mobara

CHIBA-KEN

Katsuura

Kamogawa

Tateyama

PACIFIC OCEAN

0 ____ 50 kilometers
0 ____ 30 miles

◁4

◁3

◁2

◁1

△A △B △C △D

---

coming from Kansai or Tokyo you must take the Kodama Shinkansen and not the super expresses (*hikari* or *nozomi*). If you have no JR pass, you can take the Odakyu line from Shinjuku Station either to Odawara or to Hakone Yumoto. The best of the Odakyu trains is the luxury Romance Car; it costs about the same as the shinkansen. Whatever line you take, change at Odawara or Hakone Yumoto for the local Hakone-Tozan line to Gora.

The fastest and cheapest way to get to Nikko, site of a magnificent 17th-century shrine honoring the shogun Tokugawa Ieyasu, is to take the Tobu Nikko line from Tobu Asakusa Station. The journey time by limited express is just under two hours. Rapid train (*kaisoku*) takes only 15 minutes longer than the express, but costs almost half. If (and only

Area of map detail

Tokyo

if) you have a JR rail pass, you might consider using it to go to Nikko, but it is much slower and less convenient: You take the Tohuku Shinkansen from Ueno Station and change at Utsumomiya for an hourly train to Nikko. ■

Yokohama

IT SEEMS JUST A CONTINUATION OF TOKYO'S GIGANTIC urban sprawl, but Yokohama is Japan's second largest city and its largest port. Yokohama has a fascinating history as one of the first ports opened to foreigners in 1858, but the 1923 earthquake and wartime destruction have left little of the old city behind.

The central Kannai district is being transformed with architecturally striking new developments. This applies even more spectacularly to the Minato Mirai 21 development to the west, dominated by the **Landmark Tower,** at 971 feet (296 m) one of the tallest buildings in Japan. While you are there, you could take in the **Yokohama Maritime Museum** *(Nippon Maru Memorial Park, tel 045/221-0280)*, which has displays about Japanese and world shipping, as well as *Nippon Maru,* a beautiful tall ship (built 1930). The port was the point of departure for Japan's once-colossal silk trade, as evidenced in the **Silk Museum (Shiruku Hakubutsukan),** whose fascinating exhibits focus on silk processing, textiles, and trade.

On the promontory to the south is the **Sankei-en Garden** *(58-1 Honmoku San-no-tani, Naka-ku, tel 045/621-0634)*. Laid out in 1906, it incorporates a 15th-century pagoda and other buildings moved from different parts of Japan.

For many, however, Yokohama's star attraction lies in Japan's largest **Chinatown** and its wealth of restaurants, sundry goods stores, and pharmacies. ■

Yokohama
🅰 109 C2
Visitor information
✉ Yokohama Station, 2-16-1 Takashima-cho
☎ 045/441-7300

Silk Museum
✉ Yamashita-cho, Naka-ku
☎ 045/641-0841
🕐 Closed Mon.
💲 $

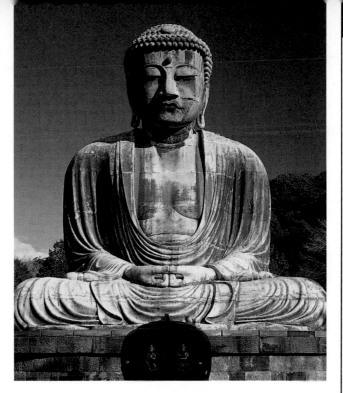

Cast in 1252, the colossal Daibutsu (Great Buddha) sits serenely, unmoved by wars and natural disasters over the centuries.

Kamakura

OVERLOOKING SAGAMI-WAN BAY, KAMAKURA, FOUNDED in 1192, was perfect as both a samurai stronghold and a temple city; it was the capital of Japan until 1333. Badly damaged during the Kanto Earthquake of 1923, it was spared Allied bombing in World War II. Now a plush residential town on Tokyo's outer commuter belt, hilly Kamakura has enough historic buildings intact or restored to justify its reputation as one of the must-sees in Japan.

Kamakura
🗺 109 C2
Visitor information
✉ 1-1-1 Komachi
☎ 0467/22-3350

Kokuhokan National Treasure Museum
☎ 0467/22-0753
🕐 Closed Mon.
💲 $

Kamakura's sights (65 temples and 19 shrines) are far too many to be visited in a single day. They are largely distributed on a loop around Kamakura Station, with most of the major ones to the north. The five most important Zen temples of the Rinzai sect, collectively known as the Kamakura Gozan, still stand, but only Engaku-ji and Kencho-ji Temples—the most popular with sightseers—retain period buildings. Both of these are closer to Kita-Kamakura, the station to the north. The famous Great Buddha, however, sits farther southwest and is reached more comfortably by bus or local train from Kamakura Station.

One way to cover the area is to arrive at Kita-Kamakura and zig-zag your way through the temples and sights. Or begin with a round trip to the Great Buddha in the south and return to Kamakura Station. From there, go northeast along Wakamiya-oji, the wide main boulevard, to the National Treasure Museum and Tsurugaoka Hachimangu Shrine, then continue northwest to Kita-Kamakura Station. There are recommended hiking routes on a bilingual map posted outside Kamakura Station. Copies are available from the visitor center.

Kamakura's colossal **Daibutsu (Great Buddha)** sits in the precincts of Kotoku-in Temple *(Tel 0467/22-0703)* and is one of the two largest pre-modern bronze Buddhas in Japan, (the other is in Todai-ji in Nara; see pp. 241–43). Cast in 1252 and 37 feet (11m) high, this seated Buddha was once housed in a vast wooden hall that was swept away by a tidal wave in 1495. With its serene countenance enhanced by the elegant flow of drapery, this is a great work of art. The statue is hollow—a ladder inside provides access to shoulder level.

Less than a quarter of a mile south is **Hase-dera Temple** *(Tel 0467/22-6300)* with a breathtaking view over Sagami Bay. Founded during the early eighth century, this temple was rebuilt by the shogun Ashikaga Yoshimasa (who also built Kyoto's Ginkaku-ji) in 1459. The temple stands beyond a beautiful garden in the precinct. Close to the steps to the buildings, as well as to the west of the compound, are serried ranks of hundreds of statues of Jizo, typically festooned with bibs and children's toys. The patron deity of travelers and children, Jizo is venerated especially by women as the guardian of the souls lost in terminated pregnancies. The main Amida Hall and Kannon Hall are open to the public (unlike in most temples). They contain fine Buddha figures, but Kannon Hall is renowned for its great *juichimen* (11-faced) statue of Kannon. Carved in 721 from a giant camphor log, the splendidly gilded figure stands 30 feet (9 m) high—the tallest wooden statue in Japan. The Buddhist deity of compassion,

Kannon is represented here with one main face and ten subsidiary ones; sometimes the figure is depicted with a thousand arms. Kannon was later mainly represented as female, but this statue predates the trend.

Presenting a wealth of exhibits revealing facets of Kamakura's rich history, the **National Treasure Museum (Kokuhokan)** is noted for its collection of temple treasures and fine Buddhist works of art.

Tsurugaoka Hachiman-gu Shrine is dedicated to Hachiman, god of war. The original 11th-century shrine burned down in 1191, but was rebuilt on nearby Tsurugaoka—the hill of cranes—the same year. Fire struck again six centuries later; most of the current structures date from 1828. Noted for its panorama over the town and the bay, the shrine is cherished for the beauty of its fine vermilion buildings in a leafy setting—but most of all for historical associations dear to the Japanese. On the square at the foot of the steps leading to the shrine is the Mai-den (dance stage), revered as a replica of the one on which Shizuka, beloved of the ill-fated hero Minamoto Yoshitsune (1159–1189), performed centuries ago. Nearby stands a huge *ginkgo* tree—the very one beneath which the son of Yoritomo (see p. 31) was assassinated in 1219.

Engaku-ji Temple *(Tel 0467/22-0478)* is the first temple you come to, about 110 yards (100 m) southeast of Kita-Kamakura Station. It was founded in 1282 to commemorate those who fell during the Mongol Wars (see p. 32). Destroyed and rebuilt several times, most of the buildings finally succumbed to the earthquake of 1923; current structures are mainly concrete reproductions, but the beautifully carved two-story sanmon gate of 1780 survives, as does the great

Tsurugaoka Hachiman-gu Shrine

✉ 2-1-31 Yokinoshita
☎ 0467/22-0315
$ $
🚉 JR Yokosuka Line: Kita-Kamakura

bell, cast in 1301. Closed to the public, the oldest extant building is the Shariden Hall, which contains a reliquary said to hold one of the Buddha's teeth. The compound has two small gardens: Obai-in, a mausoleum for the 13th-century Hojo family rulers, and Butsunichian, where green tea is served.

About 280 yards (250 m) southwest of Engaku-ji and across the train tracks, **Toke-ji Temple** *(Tel 0467/22-1663)* is set in a leafy valley. A former nunnery, this temple is also known as Enkiri-dera (Divorce Temple). In the 1600s, divorce—exclusively a male privilege—came to be recognized as the only refuge for battered wives. A year spent here made a woman's divorce official. The temple's directives inspired the first national divorce law in 1873. The complex embraces **Matsugaoka Treasure House,** a small museum exhibiting items relating to the temple's history.

Kencho-ji Temple *(Tel 0467/22-0981),* about half a mile (600 m) southwest of Kita-Kamakura, stands among majestic cedars. It is the most important of Kamakura's five main Zen temples. Founded by a Chinese Zen master in 1253, it was formerly a seminary and is now the headquarters of the Rinzai sect. The current buildings date from the mid-17th century; cast in 1255, the great bronze bell near the sanmon gate is a National Treasure. Behind the main Ryuoden (Dragon King Hall) is a fine garden laid out by the Zen master Muso Kokushi. ■

A display of *yabusame*—**archery on horseback—at Tsurugaoka Hachlmangu Shrine during the Kamakura Festival**

Nikko

Shin-kyo Bridge is one of the most famous sights on the way to Nikko's renowned Tosho-gu Shrine.

Nikko

109 C4

Visitor information

✉ Tobu Nikko Station,
4-3 Matsubara-cho

☎ 0288/53-4511

Rinno-ji Temple

✉ 2300 Sannai

☎ 0288/54-0531

$ $$$ Multiple entry
ticket for Rinno-ji,
Tosho-gu, &
Futaarasan

EVEN IF YOU PLAN TO STAY ONLY IN TOKYO, YOU SHOULD consider taking one day to visit Nikko, just 80 miles (128 km) north. Some of Japan's greatest historic sites are here. Nikko lies on the southeastern edge of Nikko National Park, an alpine wonderland for hikers in summer and skiers in winter, abounding with lakes, waterfalls, and *onsen* (hot springs).

The elegantly curved vermilion **Shin-kyo (Sacred Bridge)** spans the Daiya-gawa River, taking you from the east section of the city to the main temple and shrine area. Two *torii* (gateways) mark the ends of Shin-kyo, which was formerly used only for ceremonial purposes. Built in 1636, it commemorates an old legend about the eighth-century priest Shodo Shonin , said to have crossed the river on this spot on the backs of two gigantic serpents. The bridge was reconstructed in 1907, shortly after being washed away in a flood.

Rinno-ji Temple is on the right along the main Omotesando Avenue to the Tosho-gu Shrine, which is less than a quarter of a mile farther north. Founded by the priest Shodo Shonin during the eighth century and maintained by the Buddhist Tendai sect, the

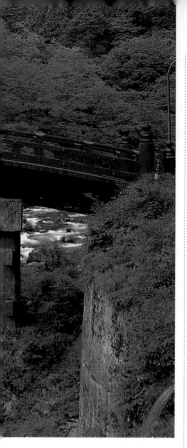

When the great shogun Tokugawa Ieyasu died in 1616, Nikko was selected as the site for his mausoleum. At Ieyasu's request, this was a modest affair, but in 1634 Ieyasu's grandson, Iemitsu, began building **Tosho-gu Shrine** on a scale commensurate with his grandfather's stature. Some 15,000 craftsmen, among them the finest carpenters, carvers, and painters in the land, worked on the project, the cost of which today would translate into hundreds of millions of U.S. dollars. Incorporating some 2.5 million sheets of gold leaf, the shrine's lavish buildings remain paradigms of the ornate style of the late 16th-century Momoyama period. They have both admirers and detractors: The Tosho-gu structures are a far cry from the simple elegance of classic Japanese taste, reflecting the rococo excess of Ming dynasty China and the parvenu taste of military dictators. Still, if they tend to be massive and overdecorated as a whole, charm and subtleties lie in a wealth of detail, particularly in the hundreds of intricate polychrome carvings, many based upon designs supplied by major exponents of the Kano school of painting. Several of the buildings are designated Important Cultural Properties and National Treasures.

As you proceed through a giant stone torii gateway along Omote-sando Avenue leading to the shrine, on your left is a five-story pagoda built in 1818 to replace a 1650 original destroyed by fire. Flanked by two fierce protective kings and featuring ornate carvings, the great vermilion Omotemon is the true gate to the Tosho-gu Shrine. Beyond this are the Sanjinko, three storehouses containing sacred trappings for the shrine's great festivals (Warrior Processions, May 18 and October 18). The last of these

A stone *torii* gateway along the approach to the Tosho-gu Shrine. The font in the foreground is for orthodox Shintoists to rinse hands and mouths before entering the sacred precinct.

temple is renowned for its Sanbutsudo (Hall of the Three Buddhas), erected in 1648. The three large gilded and lacquered statues inside represent the thousand-armed Kannon on the left, the Amida-Nyorai Buddha in the center, and the unusual Bato (horse-headed) Kannon on the right. Featuring a horse's head jutting from the forehead, this incarnation of the deity of compassion is devoted to animal welfare. The nearby Gohotendo, containing other statues, is notable for the Sorinto, a large bronze pillar inscribed with 10,000 sutras (Buddhist texts) and bearing 24 bells. Exhibiting various items connected with the temple's history, the Treasure Hall (Homutsuden) has a beautiful garden behind it.

Tosho-gu Shrine
- ✉ 2301 Sannai
- ☎ 0288/54-0560
- 💲 $$$ Multiple entry ticket

The riot of carvings that adorn the structures of Tosho-gu Shrine goes way over the top, but the beauty of the experience lies in the charm of the details (right).

structures displays fanciful carvings of elephants. The unpainted Shinkyusha (sacred stable), containing a single effigy of a white horse, bears a delightful bas-relief sequence of monkeys, including a famous "Hear No Evil, Speak No Evil, See No Evil" trio. Monkey spirits were once believed to protect horses. Beyond this is a granite water cistern; Shinto worshipers

pause here to wash hands and rinse mouths before proceeding into the sacred precinct.

Beyond the next torii gateway and up more stairs, you will find a drum tower on the left and belfry to the right, beyond which lies the Yakushi-do (extra fee for access), a Buddhist structure featuring a huge ink drawing on the ceiling of the "Naki-ryu" (roaring dragon). The

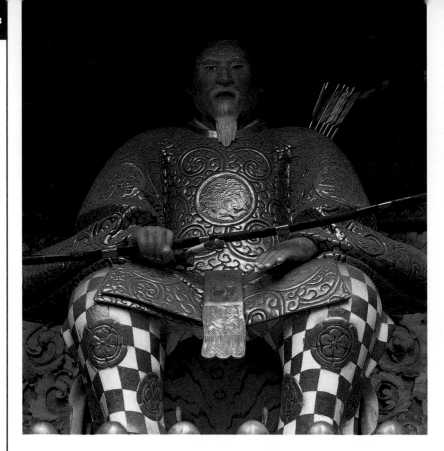

Carving of a mythical temple guardian at Tosho-gu Shrine

17th-century original was lost with the building in a fire in 1961. The current reproduction offers the same novelty: As visitors clap their hands, the reverberations are said to sound like a dragon's roar.

Back along the main path and up more steps is the amazing 36-foot (11 m) **Yomeimon** (Gate of Sunlight). The ornamentation seen so far reaches a florid climax here: The structure is alive with 400 gilt polychrome carvings of Kano-school design depicting giraffes, lions, dragons, birds, flowers, and phoenixes, along with Chinese children, sages, and immortals. One of the columns has been deliberately carved upside down to appease evil spirits; it was believed that the lavish artistic overkill might otherwise have aroused their

ire. Beyond the gate to the left is the **Mikoshigura**—a building housing *mikoshi*, sacred palanquins carried in festivals. Straight ahead are the gorgeously decorated Haiden (Oratory) and Honden (Main Hall).

To the right of the Yomeimon is a corridor leading to the Sakashita-mon Gate. Just before the gate is another small portal, whose lintel features a much cherished carving of a sleeping cat—the "Nemuri-neko"—by 17th-century sculptor Jingoro. Beyond the gates, a long stone stairway through a cedar grove leads to Ieyasu's tomb, whose austere design by now comes as something of a relief. Southwest of the shrine itself, just below the pagoda is the **Tosho-gu Homotsukan Treasure**

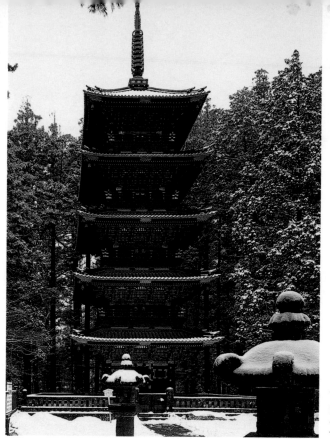

**Futaraasan-jinja
Shrine**

✉ Sannai

☎ 0288/54-0535

$ $

**The five-story
pagoda near the
entrance to
Tosho-gu Shrine**

House. The museum exhibits historical items pertaining to the Tokugawa shoguns, including armor, swords, and paintings.

FUTAARASAN-JINJA SHRINE & TAIYUIN

There are three Futaarasan shrines, dedicated to the deities of Mount Nantai-san (formerly Futaara-san), in the Nikko area. The Okumiya (Inner Shrine), near the peak of the mountain itself, is the most sacred; the Chugushi (Middle Shrine) stands by Lake Chuzenji-ko; the third, beside the Daiya-gawa River, was called Honsha (Head Shrine). Founded by the priest Shodo in the eighth century, these shrines had Buddhist connotations originally but were given exclusive Shinto status in 1868. To reach the riverside

Futaarasan-jinja Shrine, from Omotesando Avenue turn left along the Ue-Shinmichi path at the crossing before the Omotemon Gate. The buildings date back to 1619. The ornate lacquered *karamon* (Chinese gate) stands before the main hall; both the hall and oratory are designated Important Cultural Properties. The shrine stands amid magnificent cedar trees; from here you can take a fine stroll toward the Nantai-san foothills.

West of Futaarasan is **Taiyuin** (also called Taiyuin-byo), the mausoleum (1653) of the builder of the Tosho-gu Shrine, shogun Tokugawa Iemitsu. To find it, as you go north toward Tosho-gu along Omotesando Avenue, turn left into the Shita-Shinmichi path just before the stone torii gateway.

Yumoto Onsen

 Bus from JR Nikko Station (stop No. 3) Journey time approx. 80 mins.

Lake Chuzenji-ko

Bus from JR Nikko Station (stop No. 2) to Chuzenji Onsen. Journey time approx. 50 mins.

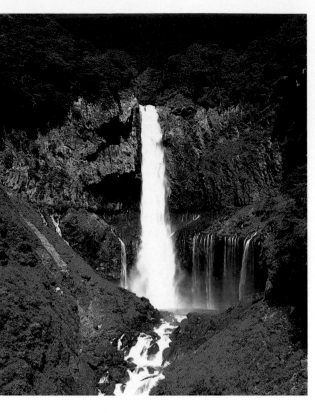

The Kegon-no-Taki Waterfall is one of the highlights of Nikko National Park.

Woman dressed in Sumarai-era costume at Nikko Edo Village, a historical theme park

The precinct embraces several Import-ant Cultural Properties. Taiyuin is beautifully ornamented but less bombastic than Tosho-gu.

OUTLYING NIKKO

If you have an extra day or more to spare, the 540-square mile (1,400-sq km) area of Nikko National Park offers scenic wonders and outstanding hiking trails. With its dramatic mountain backdrop, **Lake Chuzenji-ko** can be admired on foot or by taking a cruise or hiring a rowboat. You'll enjoy fine views of the lake from Chanokidaira, where the viewing platform is accessible by cable car from Chuzenji Onsen.

Nearby is the spectacular 318-foot (97 m) **Kegon-no-Taki Waterfall,** renowned for the display of rainbows in the spray on sunny days. **Yumoto Onsen** resort has a reputation for its traditional hot spring experience; you can reach it by bus or on foot from Chuzenji-ko. Its onsen hotels are perfect for relaxing after an afternoon of exhilarating mountain hiking from Ryuzu Waterfall to the north of Chuzenji-ko. Southeast, on the Kinugawa line from Nikko, Kinugawa Onsen is a gaudier, more conventional onsen resort than Yumoto, but for those traveling with children it has the advantage of being close to **Nikko Edo Village (Nikko Edo Mura),** a theme park with reconstructed period buildings and inspired samurai-oriented attractions. Adults might find this tacky, but kids often love it. ■

Fuji-san with the shinkansen: a cherished contemporary icon

Fuji-Hakone-Izu

The image of Japan's premier natural wonder is everywhere—on postcards, calendars, travel brochures, and old woodblock prints. Split between Yamanashi and Shizuoka Prefecture, Fuji-san is the centerpiece of Fuji-Hakone-Izu National Park. The whole area is scenically magnificent. The train lines and highways run parallel to the former Tokaido (Eastern Sea Road), which in feudal times connected Edo (Tokyo) with Kyoto and Osaka.

Hakone is renowned for its views of Fuji-san, particularly as mirrored in beautiful Lake Ashino-ko. With the region's many onsen resorts, its fuming volcanic valleys, the scenic Fuji Five Lakes area nearby, and the presence of Fuji-san itself, this is not surprisingly one of the most cherished areas for recreation and relaxation in Japan. Hakone makes a perfect day trip from Tokyo, but with so much to see and some outstanding hotels (especially the landmark Fujiya, one of Japan's first Western-style hotels), treating yourself to a stopover will make this a more leisurely experience.

One proviso is the weather: If it is cloudy or wet, Fuji-san often totally vanishes. Also, you should be aware that it is very crowded on weekends.

The giant waterside *torii* gateway of Hakone Gongen shrine and the Fuji-san backdrop both contribute to the legendary beauty of Lake Ashi-ko.

Hakone

🅼 109 B2

Visitor information

✉ Hakone Yumoto

☎ 0460/5-8911

Hakone Open-Air Museum

✉ 1121 Ni-no-Taira

☎ 0460/2-1161

🕐 Closed Thurs.

💲 $$$$

HAKONE

From Tokyo, the JR Tokaido Shinkansen (the Kodama train) stops at Odawara. From here change to the Hakone Tozan line to Gora. On the way to Hakone you could stop off at Chokoku-no-mori to see the **Hakone Open-Air Museum (Chokoku-no-Mori Bijutsukan),** a highly regarded repository of 19th-century and contemporary Japanese and Western sculpture; there is a pavilion devoted to Picasso, and 26 sculptures by Henry Moore are displayed outdoors.

From Gora take the funicular railway for a ten-minute trip to the summit of Mount Soun-zan. You can alight at any or all of the four stops on the way. Koen Kami is the stop for the **Hakone Art**

Museum (Hakone Bijutsukan, *one minute's walk from the station, tel 0460/2-2623, closed Thurs.),* noted for its collection of fine Chinese and Japanese ceramics.

From Soun-zan you take a cable car (*ropu-ue,* or "ropeway") to Togendai. Within ten minutes, the car passes over a valley of jagged rocks, craters, and bubbling mud, where steam jets from the crevices and fumaroles belch sulfurous vapors. This is **Owakudani** (Valley of Greater Boiling), where you should alight. Weather permitting, there is a fine view of Fuji-san to the northwest. You can take a closer look at the inferno from the Owakudani Exploration Path circumventing it, and perhaps allow yourself to be tempted into sampling an egg cooked (if that is the word) in the volcanic mud by a vendor on the way. Black-shelled and distinctly sulfurous, the eggs are supposed to be good for you. The **Natural Science Museum (Owakudani Shizen Kagakukan)** there tells you more about the geology, geography, and flora and fauna of the Hakone area. The building alongside the cable car station houses a panoramic restaurant, though the food is pretty unexciting.

Board the cable car again to make the spectacularly scenic descent toward **Lake Ashino-ko.** The cable car will stop en route only if someone wants to alight. On a fine day Fuji-san will be perfectly mirrored in the lake's calm surface; you can take a closer look by taking a ferry from Togendai, where the cable car terminates, to Hakone-machi or Moto-Hakone. The trip takes about 40 minutes; tickets should be purchased from the cable car terminal before boarding. If you are on a day trip with a train to catch back to Tokyo, you can catch the bus back to Odawara from Hakone-machi (outside the pier building) or Moto-Hakone (from Hakone Barrier) every 10 or 20 minutes.

The two stops, about half a mile (1 km) apart, have worthwhile sights nearby. Almost 220 yards (200 m) to the north of Hakone-machi is **Hakone Barrier (Hakone Sekishoato).** The original structure vanished long ago, but the replacement on the same spot reproduces the checkpoint set up for intercepting travelers along the old Tokaido Road between Kyoto and Edo. From here the Sugi-namiki, a splendid avenue of cryptomeria trees planted over 350 years ago, parallels the main road for about three-quarters of a mile (1.2 km) to Moto-Hakone.

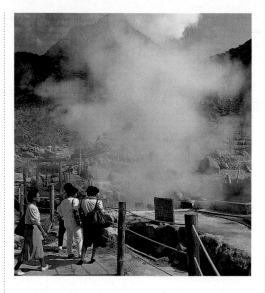

Hakone Gongen Shrine stands among dense woods in the foothills of Mount Koma. Marked by a huge red torii gateway emerging from the lake north of the Moto-Hakone bus stop, it is one of central Japan's largest shrines, founded some 1,200 years ago. Minamoto Yoritomo hid here in 1180 after a defeat during his ultimately successful campaign against the Taira clan. The shrine features a soaring cedar grove along the approach and a treasure hall with important historical relics.

If you have plenty of time, there is a popular hiking route along a preserved section of the old Tokaido Road from Moto-Hakone to Hakone-Yumoto. Paved as far as the Amazake-Jaya teahouse, the walk takes 3 hours 30 minutes and passes Saun-ji, Shogen-ji, and Soun-ji temples. As the area's most popular onsen resort, Hakone-Yumoto is predictably garish, but it's a good choice for the onsen experience. Moreover, a stopover with a long soak in hot water might be just what you need after a good hike.

(continued on p. 127)

Walkways wind past sulfurous fumaroles and boiling pools in Hakone's volcanic Owakudani—the Valley of Greater Boiling.

Natural Science Museum
☎ 0460/4-9149
💲 $

Climbing Fuji-san

The paths zigzagging up the slopes of Fuji-san are fairly regular; the ascent is less a climb than a hike. There are four main routes. If you reached the area from Tokyo via Oda-wara, opt for the northern Kawaguchi-ko route. Buses to Kawaguchi-ko 5th Station leave from Kawaguchi-ko town until late in the evening. Since this service is suspended only from mid-November through February, you *could* make an out-of-season ascent, but the weather on Fuji is extremely unpredictable even at the best of times. In winter, when the mountain is covered in snow, the ascent can be very dangerous. There is also a direct bus service all the way from Shinjuku Station in Tokyo to the Kawaguchi-ko 5th Station.

Before you start out, check ahead for the weather conditions. Call the English-language information line *(Tel 0555-23-3000)* for a recorded message, or contact Fuji-Yoshida visitor information service *(Tel 0555/24-1236)*. Either way, bear in mind that the weather at the summit is notoriously unpredictable, changing between rain, sunshine, wind, and snow without warning.

Climbers approaching the region from the southwest make their ascent from the

Like a river of light, climbers bearing flashlights ascend Fuji-san at night in time to reach the summit for the *goraiko*—the greeting for the first rays of the rising sun.

Fujinomiya-Mishima 5th Station; buses to the latter run from both the Shin Fuji and Mishima Stations on the JR Shinkansen line. The other options are the Gotemba and Subashiri 5th Stations to the east, but the distance from these to the summit is greater.

The ascent

The five- to seven-hour ascent (4 miles/6 km from Kawaguchi-ko) can be made either during the afternoon with an overnight stop at one of the stations, or in darkness to reach the top in time for sunrise. To a small number of Shinto pilgrims in white tunics, this is a ritual celebrating the sun goddess Amaterasu, mother of Japan. To millions of others, it is a secular must on the lifetime calendar.

Most climbers ascend from Kawaguchi-ko 5th Station. Along with inane Fuji-san trinkets, the souvenir stores here sell useful equipment. You will need a water bottle, perhaps a sunhat, and a staff, optionally sporting a flag and/or, pilgrim-fashion, a tinkling bell. The staffs are branded with commemorative logos at each station, and climbers hammer the bells as well as coins—just for luck—into a *torii* gateway near the shrine at the summit. No mountaineering experience is necessary: Solid iron chains serve as handrails on the rockier passages lower down. A trip from high summer into bleak midwinter, the climb makes a warm waterproof jacket, gloves, strong shoes or hiking boots (they will get scuffed), and woolen clothing essential. If you're climbing at night, don't forget to take a flashlight.

The summit

Hikers, Boy Scouts, families, pilgrims, and pensioners arrive panting through the stone torii gateway spanning the last few steps of the pathway to the 10th Station at the summit. A featureless expanse of chocolate brown chunks of stone, the summit is Martian in its desolation. There is a meteorological station on the crater rim, itself a rigorous walk. The 10th Station, 30 years ago a single hut, is now more like a small shantytown.

With the frequent arrival of fog, rain, or flurries of snow, everyone retreats indoors to huddle around an oil stove in the center of a room reminiscent of Klondike during the gold rush. Consisting of noodle soup or curry rice at twice the prices five miles down, the food (not included in the price) is legendary for its poor quality. You can carry your own provisions if you don't mind the weight. The cold prompts a roaring trade in alcoholic beverages from vending machines—even bottled water is

expensive up here, and there is no other kind. Handed a soiled, clammy sleeping bag, you retire to a rough wooden bunk or a mattress on the floor. Keep your outer garments on: The night is short but bitterly cold. At 4 a.m. everyone runs outside with flashlights to take up position to watch the sunrise.

As the sun rises through the mist in an amazing array of picture-postcard hues, all arms are raised to the hearty cheer of "Banzai! Banzai!" If the skies are clear, with clouds drifting far below mirrored in the still waters of the lakes, the view is utterly spectacular.

After a breakfast of *o-nigiri* rice patties and thin *miso* soup, it is time to descend. Despite the views over the lakes and the conical shadow of the mountain on the plain when the sun is behind you, it is a great relief to come into greenery again. You may find yourself pondering the old Japanese adage: Everyone should climb Fuji-san once, but only a fool would climb it twice. ■

A tranquil view of
Fuji-san at sunset

(continued from p. 123)

FUJI-SAN

The world's most beautiful volcano, its image immediately recognizable, Fuji-san is the highest mountain in Japan at 12,388 feet (3,776 m). Fuji-san last blew its top in 1707. The spectacular three-week eruption terrified the citizens of Edo 75 miles (120 km) away, turning skies dark during the daytime and coating the city with ash. The volcano is now dormant, but another eruption cannot be ruled out.

Of all the mountains worshiped in Shinto mountain cults, Fuji-san is the almighty; it has been revered as sacred since prehistoric times. Its sanctity is official: Following five years' wrangling over the legal ownership of the peak between the local government and Fuji's own Sengen-jinja Shrine, a hearing ruled in the latter's favor in 1962.

Forbidden to women until 1868, it is now ascended annually by over 250,000 people of both sexes and all ages during the July–August climbing season. As many as one-third of the climbers hail from abroad. If you want to climb Fuji-san, note that the season extends through July and August. You may be tempted to avoid the crowds by ascending outside these months, but the visitor stations on the mountain open only shortly before the season and close soon after (see pp. 124–26).

With its outstanding scenery, including densely forested mountains and idyllic views of Fuji-san, the nearby **Fuji Five Lakes (Fuji-go-ko)** area has not gone unnoticed; the banks of the larger

Mount Fuji-san

▲ 109 B2

Visitor information

▲ Fuji Yoshida, outside the station

▲ 0555/22-7000

lakes, **Lake Yamanaka-ko** and **Lake Kawaguchi-ko,** have been substantially developed, particularly the latter. Kawaguchi-ko is the preferred starting place for ascending Fuji-san on the north side; buses from here will take you up to the 5th Station. (The routes up the mountain are interspersed with stopping points known as stations; they culminate in Station 10 at the summit.) Up from the lakeside are some of Japan's choicest property developments for corporate and individual holiday homes, as well as vacation lodges for schools and colleges; the area abounds with facilities for sports, including tennis and golf, as well as fine hotels. The areas around Lakes Sai-ko, Shoji-ko, and Motosu-ko are a good deal more pristine, but the only really leisurely way to explore them is by car.

IZU-HANTO

The southern end of Fuji-Hakone-Izu National Park flanks the Izu-Hanto Peninsula, famous for its hot spring resorts and fine coastal scenery. Being so close to Tokyo, this is the country's most popular coastal resort area and can often be overcrowded. Where the famous scenic assets have been undermined by indiscriminate hotel development, resorts such as **Atami** have become tawdry and overpriced. This said, Atami possesses the **MOA Museum of Art (MOA Bijutsukan,** tel 0557/84-2511, closed Thurs.); its famous collection of Chinese and Japanese art includes several National Treasures and Important Cultural Properties. The area as a whole, which includes the Izu Seven Isles offshore, has a reputation for wonderful fresh seafood. The less ostentatious hot spring *ryokan* (traditional inns) around Shimoda, where Commodore Perry landed with his Black Ships in 1853 (see p. 36), can offer a very pleasant and peaceful off-peak getaway. But unless you are in Japan for some time, Izu-Hanto, unlike Fuji-Hakone, should not be a high priority. ■

Volcanoes & earthquakes

The most active volcanoes are those in Kyushu (notably Aso, Unzen, and Sakurajima). However, the presence of hot springs, geysers, pools of boiling mud, and emanations of sulfurous fumes in the land around the foothills of many others, including Fuji-san, belies their dormancy. Volcanic activity and the movement of tectonic plates deep underground make Japan particularly earthquake prone. Japan experiences as many as 2,000 earthquakes annually, many too small to be recorded except on sensitive seismographic equipment. Registering over 8 on the Richter scale, temblors such as the Great Kanto Earthquake of 1923 and the one that struck Kobe in 1995 have caused devastating damage and loss of life. The Kanto plain is considered especially vulnerable. For centuries, major earthquakes have hit the Tokyo-Yokohama region roughly once every 70 years, so the next one is widely regarded as overdue.

Strong earthquakes offshore trigger tsunami—colossal seismic waves that can have calamitous effects when they come crashing inland. Much of Kamakura was destroyed by a tsunami in 1495, and one wrecked the island of Okushiri-to off Hokkaido in 1993.

(See also Earthquakes on p. 357 of Travelwise.) ■

Japan's second largest island, Hokkaido is home to only five percent of the population. It is still seen as the nation's last frontier—an area of wilderness with breathtakingly beautiful landscapes comprising lakes, mountains, and volcanoes.

Hokkaido

Colossal ice sculpture at the Snow Festival in Sapporo

Hokkaido

THE JAPANESE HAVE ALWAYS REGARDED HOKKAIDO, their second largest island, as a wilderness. During the feudal era it was seen as a wasteland, called Ezo, inhabited only by the indigenous Ainu peoples(see p. 136). Today its wide open spaces attract growing legions who enjoy unspoiled nature and the great outdoors. With the Japan Sea on its west coast, the Pacific Ocean to the southeast, and the Sea of Okhotsk to the northeast, the prefecture of Hokkaido represents 22 percent of the national landmass but holds only 5 percent of the population.

Although there were lonely outposts in southern Hokkaido during the feudal era, exploitation of the island began only in 1859, when Hakodate was opened as one of Japan's first five treaty ports (those opened to foreign trade by treaty). Development started in earnest after the Meiji Restoration in 1868, but demographic and economic growth really took off after World War II, when millions of Japanese who had colonized Manchuria after its occupation in 1931 were repatriated. Most settled in the south of Hokkaido, particularly in the capital, Sapporo.

Hokkaido's wilderness, some of it still wild enough to be roamed by brown bears, is pristine; it possesses breathtakingly beautiful landscapes comprising dense forests, mountains, and lakes—the latter often in the calderas of extinct or dormant volcanoes. Many other volcanoes here are among Japan's most active, and the abundant hot springs dotted about the island include some of the country's favorite *onsen* resorts. The best known is Noboribetsu Onsen, 72 miles (116 km) southeast of Sapporo. It is within Shikotsu-Toya National Park, the most easily accessible of Hokkaido's several national parks.

The island's climate is Siberian, with long, cold winters and short, cool summers, but the adversity of a harsh winter has been turned into an asset. Two of Japan's finest ski resorts, Furano and Niseko, offer just some of Hokkaido's winter sports options. Many Japanese travel to Sapporo especially to see the huge, elaborate ice sculptures in Odori Park during the Snow Festival in February, and it is becoming increasingly popular to travel all the way up to the remote port of Abashiri in

Area of map detail

Daisetsuzan National Park in midwinter

the northeast to see the drift ice in winter.

Although Hokkaido has coal and iron ore and automobiles and electronics industries, it thrives for the most part on forestry products and agriculture. This is the one place in Japan where you're likely to see wheat fields. It is also ideal for fruit growing and dairy farming; Hokkaido supplies 90 percent of Japan's milk products. With rich fishing grounds offshore and plentiful rivers, the island is the country's premier supplier of trout, salmon, crab, scallops, and other seafood —it's *the* place to eat them. Hokkaido is reached either by ferry from the north of Honshu or increasingly through the 33-mile (54 km) Seikan Tunnel, the longest undersea link in the world. If you seek familiar or stereotypical Japanese cultural traits, you will be disappointed: There are temples and shrines to be sure, but much less in evidence than elsewhere. Traditional Japanese architecture and some aspects of traditional culture seem never to have made it to Hokkaido.

Travel here is also different. The distances between population centers can be considerable and journeys much longer. You can fly, but if you plan to explore the island by train, you will need a rail pass. Transport between remote points in some of the national park areas can be sparse; many people find a car or a motorcycle by far the most convenient way to travel in Japan's only wild frontier. ■

Sapporo & beyond

Sapporo
⚠ 130 B3
Visitor information
✉ International
Information Corner
☎ 011/213-5062

**Shokubutsu-en
Botanical Gardens**
✉ N3 W8, Chuo-ku
☎ 011/221-0066
🕐 Closed Mon. Garden
(except greenhouse)
closed Nov.–May
💲 $$; Greenhouse $

THE FIFTH LARGEST CITY IN JAPAN, SAPPORO IS DYNAMIC
and modern but has little to offer in the way of traditional sights.
American urban planners helped lay out the city in 1871, and even
today it feels as though its citizens have only just arrived; perhaps this
is why they seem to welcome foreign visitors almost as traveling com-
panions. Friendly and cosmopolitan, Sapporo is certainly worth an
overnight stop, at the very least as the main transport hub to other
parts of the island.

Crossed east to west by **Odori-
koen Park,** which cuts a swath of
lawns, trees, monuments, and foun-
tains through the center of the city,
Sapporo is surprisingly green.
Odori is unfortunately crowned at
its eastern end by the 482-foot (147
m) TV Tower, which is every bit as
hideous as its Tokyo equivalent.

The legacy of the American urban
planners is a city that is uncom-
monly easy to get around in. Unlike
elsewhere in Japan, addresses follow
a simple numbered grid system:
The Sapporo railroad station, for
instance, is at North 5, West 3.

Sapporo's sights are mainly
concentrated in the center. Among

Commission. Built of redbrick in the 19th-century neo-baroque style popular in Meiji Japan, it looks attractive in its setting of lawns and greenery but is less likely to impress visitors used to similar buildings in the West.

Architectural pride is reserved for the **Clock Tower (Tokei Dai),** the symbol of Sapporo and the single most photographed sight in the city. Built of wood in 1878 for Sapporo Agricultural College, it resembles a charming old New England schoolhouse and stands incongruously dwarfed between adjacent towers of concrete, some 440 yards (400 m) south of Sapporo Station.

Sapporo has a reputation as an indoor city; if the crowds appear to thin in winter, you can be sure they're down in the huge underground shopping mall in Susukino or the 0.75-mile (1 km) Tanuku-koji shopping arcade, with shops that have been operating there for a hundred years. These areas lie to the south of Odori. The latest addition is the futuristic **Sapporo Factory** (N2 E4, tel 011/207-5000), just south of Sapporo Station, a shopping and leisure complex featuring trees, streams, an old redbrick brewery, and other buildings, all within an atrium spanned by the largest glass roof in Japan.

Sapporo Beer Garden (Sapporo Biiru-en) and **Sapporo Beer Museum (Biiru Hakubutsukan),** located east of the station, is owned by Hokkaido's most famous brand name and focuses on the brewery built by the company in 1891. Free guided tours of the brewery and museum are followed by free samples of the brews. The adjacent beer garden is a vast beer hall and restaurant and one of the most popular spots in town.

Not to be outdone, the

them, about 550 yards (500 m) southwest of the station, are the **Shokubutsu-en Botanical Gardens,** a lovely oasis of green established in 1884. In addition to thousands of varieties of (mainly alpine) plants and trees, both local and from around the world, the gardens include the **Ainu Museum (Hoppo Minzoku Shiryoshitsu)** displaying historical Ainu crafts and artifacts. Also on the grounds is the first museum devoted to local wildlife—alas, of the stuffed variety.

Other buildings surviving from early days are the **Old Hokkaido Government Building** (1888, *no admission);* when Hokkaido was just beginning to attract mainland settlers, the building was called the Colonization

Diners at the Sapporo Beer Hall indulge en masse in "Ghengis Khan" style barbecued lamb—a Hokkaido specialty.

Sapporo Beer Garden and Beer Museum

 N7 E9, Higahishi-ku

011/742-1531 (beer garden); 011/731-4368 (museum)

Shuttle buses leave every 15 mins. from outside Seibu store

The entrance to
Ramen Yokocho—
Ramen Alley: Be
they ever so
humble, the
noodle stores
along here are
revered for
serving the best
of their kind.

Historical Village of Hokkaido

✉ Konoppporo, 50-1
Atsubetsu-cho,
Atsubetsu-ku

☎ 011/898-2692

🕐 Closed Mon.

💲 $$

🚌 JR bus from Shin
Sapporo subway

Otaru Municipal Museum

✉ 2-1-20 Ironai,
otaru-shi 8-min.
walk due NE from
Otaru Station

☎ 0134/33-2439

💲 $

Susukino amusement quarter to the south of the town center counts some 6,000 bars, restaurants, and places of entertainment —from swanky crab restaurants to cabarets very much in the red light category. Located due south of Sapporo Station, Susukino's **Ramen Alley (Ramen Yokocho)** is the main rival to Fukuoka's *yatai* (see p. 320) for the best ramen noodles in Japan. This narrow alley of about a dozen tiny noodle restaurants is so popular that you will probably have to wait your turn. The noodles with crab are more than worth the wait.

If you wonder about the Hokkaido of the past, you can visit the **Historical Village of Hokkaido (Hokkaido Kaitaku-no-mura),** just beyond the eastern boundary of the city. This impressive open-air museum combines some 60 buildings dismantled in Sapporo and other parts of Hokkaido and erected here. They include Sapporo's old main train station, homes, stores, and businesses, as well as structures from farming and fishing villages.

Transport around the 133-acre (54 ha) site is provided by sleigh in winter and horse-drawn trolley the rest of the year.

On the coast west of Sapporo is **Otaru,** once one of the most important commercial and fishing ports on Hokkaido and still a ferry terminal. Just 40 minutes from Sapporo by local train, this attractive city is now virtually a suburb of the metropolis. Many people who can't find a room in Sapporo (or prefer something homier or more picturesque) opt to stay here instead. There are several Western-style buildings dating back to Otaru's Meiji-era heyday, among them the recently restored Offices of the Nippon Yusen Co. Ltd., built in 1906 by Shijiro Satate, a pupil of British architect Josiah Conder.

Otaru's most interesting buildings are concentrated east of the city around the port; almost all are **warehouses** dating to the 1890s that have been restored and converted into, among other things, attractive shopping areas, cafés, and microbreweries. One of them, built in the Chinese style in 1893, is the **Otaru Museum (Otaru-shi Hakubutsukan),** which evokes interesting facets of local history. Endlessly described as "romantic" in local tourist brochures, the 0.8-mile (1.3 km) **Otaru Canal Walk** takes you past streetlamps and warehouses. How romantic it is depends on which side of the canal you are facing; the factories over on the eastern bank are less than picturesque. If its historic assets don't quite measure up to its equivalent in Hakodate (see pp. 140–41), Otaru lacks neither color nor atmosphere. Another asset is for connoisseurs of sushi: Some of the finest, freshest fish in Japan is to be found in the restaurants in Hanazono, about 450 yards (400 m) southeast of the station. ∎

Shikotsu-Toya National Park

A view of Hokkaido's lush scenery over Lake Toya-ko in summer

CLOSE TO SAPPORO, THIS PARK OF NEARLY 230 SQUARE miles (600 sq km) combines some of Hokkaido's most beautiful scenery with an abundance of hot springs, making it the island's most popular destination. It gets its name from Lake Toya-ko to the southwest and Lake Shikotsu-ko in the east, which are the highlights of the two areas that constitute the park's main sections. A third area, north of Toya-ko, centers on the perfectly conical Mount Yotei-san, often called Ezo-no-Fuji for its resemblance to its more famous counterpart on Honshu.

The northernmost ice-free lake on Hokkaido, scenic **Shikotsu-ko** is surrounded by volcanic mountains; a paradise for walkers, climbers, and nature lovers in summer, it remains popular all year round with fishermen. Despite being only about an hour from Sapporo, the 30-square mile (77 sq km) caldera lake is remarkably unspoiled. The gateway is **Shikotsu Kohan,** a village lying in the woods on the lake's eastern shore. Even the *onsen* have remained rustic, with the emphasis on *rotenburo* (outdoor baths). A long soak is the perfect way to finish a good day's hike around the

local peaks. Among the hiking options, **Monbetsu-dake** (2,841 feet/866 m) is closest to the village and easiest to summit (less than two hours). **Eniwa-dake** (4,331 feet/1,320 m) is the hardest: A round-trip hike takes five to six hours and should be abandoned if it rains. **Tarumae-zan** (3,405 feet/1,038 m) to the south is the most popular walk—and the most volcanic. It takes about half an hour to reach the summit from Station 7, itself accessible in three hours from Shikotsu Kohan on foot. The alternative is to take a taxi, as there is no bus. Transport round the Shikotsu

Shikotsu-Toya National Park
🗺 130 B3
Visitor information
✉ 144 Toya-ko Onsen-machi
☎ 0142/75-2446

Ainu elder at Poroto Kohan conducts a salmon-welcoming ceremony.

The Ainu

The Ainu were the original inhabitants of Honshu. Light-skinned and often wavy haired, they are unrelated to the Japanese; anthropologists believe they are descendants of Caucasians from prehistoric Siberia. The forebears of the Japanese drove Ainu settlers in Honshu northward, and by the ninth century the Ainu inhabited Ezo (today's Hokkaido). Their culture, which embraces carving and wood-craft, vividly patterned textiles, and epic songs, has no close relatives.

Today the Ainu are thought to number about 24,000. Inter-marriage between Ainu and Japanese has been established for so long that recent surveys show there are only about 200 people left with all four grandparents of pure Ainu descent. ■

Noboribetsu Onsen

🗺 130 B3

Visitor information

✉ Outside bus station

☎ 0143/84-3311

lake area is at best highly sporadic, so a car comes in handy, though most hotels and youth hostels rent bicycles on a daily basis.

Toya-ko, the smaller of the park's two lakes, has an island right in the center, with an animal popu-lation that includes Ezo deer (Hokkaido was formerly called Ezo). The more popular of the two lakes, with an abundance of hot springs all around the shore, Toya-ko draws onsen enthusiasts throughout the year. Just to the south is the highly active **Mount Usu-zan,** which shouldn't be missed by anyone interested in volcanoes. The latest eruption in spring 2000 caused widespread evacuations of the area. Check with the local authorities if you plan to visit this area. Usu-zan is the parent of the volcano known as **Showa Shin-zan** (New Mountain), which first appeared in a farmer's field at the eastern foot of Usu-zan in 1943; it is now more than 1,320 feet (400 m) high, and growing. Unless informed otherwise, you can safely take a cable car up to an impressive view of the infernal landscape inside the crater rim and beyond the lake to Yotei-san in the distance.

Near the park's southern coast is **Noboribetsu Onsen,** which boasts the greatest volume of hot spa water in Japan. Whatever scenic attractions may have been here are now undermined by a glut of monster resort hotels. Noboribetsu does have the advantage of an awe-inspiring **Hell Valley (Jigokudani),** with viewing platforms and wooden walkways spanning a desolate, evil-smelling landscape belching sulfurous fumes and steam from fissures in discolored rocks, not to mention the poisonous-looking, violently bubbling Oyunuma Pond.

Farther southeast is the coastal town of **Shiraoi,** noted for the reconstructed Ainu village at **Poroto Kotan.** Although the town features performances for tourists, it was set up by the Ainu themselves and boasts a particularly good Ainu museum. ■

Showa Shin-zan, a volcano that first appeared only about 60 years ago, is still on the rise.

Poroto Kotan Ainu Museum

✉ 2-3-4 Wakakusa-cho, Shiraoi-cho,
☎ 0144/82-3914
💲 $$
🚃 Train: JR from Noboribetsu Station to Shiraoi Station

From Mount Hakodate, the view over the city after dark presents a galaxy of lights.

Hakodate & beyond

HAKODATE, ON OSHIMA-HANTO PENINSULA IN THE FAR southwest of Hokkaido, is one of the main terminals for ferries from Honshu—and also one of the most rewarding cities to visit in the prefecture. No other city has quite so many buildings and reminders evoking Meiji- and Taisho-period Japan.

Hakodate

130 B2

Visitor information

12-14 Wakamatsu-cho (outside station)

0138/23-5440

JR services from Aomori (2 hrs.). From Sapporo (3 hrs. 30 mins.)

Though Hakodate is a popular gateway to Hokkaido, many Japanese visitors confine their trips to the Hakodate area alone, which has most of the attractions found elsewhere on the island.

In 1864 the shogunate built **Goryokaku** (Five Corner Fort) to defend this important outpost from foreign aggression. Ironically, it was besieged by Japanese soldiers during the Hakodate War of 1869, when the shogun's troops made

a futile last stand against the imperial forces during the Meiji Restoration. The citadel itself, an early attempt at a Western-style fortification, has disappeared, but the curious star shape of the walls is still much in evidence on a hilltop east of the city as the highlight of popular **Goryokaku-koen Park.** The moat serves as a boating pond, and the whole star shape becomes a vast floral centerpiece during the cherry blossom

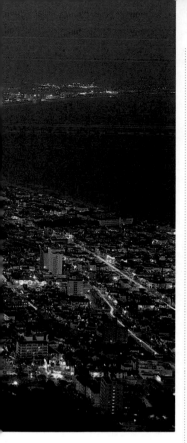

brewing their own beer. Streetcars are still the city's main form of public transportation; one dating from 1913 is still in service for tourists.

Painted signs and mountains of bright orange king crabs and hairy crabs characterize Hakodate's colorful Morning Market *(asa ichi)*, just south of the railroad station. It comprises some 400 stalls selling fish, seafood, fruit, and other local

season. Adjacent **Goryokaku Tower,** though hideous, is worth ascending to appreciate the shape of the citadel.

The city lies on a narrow spit of land, with the sea to the north and south. Beside the town is the 1,100-foot (335 m) **Mount Hakodate,** accessible either on foot or by cable car. The view from the top is spectacular. **Motomachi,** the western side of town, occupies part of the slope; it is renowned for buildings from the city's late 19th- and early 20th-century heyday . Most of these structures are open as museums (see pp. 140–41). Old buildings also pepper the area near the waterfront; warehouses have been preserved and transformed into attractive shopping areas, exhibition spaces, and café-restaurants

produce, both wholesale and retail. Open for breakfast, the local noodle restaurants are famed for their seafood soup dishes. The market opens at 4 a.m. with the sale of fresh catches and closes in the early afternoon, though some stalls remain open for tourists. Some of the wooden buildings in the picturesque alleyways out back look as if they have been around as long as Hakodate itself.

On the eastern side of the city is Yunokawa Onsen spa area; just over half an hour to the north is scenic Onuma Quasi-National Park (see p. 142). Beautiful **Cape Esan-misaki,** about 37 miles (60 km) east of the city, is cherished for two volcanic peaks carpeted with azaleas and alpine plants in late spring and summer. ∎

Hakodate is filled with fine historic buildings.

The Old Public Hall in Hakodate is the star attraction among many historic buildings.

A walk in Hakodate

Hakodate is a small city. If you have seen Goryokaku-koen Park and the Morning Market, you can take this walk around Motomachi and the waterfront area after lunch.

Take the streetcar or bus to **Hakodate Dokku-mae** or a taxi to the **Foreigners' Cemetery (Gaikoujin Bochi) ❶**. If you're coming from the streetcar/bus stop, head southwest up Uomi-zaka, take the first right, and stay on the same road. The cemetery is on the right, overlooking the bay. A poignant reminder of Hakodate's cosmopolitan history, it contains the graves of Americans (including two of Commodore Perry's sailors, who died on the trip in 1854), British, Chinese, and Russians. From the cemetery, head southeast for about 220 yards (200 m), until you come to the **Old Russian Consulate (Kyu Roshia Ryoji-kan),** built in 1908 to replace the original of 1858. The redbrick exterior is not imposing, but the interior conveys the atmosphere of the czarist era.

After leaving here, walk downhill and take the fifth street on the right, walking four blocks to reach the **Chinese Memorial Hall (Chuka Kai-kan) ❷** *(Tel 0138/22-1211)*. Rebuilt after a fire in 1907, it looks as though it belongs in old Shanghai—which, in a sense, it does. Completed in 1912, it was constructed by builders, carpenters, and sculptors especially imported from Shanghai. As you exit, turn right, then take the second right, and you will find yourself before the green **Soma Company building ❸,** a neoclassical wooden office building of the early Taisho period (1912–1926) that still functions as such. Located right on the main street, it's one of the most photographed buildings in Hakodate—especially with a tram passing by, when the pairing looks exactly as it did some 90 years ago. The broad avenue going uphill in front of the building leads to the main sights of **Motomachi.** As you walk up, the white building with the blue-trimmed arched windows on your left is the **Old British Consulate (Kyu Igirisu Ryoji-kan) ❹** *(Tel 0138/27-8159)*. In service from 1859 to 1934 and now a popular setting for weddings, the consulate contains a museum and a cozy tearoom (complete with a wax effigy of a Buckingham Palace guard) construed in Japan as "English-style."

At the top of the avenue is **Motomachi-koen Park,** dominated by an imposing gray wooden building with an elegant Grecian portico: the **Old Branch Office of the Hokkaido Government (Kyu-Hokkaido-cho Hakodate-shicho chosha) 5.** Built in 1909, it contains an interesting museum of early photography, including what is allegedly the first snapshot ever taken in Japan: Commodore Perry during his trip to Hakodate in 1854. Just behind here is the **Old Public Hall.** Built of wood in the colonial style by a Japanese architect in 1910, this delightful building has been repainted in grayish mauve with yellow highlights around the windows and decorative friezes.

From Motomachi-koen Park, take the cobbled lane on the right. About 380 yards (350 m) farther on your left, you'll see the candy-box charm of the **Russian Orthodox Church (Hakodate Harisutosu-sei Kyokai) 6,** built in 1916. Almost alongside, on the other side of the lane, is the 1924 Gothic-style **Roman Catholic Church (Katorikku Motomachi Kyokai).** On the same street lies the **Episcopal Church (Sei Yohane Kyokai),** built by missionaries in 1874 and demolished to make way for some futurist renovations in 1979. Just east of it is the **Mount Hakodate Cable Car Station,** which takes you to the summit for a spectacular view over the city and harbor.

Down again after enjoying the view of the town and port, walk in a northwesterly direction for about 15 minutes toward the

See area map page 130–31
Foreign Cemetery
3.5 miles (5.6 km)
4 hours
Railway Station

NOT TO BE MISSED

- Chinese Memorial Hall
- Soma Company office building
- Old British Consulate
- Old Branch Office of the Hokkaido Government

waterfront. As you reach the road running parallel to the seafront, you'll see to your right a large redbrick building with high rounded arches—the **Old Hakodate Post Office (Kyu-Hakodate Yubinkyoku) 7.** A post office until 1955, it has been converted into a glass studio and shopping precinct. Around back are a number of 19th-century warehouses made into attractive stores, exhibition and event spaces, and café-restaurants. Among the warehouse developments are **Bay Hakodate** and **Hakodate History Plaza** just behind the old post office, the **Hakodate Beer** microbrewery-restaurant farther north along the waterfront, and the **Kanemori warehouses** to the southwest. You can continue past the Morning Market to the station if you intend to travel on from the town, but dinner on the waterfront is a perfect way to wind up a walk in Hakodate. ■

Onuma Quasi-
National Park
🏔 130 B2
Visitor information
☎ 0138/23-5440
   (Hakodate)
🚉 Train from
   Hakodate. Journey
   time 20 mins.

Onuma Quasi-National Park & the south

LOCATED TOWARD THE EAST OF THE OSHIMA HANTO
Peninsula in western Hokkaido, Onuma Quasi-National Park is just
north of Hakodate. At the center is 3,717-foot-high (1,133 m) Mount
Komaga-take, an active volcano famed for the beauty of its craggy
peaks and gentle slopes, which in summer are carpeted with spectacular displays of alpine flowers.

**Wild swans
winter on
islands in Lake
Konuma-ko.**

Walkers and climbers are rewarded
with views south of the mountain
over the twin lakes **Onuma,** which
gives the park its name, and

Konuma. Both are outstanding
beauty spots. Onuma, whose waters
reflect Komaga-take, is dotted with
scores of tree-covered islets famed
for their display of autumnal color.
Lake Konuma-ko is no less
scenic; Ezo deer roam its perimeter,
and the lake's three islands are the
winter habitat of wild swans.

Southwest of the park, near the
point of the peninsula joined to
Honshu by the Seikan Tunnel, lies
Matsumae, virtually the only
place on Hokkaido that retains vestiges of its feudal past. Its castle is a
reproduction of the original built
in 1854 and destroyed after the feudal era ended in 1868, though the
main gate is original. ■

Daisetsuzan National Park & central Hokkaido

RIGHT IN THE CENTER OF HOKKAIDO AND IN EVERY WAY the island's heart—at least to the nature lover—Daisetsuzan National Park covers some 890 square miles (2,300 sq km), making it Japan's largest national park. Its backbone is a mountain range known as the "roof of Hokkaido," culminating in the 7,513-foot-high (2,290 m) Mount Asahi-dake, the island's highest peak. The park and its mountains are famed for beautiful valleys, steep cliffs, and spectacular waterfalls, in addition to the hot springs sprinkled about the foothills. Most notable is Sounkyo spa in the north of the park, which is also the main staging point for a variety of mountain walks in the region.

Above: Sounkyo Gorge

Below: Lavender fields near Furano in central Hokkaido

Daisetsuzan National Park
⚠ 131 C4

Sounkyo Gorge
⚠ 131 C4
Visitor information
✉ Bus terminal
☎ 01658/5-3350

Asahikawa
⚠ 131 C4
Visitor information
✉ Asahikawa Station
☎ 0166/22-6704

Furano
⚠ 131 C4
Visitor information
☎ 0167/23-3388
🚃 Train: JR Furano line from Asahikawa. Journey time 75 mins.

One excellent area for hiking is the 15-mile (24 km) **Sounkyo Gorge,** with its rich tapestry of color in the fall and lovely waterfalls, some of which cascade 500 feet (150 m) down a sheer drop, in particular over the Obako and Kobako cliffs. South of Asahi-dake is the park's other great gorge, **Tennin-kyo,** again with waterfalls in beautiful sylvan settings, as well as a number of hot springs.

Twenty five miles (40 km) northwest of Daisetsuzan National Park is **Asahikawa,** Hokkaido's second largest city. Though of little interest to travelers, it is an important transportation hub; many people therefore opt to stay here out of sheer convenience. Some use it as a gateway to the park if they plan to visit on a day trip, but this is not a truly satisfactory option: You would be better off staying in the park itself, especially in a scenic area such as that around Sounkyo Gorge.

About 30 miles (50 km) southwest of Asahikawa is **Furano**—an area important for its winter sports, scenery, and agriculture. Furano resort has some of the best snow conditions in Japan, and it often hosts international ski events. A major producer of grapes, potatoes, beans, asparagus, and other vegetables, the area around the Tokaichi foothills has become popular among Japanese tourists for its vast fields of lavender. ■

Rishiri-Rebun-Sarobetsu National Park & the far north

UP IN THE FAR NORTHWEST OF JAPAN, THIS NATIONAL park comprises the beautiful and hiker-friendly islands of Rishiri and Rebun; on the mainland opposite is the Sarobetsu Plain, a strip of coastal swampland some 21 miles (34 km) long.

Just to the north of the Sarobetsu Plain, the remote coastal town of **Wakkanai** has a reputation for bleakness. Many Japanese come here just to see the view over the disputed island of Sakhalin (presently in Russian possession) to the north, then go on to nearby **Cape Soya-misaki**—the northernmost point in Japan—just to say they've been there. As far as the average traveler is concerned, Wakkanai is primarily a jumping off point for the two breathtakingly lovely islands a short distance from the western coast.

The rounded island of **Rishiri-to** is crowned by a conical volcano often compared to Fuji-san, the magnificent 5,646-foot (1,721 m) **Rishiri-zan.** This is the island's main draw; there are several trails to the summit, including one for serious climbers. None of the routes is especially easy. To ascend and descend Rishiri-zan takes about ten hours, but there are less strenuous walks through lower, greener hills dotted with alpine flowers, notably to the scenic **Hime-numa Pond.** The visitor information center at the island ferry terminal in Oshidomari has maps and guides describing the various trails in English, although the staff does not speak English. If you're planning to climb, bring proper clothing, as it can be bitterly cold, with plenty of ice and snow even in high summer. You

will also need to carry water; there is none on the mountain.

If you are not of the mountaineering persuasion, the visitor center rents out bicycles. The single road around the island links various picturesque fishing hamlets with the ports of **Oshidomari** in

Rishiri-Rebun-Sarobetsu National Park

🏔 130 B6

Visitor information

✉ Wakkanai

☎ 0162/33-1100

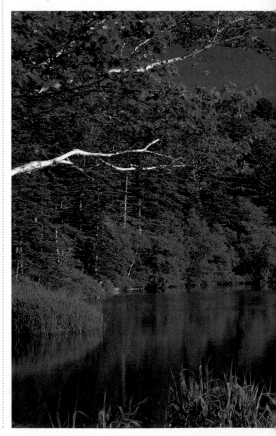

the north and **Kutsugata** in the west, where there are the largest number of places to stay.

Rebun-to, a narrow, wedge-shape isle some 9 miles (15 km) long, is smaller than Rishiri but more interesting—at the very least for the sheer variety of its scenery. Famous for carpets of hundreds of varieties of alpine flowers in summer, its rolling hills culminate in the 1,607-foot (490 m) **Rebun-dake.** The most popular hiking routes on Rebun run along the west coast, taking in cliffs, remote fishing hamlets, and a striking array of both wooded and marine scenery. Details of the trails are available at the hotels and youth hostels on the island, many of which organize hiking parties. Because the trails pass through remote areas, it is better to avoid hiking on your own.

There are two main ports, Kafuka in the south and smaller Funodomari in the north; both offer a range of accommodations, as do the villages of Motochi in the southwest and Shiretoko on the southern tip. Bicycle rental is available from most hotels and *minshuku* (see p. 359), and all communities are linked by a bus service. Rebun and Rishiri are at their best from June to September.

The **Sarobetsu Genya Plain,** the remaining area of the park, is famous for its colorful summer flowers, especially irises, lilies, and rhododendrons. ∎

Mount Rishiri-zan famously graces remote Rishiri-to.

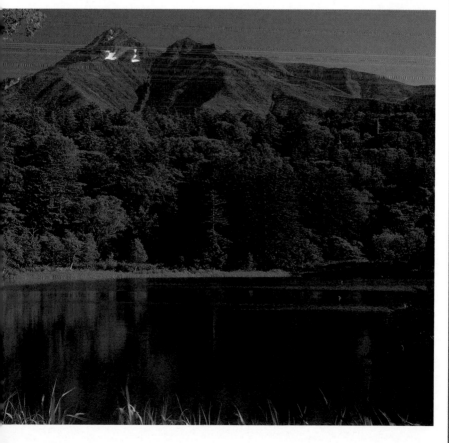

The northeast: Abashiri & Shiretoko National Park

AT THE MOUTH OF THE ABASHIRI-GAWA RIVER ON THE SEA of Okhotsk is Abashiri, a port for the trout and salmon fishing industry. From December to March, when the port closes down as the bay fills with ice floes, it's a lonely place.

Museum of Northern Peoples (Hoppo Minzoku Hakubutsukan); it provides insights into the Ainu, Siberians, Eskimos, and Amerindians—and the connections among them. In Mombetsu, 56 miles (90 km) north of Abashiri, is **Okhotsk Ryuhyo Museum (Okhotsk Ryuhyo-kan,** *245-1 Tento-zan, Abashiri, tel 0152/43-5951).* With its subzero temperatures and great blocks of ice, it seems designed to show summer visitors what they missed from the pack ice in winter. Hardier visitors are coming increasingly to Mombetsu to see the ice floes on the Sea of Okhotsk in midwinter; come February, the sea is frozen out to the horizon, and popular sightseeing excursions are provided aboard an icebreaker.

Above all, Abashiri is the gateway to **Shiretoko National Park,** Japan's only true wilderness. Occupying the last 30 miles (50 km) of a rugged peninsula extending some 45 miles (70 km) and pointing like a finger into the Sea of Okhotsk, Shiretoko includes peaks and dense forests. The road runs along the coast to the town of **Utoro** on the west and connects with the small town of **Rausu** in the east. Beyond it there are no more roads: *Shiretoko* is the Ainu word for "world's end." Fox, deer, and bear roam the last 25 miles (40 km) of the peninsula. The area can be explored on foot or by sightseeing boat from Utoro (a 3-to 4-hour trip around the cape).

Say "Abashiri" to most Japanese of the baby-boomer generation, and—strange as it seems—they fondly think back to a prison rather than to the town. It's all due to a gangster-movie series cherished during the early 1970s, featuring tattooed antiheroes in a snowbound maximum-security lockup. Built on **Mount Tento-zan** near the city in 1890, the real thing has been moved to new premises, and the old one has been turned into **Abashiri Prison Museum (Hakubutsukan Abashiri Kangoku,** *Tel 0152/45-2411).* Now populated with wax figures, Japan's Alcatraz is a grim if fascinating reminder of the harsh, chilly conditions endured by jailbirds in prewar Japan. Also on Tento-zan is the interesting **Hokkaido**

Abashiri

🅰 131 D4

Visitor information

☎ Outside Abashiri Station

☎ 0152/44-5849

🚆 Train: JR Abashiri from Sapporo (5 hrs. 19 mins.)

Hokkaido Museum of Northern Peoples

☎ 0152/45-3888

🕐 Closed Mon.

💲 $$

These Hokkaido brown bear cubs may grow up to weigh some 880 pounds (400 kg).

Some 6 miles (10 km) northeast of Utoro is one of the park's highlights, the beautiful **Shiretoko Five Lakes (Shiretoko-go-ko),** where wooden walkways encircle bodies of water in virgin forest crisscrossed by hiking paths. Another 6 miles (10 km) farther on is **Kamuiwakka-no-taki,** an *onsen* area characterized by a warm-water river offering the novel experience of bathing in cascades and waterfalls of hot water. Bring swimwear and shoes with soles capable of gripping slippery rock; otherwise you will fall prey to vendors waiting to rent out straw sandals at inflated prices.

Of the many walks within Shiretoko park, the most popular is the ascent of **Rausu-dake** (5,450 feet/1,661 m), the highest peak in the volcanic range at the park's center. Allow up to five hours for the climb. From the peak you can walk north to **Io-zan** (5,125 feet/1,562 m), the volcano that heats the water at Kamuiwakka-no-taki; the trek to the peak and back takes around eight hours.

Many people planning serious hikes in the area swear by the **Shiretoko Iwaobetsu Youth Hostel** some 3 miles (5 km) north of Utoro, which organizes them. Remember, if you're planning to explore the remote tip of the peninsula, traveling in a group is essential. With an estimated 600 bears on the loose out there, you would not want to take a chance—especially not in the fall, when they're out to fatten themselves before hibernating through the winter. ∎

The Sea of Okhotsk freezes over in winter, leaving icebreakers to push through the floes.

Shiretoko National Park
⛰ 131 E5
Visitor information
✉ Shari Station
⛰ 01522/3-2424
🚆 Train: JR Senmo line to Shari from Abashiri, then bus to Utoro Onsen (60 mins.) or Iwaobetsu (70 mins.)

Often shrouded in mist, mysterious Lake Mashu-ko was held in awe by the Ainu, to whom it was a specially sacred place.

The east: Akan & Kushiro-Shitsugen National Parks

SOUTHWEST OF THE SHIRETOKO PENINSULA, TOWARD THE center of the eastern wing of the island of Hokkaido, lies Akan National Park, an idyllic preserve of dense virgin forest, clear lakes, and volcanic mountains. The town of Abashiri (see p. 146) to the north is the most convenient access point for the park.

Akan National Park

📍 131 D4

Visitor information

☎ 0154/67-2254

🚌 Bus: Akan bus from JR Kushiro Station to Akan Kohan

Often regarded as the eastern equivalent of Shikotsu-Toya (see p. 135) and likewise endowed with hot springs, Akan is less accessible and so less crowded. The park encompasses three main lakes: Akan in the southwest, Mashu to the east, and Kussharo just north of center. Dotted with small islands and surrounded by forests, **Lake Akan-ko,** with its alpine scenery, is famous for the curious plant balls called *marimo (Aegagropila sauteri)* that form in its water. A species of pondweed growing in a perfectly spherical shape, the marimo are not much larger than a baseball but can take 200 years to form.

Akan-ko offers a multitude of hot springs, especially in the resort of **Akan Kohan** on the southern shore. Although the area is very

Hokkaido's national parks are home to a variety of wildlife.

six hours. However, the most interesting local hike is up **Me-akan-dake** (4,918 feet/1,499 m), which is not only the highest mountain in the park but also one of the most active volcanoes in Japan. Me-akan has erupted 15 times since 1800, most recently in 1988. There are a number of ways to reach the summit; the most common is via a trailhead at lovely **Lake Onneto-ko,** nestled in the depths of a thick forest. The lake is accessible from Akan Kohan by bus. If you are going to climb Me-Akan, take warm, waterproof clothing, as the

touristy and marred by the usual monster *onsen* hotels, it is a convenient base for climbing 4,498-foot (1,371 m) **O-akan-dake.** With its trailhead some 3 miles (5 km) northeast of Akan Kohan, it can be ascended and descended in about

Bears on Hokkaido

Hokkaido is home to the brown bear *(ursus arctos)*. Bears are shy of humans and make themselves scarce, but can be very dangerous if frightened or hungry. In bear areas, always travel in a group. Avoid hiking just after sunrise and at dusk. Carry a bell or something to warn any bears of your approach. If you do encounter a bear, don't shout or turn your back. Instead, move slowly backward; unless you really have to, don't run. If you spy a cub, don't approach it—the mother is usually close by.

Bears have always been sacred to the Ainu, an honor lost on the animals, who were sacrificed and eaten. Raised in captivity, some bears are now confined in hideous concrete reserves. ■

Japanese cranes make their winter home in the bird sanctuary in Kushiro Marsh.

Kawayu Onsen

🚉 Train: JR Senmo line to Kawayu Onsen Station (55 mins. from Shari, 65 mins. from Kushiro), then bus to town center (10 mins.)

Kushiro-Shitsugen National Park

🅰 131 E4

Visitor information

✉ Information counter inside JR Kushiro Station

☎ 0154/22-8294

🚌 Bus: Akan bus from JR Kushiro Station to (30 mins.)

weather is notoriously unpredictable. Once you reach the unearthly landscape near the summit, with its discolored ponds and steaming vents, you might find the air a little too sulfurous for comfort.

Lake Mashu-ko is a caldera lake surrounded by sheer cliffs. More than just an intense shade of blue on a clear day, the exceptionally pure lake water happens to have one of the world's highest transparency ratings, with visibility to a depth of 115 feet (35 m). A good base in the area is the wooded resort of **Kawayu Onsen** to the west of the lake, which is much more pleasant and unspoiled than Akan Kohan. Just south of Kawayu Onsen, another great volcanic hiking opportunity looms in the form of **Io-zan** (Sulphur Mountain). At only 1,680 feet (512 m) it's a less arduous trek than Me-Akan, taking under an hour. In geothermal terms, however, Io-zan pulls out all the stops: Its fascinating, extraterrestrial-looking landscape is alive with bubbling pools and vents belching sulfurous steam.

Kawayu is roughly midway between Mashu-ko and **Lake Kussharo-ko.** The largest lake on Hokkaido, Kussharo has a circumference of 35 miles (57 km) and is very popular for swimming in summer. At **Sunayu Onsen** on a beach on its eastern shore, the heat of the underground water rises to warm the sand.

South of Akan National Park is the newer **Kushiro-Shitsugen National Park.** The main attraction here is **Kushiro Marsh,** Japan's largest wetland (75 square miles/200 sq. km) and a bird sanctuary *(Kushiro Marshland Observatory, 6-11 Hokuto, Kushiro-shi, tel 0154/56-2424).* The main draw is the endangered Japanese red-crested crane; some 400 survive in the park, which is their winter habitat. Opened in 1958, the Japanese Crane Reserve continues its research into breeding and artificial incubation (not open to the public). The park is reached from the city of Kushiro, the industrial hub of eastern Hokkaido; the city is also the main southern gateway to Akan National Park. ∎

Tohoku is renowned for its mountain scenery and fertile countryside, seascapes, cold winters, and the historical assets of its old towns. The people are especially welcoming and their festivals rousing. This is Japan for connoisseurs.

Northern Honshu (Tohoku)

A Japanese macaque gets in hot water in winter.

Snug in their snowhouses, children hold parties during the Kamakura festival in February.

Northern Honshu (Tohoku)

TOHOKU MEANS "NORTH EAST," BUT WHEN THE POET BASHO (1655–1694) made his famous journey to the eponymous region at the top of Honshu in 1689, it was just the "deep north." Mountainous, wild, and often bitterly cold in winter, Tohoku was extremely remote in those days. Some of it still is.

Like much of the Sea of Japan side of Honshu, western Tohoku is known as *yuki guni* (snow country). Tohoku was the last dwelling place of the Ainu people on Honshu before they were driven to Hokkaido about a thousand years ago; until recently, much of it was backward and desperately poor.

In this happily affluent era, the area's remoteness is an asset; in a word, Tohoku is beautiful. Topped by the additional attraction of plentiful *onsen* resorts, it boasts outstanding alpine scenery in Yamagata-ken and Akita-ken. Tohoku's days of remoteness are definitely numbered. Indeed, some sites—notably Sendai, the most important regional capital—have been anything but remote for centuries. Just outside the city on the Pacific coast is lovely Matsushima Bay, long regarded by the Japanese as one of the nation's Three Great Sights. Famous too is the old castle town of Hirosaki in Aomori, especially in springtime,

Area of map detail

Tokyo

when millions travel there to contemplate the castle standing over a sea of cherry blossoms. Meanwhile, in Iwate-ken, the little town of Hiraizumi still contains vestiges of a glorious past fading some 900 years ago, including Chuson-ji Temple, in which the fabulously sculpted golden altarpiece is one of the country's greatest designated National Treasures. ■

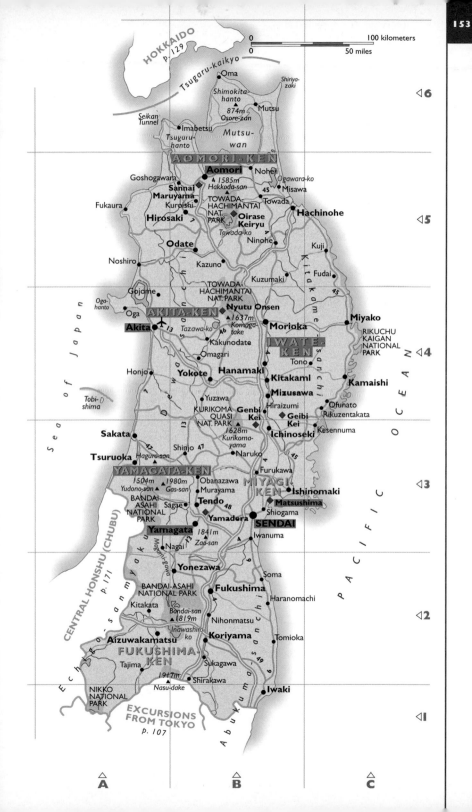

HOKKAIDO p.129

100 kilometers
50 miles

Tsugaru-kaikyo

Oma

Shiriya-zaki

Shimokita-hanto

6

874m Osore-zan

Mutsu

Seikan Tunnel

Imabetsu

Tsugaru-hanto

Mutsu-wan

AOMORI-KEN

Goshogawara

Aomori

Noheji

Ogawara-ko

5

Sannai Maruyama

1585m Hakkoda-san

Misawa

45

Fukaura

Kuroishi

TOWADA-HACHIMANTAI NAT. PARK

Towada

Hachinohe

Hirosaki

Oirase Keiryu

Towada-ko

Ninohe

Odate

Kuji

Noshiro

Kazuno

Fudai

Kuzumaki

Gojome

TOWADA-HACHIMANTAI NAT. PARK

Oga-hanto

Oga

AKITA-KEN

Nyutu Onsen

Miyako

RIKUCHU KAIGAN NATIONAL PARK

4

Akita

13

1637m Komaga-take

Morioka

Tazawa-ko

IWATE-KEN

Kakunodate

Honjo

Omagari

Tono

Yokote

Hanamaki

Kitakami

Tobi-shima

Yuzawa

Mizusawa

KURIKOMA QUASI NAT. PARK

Genbi Kei

Hiraizumi

Geibi Kei

Ofunato

Rikuzentakata

Kamaishi

Sakata

1628m Kurikoma-yama

Ichinoseki

Kesennuma

Shinjo

47

Naruko

45

Tsuruoka

Haguro-san

YAMAGATA-KEN

Furukawa

3

1504m Yudono-san

1980m Gas-san

Obanazawa

Murayama

MIYAGI-KEN

Ishinomaki

BANDAI-ASAHI NATIONAL PARK

Sagae

Tendo

48

Matsushima

Shiogama

Yamadera

SENDAI

Yamagata

1841m Zao-san

Iwanuma

Nagai

Yonezawa

Soma

BANDAI-ASAHI NATIONAL PARK

Fukushima

Haranomachi

2

Kitakata

Bandai-san 1819m

Nihonmatsu

Inawashiro-ko

Aizuwakamatsu

Koriyama

Tomioka

FUKUSHIMA-KEN

Tajima

Sukagawa

1917m Nasu-dake

Shirakawa

Iwaki

NIKKO NATIONAL PARK

EXCURSIONS FROM TOKYO p.107

CENTRAL HONSHU (CHUBU) p.171

Sea of Japan

PACIFIC OCEAN

A

B

C

1

Aomori-ken

AT THE VERY NORTHERN TIP OF HONSHU, AOMORI IS Japan's world's end. The winters are harsh and Siberian; up on the far northeastern Shimokita-hanto, even the monkeys—the world's northernmost—have adapted to the conditions by growing longer coats than their relatives elsewhere in Japan. It may sound bleak, but Aomori's numerous archaeological sites prove that the region is sufficiently rich in natural resources to have attracted human beings since Neolithic times.

Sannai Maruyama Iseki
- 153 B5
- Sannai Maruyama, Aomori-shi
- 0177/22-1111
- Bus: from JR Aomori Station (30 mins.)

Aomori City
- 153 B5
- **Visitor information**
- Aomori Station (just in front)
- 0177/23-4670
- Train: Tohoku Shinkansen from Tokyo via Morioka (4 hrs. 50 mins.)
- Tokyo (Haneda) to Aomori airport (1 hr. 10 mins.)

Munakata Memorial Museum
- 2-1-2 Matsubara
- 0177/77-4567
- Closed Mon.
- $
- Bus: from Aomori Station (15 mins.)

Featuring reconstructed Jomon-period (see p. 28) dwellings and open to the public, the most famous sites are in Korekawa, near the town of Hachinohe on the east coast, and especially at **Sannai Maruyama Iseki,** the impressive site of a village 5,000 years old just south of Aomori city. Until the 1970s Aomori was regarded as a cultural backwater; today it is revered as a nostalgic repository of customs, festivals, and folklore.

Aomori is famous for horses, although much less so than in premodern times; always an agricultural region, it now prospers as a leading national provider of rice, vegetables, and fruit and is a major producer of processed foods. With coastlines on both the Pacific and the Japan Sea, Aomori is renowned for its fish and seafood.

As in much of Tohoku, Aomori's natural beauty spots, beaches, ski resorts, and proliferation of *onsen* spas attract increasing numbers of Japanese but few foreign tourists.

The capital, **Aomori,** lies in the north of the prefecture between Tsugaru-hanto and Shimokita-hanto. Blitzed during World War II, the city is entirely modern. Nevertheless, this is another of those cities that prove indispensable to travelers exploring a region—in this case, especially those going on to Hokkaido. If you do stop over, take a look at the **Munakata Memorial Museum (Munakata Shiko Kinenkan),** devoted to the eponymous modern woodblock print master (1903–1975), a native son. Despite Aomori's plentiful hotels and *ryokan,* be warned: The city's accommodations are often fully reserved during holiday periods, especially for the Nebuta festival.

Aomori-ken is divided into three peninsular districts: the Shimokita in the northeast,

Aomori arts & crafts

A woodblock master of international renown, Munakata Shiko (1903–1975) was a leading member of the *mingei* (folk art) movement. Evidencing his Aomori roots, his works reflected the dynamic designs of the Nebuta festival's illuminated floats (see p. 156), which are in turn inspired by

Tsugaru tako-e—the colorful paintings on paper kites produced in the Tsugaro region. Woodcraft is another regional specialty, notably the dappled, polychrome *Tsugaru-nuri* lacquerware and a variety of charming lathe-turned toys. *Kogin* embroidery, used on clothing and souvenirs, dates to feudal times. ■

Nambu to the southeast, and Tsugaru in the west. **Shimokita-hanto** is known for the weird, strangely twisted cliff formations along the rocky **Hotoke-ga-ura** coast on its western side, but "weird" is even more fitting to describe **Mount Osore-zan** (Mount Dread), a sacred mountain revered as a gateway to the world of the dead. Some say it is one of the most haunted places on Earth.

Ravens caw across a desolate volcanic landscape with sulfurous fumes drifting from rocky fissures, and little piles of stones decorated with toys commemorate the souls of departed children. During the Bon festival for the dead at the end of July, thousands come up here to pray at **Entsu–ji Temple.** Many consult with *itako* (elderly, often blind female mediums) to talk to departed relatives.

Far off the beaten tourist track, old-style rustic onsen such as Tsuta Onsen abound in Aomori-ken.

Hirosaki

 153 B5

Visitor information

✉ Hirosaki-koen

☎ 0172/32-0524

🚆 Train: JR limited express from Aomori (30 mins.)

Hirosaki-jo Castle

✉ Hirosaki-koen

☎ 0172/33-8733

💲 $

Chosho-ji Temple

✉ 1-23-8 Nishi-shigemori

☎ 0172/32-0813

💲 $

The floats at Aomori's Nebuta Matsuri festival epitomize Japanese folk art.

Scenic areas in the Nambu district include the **Oirase Keiryu Gorge,** where torrents wind through 9 miles (14 km) of woodland, and—the source of the Oirase-gawa River—**Lake Towada-ko,** in a crater with a 25-mile (40 km) perimeter; with its clear blue waters, this is one of Japan's most beautiful lakes.

Tsugaru-hanto is of interest mainly for its scenery, from rugged Cape Gongen to the central mountain of Hakkoda-san (5,200 feet/1,585 m). West of Tsugaru are the Shirakami Mountains, declared a UNESCO World Heritage Site for possessing one of the largest virgin beech forests in the world.

Tsugaru also harbors one of Tohoku's few historical places: the old castle town of **Hirosaki.** The feudal domain of the Tsugaru clans, Hirosaki flourished during the Edo period as one of the area's most important towns. Today its reputation resides in the charm of the town itself (the preservation areas, that is) and its castle, but probably most of all for the 5,000 or so cherry trees blossoming on the castle grounds. These make Hirosaki a premier destination for *hanami* (flower-viewing) parties and, during the Hirosaki Cherry Blossom Festival (Apr. 23–May 5), the town receives some two million tourists.

Built in 1611 and still surrounded by three moats, **Hirosaki-jo Castle** retains several original gates and towers. Lightning destroyed the five-story main keep in the 18th century; the current three-story replacement dates from 1810 and has a museum devoted to samurai armor and artifacts. Like the castle, the town's other sights—the Historical House Preservation Area and **Zenrin-gai,** the Zen temple district with its impressive 17th-century **Chosho-ji Temple**—are concentrated in the more attractive west side of town. The town also preserves several charming Western-style buildings where 19th-century missionaries lived. ■

Nebuta

Spectators from all over Japan come to Nebuta Matsuri, when thousands of revelers dance in a parade (whose origins are forgotten) featuring colossal illuminated floats. One theory is that the festival commemorates a legend about the ninth-century warrior Sakanoue-no-Tamuramaro, who led imperial forces to the far north to conquer local tribes. Tamuramaro's successful strategy consisted of placing huge lanterns around the hills at night; when the hapless tribesmen came out to investigate the lanterns, they were captured. The *nebuta*, which represent the lanterns, are gigantic illuminated paper structures colorfully painted with mythical figures. ■

Akita-ken

Lake Tazawa-ko is immensely popular with Japanese holidaymakers.

IN THE NORTHWEST OF TOHOKU, AKITA-KEN ENCOMPASS-es high mountain ranges in the north, east, and south; 70 percent of the land is forested. The mountains of Akita are renowned for Lakes Towada-ko and Tazawa-ko (see p. 158), for the sylvan Hachimantai Plateau, and for their sheer scenic beauty. Ski resorts abound, and being volcanic, the mountains have plenty of hot springs, notably those in the remote resort of Nyuto Onsen (see p. 158). Jutting 12.5 miles (20 km) into the Sea of Japan, the Oga-hanto Peninsula, with its green hills and craggy coastline, is a favored destination in summer, but transportation dwindles to a bare minimum in winter. The region's most interesting town by far is Kakunodate (see pp. 158–60), famed for one of the largest and best-preserved samurai districts in the country.

Winters are cold and snowbound on Akita's higher ground, but the plain on the milder seaward side is subject to the high rainfall common to much of the west coast of Japan. There can be seasonal extremes of temperature; situated halfway down on the coastal side, the prefectural capital of Akita City records temperatures dropping to 14° F (-10° C) in winter and soaring to 93° F (34° C) in summer. Particularly lush, the agricultural lowlands take in productive rice-growing districts, some yielding the highest quality crop in the country.

Archaeological finds have shown that the region was inhabited at least 20,000 years ago, probably by tribes related to the Ainu (see p. 136). The army of the Yamato court took Akita in 658 and drove the Ainu ever farther north; Akita city grew out of a permanent garrison established in the eighth century. In 1602, the year before he founded

Tazawa-ko

⚠ 153 A4

Visitor information

✉ JR Tazawa-ko Station

☎ 0187/43-2111

🚆 Train: Akita
Shinkansen from
Tokyo Station to JR
Tazawa-ko Station
(3 hrs.)

Nyuto Onsen

⚠ 153 A4

Visitor information

🚆 Bus from JR Tazawa-
ko Station (40
mins.)

Kakunodate

⚠ 153 A4

Visitor information

✉ Kakunodate Station
(just outside)

☎ 0187/54-2700

🚆 Train: Akita
Shinkansen from
Tokyo Station to
Kakunodate Station
(3 hrs. 11 mins.)

**Revelers balance
weighty tiers of
lanterns at the
Kanto festival
held in Akita city
in August.**

the national government that
would last for centuries, the shogun
Tokugawa Ieyasu appointed the
Satake clan as the first lords of
Akita. The Satake later moved to
Kakunodate, and until the fall of
the shogunate in 1867, rule of the
province was shared by families collectively constituting the Akita clan.

The city of **Akita** is pleasant
and equipped with hotels to provide a comfortable stopover or a
base for visiting the region. In itself,
the city has few sights to attract
visitors. Except for the ruins of the
foundations and a recent reconstruction of a lookout tower—
both in **Senshu-koen Park—**
nothing remains of Satake-jo Castle
or the old town. But in August the
city comes into its own with the
colorful **Kanto festival** (August
4–7), when crowds arrive for the
spectacle. The parade features some
200 men using their foreheads,
hips, shoulders, and palms to
balance clusters of lighted paper
lanterns atop tall, thick bamboo
poles. The poles, each bearing 20
lanterns, weigh about 110 pounds
(50 kg) a piece.

At 1,394 feet (425 m), **Lake
Tazawa-ko** is the deepest lake in
Japan. It is renowned for the views
of the surrounding peaks, notably
Mount Komaga-take, and their
reflections in the intense blue of its
crystal-clear water. The Tazawa-ko
area has several nearby ski resorts
but lures visitors year-round. A
favorite with Japanese vacationers,
the lake can be chockablock with
swimmers, rented rowboats, and
pleasure boats in high summer;
choose off-peak periods to make
the most of its great scenery. You
can tour its 12-mile (20 km) circumference by bus, but the most
pleasant way is to rent a bicycle
from one of the outlets on either
side of the Tazawa-kohan bus
terminal. The area has plenty of

accommodations in all categories,
including campgrounds.

If you like walking, buses
from Tazawa-kohan take 50 minutes to reach Komagatake-
Hachigome. From there it is just
over an hour's walk to the summit
of **Mount Komaga-take** (5,369
feet/1637 m), the starting point for
several hiking trails through fine
alpine scenery. If you have the sta-
mina, one option is to make a day's
trek north over Mount Eboshi-dake
and then down to the group of
remote spas at Nyuto Onsen.

Reachable by bus from Tazawa-
kohan, **Nyuto Onsen** comprises
six spa resort hotels (all Japanese-
style *ryokan*) in a beautiful mountain setting crisscrossed with
hiking trails. Several of the baths,
if not all the ryokan owning them,
have reputations going back to the
Edo period (1603–1868). Featuring
both indoor baths and *rotenburo*
(rustic baths in the open air),
they could be the perfect place for
an onsen experience. Even in the
snow you will not feel the cold;
there is nothing like contemplating
the scenery as you luxuriate in
hot water. Nyuto's remoteness has
boosted its fame, so be sure to make
your accommodation reservations
in advance.

Around 15 minutes west of
Tazawa-ko is **Kakunodate,** the
prefecture's most famous town.
Between late April and early May,
thousands go there to see the fantastic tunnels of blossoming cherry
trees planted along a 1-mile (1.5
km) stretch of the **Hinokinai-
gawa River.** But the trees, planted
as recently as 1934, are a recent
complement to some substantial
historical attractions. Founded as
a castle town in 1620 by Akita clan
lord Yoshikatsu Ashina,
Kakunodate succumbed to fires
over the years. However, it was
flooding that determined its

Aoyagi-ke

26 Higashi-
Katsuraku-cho
☎ 0187/54-3257
$ $$

**Denshokan
Museum**

10-1 Omotemachi-
shita, Kakunodate-
machi
☎ 0187/54-1700
$ $

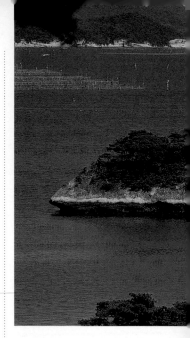

relocation farther south along the river. All that remains of the castle is the hill upon which it stood; the original town center, which lay to the north of it, has vanished. The new town, still divided into a northern samurai quarter and a southern quarter for merchants, contains a substantial number of old wooden houses. The most impressive are concentrated in **Buke-yashiki,** the unmissable old samurai quarter.

The houses stand behind wooden walls and stately gateways on a long avenue flanked by weeping cherries, many of them planted 300 years ago. Although most of the houses are privately owned, six of them—Kawarada, Aoyagi, Odano, Iwahashi, Ishiguro, and Matsumoto—are open to the public. The houses date from the twilight of the samurai from early to mid-19th century. Mainly modest rather than grand and featuring charming gardens, some display collections of heirlooms and memorabilia ranging from samurai relics to Western appliances.

The **Kawarada** house, for instance, has a tiny museum of swords and armor. The houses and their contents wistfully reflect a period midway between feudal power and rural middle-class gentility. **Aoyagi-ke** is the favorite with the public. Its compound, more opulent than the others', embraces several houses, five of which are museums. One is devoted to swords and armor, another to painting and calligraphy, and the rest present a fascinating miscellany of crafts, ceramics, household appliances, implements, and possessions. Concentrating on technical appliances from the 1870s through the 1920s, the collection in the **Haikara-kan** building includes clocks, phonographs, cameras, and even a 1917 American

"Indian" motorbike. *Haikara* means "high collar," the term used for Western shirts; it is now virtually synonymous with Meiji Japan.

With cherry blossom viewing a prime attraction, it is perhaps not surprising that the wood and bark of the cherry are the materials of choice for Kakunodate's attractive local handicrafts. The place to see the historical development and finest examples of *kabazaiku* (cherry bark craft) is **Denshokan Museum.** Working in one of the museum rooms, an in-house artisan is always happy to demonstrate his craft.

The museum is otherwise devoted to antiques, including armor, clothing, laquerware, and old and new examples of Kakunodate's recently revived Shiraiwa pottery. This is distinguished by its earthen hues, with subtle, semitransparent overglazes in lighter colors. There is a sales area offering quality local crafts at prices comparing favorably with the specialty stores around the town. ∎

Sendai & Matsushima

Pine-clad islets dot the calm waters of Matsushima-wan, revered for centuries as one of the most beautiful sights in Japan.

TOHOKU'S LARGEST CITY, SENDAI, IS THE CAPITAL OF Miyagi-ken. An important business center, it has a good number of hotels, making it a convenient base for exploring the region. Most of all, visitors use Sendai as a base for visiting nearby Matsushima-wan—which, along with Miyajima (see pp. 288–90) and Amanohashidate (Kyoto-ken), is one of the Three Great Sights of Japan.

The warlord Date Masumune built **Aoba-jo Castle** in 1602. The castle was ruined long ago, but its foundations still lie in the city park. Other vestiges of the Date legacy were obliterated with most of Sendai during the air raids of World War II. Unlike most resurrected Japanese cities, Sendai breaks the monotony of concrete by lining its boulevards with trees. Along with the usual covered shopping arcades and an exuberant street market, Sendai is home to Kokubuncho, Tohoku's largest amusement district.

The Date family mausoleum, the 16th-century **Memorial Hall (Zuihoden),** was recently reconstructed, and ornate **Osaki Hachiman-jinja Shrine,** built in 1607, miraculously survived the war. Otherwise, despite having a few attractive temples and gardens, Sendai is not known for historical sights. The surrounding hills boast hiking trails and hot springs, as well as beautiful scenery in the gorges of Futakuchi and Raira-kyo and especially near the town of **Naruko,** renowned for the curative properties of its spas. Near Sendai too is the 180-foot (55 m) **Akiu Otaki Waterfall,** among the country's most spectacular cascades.

"Matsushima, ah, matsushima, matsushima, matsushima!" This was not one of Basho's best haiku; the view over **Matsushima-wan** obviously left the 17th-century poet at a loss for words.

Sendai
🅰 153 B3
Visitor information
✉ Sendai Station
✉ 022/222-4069
🚉 Train: JR Tohoku
Shinkansen from
Tokyo (2 hrs.)

Aoba-jo Castle
🚌 Bus from Sendai
Station (20 mins.)
💲 Museum: $$$

Osaki Hachiman-jinju Shrine
🚌 Bus from Sendai
Station (20 mins.)

The curiously shaped Godai-do temple (right of center) has stood on the same spot for a thousand years.

Matsushima

⚏ 153 B3

Visitor information

✉ Outside Matsushima-Kaigan Station

☎ 022/354-2263

Kanran-tei

✉ 56 Aza-machi

☎ 022/353-3355

$ $

Zuigan-ji Temple

✉ 91 Aza-chonai (7 mins. walk from Matsushima-Kaigan Station

☎ 022/354-2023

$ $$

The panorama inspired the very place-name: *matsushima* means "pine island." With some 200 pine-covered islets sprinkled about a sweeping bay, the view is lovely. But what would Basho say today? Much blighted by cheap souvenir outlets, Matsushima sees hordes disgorged from a seemingly endless succession of tour buses. The bay is plied by vessels ranging from hired rowboats to luridly colored sightseeing junks with ornate sculpted dragons at the prow—ugly but fun; you can dine aboard while cruising the bay. The larger islands are connected by low red bridges, notably one 270 yards long (250 m) to **Fukuura-jima,** which has a botanical garden and pleasant paths to stroll.

By late afternoon, except during the peak season, the armies of day-trippers vanish and the promenade on the seafront becomes all the more pleasant for strolling. So does Matsushima itself, a relaxing little coastal town where kitsch emulations of the Japanese castle replace the usual monster concrete resort hotels.

Standing on an islet connected to the promenade by a short bridge is the **Godai-do.** This small, curiously shaped temple was erected in the ninth century and rebuilt in 1600 by Date Masamune. The interior is opened only three times a century, but you can look at the fine carvings of zodiac animals at the top of the pillars. Flanked by pines, the Godai-do charmingly complements the view over the sea.

As you leave the Godai-do, some 270 yards (250 m) to your left is the **Kanran-tei,** the "water-viewing" pavilion. Once a teahouse in Fushimi, a castle near Kyoto built by 16th-century warlord Toyotomi Hideyoshi, it was presented to Date Masamune and moved here, to a clifftop site overlooking the sea, in the late 16th century. Used as a moon-viewing pavilion by generations of Date lords, it contains a small museum exhibiting Date memorabilia.

The beauty of **Zuigan-ji Temple,** one of the great Zen temples of Japan, is a fitting human counterpart to the panorama on

Main Hall (Hon-do) feature doors lavishly carved in the Chinese style. The sliding screen doors in the chambers inside, completed in 1622, were covered in gold leaf and decorated with exquisite paintings. The current ones are copies. Beautifully restored between 1985 and 1995, the originals are now displayed in the adjacent **Seiryuden Treasure Museum,** along with fine Buddhist relics and paintings and statues of the Date family and the erstwhile temple abbots.

To the right of the temple approach, rows of **hermitages** have been carved into a solid wall of rock. Many contain images of the Buddha, hewn from the stone within. It is said that acolytes had to carve their way in and spend time meditating inside —the path to enlightenment seems arduous indeed!

The temple precinct of **Entsu-in** (also called Rose Temple), just next door to Zuigan-ji, contains the mausoleum of Date Masumune's grandson Mitsumune, set in a quiet glade of cedars. It is also notable for a lovely garden. Much of it is devoted to flowers not usually found in Japanese gardens—roses. ■

Entsuin

✉ 67 Aza-chonai
☎ 022/354-3205
💲 $

the bay, from which it lies back, approached along an avenue of cedars. Founded in 828 by the Tendai sect, Zuigan-ji became a Zen temple during the 13th century. It declined during the long era of civil wars (15th–16th centuries) and was in a sorry state of disrepair by 1604, when Date Masamune began rebuilding it.

Surrounded by split-level corridors, three sides of the imposing

---

Matsuo Basho (1644–1694)

Japanese poetry packs rich imagery and emotional power into few words. As the Zen influence gained ground from the 14th century on, the concept of "less is more" pervaded the cultural spectrum. Epitomizing it is haiku—a profoundly evocative, often elegiac verse form in which the 31 syllables of classical *tanka* poetry (the main poetic form from the 9th to 13th centuries) were slashed to 17. Of all haiku exponents, none is so revered as Basho.

Born a samurai, Basho studied at a Zen monastery before distinguishing himself as a poet. He habitually roamed the country for months on end, interspersing his travel diaries with haiku masterpieces. *The Narrow Road to the Far North,* recording a journey through Tohoku in 1689, is considered his greatest work. Frail and prematurely aged, Basho died on the road, succumbing to food poisoning at an inn on his way to Kyushu. ■

Iwate-ken

LONG KNOWN AS THE "DEEP EAST" FOR ITS REMOTENESS,
Iwate is the largest prefecture outside Hokkaido—and the least
populated. Its main historic claim to fame is the old town of
Hiraizumi, where the hero Minamoto Yoshitsune met his death.
Today Hiraizumi is just a small town, but some of the relics from its
glorious past are among the most impressive in Japan.

Morioka

🗾 153 B4

Visitor information

✉ Morioka Station

☎ 0196/25-2090

🚉 Train: JR Tohoku
Shinkansen from
Tokyo (2 hrs. 20
mins.–3 hrs. 20
mins.). For
Hachimantai take
bus from station

Morioka, Iwate's prefectural capital, is publicized as a "castle town"
(the castle was destroyed during the
1870s) and even as "little Kyoto."
But short of a pleasant river bank,
green spaces, and the occasional
district with a few mid-19th- to
early 20th-century vestiges, there is
nothing much to see. It is a congenial place nevertheless, and as the
terminal of the Tohoku Shinkansen

from Tokyo it makes a handy
stopover for visiting the prefecture.
Taking in all the sights would
require an overnight stay, but visiting Chuson-ji and Motsu-ji
Temples takes about four hours.

Iwate-ken has a lot of unspoiled
space with plenty of fine scenery,
especially in the national parks.
There is **Rikuchu Kaigan
National Park** to the east, with

its stark seascapes of rocky coves and 650-foot (200 m) cliffs, and **Towada Hachimantai National Park** *(Train: JR Tohoku Shinkansen from Ueno, Tokyo to Morioka)* to the west, in the volcanic mountain region shared with Akita-ken (see pp. 157–60) and Aomori-ken (see pp. 154–56). In addition to being another nucleus of *onsen* spas, Hachimantai is renowned for its scenery, as well as for the option of skiing until June, notably cross-country through forests. To the south is **Kurikoma Quasi-National Park,** where the alpine scenery is spectacular when aflame with colors in the fall. Kurikoma lies near Ichinoseki, the transfer point for the town of Hiraizumi.

The main avenues of modern **Hiraizumi,** unusually broad for a small rural town, faintly echo the layout of an ancient Sino-Japanese city. Hiraizumi has a strangely melancholy atmosphere; you become eerily aware of a lost city beneath your feet—underlined by such discoveries as the foundations of a 12th-century settlement when a private house was redeveloped in 1998.

Once consisting of no more than a remote garrison and two temples, Hiraizumi grew into a city of 100,000 people—the jewel of the northeast—when Fujiwara Kiyohira turned it into a regional capital in the early 12th century. Mining its own gold, producing silk, and breeding horses, Hiraizumi rivaled even Kyoto in opulence for over a century. The northeastern Fujiwara dynasty held onto Hiraizumi until, greedy for gold and horses, Minamoto Yoritomo's troops invaded the city in 1189.

It was here that Yoritomo's half-brother Yoshitsune, the great military hero whom he detested, was cornered and forced to commit suicide (see below). Hiraizumi declined rapidly and suffered a number of fires over the centuries, becoming nothing more than a backwater with an illustrious past—perhaps saved from oblivion only by the continued veneration of Chuson-ji Temple.

A bicycle is perfect for exploration, though not much use for scaling the steep hill to Chuson-ji. As in many tourist towns in Japan, you can rent bikes from an outlet next to the station.

Hiraizumi

 153 B4

Visitor information

✉ Outside Hiraizumi Station

☎ 0191/46-2110

🚃 Train: JR Tohoku Shinkansen from Tokyo. Change at Ichinoseki for JR Tohoku Honsen line to Hiraizumi (2 hrs. 45 mins.)

Yoshitsune's demise

The Fujiwara clan's last power base was Hiraizumi, which they still held when their Minamoto allies ousted the Taira at the culmination of the Heike War in 1185. Minamoto Yoritomo was the leader, but the victorious star was Yoshitsune, his younger half-brother and Japan's most revered pre-medieval hero.

Yoritomo hated his half-brother enough to conspire to murder him, whereupon Yoshitsune fled to Hiraizumi. But Yoritomo intended to turn against the Fujiwara and invade the city anyway. Faced with Yoritomo's troops, legend has it that Yoshisune committed suicide as his formidable steward, the warrior monk Benkei, died standing up in a hail of arrows.

Whatever the true circumstances, Yoshitsune died here; the Takadachi Gikeido Hall on the east side of Hiraizumi marks the spot. When the wandering poet Basho saw it in 1689, it inspired one of his most famous haiku: "The summer grass—all that remains of ancient warriors' dreams." ■

The Golden Hall (Konjiki-do) at Chuson-ji houses a tiny hall that is one of Japan's greatest National Treasures.

Chuson-ji Temple

✉ 202 Koromoseki, Hiraizumi-cho

☎ 0191/46-2211

💲 $$$$ (includes Konjiki-do, Kyozo, & Sankozo)

Motsu-ji Temple

✉ 58 Osawa, Hiraizumi-cho (7-min. walk from Hiraizumi Station)

☎ 0191/46-2331

💲 $$

Hiraizumi's finest attraction is the splendid hilltop precinct of **Chuson-ji Temple.** Founded in 850, Chuson-ji was greatly enlarged by Fujiwara Kiyohira, who built 40 halls during the 1120s. Including monks' quarters, the precinct counted 300 structures, but nearly all were destroyed during a fire in 1337. Current buildings date mostly from the late Edo period, including a fine **Noh stage** built in 1853. All that remains of the original temple is the **Sutra Hall (Kyozo)** and the breathtaking **Golden Hall (Konjiki-do),** commissioned in 1124. Housed within a large protective concrete building, this tiny hall is one of the greatest National Treasures. Intricately carved, inlaid with mother-of-pearl, lacquered, and gilded, it enshrines altars graced with outstanding golden Buddhist carvings. Beneath them lie the mummified bodies of Fujiwara Kiyohira and three of his descendants. Painted in gold on indigo paper, some of the 5,300 illustrated sutras formerly in the Kyozo are now in the nearby **Treasure Hall**

(Sankozo). Also containing several sculptures designated National Treasures, the Sankozo holds such a wealth of temple relics and Heian-period artifacts that a new annex was built to accommodate them in 1999.

Chuson-ji precinct stands atop a hill with splendid views over the surrounding plain. The approach is through a magnificent grove of tall cedars, but the slope is pretty steep. You can stop at the tiny Edo-period shrine dedicated to Yoshitsune on the way up and refresh yourself in an old thatched farmhouse charmingly converted into a café.

Motsu-ji Temple, founded in the mid-ninth century, was the largest temple in northern Japan during the 12th century. Declining along with the rest of Hiraizumi, its several pagodas, 40 halls, and 500 monastic dwellings all burned down in several fires. Built in 1989, the present **main hall** is an uninspiring emulation of the Heian-period style; the precinct's only really old building is the 17th- century **Jogyo-do** hall. Archaeologists uncovered the foundation stones of several original buildings in the late 1960s, and later excavation revealed the rocks constituting the artificial watercourses and pond of a lost **garden.** Now beautifully restored, it is the only complete extant example of a Heian-period Jodo (Pure Land) garden, landscaped on a grand scale in emulation of Buddhist paradise.

The precinct also includes an iris garden containing 300 varieties; visitors come from all over Japan to admire the flowers between mid-June and mid-July. On the fourth Sunday in May the **Gokusui-no-en** (Floating Poetry Festival) finds contestants in Heian-period garb floating cups of sake down the garden's stream. The objective is to compose a poem before your cup reaches the end—very much a garden-party game enjoyed 900 years ago.

Lush and green in spring and summer, the surrounding countryside presents fine rural scenery, as well as one or two sights: the gorges of **Geibikei** (to the east) and **Genbikei** (to the west) and, en route to Genbikei gorge, **Takkoku-no-Iwaya,** a curious rock temple with a Buddhist effigy carved in the cliff face. ■

Memorial plaques such as these are a familiar sight in Japan.

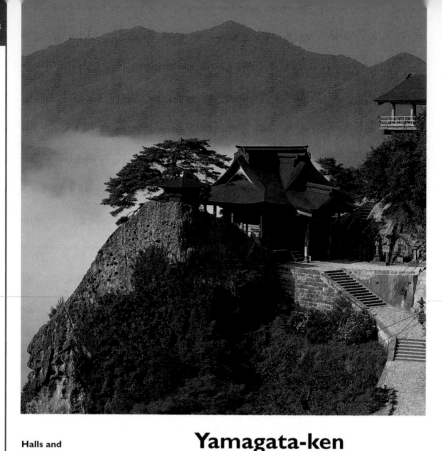

Yamagata-ken

YAMAGATA-KEN EMBRACES THE SOUTHWESTERN BOUN-dary of Tohoku. It is a prime agricultural region—in the 30 percent of it that is not mountain and forest (Yamagata means "mountain shape"). Yamagata's climate varies as much as its topography; ski resorts remain open on Gas-san in high summer, when temperatures on the plain can reach the highest recorded in Japan. Out of the four million annual tourists here, most come to ski resorts, leaving much of the prefecture refreshingly unspoiled.

Yamagata city

🏔 153 B3

Visitor information

✉ JR Yamagata Station

☎ 023/631-7865

🚉 Train: JR Yamagata Shinkansen From Tokyo to Yamagate Station (2 hrs. 30 mins.)

A boon for both farming and tourism, the Mogami-gawa River and its tributaries flow from the southwest to the northwest. Near the town of Sakata (see opposite), tour boats ply the spectacular **Mogami Gorge**—the appeal lying as much in the folk-singing skills of the boatmen as in the scenic beauty of the steep cliffs flanking the river. Yamagata thrives in winter with winter sports facilities in nearly all its mountains and at least one *onsen* (hot spring) in every village. Well known for both, **Mount Zao-san** in the southeast also attracts walkers and nature lovers year-round with its fine alpine scenery. Undamaged in World War II, Yamagata's towns suffered from Japan's ubiquitous postwar architectural brutalism; though convenient as bases for regional exploration, they retain precious few sights.

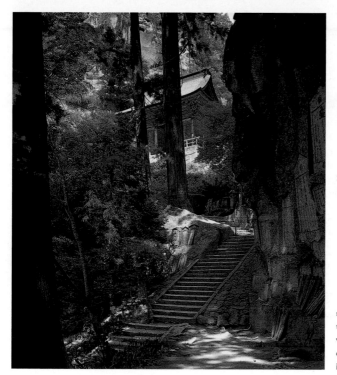

Yama-dera Temple

💲 $

🚆 Train: Senzan line
from Yamagata
Station to Yamadera

Dewa Sanzan

🅰 153 A3

🚌 Bus: Tusruoka
Station to Haguro
(35 mins.)

Sakata

🅰 153 A3

**1,100 stone
steps lead up
through the
woods to Yama-
dera Temple's
inner sanctum.**

The prefectural capital city, **Yamagata,** is a convenient base, especially for winter sports on Zao-san and for visiting **Yama-dera Temple** (also called Risshaku-ji), the Mountain Temple, one of Tohoku's most celebrated historical and religious sites. Yama-dera dates from 860, when Ennin, its founding priest, is said to have chipped away at the rocks to build the **Main Hall (Konponchu-do).** Although the structure was rebuilt in 1356, the Buddhist figure enshrined here dates to the ninth century; the flame before it has burned for over a thousand years. The temple comprises some 40 buildings perched on peaks and cliffsides; a trek for the hardy, the route from the bottom of the path to the temple winds up 1,100 stone steps through the woods, past spectacular views of the valley below, to the uppermost **Inner Sanctum (Oku-no-in).** The poet Basho wrote a haiku about Yama-dera during his Tohoku journey of 1689:

The quiet—
shrilling into the rocks
the cicada's cry.

The northwestern town of **Sakata,** on the Mogami-gawa estuary, was the main trade link with Kyoto in feudal times; sadly, it lost many historical buildings in a 1976 fire. It still has one old samurai residence, Honma-ke Kyu-hontei (Former Honma Family Residence), which harks back to the ruling Honma clan, and Sankyo Soko, a district preserving 12 warehouses built in 1893. Sakata is the ferry port for **Tobi-shima,** a tiny island off the west coast popular both as a bird sanctuary and as a resort for fishing and diving.

Tsuruoka
153 A3

Chido Museum
10-18 Kachushin-machi, Tsuruoka-shi
0235/22-1199
$$

Just south of Sakata, the city of **Tsuruoka** was the feudal domain of the Sakai family, but the only reminders today are the castle moats and the interesting open-air **Chido Museum (Chido Hakubutsukan).** Several buildings of the Sakai family in the vicinity were taken down and reerected here in a park.

Tsuruoka is convenient as a gateway to the **Three Dewa Mountains (Dewa Sanzan),** a trio of peaks ranking among the most sacred in Japan. Along with Fuji-san and On-take in Nagano prefecture, the Dewa Sanzan are the holiest of all the objects of worship of Shinto mountain cults. Because the Dewa trio—Haguro-san (1,358 feet/414 m), Gas-san (6,494 feet/1,980 m), and Yudono-san (4,933 feet/1,504 m)—respectively symbolize birth, death, and rebirth, they are supposed to be visited in that order. Of the thousands going on Dewa pilgrimages, a few belong to the *yamabushi* sects (see below) that wandered and worshiped these mountains centuries ago. Although athletic sightseers claim otherwise, visiting all three requires an overnight stopover. There are several *shukubo* (shrine or temple lodgings, see p. 359) in the Toge district at the foot of Haguro-san.

Haguro-san—the lowest and easiest to climb—is the most visited of the holy trio. Dedicated to the three deities, the **Sanshin Gosaiden Shrine** stands at the summit, along with a museum of temple memorabilia. If you are unfit you should probably stay at the bottom, but the good news is that the way up includes a waterfall and a fine 14th-century pagoda; the bad news is that from the latter there are still 2,446 stone steps to climb to the summit! You can also take a bus to the top and walk down.

Gas-san has a shrine at the top, but getting there can be quite a trial except in late summer. The mountain is best known for skiing. Snowfalls of up to 26 feet (8 m) close even the ski slopes until mid-April, which remain open until the end of July. Ideal for hiking in late summer, Gas-san is justifiably famous for its spectacular scenery.

The last of the trio, **Yudono-san** is also the holiest. The walk from the road to the shrine at the top takes only about 15 minutes. The object of worship is a rock stained bright brickred by the iron in the spring welling up around it. So sacred is it that visitors are asked to remove footwear and refrain from taking photographs. ■

Yamabushi—monks of the mountains

Kaiko-ji Temple in Sakata is famous for the remains of two monks said to have attained Buddhahood through meditating and fasting until they succumbed to deliberate self-mummification. This example is much admired by the *yamabushi*—the "monks who lie in the mountains" and follow of Shugendo, a religion embracing both Shinto and Buddhism. Believers practice austerities such as immersion in ice-cold water in midwinter or being suspended by the heels over cliff edges with a drop of hundreds of feet. Yamabushi still exist, though they practice only on an occasional basis. These days the Ideha Cultural Museum *(Toge, Haguro, tel 0235/62-4727)* runs three-day Yamabushi courses, complete with a generous ration of dire hardships. For details contact the museum. ■

The regional capital of Nagoya is Japan's third city; the beaches often vie for space with heavy industry on the coast, but with densely forested mountains and historic old towns, Chubu is the ultimate Japan sampler.

Central Honshu (Chubu)

Gardeners tend Kanazawa's Kenroku-en landscape garden.

Central Honshu (Chubu)

CHUBU, WHICH MEANS "CENTRAL SECTION," IS THE MIDDLE PART OF THE island of Honshu—the very center of Japan. Its nine prefectures have a wealth of different topographical, climatic, and cultural features. Chubu is divided into two main regions: Tokai on the Pacific side and Hokuriku on the Japan Sea.

The Onbashira-sai log-pulling festival in Nagano-ken occurs once every seven years.

Having given its name to the great Eastern Sea Road (Tokaido) route between Edo and Kyoto in feudal times, the Tokai district is still crossed by the main transportation arteries between Tokyo and the southwest of Japan. Heavily industrialized and densely populated along the coast, the area has few major tourist sites; consequently foreign travelers stopping here en route to the district of Kansai (see pp. 197–260) are comparatively few. For those on their way to Hokuriku and the Japan Alps, the Nagoya region is a convenient gateway. Although it is one of the most industrialized areas of all, it still has some see-worthy scenic and historical sights.

Hokuriku has a great deal to recommend it. From Nagoya you can move up toward Nagano via the delightful Kiso Valley, or through Gifu to Kanazawa in the west, or north to Takayama. Historical and cultural destinations of major importance, Kanazawa and Takayama also have the advantage of being less touristic than towns in Kansai. Off the coast of Niigata-ken is lovely Sado-ga-shima; once reserved for political exiles, it is now a peaceful, scenic vacationland for those fleeing the crowds and pressure of urban Japan. ∎

0   100 kilometers
0   50 miles

Area of map detail

Tokyo

6

Sado-gashima
Donden-yama ▲
Ryotsu
Aikawa
Sawata
Mano
Ogi

Murakami
Shibata
Niigata
Niitsu
Shirone
NIIGATA-KEN
Sanjo
Tochio
Nagaoka
Kashiwazaki
Ojiya

BANDAI-ASAHI NATIONAL PARK

5

NORTHERN HONSHU (TOHOKU)
p. 151

Joetsu
Itoigawa
Arai
2446m
Myoko-san ▲
Iiyama
JO-SHIN-ETSU KOGEN NATIONAL PARK
Jozu
Nakano
Tokamachi
Nagano
Suzaka
Omachi
Ueda
Matsumoto
Saku
Kamikochi
Shiojiri
NAGANO-KEN
Okaya
Suwa
Kisoji
Chino
3063m
ntake-san ▲
Fukushima
Agematsu
Nirasaki
Tsumago
3192m
Iida
MINAMI-ALPS NAT. PARK
3120m
Ena
awa
Fujinomiya
SHIZUOKA-KEN
ICHI-KEN
Shibara
Fuji
Shimizu
Shizuoka
Kakegawa
Fujieda
Yaizu
Toyohashi
Kosai
Hamamatsu

HUBU SANGAKU NATIONAL PARK
3190m
Hotaka-dake ▲

Nasu-dake 1917m
NIKKO NATIONAL PARK
Imaichi
Otawara
Kitaibaraki
TOCHIGI-KEN
Hitachi
Numata
Shibukawa
GUMMA-KEN
Utsunomiya
Katsuta
Kiryu
Oyama
Mito
Nakaminato
Shimodate
Maebashi
IBARAKI-KEN
Takasaki
Koga
Tsuchiura
Kumagaya
Kasukabe
SAITAMA-KEN
Kawagoe
Toride
Urawa
Narita
CHICHIBU-TAMA NATIONAL PARK
Kawaguchi
Ichikawa
Choshi
Kofu
TOKYO-KEN
Hachioji
TOKYO
Funabashi
Kawasaki
Chiba
YAMANASHI-KEN
Fujiyoshida
Tokyo-wan
Mobara
KANAGAWA-KEN
Gotemba
YOKOHAMA
CHIBA-KEN
FUJI-HAKONE-IZU NAT. PARK
3776m
Fuji-san ▲
Kamakura
Futtsu
Odawara
Yokosuka
Boso-hanto
Katsuura
Mishima
Miura
Kamogawa
Atami
Sagami-nada
Numazu
Tateyama
Ito
Izu-hanto
O-shima
Shimoda
Suruga-wan

4

3

2

IZU SHICHITO

Nii-shima

Kozu-shima

Miyake-jima

Mikura-jima

1

△ C
△ D
△ E

Nagoya-jo Castle,
destroyed in
World War II, was
impressively
replicated in
concrete in 1959.

Aichi-ken

ALTHOUGH IMPORTANT AGRICULTURALLY, AICHI-KEN IS better known for its industrial output: electronics, chemicals, food products, ceramics, textiles, and 40 percent of the nation's cars. Because of this and the drab highway scenery on the flatlands, most travelers to Japan give Aichi a miss. For those with time to spare, however, it has its rewards. The regional capital, Nagoya, may have few sights to recommend it, but as a major transport hub with an abundance of good hotels it makes a convenient base for exploring the Tokai region and the southern Japan Alps.

Nagoya
🅼 172 B2
Visitor information
✉ Nagoya Station
✉ 052/541-4301
🚄 2 hrs. from Tokyo,
   1 hr. from Osaka
   (Shin Osaka Station)
   on the JR Tokai
   Shinkansen line

Nagoya-jo Castle
✉ 1, 1 Honmaru,
   Naka-ku
☎ 052/231-1700
💲 $$
🚇 Shiyakusho subway
   station on the Meijô
   line, then 5 min.
   walk north

Coastal Aichi-ken is dotted with beach resorts and *onsen* spas, but there is little of cultural or historical interest. Also, the resorts and spas are scattered; to make the most of them, you will need plenty of time or a car. North of the coast, Aichi-ken shares mountains with Nagano-ken and Gifu-ken; if you have your own transportation, you can cover miles of idyllic sylvan scenery crossed by torrents and rivers, many offering fishing and swimming. The jewel in Aichi's crown is the delightful historic hill town of Inuyama (see p. 176), with the oldest original castle in Japan.

Nagoya is Japan's fourth largest city and has an airport served by both domestic and international flights. The city has an efficient subway network (English-language maps are available at subway stations and the visitor information center) and is easy to get around.

Inhabited since prehistoric times, Nagoya rose to prominence in the 16th century as Japan's three greatest shoguns completed the process of unifying the country (see p. 33). While Oda Nobunaga and Toyotomi Hideyoshi were from Nagoya, Tokugawa Ieyasu, founder of the military dynasty that ruled Japan until 1867, was born in Okazaki, 38 miles (60 km) southeast. (Retaining several old temples connected with Ieyasu, Okazaki may interest Ieyasu enthusiasts, but its castle was destroyed a century ago, and what you see today is a concrete reproduction.) Nagoya was virtually obliterated by World War II air raids, and the vestiges associated with its great warrior sons went with it.

Nagoya-jo Castle was built by Tokugawa Ieyasu for his son Yoshinao in 1612. The pride of the city, it was famous for the *shachihoko*—the golden dolphins topping the gables on the roof of the keep. Destroyed in 1945, it was rebuilt in 1959. Complete with new dolphins, the reinforced concrete copy still conveys the outward splendor of the original. An elevator takes you to the viewing platform at the top, where there is a fine panorama over the city and surrounding plain. A **museum** on the lower floors displays Tokugawa treasures and artifacts. The castle is set in elegant **Ninomaru-teien Garden,** which has an attractive teahouse.

Established in the third century, **Atsuta-jingu Shrine** houses the ancient Kusanagi Sword—one of the three treasures used in the imperial enthronement ceremony (the others are the Mirror at Ise Grand Shrine and the Jewel at the Imperial Palace in Tokyo). Atsuta is of similar vintage to Ise (see p. 259) and is likewise built of unadorned cedarwood. Set in a grove of camphor trees, the precinct includes a Noh stage hosting occasional performances and a **treasure hall** displaying Shinto relics, including swords and bronze mirrors. The Kusanagi Sword is not on display; no one except high priests and emperors have ever seen it. As one of Japan's most sacred shrines, Atsuta receives millions of devotees, especially during the New Year.

From Nagoya Station take the subway to Ozone, where a short walk south leads to the **Tokugawa Museum of Art (Tokugawa Bijutsukan).** The 10,000 items that make up the Tokugawa family treasures include ceramics, paintings, calligraphy, armor, and swords. The star attraction is the celebrated 12th-century *Genji Scroll*, the oldest surviving set of text and illustrations of Lady Murasaki's great 10th-century novel, *The Tale of Genji* (see p. 45). Because of its extreme fragility, the original is exhibited only once a year; what you normally see is a reproduction.

Atsuta-jingu Shrine
- ✉ 1-1-1 Jinju, Atsuta-ku
- ☎ 052/671-4151
- 🕐 Treasure hall closed last Wed. and Thur. each month
- 💲 Treasure Hall $
- 🚉 Train: Jingu-mae on the Meitetsu line

The Tokugawa Museum of Art
- ✉ 1017 Tokugawa-cho, Higashi-ku
- ☎ 052/935-6262
- 🕐 Closed Mon. and mid-Dec. through the New Year period
- 💲 $$$
- 🚉 Subway: Ozone on the Meijo line

Hand-enameling at Noritake china works in Aichi-ken, where traditional craftsmanship and heavy industry coexist

Osu Kannon Temple is the focus of Nagoya's most colorful neighborhood.

Inuyama

M 172 B3

Visitor information

Inuyama Station

0568/61-6000

Train: Inuyama is 30 mins. from Shin-Nagoya Station (near the JR Nagoya Station) via the Meitetsu-Inuyama line express (or 45 mins. by ordinary train). Note that the stop for the area's sights is not Inuyama, but Inuyama-Yuen

About one mile (1.5 km) east of the station, the focal **Sakae** district comprises restaurants, bars, shopping centers, and a colossal underground mall. **Osu,** to the south, is a more animated downtown neighborhood with a colorful arcade leading to the popular **Osu Kannon Temple,** which holds a good flea market on weekends. Nagoya Port, on Ise-wan Bay, is the country's third largest port.

On the south bank of the Kiso-gawa River on the boundary between Aichi-ken and Gifu-ken, the pleasant town of **Inuyama** and its surroundings are a favorite Nagoyite weekend excursion. Along with fine scenery and a historic castle, it has some unusual sights, including the remarkable Meiji Village architectural museum and Japan Monkey Park, which may be of interest to children. If you don't like zoos, be aware that some of the primates are confined to cages.

The small four-story **Inuyama-jo Castle,** set on a cliff overlooking Kiso-gawa, is one of Japan's finest castles. In fact, built in 1537, it is the oldest still in its original state. It is also the only one privately owned, having remained the property of the Naruse family since 1618.

The castle's survival is miraculous: When it was seized from its owners in 1871, the buildings surrounding the keep were destroyed. Damaged in an earthquake in 1891, the castle was returned to the Naruse family in 1895 on condition they restore it—and they did. The viewing platform on the top offers a wonderful panorama over the river and valley. A three-minute walk east of the castle, on the grounds of the Meitetsu Inuyama Hotel, is the **Uraku-en Garden.** In the garden is the **Jo-an,** a celebrated 17th-century teahouse (moved here from Kyoto) where visitors can drink green tea.

Inuyama-jo Castle
✉ 440 yards (400 m) SW of Inuyama-Yuen Station
💲 Castle $; Uraku-en $$$ (green tea in Jo-an teahouse $)

Tea utensils in a reconstructed interior at the Tokugawa Museum of Art

Tagata-jinja Shrine, a short distance south of Inuyama, opposite Tagata-jinja-mae Station, is one of Japan's 40 or so remaining phallic shrines. Tagata is renowned for its rousing Bumper Harvest Festival (Tagata Honen Sai, March 15). The English-language shrine leaflet tells us the purpose of the festival "is to offer the huge penis to the shrine, praying for world peace, the growth of all things and a pumper [sic] crop." The monster wooden phallus leading the parade is enshrined in the main hall, and many more are displayed in an array of improbable sizes in the adjacent building. Exhibiting rocks and stones suggesting male and female genitalia, parts of the precinct are also festooned with small *ema*—votive plaques left by those entreating the gods to find them partners or grant offspring. Stronger on content than form, the shrine buildings are disappointingly utilitarian.

Tagata's female counterpart is the more demure **Oagata-jinja Shrine.** Set in wooded hills and attractively constructed, it provides insights into feminine Shinto practices: Girls leave their dolls here to be burned as a kind of rite of passage to womanhood. A central feature is an open-sided pavilion with a miniature *torii* gateway; some women believe crawling through it will increase their fertility.

Inuyama's most curious attraction is **Meiji-mura Village** *(1, Uchiyama, Inuyama-shi, tel 0568/67-0314).* Set beside man-made Lake Iruka-ko in a park, 20 minutes by bus from Inuyama Station, this open-air museum, created in 1965, is where lucky buildings go when they die. More than 60 important early Western-style structures have been moved here from other locations in Japan and rebuilt. Highlights include the facade and lobby of Frank Lloyd Wright's Tokyo Imperial Hotel, Kyoto's St. John's Church, and the old Sapporo telephone exchange. You can ride around the village on antique streetcars and a steam railroad. Meiji-mura makes a perfect outing for children. Including shops and restaurants, it covers a substantial area, so set aside half a day for a visit. ■

Tagata-jinja Shrine
✉ 152 Tagata-cho, Komaki-shi
☎ 0568/76-2906
🚆 Train: Tagata Jinja-mae Station (10 mins. from Inuyama on the Komaki line)

Oagata-jinja Shrine
✉ 15 mins. walk east of Gakuden Station
🚆 Train: Gakuden Station (8 mins. from Inuyama on the Komaki line)

Kanazawa & beyond

CALLED HOKURIKU, THE NORTHERN REGION OF CHUBU encompasses four prefectures: Ishikawa-ken, northern Gifu-ken, Nagano-ken, and Niigata-ken. Mainly mountainous, the region offers aspects to please most travelers, but the old towns of Kanazawa (Ishikawa) and Takayama (Gifu) offer an array of additional historical and cultural assets to make them the firm favorites in the Hokuriku region.

Ishikawa-ken lies on the northwestern side of Honshu, extending north to the **Noto-hanto Peninsula** on the Sea of Japan. Tourism and resorts flourish on the east of the peninsula, but a beautiful coastline and peaceful fishing villages to the west demand exploration if you have time and—preferably—a car. In Ishikawa's southeast is the sacred mountain of Haku-san—revered for its spectacular alpine scenery, camping and hiking in summer, and *onsen* bathing and skiing in winter. The most famous destination is the prefectural capital of Kanazawa, a former castle town retaining many facets of its illustrious past as a center of culture and craft.

Gifu-ken includes the old province of Hida, of which the capital was **Takayama** on the western slopes of the Japan Alps. This delightful town is the region's main destination for visitors.

Lovers of mountain scenery should head for **Nagano-ken.** The capital city of Nagano in the north and Matsumoto in the center are the main bases for mountain activities. The **Kamikochi Valley,** west of Matsumoto, can claim to have the finest mountain scenery in all Japan, while the beautiful **Kiso Valley,** carved by Kiso-gawa

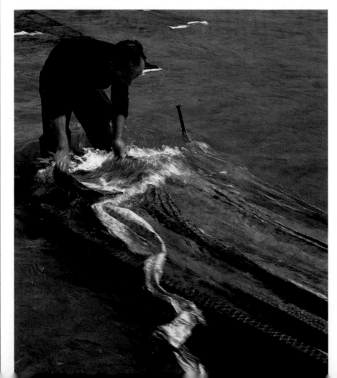

Kanazawa

🅐 172 B4
Visitor information
✉ Kanazawa Station
☎ 076/232-6200
🚆 Train: JR Joetsu Shinkansen from Tokyo to Nagaoka, change for limited express (4 hrs. 30 mins.–5 hrs.)

Washing silk kimono textiles in the river is part of the *yuzen* dyeing process for which Kanazawa is famous.

through the central range of the Japan Alps, is an area steeped in legend.

Niigata-ken's capital, **Niigata,** is the most important coastal city on the Sea of Japan. For most visitors, however, it serves only as the gateway to the prefecture's star attraction: Sado-ga-shima Island (see pp. 193–96).

Kanazawa was the capital of the old fiefdom of Kaga, which came to be governed by the Buddhist Jodo Shinshu sect as an autonomous republic from 1488. Conquered by shogun Oda Nobunaga in 1583, it thrived as a prominent center for arts and crafts, including ceramics, textiles, and paperware, as well as traditional *Kaga ryori* cuisine (see p. 370) and *wagashi* (Japanese confec-

tionery). These all still continue today. The Noh theater also flourished in Kanazawa, and the Ishikawa Prefectural Noh Theater (see p. 385) is now one of Japan's most important centers for Noh. The city sprawls and its sights are scattered, which can be frustrating if you have limited time. However, main bus lines run between the station and major sights. With fine food and many a good *ryokan,* a stopover in Kanazawa is always a good idea. Be sure to stop at the **visitor information center** when you arrive at Kanazawa station, to pick up the excellent illustrated pamphlet mapping the city and its bus routes in English.

Katamachi, the town center, is nondescript, with department stores and the usual amenities;

The Kenroku-en Garden, one of Japan's most famous, blazes with early summer azaleas.

Kenroku-en Garden

- ✉ 1 Kenroku-machi
- ☎ 076/221-5850
- 💲 $
- 🚌 Buses 11 and 12 run from Kanazawa Station to Kenrokuen-shita (or the Dewacho stop for Seisonkaku)

Graced with an elegant two-story tower, the Ishikawamon Gate is all that remains of Kanazawa-jo Castle.

Saihitsu-an

✉ 1-3-16 Naga-machi
☎ 076/264-2811
💲 $$

Kanazawa-shi Shinise Kinenkan

✉ 2-2-45 Naga-machi
☎ 076/220-2524

Nomura house

✉ 1-2-32 Naga-machi
☎ 076/221-3553
💲 $$$

north of the center is lively Yoko-Yasuecho shopping arcade, and just south of this is Omicho market, which sells produce for Kanazawa's fine cuisine and some of the best seafood in Japan.

Having survived World War II unscathed, Kanazawa abounds in historical sights. Several are in or near the **Kenroku-en Garden.** Designated one of the three great gardens of Japan, Kenroku-en is named after the *kenroku* (six combinations) considered ideal for gardens: spaciousness, serenity, venerability, scenic views, subtle design, and coolness provided by watercourses. Originally the stroll garden of Kanazawa-jo Castle, it was enlarged and completed in 1819 and opened to the public in 1871. There are 12,000 trees of 150 varieties in this masterpiece of landscaping, which includes artificial hills, ponds, and waterways flanked by irises in season. Kenroku-en's scale, impressive as it is, precludes the intimacy of a true garden—it is better described as a park. It can get very crowded between 11 a.m. and 3 p.m.

Just to the north outside Kenroku-en is the impressive **Ishikawamon Gate,** the last surviving structure of Kanazawa-jo, which burned down in 1881. At the southern end of the garden the refined **Seisonkaku Villa,** built in 1863, is noted for the delicacy of its interiors. The grounds include a teahouse and a garden with gnarled pines and streams meandering beneath the veranda.

About half a mile west of the villa, the old earthen walls flanking the lanes of the Nagamachi samurai quarter make the area picturesque, but most of the buildings are private—and few are original structures. In the 1910s the remains of **Nomura house (Nomura-ke)** were restored by a shipping magnate, who added part of a samurai house he owned in his hometown. Although not quite authentic, the building is highly evocative. Viewed from the veranda or from upstairs while sipping green tea, the exquisite little garden of rocks and watercourses is a masterpiece of miniature landscaping. Nearby stands the **Saihitsu-an,** an old teahouse that is now a silk dyeing house. Here you can watch *kaga yuzen* artisans intricately hand painting silk textiles (children are not admitted). The **Kanazawa Shinise Memorial Hall (Kanazawa-shi Shinise Kinekan),** once a wooden pharmacy in the center of town, has been dismantled and reerected here as a museum exhibiting local crafts and showing shop interiors of the late 1800s.

Three old geisha districts remain in Kanazawa. Kazue-machi along Asano-gawa River is picturesque, as is the Nishi-Chaya-gai quarter in the southwest. The finest is **Higashi-shaya-gai** to the northeast. The streetlights and buildings here remain unchanged since the 19th century, although the geisha who once frequented it are now reduced to a mere 20 or so. The 180-year-old **Kaikaro** is a teahouse, its decor an inspired blend of the traditional and the contemporary, featuring an inner garden of shards of glass. A few doors away is **Shima** *(1-13-21 Higashiyama, tel 076/252-5675),* a delightful old geisha house with original fixtures and furnishings, now a museum.

On the slopes of tranquil **Teramachi,** the temple district in the south of town, are some 70 temples and shrines. None is major

but several are interesting, among them Gannen-ji, visited by the 17th-century poet Basho, Akan-ji (also called Neko-dera—Cat Temple—a former feline cemetery), and Daien-ji Temple, which has a fine Zen garden. West of Teramachi is the famous **Myoryu-ji,** also known as Ninja-dera, the Ninja Temple. The first impression on entering is of nothing special, but appearances are deceptive—intentionally. Built in the 1640s, it presents an ingenious labyrinth of 21 secret chambers, hidden stairways, and trapdoors designed as escape routes, particularly for ninja— secret agents practicing the martial art of *ninjutsu* (the art of stealth). The effect is odd and unsettling. Conducted in Japanese, tours include demonstrations of trick devices and ninja techniques. ∎

The music behind these facades in the old Higashi geisha quarter fell silent long ago, but they retain their charm.

Myoryu-ji Temple
- ✉ 1-2-12 No-machi
- ☎ 076/241-2877
- 💲 $$$ (tours must be booked ahead through the visitor information center)

Kanazawa ceramics

A great center for ceramics since feudal times, Kanazawa is renowned both for Ohi and Kutani pottery. Craft shops selling ceramics dot the town, and the cream of antique ware is displayed in museums such as the **Ishikawa Prefectural Museum of Traditional Products and Crafts** and the **Ishikawa Prefectural Museum of Art,** both near the Kenroku-en Garden. In the southwest of town the **Kutani Pottery Kosen Kiln** welcomes visitors. You can arrange to visit workshops through the visitor information center. Just north of Kenrokuen gardens, the **Ishikawa Local Products Shop** features local art, crafts, and food; it also has a restaurant. ∎

Takayama

DELIGHTFUL TAKAYAMA, ON THE WESTERN SLOPES OF THE Japan Alps in Gifu-ken, was the capital of the old province of Hida. The very name Takayama, meaning "high mountain," conveys uncommon remoteness for what was once an important town. Its carpenters reputedly played a large part in the building of ancient Kyoto and Nara. As its reputation for woodcrafts spread around Japan, Takayama continued to prosper. It suffered a decline during the modern era, but its very remoteness has helped preserve it.

Above: Floats and crowds flow over the bridges during Takayama Festival. Right: Kusakabe-ke, an old merchant house, is now a museum.

Takayama
🅰 172 B3
Visitor information
✉ Outside station
☎ 0577/32-5328
🚆 Train: Express Hida from Kyoto (3 hrs. 40 mins.)
✈ Tokyo Haneda airport to Toyama (1 hr.)

Kusakabe Folk Museum
✉ 1-52 Ojin-machi
☎ 0577/32-0072
$ $$

Today the town retains sufficient historical sights to justify the hackneyed designation "Little Kyoto"—mainly for its Teramachi temple district. Yet Takayama is nothing like Kyoto; no realm of samurai, priests, and literati, it grew up as a town of farmers, artisans, and merchants. Its charm lies in the remarkably well-preserved streets of merchant houses and venerable sake breweries concentrated in the **Sanmachi Suji** district, which also contains shops, taverns, and inns of similar vintage. Takayama's role as the hub of a rich folk culture is evidenced in its museums.

Although Takayama is small, it takes a good day to do justice to the sights on the east side of the Miya-gawa River alone; a stopover is highly recommended. Friendly and laid-back, this is not a place to rush around. You might be tempted to sample the excellent local sake; Takayama has a reputation for the

quality and conviviality of its traditional inns. Expect *sansai* (mountain vegetables) with your meals, and in restaurants make a point of sampling Hida beef, which rivals that of Kobe for quality.

If you visit in spring or autumn, don't miss the **Takayama Festival** on April 14–15 and October 9–10. Famous throughout Japan, the procession features ornate floats (*yatai*) with antique *karakuri* automatons performing mechanical feats. If you cannot make the show, you can see the floats at the **Festival Floats Exhibition Hall (Takayama Yatai Kaikan,** *53-1 Sakuramachi, tel 0577/32-0881*) in Sakurayama Hachimangu shrine at the north end of town.

Hida Kokubun-ji Temple, northeast of the station on the west river bank, was founded by Nara's pious emperor Shomu in 746. It has been burned down and rebuilt

since, so all that remains of the
original is a ginkgo tree thought to
be 1,200 years old; next to it stands
a three-story **pagoda** from 1821.
The oldest current structure is the
16th-century **Main Hall.** Among
the temple's treasures are two fine
Buddhist statues carved in the
Heian period (794–1185) and a
12th-century sword thought to
have belonged to a warrior of the
Heike clan—the last rulers of Kyoto
during the Heian period.

**Kusakabe Folk Museum
(Kusakabe Mingeikan)** is located on the eastern bank of Miya-
gawa. The building, built in 1879 as
a merchant's home and warehouse,

is a fine example of Takayama carpentry. Now a museum, it displays
all the fixtures it contained when
open for business during the 19th
century. Next door, the interior of
Yoshijima-ke House *(1-51 Ojin-
machi, tel 0577/32-0038, closed Tues.
Dec.–Feb.)* is not to be missed. A
masterpiece of traditional Japanese
domestic architecture, its soaring
framework of huge crossbeams
and posts stretches high up under
the roof.

Also on the eastern side of town
is **Shiroyama-koen Park.** The
park is on the site of the feudal
castle built by the Kanamori lords
in 1590 and dismantled when the
Tokugawa shogunate took over in
the late 17th century; all that
remains are the walls and foundations. Shiroyama-koen is renowned
for its alpine views and display of
cherry blossoms in spring.

Shoren-ji Temple in the
northwestern part of the park originally stood in Shirakawago, some
20 miles (32 km) northwest of
Takayama. It was moved and
reassembled here in 1960, when the
lake formed by a new dam drowned

its site. The 1504 **Main Hall** is much admired as an example of Muromachi (1338–1573) temple architecture. There is a pleasant landscape garden adjacent.

If you follow the paths through Shiroyama-koen, you will come to **Teramachi,** the temple district. The Higashiyama Walking Route (2 miles/3.5 km) is well signposted in English throughout. If you have visited Shoren-ji, you can take the path due south, following the loop around **Dairyu-ji Temple** and then bearing right up to **Ena-jinja Shrine.** The path from here follows the Teramachi route, which runs straight along the northeastern side of town. Though not of major importance, the 13 temples and five shrines you pass along the way are highlights on an enchanting walk. The path winds west to Yasugawa-dori, the street crossing the rivers into the center of town. Alternatively, you can approach Teramachi by starting from Yasugawa-dori and following the path due southeast.

Sights on the western side of town include the **Historical Government House (Takayama Jinya),** reached by walking east to the end of Hachikenmachi-dori. The palatial structure on the left is one of the only government buildings surviving in Japan from the Edo period. It was originally erected by the

Kanemori rulers in 1615. Rebuilt 200 years later, it remained the seat of government in Takayama even after the abolition of the shogunate in the 19th century. Entered via an imposing gate through massive surrounding walls, it includes administrative rooms, a granary harking back to the days when fortunes were counted in rice, court rooms, and a torture chamber.

Hida Folk Village (Hida Minzoku Mura) is a 20-minute walk southwest of Takayama Station or reachable by bus. This open-air museum should be a high priority when visiting Takayama. More than 30 fine old farmhouses and rustic buildings from around Takayama and the Hida area have been dismantled and rebuilt in a landscape designed to evoke their original setting. The spacious village complex is on hilly ground overlooking the town. Featuring high thatched roofs and interiors with beams blackened by the smoke of cooking fires, the buildings provide fascinating insights into the simple, often harsh lifestyle of rural Japan until less than a century ago. Their original fixtures and farming tools include a water mill and workshops where artisans (weavers, dyers, woodcarvers, basket-makers) and others demonstrate local crafts. It takes two to four hours to stroll around the village, which includes restaurants and craft shops. ■

An interior in Takayama reveals its massive crossbeam roof structure.

Historical Government House

✉ 1-5 Hachiken-machi

☎ 0577/32-0643

$ $$

Hida Folk Village

✉ 1-590 Kamiokamoto-cho

☎ 0577/34-4711

$ $$$

🚌 Bus: from number 6 gate at the station to Hida-no-Sato (fast bus takes 10 mins., slow bus 30 mins.)

Takayama markets

There is plenty of local color in Takayama's morning street markets *(asa-ichi),* which trade daily in produce and flowers grown by local farmers as well as in handicrafts. Both are open from 7 a.m. to noon, one at Jinya-mae near the Historical Government House and the other on the eastern bank of

the Miya-gawa River, across from Kajibashi bridge.

The old town center of Sanmachi Suji holds an antique market on the 7th of each month from May through October. Good pieces won't come cheap, but they are still priced substantially lower than in Kyoto or Tokyo. ■

The street leading to Zenko-ji Temple is the most picturesque spot in this pleasant but unremarkable town.

Nagano-ken

WITH NO SHORTAGE OF MOUNTAINS, OTHER PLACES IN Japan could qualify, but to the Japanese Nagano-ken is *the* alpine prefecture. Western-style mountaineering was first introduced more than a century ago; in 1998, Nagano city was host to the Winter Olympic Games. Apart from winter sports, visitors can enjoy mountain hiking in summer, especially around Kamikochi. An old castle town, picturesque Matsumoto boasts one of Japan's most magnificent examples; the surrounding mountains present great natural beauty and a wealth of hot springs. South of Matsumoto, an inspiring blend of mountain scenery and history pervades the Kiso Valley.

Nagano

🗺 173 C4

Visitor information

✉ JR Nagano Station

🗺 026/226-5626

🚆 JR Shinkansen from Tokyo (1 hr. 35 mins.) or JR Chuô Honsen line from Nagoya (2 hrs. 50 mins.)

After coming under the spotlight in 1998, Nagano reverted to its mundane routine as prefectural capital. A small modern city, it has few sights, but it is friendly and cosmopolitan, and it makes a comfortable base for trips into the surrounding mountains. The town's one truly outstanding historic and religious asset is **Zenko-ji Temple.** So important is it that Chuo-dori, the main street, runs northward up to it in a dead straight line, a distance of one mile

colossal **Main Hall (Hondo)**
stands on a site northeast of its
original counterpart. The **Nio-
mon,** first of the two massive
gates along the approach, was
rebuilt in 1918.

The imposing facade of the
Main Hall does justice to the
magnificence of the lofty interior.
Incense wafts high up into the
gilded shadows of an ornate
coffered ceiling hung with gigantic
gold lamps; the atmosphere is awe-
inspiring. Scribes are on hand to
commemorate pilgrims' visits with
a temple seal; for a small fee they
will stamp your notebook (visitors
can collect stamps from temples
and shrines throughout Japan) and
embellish it with votive calligraphy.

One of the main attractions—a
ticket to heaven—is to touch the
key of paradise (an icon set in
wood) beneath the main altar.
Claustrophobes, be warned: to
touch the key you need to grope
along the wall through a long, narrow tunnel in pitch darkness. If you
fail to touch the key, take heart: The
relief at seeing a glimmer of light at
the end is symbolically equated
with enlightenment.

The precinct is frequently
crowded and the atmosphere festive; outside the gate, craft shops,
cafés, and restaurants line a pleasant avenue leading to the town
center. ∎

**Above right: Dedi-
cated to travelers,
children, and the
unborn, *jizo* sta-
tues flank the
approach to
Zenko-ji Temple.**

Zenko-ji Temple

✉ 491 Motoyoshi-cho

🚌 Bus from the
station to Daimon
(10 mins.)

💲 Main Hall free;
Inner Sanctum and
walk in the dark
(okaidan meguri)
$$

(1.5 km) from Nagano Station.
Founded around 660, Zenko-ji's
all-embracing tradition of worship
reflects the dawn of Buddhism in
Japan, but it belongs to no specific
sect and is revered by all. Zenko-ji
has admitted women both as wor-
shipers and priests for centuries,
even when most sacred precincts
were male preserves. Of paramount
importance to pilgrims, it receives
up to eight million visitors annual-
ly. Those numbers are swelled every
seven years for the Gokaicho cere-
mony honoring the Ikko Sanzon
Amida Nyorai statue. Too sacred
for mortal eyes, the statue tradi-
tionally remains hidden. The next
Gokaicho takes place in 2006.

The temple's destruction in
1700 prompted a reorientation of
the compound; built in 1707, the

Matsumoto

Matsumoto

🗺 173 C4

Visitor Information

✉ Outside JR
  Matsumoto Station

☎ 0263/32-2814

🚉 JR Shinonoi line
  from Nagano (55
  mins.). JR Chuo
  Honsen Line's
  "Azusa" limited
  express from
  Shinjuku Station,
  Tokyo (2 hrs. 45
  mins.). JR Chuo
  Honsen line from
  Nagoya (2 hrs. 30
  mins.)

MATSUMOTO, IN THE CENTRAL HIGHLANDS, IS THE southwestern equivalent of Nagano (see p. 186) and is similarly used as a base for mountain excursions and activities. The city is bland in the center but retains some venerable back streets. The Metoba-gawa River flows through Matsumoto east to west, and the townscapes along the banks present an engaging jumble of old and new.

Ruled by the Ogasawara clan in the 14th and 15th centuries and taken over by the Ishikawa in the 16th, Matsumoto was a castle town. **Matsumoto-jo Castle** *(4-1 Marunouchi, tel 0263/32-2902)* ranks as one of Japan's most magnificent. Only a hint of white accentuates the black wooden walls

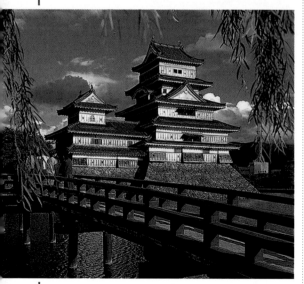

Matsumoto-jo Castle is one of the finest and most authentic surviving samurai castles in the country.

and dark-tiled roofs of this National Treasure, nicknamed Karasu-jo (Crow Castle). The name is said to derive from its shape, but more probably it shares the sobriquet with other black castles in contrast to the "White Egret" castle of Himeji (see pp. 256–57). First constructed in 1504, the castle reached its final form in the 1590s. Up steep wooden staircases, there is

a spectacular alpine panorama from the viewing platform on the five-story **main keep.** The interior—actually six floors (Japanese castles have five stories outside and six inside)—displays an arsenal comprising guns, swords, and armor. The castle never saw any action—hence its excellent state of preservation. Among its turrets, the most famous is the moon-viewing turret.

Nihon Minzoku Shiryokan Museum, attached to the castle, showcases many exhibits, including the Honda Clock Collection of fine antique pieces. **Nihon Ukiyo-e Hakubutsu-kan Museum** *(2206-1 Koshiba, Shimadachi, tel 0263/47-4440, closed Mon.)* has the country's largest collection of *ukiyo-e,* or woodblock prints. The Nihon Museum is just a seven-minute taxi ride from the station; most of the town can be comfortably covered on foot.

Matsumoto is noted for scenic spots less than 30 minutes away by bus, notably the 6,500-foot (2,000 m) **Utsukushigahara Plateau (Utsukushigahara-kogen),** famed for breathtaking mountain views and carpets of alpine flowers. The plateau also boasts popular spas, **Utsukushigahara Onsen** and adjacent **Asama Onsen** at the foot. Matsumoto is a stepping-stone to Kamikochi Valley, the gateway to the Japan Alps. Hikers and cyclists crowd into the city in summer, when hotel reservations should be made well in advance. ■

Kamikochi Valley

Kappa-bashl suspension bridge spans Azusa-gawa River in the Kamikochi Valley.

THE KAMIKOCHI VALLEY, CUTTING THROUGH THE Japan Alps west of Matsumoto, is a narrow glen in Chubu Sangaku National Park. Kamikochi lies at 5,000 feet (1,525 m) above sea level between Mount Yake-dake to the southwest, Mount Kasumizawa-dake to the east, and the Hotaka range to the north. Averaging 10,000 feet (3,050 m), these peaks are among the nation's highest—a challenge to serious climbers. Hikers, campers, and nature lovers all cherish the area, too. After kaleidoscopic displays of alpine flowers in summer and blazing colors in the fall, Kamikochi is closed from November through May.

Following the Azusa-gawa River east to west, the main attractions of the area are **Taisho-ike,** a pond formed after the eruption of Yake-san in 1915, and—an hour's hike away—**Kappa-bashi,** a suspension bridge over Azusa-gawa with a spectacular view of Mount Oku-Hotaka-dake. Another good hour farther east is **Myojin-ike** pond. Kamikochi Valley extends to Yoko'o, about 4 miles (6 km) farther on. You should have mountain trekking experience and proper equipment to venture beyond here; the area is more remote and the ground steep-er, while temperatures are known to dip below freezing even in summer. Kamikochi offers a wealth of hiking routes. There is an information office at the bus terminal, but you would do better seeking advice about trails and accommodations in English at visitor information centers in Matsumoto or Takayama. From mid-July to mid-August and again in October, the region is so crowded that advance booking (not to say avoidance) is essential. Note that during the rainy season in June, Kamikochi's scenic marvels tend to vanish in the drizzle. ■

Kamikochi

🅰 173 C4

Visitor information

✉ Kamikochi bus terminal

☎ 0263/95-2405

🚆 Matsumoto Dentetsu Line to Shin-Shimashima from Matsumoto station (30 mins.), then 1 hr. 20 mins. by bus to Kamikochi (bus service runs from late April to mid-November only)

Kiso Valley (Kisoji)

One of the gems of the Kiso Valley, Tsumago has been restored to look just as it did a century ago.

KISOJI, EMBRACED BY THE MOUNTAINS OF NAGANO-KEN, is celebrated in a song known to every Japanese schoolchild. Many legends haunt Kisoji, its 230 square miles (600 sq km) of soaring cedar forests having yielded the trees used to build the most sacred Shinto shrines. To the west (weather permitting) the skyline is dominated by 10,049-foot (3,063 m) Mount Ontake-san, an active volcano held sacred to Shinto.

Kisoji

🗺 173 C3

Visitor information

�æ Train: JR Chuo Honsen line Matsumoto–Nagoya

Narai

🗺 173 C3

Visitor information

✉ Tourism section, Town Hall

☎ 0264/34-2001

Agematsu

🗺 173 C3

Visitor information

✉ Outside the station

☎ 0264/52-4820

Kisoji lies along the Nakasendo (the old "through the mountains" road), the alternative to the Tokaido trunk road from Edo to Kyoto in feudal times. The road's historical post towns of Narai, Tsumago, and Magome became increasingly remote after the decline of the Nakasendo and the increase in rail travel, but gained architectural recognition during the late 1960s. Since then they have been strictly preserved and painstakingly restored. Although Kisoji's townships are linked by rail, many beauty spots, historical sites, secluded shrines, and temples are a good bus ride away from the stations; to do justice to this wonderful region, you need a minimum of three days.

Kisoji's once-flourishing forestry industry declined from the 1950s as a result of poor management, bringing down the regional economy. Recent years, however, have seen a modest revival. Village workshops, craft centers, and folk museums provide ubiquitous evidence that Kisoji maintains its centuries-old reputation for woodcraft and lacquerware. Today it depends heavily on the five million tourists it receives annually. The majority are daytrippers, so the region is enchantingly tranquil and unspoiled once the hordes go home. The deeply forested hills of larch and cedar present spectacular hiking possibilities, and their many torrents make them a fishing

Mountain paradise

Venerated since prehistoric times, Mount Ontake-san is the object of a Shinto cult. The first Ontake shrine is said to have been erected in 920, but Ontake-kyo (Ontake religion) was developed during the 18th century as an animistic composite of shamanism and *ryobushinto*—a meld of Shinto and Buddhism outlawed during the "purification" of Shinto in the 1870s. Ontake-kyo counts around two million followers. Every year some 150,000 pilgrims ascend the slopes of Ontake to a shrine near the summit (the volcano is active, so access to the crater is prohibited). Many start with ritual purification by standing under the Kiyo-taki Waterfall, in the forest near Otaki-mura. Believers erect commemorative stones called *reijin-no-hi*, believing them to be their ticket to a mountain paradise when they die. Shrouded in mist and mystery, the stones stand in their hundreds of thousands on wooded slopes and dells in the vicinity of Ontake-jinja Shrine. ■

Ontake-kyo: melding Shinto with Buddhism

paradise. Spring and summer come quite late to Kiso, where the winters can be bitterly cold. But you can always warm yourself beside a square, sunken *irori* fireplace and enjoy good mountain fare, including *sansai* (mountain vegetables), river fish, and (seasonally) stews of wild boar.

Narai, once dubbed "Narai of the 1,000 houses," was the most important post town on the Nakasendo. There are far fewer than 1,000 today, but venerable houses still flank the 0.75-mile (1.2 km) main street, which looks much as it did 200 years ago, down to the old wells for slaking travelers' thirsts. Just behind it are charming rustic shrines and temples. Some houses are now museums and craft shops; others, such as the sake brewery, an old lacquerware workshop, and the famous Echigoya Inn, maintain their ancestral function.

You can visit a large lacquerware store and museum in **Hirasawa,** about half a mile (1 km) north. About the same distance north of this is **Niekawa,** which maintains a replica of its old *sekisho* (barrier station), where the identities of travelers were checked.

Kiso Fukushima is Kisoji's largest town. Part of it was badly damaged by fire in 1947 and subsequently rebuilt. The old section on the hill, overlooking the Kiso-gawa River, was largely spared and retains an antiquarian charm. As at Niekawa, there is a handsome replica of the old barrier station. Above all, Fukushima is the gateway for those climbing Ontake-san. Taking about 70 minutes, buses from Kiso-Fukushima Station go to

Kiso Fukushima

🅰 173 C3

Visitor Information

✉ Outside the station

☎ 0264/22-4144

🚆 Train: JR Chuo Honsen line from Matsumoto (40 mins.)

A Narai craftsman shapes bentwood bowls.

**A postman sports
Edo-period garb
in Tsumago.**

Nakanoyu Onsen, the starting point of the main trail up the mountain. From the trailhead it takes almost four hours to hike through the cedar forests to the summit.

Perched riverside, the otherwise unremarkable town of **Agematsu** offers a breathtaking view over the Kiso-gawa gorges. Known as a center for woodcraft, the town's factories and workshops are open to the public. The scale of these operations is somewhat industrial, but the scent of cedar is heavenly.

Tsumago is the jewel in Kisoji's crown. Another important post town and 15 miles (25 km) southwest of Agematsu, it has been officially protected since 1968; the town's buildings have been beautifully restored, with communication lines buried underground and TV aerials hidden. Highlights include a palatial wooden official residence (now the local museum) and a post office, both dating from the 1860s.

Tsumago's only drawback is that it feels rather like a museum, particularly as the often daunting crowds of visitors vastly outnumber the residents. Best appreciated in the evening and early morning, Tsumago is a delightful place to stay. The 18th-century house on the main street, famous for the tree growing right against its facade and featured on local postcards, is still a *ryokan* (inn).

The picturesque town of **Magome** was the birthplace of poet and novelist Shimazaki Toson (1872–1943), one of the first writers to combine Japanese sensitivities with Western forms of expression; a modern museum building is devoted to his life and art. However, too many of the old houses—damaged by fire and restored—have been turned into tourist cafés and kitschy souvenir shops. Compared with Narai or Tsumago, Magome feels disappointingly like a theme park. ■

Tsumago
🗺 173 C3
Visitor information
✉ Main street
☎ 0264/57-3123
🚉 Train: JR Chuo Honsen line from Matsumoto to Nagiso (1 hr.), bus to Tsumago (10 mins.)

Magome
🗺 173 C3
Visitor information
✉ Opposite Toson Kinekan
☎ 0264/59-23363
🚉 Train: JR Chuo Honsen line from Matsumoto to Makatsugawa (1 hr. 30 mins.), bus to Magome (30 mins.)

Magome to Tsumago Walk

Some 6 miles (9.5 km) long, this three-hour hike follows the old Nakasendo route. But for the first 2 miles (3 km), so does the modern road. If you feel traffic would mar your appreciation of the scenery, take the bus from Magome to Magome-toge Pass (listen for the name), and then start walking the hamlets of O-daki, Kudaritani, Otsumago, and Tsumago. Depending on the season, you will see mountains reflected in the flooded rice fields, lush shades of green, or vivid autumn hues—a perfect prelude to the old houses of Tsumago, where time seems to have stood still. The visitor information center can arrange for luggage to be forwarded between Magome and Tsumago. ■

Sado-ga-shima

Alpine flowers
enliven the
seascape at
Onogame in early
summer.

COVERING 330 SQUARE MILES (855 SQ KM), SADO-GA-shima is one of Japan's largest islands. Its verdant northern and southern mountain ranges are separated by a lush agricultural plain; carpeted with alpine flowers, Mount Donden-yama offers spectacular views.

Medieval warlords, wary of creating martyrs, sent their more noble, pious, or learned enemies into exile. The banishment of choice was remote Sado-ga-shima, separated from the mainland by a 22-mile (35 km) strait notorious for its treacherous winter seas. Sado Kinzan Gold Mine was founded in 1601 to dig gold discovered in the hills near Aikawa and flourished under the shogunate's control during the Edo period. The gold made little difference to the islanders, whose existence depended (as it does today) on rice farming and fishing. Having closed as a mine in 1867, Sado Kinzan is now one of the main attractions in a region that relies heavily on tourism for revenue.

Sado's scenic assets belie its gloomy past. The island lures legions of modern exiles in spring and summer with endless opportunities for hiking, cycling, camping, swimming, wallowing in hot springs, and feasting on superlative seafood. Sado has accommodations to suit all budgets. Many of its quiet Japanese-style inns lie in charming country surroundings.

The island's secluded temples and shrines, often historically associated with illustrious exiles, cluster in peaceful little towns such as **Mano** and **Sawata** on the west coast and the central plain. Emperor Juntoko, who died in exile in 1242, is buried in the **Mano Goryo** mausoleum near Mano.

The coast is dotted with fishing villages, notably attractively restored Shukunegi in the south (see p. 196) The rugged coastline

Sado-ga-shima

🅰 173 C6

Visitor information

✉ Near ferry terminal at Ryotsu

☎ 0259/23-3300

🚢 Ferry: from Niigata to Ryotsu port (2 hrs. 20 mins.). Jetfoil: from Niigata (1 hr.)

features striking volcanic rock formations, especially along **Senkaku-wan,** a bay on the north coast. Although predictably crowded in high summer, Sado remains unhurried and refreshingly unspoiled, attracting young people fond of outdoor activities and fugitives from the pressures of modern Japan. For all that, it does not exert much of a hold on its constantly declining population. Job opportunities are too few to attract the young, and the relatively advanced age of many locals may seem surprising. From November through April, bus services are halved and accommodations close as islanders batten down to face harsh winters.

You could spend one night on Sado and take tours, but a stay of three or four days would be much more worthwhile. The towns are all connected by bus, and services run about once an hour. Cycle rentals abound, or you can rent a car.

Most people reach Sado by ferry from Niigata on the Honshu mainland, a journey of some two and a half hours, docking at Ryotsu, on a bay in the center of the east coast. The island capital, **Ryotsu,** lies on a strip of land separating Lake Kamo-ko from the sea. Catering mainly to Japanese package tours, this is Sado at its most developed and least attractive, but it is convenient as a base for transportation all over the island. The famous Sado Okesa dance (see p. 196) originated here, so this is the place to see it. If you miss it at a festival, there are sometimes professional performances, along with Ondeko drumming and dancing (see p. 195), at the **Ryotsu Kai-kan Hall** north of town.

A more pleasant but less convenient way to visit the island is to take the ferry from Naoetsu (south along the coast from Niigata) to Ogi, then make your way west and north. **Ogi** is the gateway to one of the island's most attractive regions. The modern ferry terminal building is deceptive: This is a sleepy fishing town small enough to cover on foot, consisting of a single main street lined with weather-beaten shops and houses—as perfectly unremarkable as it is charming.

Above left: Fisherwomen still use rotund *tairabune* near Ogi, though the boats are now mainly tourist attractions.

Ogi

🗺 173 C5

Visitor information

✉ Outside the ferry terminal

☎ 0259/86-3010

🚌 Bus: From Sawata (65 mins.)

⛴ Ferry: from Naoetsu, Honshu (2 hrs. 30 mins.)

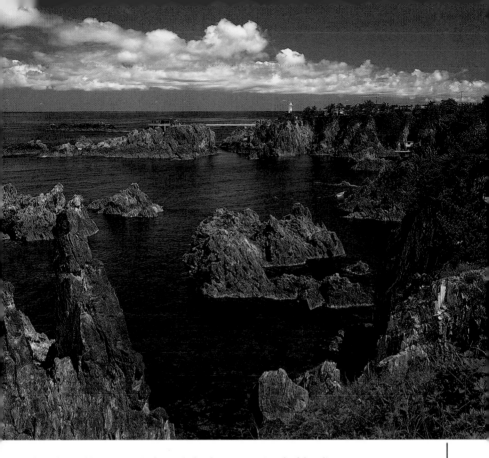

The only notable attraction is the **taraibune** **fishing boat pier** just west of the port. The tub-shaped vessels called taraibune were used by fisherwomen for gathering squid and seaweed; they hold about four adults and are now reserved mainly for tourists. You can either rent one yourself or be paddled around the bay by a woman in colorful traditional garb (in which she would not be seen dead anywhere else).

The area west of Ogi is rural, and there are delightful scenic walks along the coast and just inland. The only road leads to Shukunegi, 2.5 miles (4 km) farther on. Along the way two temples lie

Volcanism forged the craggy coastline of Senkaku-wan Bay.

Kodo drummers

Accompanying dancing and parades, traditional Japanese festival combos incorporate flutes with a gamut of percussion instruments including giant upright *taiko*, hand-drums and wooden clappers—all orchestrated with dexterous precision. Among them, Sado's *ondeko* drumming is paramount; founded in 1981, its Kodo troupe stands at the pinnacle of the art. Kodo drummers train long and hard, living according to a monastic regime near Ogi in the south. The Kodo organization created Sado's international three-day Earth Celebration festival of music and dance (third week of August). ■

Sadokoku Folk Museum

✉ 270–2 Shukunegi, Ogi-machi

☎ 0259/86-2604

💲 $$

Sado Gold Mine

✉ 1305 Oaza Ahimo-Aikawa, Aikawa-Machi

☎ 0259/74-2389

💲 $$

An oni-daiko dancer on Sado-ga-shima

across the rice fields in wooded glades: **Shiawase-jizo Temple** has a statue, 59 feet (18 m) high, of Jizo, patron deity of travelers and children, while **Iwaya-san Temple** features a cluster of ancient statues in a cave. On the way to Shukunegi, don't miss the extraordinary **Sadokoku Folk Museum (Sadokoku Ogi Minzoku Hakubutsukan).** Housed in a wooden former school complex, it is devoted to some 200 years of local history. The eclectic exhibits include farming and fishing implements, clothing, dolls, lamps, home altars, shop signs, kitchenware, clocks, radios, phonographs, and telephones. One shed contains a full-size reconstruction of a treasure ship used for carrying Sado's gold to the mainland.

Shukunegi village, a conservation area, is wedged snugly between the rocks on the bay. Separated by an arm's length along narrow alleys, the houses look much as they did a century ago; the official residences have been beautifully restored and are open as museums.

During the Edo period, when gold mining reached its peak, the northwestern coastal town of **Aikawa** had a population of 100,000—greater than modern Sado's. Declining since the mine's closure in 1867, it currently stands

at 10,000. The town itself is congenial but offers little to detain a visitor beyond the **Aikawa Folk Museum (Aikawa Kyodo Hakubutsukan),** which displays relics from the gold-mining days and modern woodblock prints by noted local artists. There is a pleasant scenic walk among the leafy (if mainly funereal) temples up the steep slope east of town.

The major draw is the **Sado Gold Mine (Sado Kinzan),** a 10-minute bus ride (or 40-minute walk) east of town. Opened in 1601, it was exploited by the shogunate for more than 250 years and was then worked sporadically until the mid-1990s. Although skilled miners were voluntary recruits, those carrying water down the shafts were vagrants forcibly sent from the mainland. An unusual museum, the old Sodayu-Ko section of the mine retains the wooden pumping gadgetry in the narrow tunnels in which Edo-period miners toiled. The tunnels are now populated with animatronic wax figures representing miners at work, complete with sound effects. The museum's exhibition hall has an outstanding model of the town and its mining operations in feudal times. On a hilltop near Sado Kinzan is Doyu-no-wareto, the original open-pit mine that split the peak of the mountain in two. ∎

Sado dancing

Sado's folk culture, on display during local festivals and often performed for tourists, is very much alive. The most famous form is *Sado okesa, a* combination of melancholy ballads and graceful dancing by women. Festivals also feature *tsuburosashi,* a ribald old comic dance with phallic overtones, as well as the furious *ondeko* drum-

ming that traditionally accompanies such dances and *oni-daiko,* a masked demon dance. The best place to appreciate Sado dancing is during a *matsuri* (festival), but the larger towns, including Ryotsu, Aikawa, Ogi, and Sawata, often stage performances nightly during the high season. Check with the local visitor information center for programs. ∎

With more than a thousand years of history, Kyoto constitutes Japan's heartland for traditional culture. Nara is even older. And there is much more to discover, for this is Kansai—the region wherein resides the very spirit of Japan.

Kansai

**Statue at Fushimi Inari
Taisha Shrine**

At Ninnai-ji Temple, the oldest buildings date from the 17th century.

Kansai

KANSAI MEANS "WESTERN PROVINCE." NEVER MIND THAT MID-20TH-century administrators changed the area name to "Kinki"; the Japanese still prefer to call the province by its feudal name of Kansai. It's easy to see why: Among the seven prefectures it covers are Kyoto and Nara—the very cradles of Japanese civilization. Founded more than 1,200 years ago, Kyoto is still the nation's prime temple town and its greatest repository of traditional culture. Among the temples in slightly older Nara are some of the oldest wooden buildings still standing on Earth. Small wonder, then, that Kansai boasts the most popular tourist destinations in Japan.

In Mie-ken on Kansai's eastern confines is Ise-jingu, the main shrine of Shinto for nearly 1,800 years. Founded in 552, Asuka was Yamato's first capital; Nara became the new capital in 710. The grandest old city was Kyoto. Founded in 794, it remained the imperial capital for over a millennium; its wealth of historical and cultural assets make it the single greatest tourist destination in Japan.

Hanshin, Kansai's heavily industrialized coastal area, embraces the cities of Kobe and Osaka. Kobe, capital of Hyogo-ken, still reflects the cosmopolitanism it acquired as a 19th-century treaty port. Osaka, rising to prominence during the Edo period as a mercantile and industrial hub, is now the nation's third largest city. Pleasantly situated on a hill overlooking the bay of Osaka-wan, Kobe has largely recovered from the devastating earthquake of 1995, but like Osaka it has little to offer visitors in search of historical sights. Just west of Kobe, however, is magnificent Himeji-jo Castle—the finest of all surviving Japanese castles.

The east of Kansai is the gateway to Shikoku and Seto-naikai Inland Sea via Awaji-shima Island and the giant Naruto Ohashi Bridge. The peaceful Buddhist sanctum of Koya-san, a mountain retreat offering the public firsthand experience of temple life, lies to the south in hilly and remote Wakayama-ken, famous for its rugged coast. In Shiga-ken, on Kansai's northeastern area, is Biwa-ko,

0 | 75 kilometers
0 | 50 miles

WESTERN HONSHU (CHUGOKU) p. 261
CENTRAL HONSHU (CHUBU) p. 171

◁4

Hamasaka
Toyooka
Miyazu
Amanohashidate
Maizuru
Nagahama
Yoka
Fukuchiyama
Ayabe
KYOTO-KEN
Biwa-ko
Hikone
SHIGA-KEN
Yamasaki
HYOGO-KEN
Hiei-zan 848m
Otsu
Yokkaichi

◁3

Nishiwaki
Sanda
KYOTO
Kusatsu
Suzuka
Himeji
Kakogawa
Amagasaki
Uji
Ueno
Tsu
Ise-wan
Ako
Takasago
Akashi
Nara
Matsusaka
KOBE
Sakai
OSAKA
25
MIE-KEN
Toba
Harima-nada
Naruto Ohashi Bridge
Kansai
OSAKA-KEN
Kashihara
Ise Jingu
Ise
Shima-hanto
Awaji-shima
Osaka-wan
Kishiwada
NARA-KEN
ISE-SHIMA NAT. PARK
Onarutu Bashi Bridge
Sumoto
Hashimoto
Nagashima

◁2

△ A
Wakayama
Koya San
KOYA-RYUJIN QUASI-NAT. PARK
Owase
Arida
Kii-hanto
Kumano
Gobo
WAKAYAMA-KEN
Hongu
Tanabe
Nachi-no-taki
Shingu
Nachikatsuura
◁I
Kushimoto
O Shima
△ B
△ C
△ D

Kii-suido

Area of map detail

Tokyo

Archery competition at Fushimi Inari Taisha Shrine

Japan's largest lake—probably best appreciated from Hikone, where there is a fine castle.

There is much to see in Kansai. Although Tokyo is less than three hours from Kyoto by train, overseas visitors often choose to confine their stay in Japan to this, Japan's historical heart. Following the opening of Kansai International Airport in 1994, the number of direct overseas flights is growing sufficiently to make this option worth considering. ■

Kyoto

Kyoto has everything visitors could wish for, with more than 1,800 temples, hundreds of shrines, historical buildings and neighborhoods, famous gardens, and beauty spots among wooded hills. As Japan's seventh largest city, however, Kyoto has not escaped some redevelopment, especially to the south. The Kyoto Station building, completed in 1997 with a colossal central concourse and shopping mall is architecturally impressive, but you emerge from it into a modern city as nondescript as any. You need not go very far, however, to find traditional beauty.

There is more in Kyoto than anyone could see in months, let alone a few days. This makes it vital to plan your sightseeing schedule. It is easy to go overboard visiting temples. Like most Oriental art and architecture, Japanese examples tend toward a certain uniformity; what constitutes the best lies in age, subtleties, details, and settings. Random sightseeing can induce you to dismiss the temples on a "seen one, seen 'em all" basis long before you reach the best. Begin by visiting the city information office (see p. 202), even if only to pick up a map to the Kyoto bus and subway system. The helpful staff speaks English.

The center of Kyoto is a modern city with main shops and amusements. It includes a few sights, notably Nishi Hongan-ji Temple and Nijo-jo Castle. Crossing over the Kamo-gawa River to the east, you discover traditional Kyoto. Eastward from the old geisha district of Gion you can stroll uphill through venerable streets to Kiyomizu-dera Temple, walking along the canal on the Path of Philosophy up to Ginkaku-ji (the Silver Pavilion). To the north lie such sights as Kinkaku-ji (the Golden Pavilion) and Ryoan-ji nearby, with its world-famous Zen rock garden. Westward and over the Kagura-gawa River is hilly Arashiyama, where many more temples nestle in sylvan settings of bamboo, cherries, and maple trees.

Kyoto is also renowned for the quality of its handicrafts and its cuisine. ∎

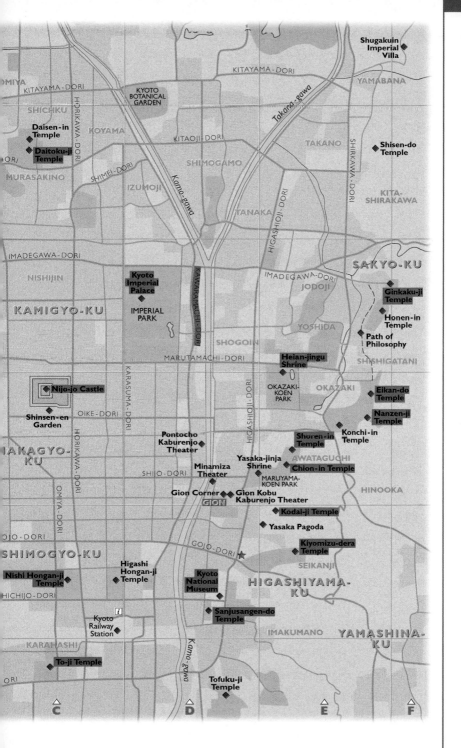

KITAYAMA-DORI
YAMABANA
Shugakuin
Imperial
Villa
OMIYA
KITAYAMA-DORI
KYOTO
BOTANICAL
GARDEN
SHICHKU
KOYAMA
KITAOJI-DORI
TAKANO
Daisen-in
Temple
Shisen-do
Temple
ORI
Daitoku-ji
Temple
SHIMEI-DORI
SHIMOGAMO
KITA-
SHIRAKAWA
MURASAKINO
IZUMOJI
TANAKA

IMADEGAWA-DORI
SAKYO-KU
NISHIJIN
IMADEGAWA-DORI
JODOJI
Ginkaku-ji
Temple
Kyoto
Imperial
Palace
KAMIGYO-KU
IMPERIAL
PARK
YOSHIDA
Honen-in
Temple
Path of
Philosophy
SHOGOIN
MARUTAMACHI-DORI
SHISHIGATANI
Heian-jingu
Shrine
Nijo-jo Castle
OKAZAKI-
KOEN
PARK
OKAZAKI
Eikan-do
Temple
Shinsen-en
Garden
OIKE-DORI
Nanzen-ji
Temple
IAKAGYO-
KU
Pontocho
Kaburenjo
Theater
Shuren-in
Temple
Konchi-in
Temple
Yasaka-jinja
Shrine
AWATAGUCHI
Minamiza
Theater
Chion-in Temple
SHIJO-DORI
MARUYAMA-
KOEN PARK
HINOOKA
Gion Corner
Gion Kobu
Kaburenjo Theater
GION
Kodai-ji Temple
OJO-DORI
Yasaka Pagoda
GOJO-DORI
Kiyomizu-dera
Temple
SHIMOGYO-KU
SEIKANJI
Higashi
Hongan-ji
Temple
Kyoto
National
Museum
HIGASHIYAMA-
KU
Nishi Hongan-ji
Temple
HICHIJO-DORI
Kyoto
Railway
Station
Sanjusangen-do
Temple
IMAKUMANO
YAMASHINA-
KU
KARAHASHI
To-ji Temple
ORI
Tofuku-ji
Temple

C
D
E
F

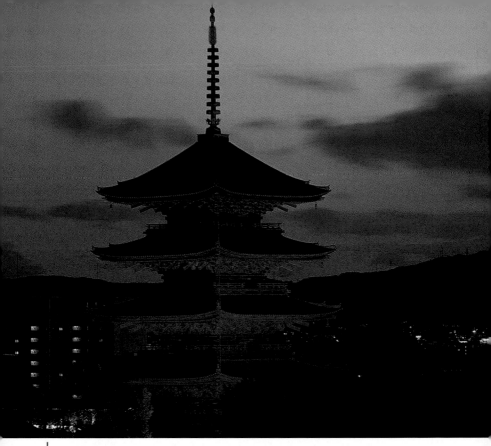

To-ji Temple pagoda at twilight: Spared during World War II, Kyoto remains Japan's greatest repository of culture.

Central Kyoto

START YOUR VISIT TO KYOTO BY EXPLORING THE CENTER of the city. You will probably arrive at Kyoto Station at the end of a three-hour train ride from Tokyo. Do not be alarmed by the modern buildings and busy streets; Kyoto has treasures aplenty for visitors. North of the station you will find two temples. The city center has a palace, a castle, and gardens as well as busy shopping arcades.

Kyoto visitor information

✉ Kyoto Tower Building

☎ 075/371-5649

Built by the shogun Toyotomi Hideyoshi in 1591, **Nishi Hongan-ji Temple,** headquarters of the Jodo Shinshu sect of Buddhism, is one of Japan's most important temples. The current buildings, erected in the 17th century, are among the finest examples of Japanese Buddhist architecture.

Behind the imposing main gate, the **Founder's Hall (Goeido)** was rebuilt in 1636 and contains a wooden sculpture of the sect's founder, Shinran, which he is said to have carved himself in the 1250s. Moved from Hideyoshi's Fushimi Castle in 1632 along with the great **Chinese gate (karamon)** in front of it, the ornate **Daisho-in Hall,** a National Treasure, is graced inside with screen doors exquisitely painted by masters of the Kano school (see p. 51). Of the two **Noh stages** north and south of the structure, the former was also brought from Fushimi Castle and is treasured as one of the oldest and finest in Japan. The three-story **Hiunkaku** pavilion, once Hideyoshi's private mansion, was moved here in 1615. Panels of birds

and flowers by the Kano school decorate the interior; the shogun even had his bathroom adorned with work by the great Kano artist Eitoku (see p. 51).

Formerly plain Hongan-ji, the temple became known as Nishi (West) Hongan-ji when **Higashi Hongan-ji Temple,** its eastern counterpart, went up nearby. A renegade abbot left the Jodo Shinshu sect to found a rival school, and Higashi Hongan-ji was built in 1602 to house it. Burned in a fire and reconstructed in 1895, the temple rivals its predecessor in sheer size; the colossal main hall is the largest wooden structure in Kyoto.

From Kyoto Station, Nishi Hongan-ji is a ten-minute walk northwest; Higashi Hongan-ji is

An ornate
gateway at Nijo-jo
Castle

**Nishi Hongan-ji
Temple**

- 201 C2
- Monzen-cho,
  Shimogyo-ku
- 075/371-5181
- City Bus: 9 to Nishi
  Honganji-mae
- Grounds of Nishi
  Hongan-ji freely
  accessible; entrance
  to buildings (tours
  conducted in
  Japanese) subject to
  permission, which
  must be applied for
  at least 7 working
  days prior to your
  visit. Applications
  should be made
  through a visitor
  information center
  or JNTO office
  overseas. Or write
  to above address
  with details of your
  proposed visit and
  party size using SAV
  and international
  postage coupons.

Jodo Shinshu sect

Founded by the priest Shinran (1173–1262) in 1224, the Jodo Shinshu (Pure Land New Faith) sect of Buddhism rejects the need for vegetarianism, asceticism, and celibacy for the priesthood. Instead, it teaches that enlightenment may be achieved simply through repeatedly chanting a sutra exalting the Amida

Buddha: *"Namu Amida Butsu."* Seen as a political threat, the sect was persecuted. But so great was its following that Toyotomi Hideyoshi realized that his campaign to unify Japan would fail without it; he built Nishi Hongan-ji in Kyoto in 1591. Jodo Shinshu now counts 12 million followers worldwide. ■

Ornate gate at Nijo-jo Castle, with detail at right

Nijo-jo Castle

🅰 201 C3

✉ Nijojo-cho, Nijo-dori, Horikawa Nishi-iru, Nakagyo-ku

☎ 075/841-0096

🚇 Subway: Nijojo-mae City Bus: 9, 12, 50, 101 stop at Nijojo-mae

💲 $$ (including garden)

five minutes north of the station.

After founding Kyoto's ancestral capital in 794, the emperor Kammu had **To-ji Temple** constructed two years later. Repeatedly burned down and rebuilt over the centuries, the temple buildings were destroyed during 15th-century civil wars. The **Main Hall (Kondo,** 1606) is a National Treasure, as are some of the eighth- and ninth-century works of religious art in the **Lecture Hall (Kodo,** 1491), which contains 21 renowned statues of Buddhas and deities. To-ji possesses a substantial garden elegantly decked out with ponds, at the southern end of which is the **pagoda** built by shogun Tokugawa Iemitsu in 1644; standing 180 feet

(55 m), it is the tallest in Japan. To-ji's other attraction lies in the popular antique and flea markets held on the grounds monthly; a larger one is held on the first Sunday of every month and a smaller on the 21st. The temple is a 15-minute walk southwest of Kyoto Station.

Built in 1603, **Nijo-jo Castle** was not so much a fortress as a palatial residence for the shogun Tokugawa Ieyasu (1542–1616) during his visits to Kyoto. A fire destroyed the keep and many buildings in the 18th century; following the Meiji Restoration, the remainder—proud symbols of former samurai power—became the home of the Kyoto prefectural government in the 1870s. Modernizing zeal dictated contempt for feudal remnants; the willful damage wrought on Nijo-jo by erstwhile bureaucrats still causes culturally sensitive souls to shudder. Happily, what is left is more than impressive.

The castle passed to the imperial family in 1893, when the **Main Palace (Honmaru)** was moved here from the Imperial Palace precinct as a home for Prince Katsura. The Honmaru is open to the public only on special days.

Reached through the ornate carved **Chinese gate** (karamon), the **Second Palace (Nino-**

maru) is really the first; its five buildings are all 17th-century originals. The first and largest, the **Tozamurai,** complete with "nightingale" flooring (specially constructed so that the boards squeaked underfoot—Ieyasu took no chances with unexpected visitors), has fine carvings, coffered ceilings, and screens painted by the Kano school, notably by the master Tanyu (1602–1674). Tanyu's paintings also grace three rooms in the **second building (Shikidai).**

Exquisite paintings and carvings adorn the **third building (Ohiroma),** which was the shogun's audience chamber. Smaller but lavishly decorated, the **fourth building (Kuroshoin)** is highly regarded for its Kano-school pictures of birds. The style of the shogun's private residence, the **fifth building (Shiroshoin),** is often considered all the more beautiful for its comparative restraint. Particularly charming is a snowscape mural depicting sparrows sleeping in a bamboo grove.

South of the Ninomaru and outside the walls is the **Shinsen-en Garden,** designed by the great landscape architect Kobori Enshu (1579–1647). It was originally treeless (falling leaves were felt to emphasize the transitory nature of life), but the later inclusion of trees did not endow it with much cheer; the garden's rather gloomy atmosphere is often attributed to the fact that it is now all that remains of the precinct of the great imperial palace from Heian times. Built by the emperor Kammu in 794, the original **Kyoto Imperial Palace (Kyoto Gosho)** stood northwest of its present site for more than a thousand years before being consumed by fire in 1788. Completed in 1790, the last palace burned down in 1854. The current, smaller one was built the following year on a new site.

Still used for the imperial enthronement ceremony, the Gosho is notable for the stark simplicity of its grand-scale architecture. Containing majestic but simple silk hangings and fine painted screens, the interiors somehow lack atmosphere. This is not to say the Gosho is devoid of interest; its sheer grandeur conveys a sense of its great ceremonial importance.

The grounds embrace the elegantly landscaped **pond garden (Oike-niwa)** and lie on one of Kyoto's most beautiful public parks, particularly popular when the cherry trees blossom in April.

(continued on page 208)

Imperial Palace
- 201 D4
- Kyoto Gyoen-nai, Kamigyo-ku
- 075/211-1211
- Subway: Imadegawa
- English-language tours (50 mins.) at 10 a.m. & 2 p.m. Mon.–Fri. There is a tour at 10 a.m. every Sat. in April, May, Oct., Nov. and every 3rd Sat. during other months; check first for availability—the Imperial Palace is often used for official functions.

Imperial Household Agency
- Kunaicho Kyoto Jimushu, 3 Kyoto Gyoen, Kamigyo-ku,
- 075/211-1215

Permission to visit

There are restrictions on visiting the Imperial Palace and Katsura Villas (see p. 231). Non-Japanese visitors are generally permitted to visit the same day if they apply at the Imperial Household Agency in Kyoto (north of the palace precinct) before 9:40 a.m. You can obtain permission by using the forms provided at the visitor information office in either Kyoto or Tokyo or in JNTO offices overseas. Your application should include a stamped addressed envelope if made in Japan, or a postage coupon if from abroad. In all cases, you must bring your passport. Permission must similarly be obtained from the Imperial Household Agency for the Katsura Villas; you can apply for them all at the same time, but note that admission is restricted to people over 20 years old. ■

Geisha

Most Japanese have seen true geisha only on television or in festival parades; the onsen geisha in spa resorts may well be only hookers in fancy dress. Genuine geisha entertain the political and industrial elite in exclusive traditional *ryotei* restaurants, *cha-ya* (teahouses), and *machi-ai* (assignation houses)—all antiquarian establishments boasting inner gardens graced with flickering stone lanterns. Numbering about 100,000 before World War II, the geisha declined with the rise of the bar hostess after the war; they now number barely 8,000.

a law forbidding geisha to sleep with customers in the pleasure quarters. As a result, the profession went upscale.

Today's geisha earns a lot of money. She has to, for her wardrobe includes a collection colored according to each season. She shuns wearing the same kimono before the same customers twice. The goal of most geisha is to find a *danna*—a wealthy patron to support her as a mistress. Some have been brides for prime ministers—Katsura during the Meiji era and Yoshida in the 1950s. A scandalous affair with a geisha in 1989 felled Prime Minister Uno after just two months in office.

The geisha have their origins in the pleasure quarters—the Floating World—of 300 years ago. More than mere bordellos, the great Green Houses of the 17th-century pleasure quarters offered banquets enhanced by courtesans adept at singing and dancing. Itinerant entertainers and musicians often accompanied them, the most skilled being dubbed *otoko geisha* (male arts people). By the 1700s the best female entertainers became known as *geiko* (arts girls), a name still used in some regions. To call them by any other name in Kyoto would ruffle their fine plumage but, elsewhere, the generic "geisha" stuck.

The geisha, her face whitened and her mouth reduced to little petals of brilliant red, became a living work of art, an icon of womanhood. Spirited, garrulous, talented, and sexy, she had all the dazzle that Confucian strictures forbade in a virtuous wife. Geisha are also table entertainers, sought for their wit and powers of conversation. Even in advanced years, some geisha continue to be revered as exponents of traditional performing arts.

At first, many geisha doubled as prostitutes. Infuriated by the rivalry, the courtesans successfully petitioned the government to pass

In the old days, girls trained as geisha from childhood; nowadays they start in their late teens. Hundreds of girls still aspire to become geisha, but only three out of ten weather the harsh training as *maiko* (apprentices) at the *okiya* (geisha house), where they are strictly schooled in singing, dancing, playing the *samisen* (Japanese three-string lute), and deportment.

You might see geisha in Kyoto's Gion (see p. 218), where the *maiko*—gaudy little dolls with whitened faces—bustle along, pigeon-toed on high sandals, while the geisha glide past in their silken finery with regal nonchalance. Appearances are deceptive, however. Tokyo, where they are rarely glimpsed, has about a thousand geisha. In Kyoto, despite their higher profile, there are slightly more than 500 left.

Geisha are not as old-fashioned as they seem. Their conversational skills are utterly contemporary, and many attend corporate functions in modern dress. If geisha disappear altogether, it will not be because they are out of tune with the times, but a matter of simple economics. Catering to a dwindling elite, they have priced themselves out of the market. ■

Once generalized, the elaborate makeup and unnatural whiteness characterizing the traditional geisha are now confined mainly to appearances on stage and in festival parades. Many brides have adopted the look for mainstream weddings.

**Pontocho
Kaburenjo Theater**

201 D3

Pontocho, Sanjo-
sagaru, Nakagyo-ku

075/221-2025

Maiko dances
May 1–24

Subway: Sanjo

$$$$

**Women in
traditional dress
shop at a souvenir
store near
Kiyomizu-dera
Temple.**

(continued from page 205)

Kawaramachi, Kyoto's prime shopping district, extends eastward along Shijo-dori to the Kamo-gawa River. Here are major department stores such as Hankyu and Takashimaya, as well as fashion stores and boutiques. If you're interested in traditional handicrafts, Kawaramachi is full of specialists in local products, such as ceramics, kimono and textiles, dolls, fans, and paper umbrellas.

Traditional goods and crafts are plentiful, too, in two shopping arcades: Shinkyogoku-dori and the more upscale Teramachi-dori, off the left-hand side of Shijo-dori as you walk east. The two alleys intersect with Nishikoji-dori, a lively and colorful covered arcade that serves as Kyoto's main food and vegetable market.

To the left of Shijo-dori and flanking the western bank of Kamo-gawa, **Pontocho** is one of the two great centers for traditional, geisha-oriented Kyoto nightlife; the other is Gion (see p. 218). A long alley of low wooden buildings festooned with red paper lanterns

and housing hundreds of bars and restaurants, Pontocho makes for some enchanting nighttime strolls. Many restaurants have riverside verandas, where wealthy patriarchs are entertained by fluttering bevies of geisha in summer. Like geisha entertainment, however, these restaurants tend to be accessible only with an introduction and are astronomically expensive.

More affordable dining options lie closer to the Kawaramachi end of the alley. Bars, too, in this area tend to be exclusive and expensive; whatever the establishment, as a rule of thumb venture only into those displaying prices, menus, or food exhibits in the window. More contemporary and cheaper restaurants and entertainment (the latter becoming raunchier the farther south you walk across Shijo-dori) abound around Kiyamachi-dori, which runs parallel to Pontocho along a canal. Like its equivalent in Gion, **Pontocho Kaburenjo Theater** at the northern end of Pontocho stages dances by *maiko*—apprentice geisha—twice annually as it has since the 1870s. ■

Eastern Kyoto

The attractive garden at the Heian-jingu Shrine

WHEN YOU CROSS OVER THE KAMO-GAWA RIVER, YOU discover a city that comes closest to everyone's ideal of an older Japan. The one caveat here applies to all of Japan's famous sites: Unless you visit early in the morning or on weekdays out of season, you will have to contend with formidable crowds. Bordering lush Mount Higashi-yama, the area possesses some of Kyoto's greatest sights.

As was once the case in all Japanese cities, the realms of religion and the senses exist cheek by jowl in eastern Kyoto: The world of temples extends east toward Higashiyama, which sits next to Gion, the oldest extant geisha district in Japan.

Eastern Kyoto begs exploration on foot. Between Ginkaku-ji Temple to the north and Nanzen-ji Temple to the south is the 0.75-mile (1 km) **Path of Philosophy (Tetsugaku-no-michi)**, a pleasant stroll alongside a canal, past old wooden houses with gardens and several temples. From **Maruyama-koen Park** southward toward Kiyomizu and westward toward Gion, you discover steep cobbled lanes lined with traditional buildings; they may house

a glut of souvenir shops that are architecturally the genuine article. Traditional buildings in such profusion are unique in modern Japan.

Walk north from Higashiyama subway station for about half a mile (1 km) to the **Heian-jingu Shrine** in Okazaki-koen Park. Built in 1895 to commemorate the 1,100th anniversary of the founding of the city, the shrine is a two-thirds-scale reproduction of the Heian-period (794–1185) imperial palace. As the colossal red *torii* gateway (made of steel) towering over the approach portends, the shrine is nothing if not bombastic. Incorporating two pagodas and a complex of ornate buildings in regulation Shinto scarlet with intricate Chinese-style roofs in blue-green

Heian-jingu Shrine
- 201 E4
- 97 Nishi Tenno-cho, Okazaki, Sakyo-ku
- 075/761-0221
- City Bus: 5, 4, or 6 to Kyoto Kaikan Bijutsukan

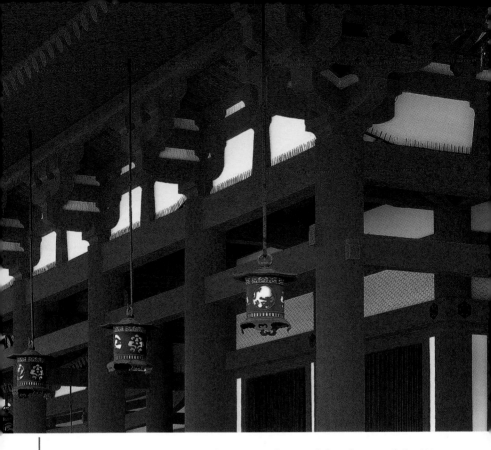

Nanzen-ji Temple

🗺 201 E3

✉ Fukuchi-cho, Sakyo-ku

☎ 075/771-0365

💲 Sanmon: $, Hojo Hall: $, Nanzen-in: $, Tenju-an: $, Konchi-in: $

🚉 Subway: Keage City Bus: Hoshojicho or Eikandomichi

tiles, the Heian shrine is certainly colorful—too new and over the top for those with antiquarian leanings. Ironically, bright colors were very much part of the picture in Heian times, though the gaudy paint has vanished from the few authentic remnants over the centuries.

With a profusion of weeping cherry trees, maples, azaleas, and lily ponds, the garden behind the shrine is attractive most of the year. Heian-jingu stages Takigi Noh theater performances at intervals and is also host to (and starting point of) one of Kyoto's great festivals, the Jidai Matsuri. Held on October 22, it features parades by celebrants attired in the lavish costumes of Heian times.

Built originally as a villa for Emperor Kameyama in 1264 and dedicated as a temple in 1293, **Nanzen-ji Temple** is one of the most important temples in Kyoto as well as the headquarters of the Rinzai sect of Zen. It is about half a mile (1 km) southeast of Heian-jingu. Standing in a spacious grove of pines that stretch back into forested hills, the subsidiary temples, some with lovely gardens, are so numerous that Nanzen-ji amounts almost to a temple city. The most notable current buildings (the original structures were destroyed) were erected in the early 17th century.

The imposing **sanmon gate,** a massive structure of dark wood in front of the entrance, was built in 1628; the climb up a steep flight of stairs inside is rewarded with a fine view over the city from the upper floor. Moved from the former Kyoto Imperial Palace, the **Hojo Hall** beyond the gate contains screen doors decorated with masterpieces by the Kano school, most notably a celebrated composition by Kano Tanyu (1602–1674) of tigers drinking in a bamboo grove. Attached to the Hojo is a fine Zen garden landscaped with shaped trees, rocks, and raked sand; you can contemplate it while sipping *macha*, the brew consumed during tea ceremonies.

About 220 yards (200 m) south of the main precinct and reached by passing under an old brick aqueduct is **Nanzen-in,** a subtemple of Nanzen-ji and once Emperor Kameyama's private villa. A beautiful garden features pines, mosses, and a pond full of variegated carp. Carrying water from Lake Biwa-ko, the raised aqueduct just south of Nanzen-in is an unusual structure in Japan, incorporating Roman-style redbrick arches. Follow the aqueduct uphill to a pine forest. The path passes under some red torii gates before reaching a lovely clearing with a small Shinto shrine honoring a sacred waterfall, beneath which hardy pilgrims undergo ritual cleansing—considered especially efficacious in winter. From here hiking trails lead up into the eastern hills.

The garden of Tenju-an, a subtemple of Nanzen-ji

Tenju-an, a subtemple constructed in 1337 near the sanmon gate, has another fine garden, but the star attraction among the gardens is at **Konchi-in,** just outside the temple compound. Using rocks, raked sand, and dwarf trees to depict a scene of mountains and islands in the sea, the garden was laid out in 1627 by Kobori Enshu and is regarded as a masterpiece.

The roads leading away from the approach to Nanzen-ji have several good restaurants (often in lovely garden settings) that specialize in *yudofu* (boiled tofu) cuisine, among them some with nationwide reputations (see p. 373).

Founded in 856, the Buddhist **Eikan-do Temple,** also called Zenrin-ji, was dedicated in the 11th century to the priest Eikan, greatly revered for his benevolence. Most of the current structures were built after the wars of the 15th century. The temple lies 440 yards (400 m) north of Nanzen-ji, on the southern end of the Path of Philosophy to the right.

To the south of the precinct, the main **Amida-do Hall** is reached via a staircase on the right. It contains the Mikaeri-no-Amida, an unusual statue showing the Amida Buddha glancing over his shoulder. Connected by cloisters and giving

Eikan-do Temple
- 201 E3
- 48 Eikando-cho, Sakyo-ku
- 075/761-0007
- $$ ($$$ in Nov.)
- Subway: Keage
  City Bus: Eikando-mae

Honen-in
- 201 E4
- Goshonodan-cho, Shishigatani, Sakyo-ku
- 075/771-2420
- Only open spring & autumn
- $ in spring; $$ in autumn. Free entrance to grounds
- City Bus: Jodoji

Ginkaku-ji Temple
- 201 E4
- 2 Ginkakuji-cho, Sakyo-ku
- 075/771-5725
- $
- City Bus: 5 from Kyoto or Sanjo Stations, or 203 from Demachiyanagi or Shijo to Ginkakuji-michi bus stop (5 mins. walk)

Honen-in Temple seen through its forest shroud

onto gardens noted for their maple trees, the other buildings display fine painted screens. South of the compound, the stone staircase on the right leads to the Taho-to Pagoda, with views over the city.

Walking north on the Path of Philosophy, you come to **Honen-in Temple.** Built in 1680 to honor the priest Honen, founder of the Jodo sect, this unassuming thatched temple appears rustic and peaceful. The narrow approach, passing through an imposing grove of trees, is flanked by areas of gravel subtly raked and shaped to complement the wooded setting. There is also a landscaped garden.

About 550 yards (500 m) north of Honen-in is the **Ginkaku-ji Temple** (Silver Pavilion). A sybarite and aesthete, the shogun Ashikaga Yoshimasa built Ginkaku-ji in 1482 as a luxurious country retreat. He intended to cover it with silver leaf to create something similar to the Golden Pavilion built by his grandfather Yoshimitsu (see p. 32), but money ran out, and Ginkaku-ji was never given its silver coating. It was turned into a temple after Yoshimasa's death.

A magnificent structure nonetheless, this is one of Kyoto's greatest sights. The surrounding garden, with its tall pines, raked sand, and pond of gorgeous carp, was designed by the great landscape architect Soami with Yoshimasa's autumn moon-viewing parties in mind. The little tea room in the Togudo Hall (1482), the oldest in Japan, is believed to be the prototype for all others. The adjacent rooms are reproductions of the ones used for incense parties.

A tree-lined path winding up the hill affords a splendid view of the grounds and the city. Early and out-of-season visits are particularly recommended for Ginkaku-ji, which can attract the biggest crowds in all Kyoto.

Located in the wooded foothills of Higashiyama is the temple of **Kiyomizu-dera,** a ten-minute walk from Gojozaka bus stop.

The temple, established in 798, is dedicated to the 11-faced Buddhist deity Kannon. The current buildings were erected by the shogun Tokugawa Iemitsu in 1633. The **main hall,** a National Treasure, is perched ingeniously atop a cliff on a massive framework incorporating 139 colossal wooden

pillars. From the veranda jutting out over a steep valley, there is a famous view (see above) over the roofs of Kyoto and Yasaka pagoda. The **Otowa Waterfall (Otowa-no-Taki),** known for its purifying properties, drops down from below adjacent buildings on a second cliff; the faithful gather here to cleanse themselves, sometimes by immersion under the fall. (The not-so-faithful line up to pass their hands beneath the cataract.) As Kyoto's most celebrated site, Kiyomizu is also the most crowded. Visiting in the early morning or on weekdays during off-peak periods (autumn and winter, excluding New Year's) is highly recommended; in winter, the temple setting is particularly lovely—and empty— in the late afternoon. Despite its

From the foothills of Higashi-yama, visitors to Kiyomizu-dera Temple can take in the view across Kyoto.

Kiyomizu-dera Temple

- ⓜ 201 E2
- ✉ 1–294 Kiyomizu, Higashiyama-ku
- ☎ 075/551-1234
- 💲 $
- 🚌 City Bus: 206 to Kiyomizu-michi or Gojozaka

overwhelming array of souvenir stores, the charm of the approach to the temple (Kiyomizu-zaka), a steep cobbled lane lined with old wooden buildings, is irresistible.

Kodai-ji Temple lies 660 yards (600 m) northwest of Kiyomizu-dera. Built in 1605 in memory of the shogun Toyotomi Hideyoshi by his widow, it boasts five ornate original buildings in a superb state of preservation. The **Main Gate (Omotemon)** was brought from Hideyoshi's Fushimi Castle, as were the two teahouses standing in the garden in the compound, designed by 17th-century landscape architect Kobori Enshu. The elaborate **Founder's Hall (Kaisando)** is noted for its ceilings and panels, painted by masters of the Kano and Tosa schools. The **Otama-ya,** Hideyoshi's mortuary chapel, is beautifully enhanced with raised lacquerwork inlaid with gold.

Left: Visitors at Kiyomizu-dera Temple catch water from the sacred fall for luck, longevity, and simply because it is the thing to do.

Kodo—the way of incense

Incense, which supposedly displeases evil spirits, permeates the air wherever Buddhism prevails—the temple, home altar, or cemetery. Incense came to Japan with Buddhism via China and Korea in the sixth century. During the Heian era (794–1185), its religious and funereal connotations were complemented by its pleasures as a perfume. Presented to emperors and clerics, chunks of priceless incense wood feature among exhibits in temple treasure halls. Collecting varieties far too precious for the common nose, Heian aristocrats entertained themselves with *kokai* (incense parties). The object was to guess the provenance of an incense as it burned—a refined game played according to strict etiquette. The shogun Ashikaga Yoshimasa collected and named 130 different varieties of incense during the 13th century. Although the practice largely died out with the shoguns, there are still devotees of Kodo—the way of incense—today. ∎

Kodai-ji Temple

⬛   201 E2

✉   526 Shimokawara-cho, Kodaijishita, Higashiyama-ku

☎   075/561-9966

⑤ $$

🚍   City Bus: 206 to Higashiyama-Yasui

Sanjusangen-do Temple

(657 Mawari-cho, Sanjusangendo, Higashiymam-ku, tel 075/561-0467) was founded in 1132 and rebuilt in 1266 following a fire. Named for the number of spaces between the pillars of the hall (sanju-san means "33"), it is renowned for its thousand-plus statues of the Buddhist deity Kannon. These stand on either side of the most famous of all, a thousand-armed Kannon carved in 1254 by master sculptor Tankei. At the far end of the hall stand 28 statues of guardian deities; along with the centerpiece by Tankei, these are designated National Treasures.

Sanjusangen-do is 220 yards (200 m) southwest of the Higashiyama-shichijo bus stop. Opposite it is the **Kyoto**

National Museum (Kyoto Kokuritsu Hakubutsukan),

which occupies two buildings. Kyoto's finest museum was built by the Imperial Household Agency in 1879 as a repository for the emperor's own collection of artworks and historical relics, and was later passed on to the city. There are about 2,000 exhibits in 17 rooms divided into sections: historical, fine arts, and handicrafts.

The fine arts section contains more than 230 items designated Important Cultural Properties or National Treasures. The exhibits from the permanent collection are changed regularly and displayed in one building, and special exhibitions are staged throughout the year in the original hall. ■

Statues of the Boddhisatva Kannon at Sanjusangen-do

Kyoto National Museum

🔺 201 D2

✉ 527 Chaya-machi, Higashiyama-ku

☎ 075/541-1151

🕐 Closed Mon.

💲 $

🚃 Subway: Keihan Shichijo
City Bus: 206, 208 to Hakabutsukan-Sanjusangendo-mae

Higashiyama walk

This walk takes in several of Kyoto's best-known sights; allow extra time if you plan to visit any of the places on the way. It will probably take a full day to follow the route and stop off for sightseeing and refreshments. If you are in a hurry, be sure not to miss Kiyomizu-dera and Chion-in Temples.

From Gojozaka bus stop, walk up Gojo-zaka slope, veering right for 550 yards (500 m) up to **Kiyomizu-dera Temple ❶**, Kyoto's most famous landmark (see p. 213). The temple buildings were erected in 1633; perched on pillars on top of a cliff, the main hall is designated a National Treasure. Having admired the view from up here, particularly beautiful in the cherry blossom season, wander down the narrow lane called **Kiyomizu-zaka.** The number of craft and souvenir stores here is overwhelming; 19th-century Western visitors did not dub the street "Tea-pot Alley" for nothing. At the bottom turn to your right down Sannen-zaka and on to Ninnen-zaka slope.

To your left is the five-story, 128-foot-high (39 m) **Yasaka-jinja Pagoda ❷,** built by the shogun Yoshinori Ashikaga in 1440. Follow the street on your right (passing Ryozen Kannon Temple, notable for a colossal statue of the Buddhist deity, Kannon, 80 feet/24 m high) to **Kodai-ji Temple ❸** (see p. 214), which dates from 1606. The grounds include an elegant garden, and the screens inside the buildings are decorated with fine paintings. Proceed north 650 yards (600 m), then cross through **Maruyama-koen Park,** a Kyoto favorite containing several landscaped gardens. At the northern end visit magnificent **Chion-in Temple ❹** (see p. 218), with its fine 17th-century buildings on a colossal scale. ■

Pontocho
Kaburenjo
Theater

Kamo-gawa

MARUYAMA-
KOEN
PARK

Gion

**Yasaka-jinja
Shrine** ⑥

SHIJO-DORI
Minamiza
Theater

GION

Gion
Corner

Gion Kobu
Kaburenjo
Theater

HIGASHIOJI-DORI

② **Yasaka
Pagoda**

KIYOMIZU-ZAKA

GOJO-ZAKA

GOJO-DORI   Gojozaka

START

⑤ **Shoren-in
Temple**

AWATAGUCHI

**Chion-in
Temple** ④

0   500 meters
0   500 yards

YAMASHINA-KU

③ **Kodai-ji
Temple**

**Ryozen Kannon
Temple**

NINEN-
ZAKA

SANNEN-
ZAKA

HIGASHIYAMA-KU

**Kiyomizu-dera
Temple** ①

SEIKANJI

From here walk 220 yards (200 m) north to
Shoren-in Temple ⑤ (see p. 219), noted
for its excellent 17th-century paintings inside
and for its landscape garden, one of Kyoto's
most famous. Retrace your steps as you leave,
and walk 550 yards (500 m) down to **Yasaka-
jinja Shrine** ⑥, the shrine favored by the
residents of Gion and known locally as Gion-
san. From here you can go on to explore Gion (see p. 218) itself, or call it a day at the
Gion bus stop, which is opposite the *torii* gateway in front of the main entrance to Yasaka. ∎

A lane leading to Kyomizu-dera Temple

▲ See area map page 200–201
► Gojozaka bus stop
↔ I mile (1.5 km)
⊕ 3–4 hours
► Gion bus stop

NOT TO BE MISSED

- Kiyomizu-dera Temple
- Kodai-ji Temple
- Maruyama-koen Park
- Chion-in Temple
- Shoren-in Temple

Chion-in Temple
- 🅰 201 E3
- ✉ 400 Rinka-cho, Higashiyama-ku
- ☎ 075/531-2111
- 💲 $
- 🚌 City Bus: 12, 46, 203, or 206 to Chionin-mae

Girls don traditional summer finery during the Gion Matsuri—one of Japan's greatest festivals, held each July.

GION

Crossing the bridge eastward over the Kamo-gawa River toward Higashiyama will find you in Gion, Kyoto's old entertainment and geisha district. Although the onslaught of concrete and neon, discos, cabarets, pachinko parlors, and traffic has changed its face irrevocably, particularly during the past 20 years, old *chaya* (teahouses), *machiya* (assignation houses), and venerable *ryokan* (inns) and restaurants still exist here and there, concentrated mainly along Hanami-koji.

Hanami means "flower watching," the blossoms in question being the geisha, the central characters in the realm popularly known as *kairyukai*—the "world of flowers and willows." With its ancient wooden facades and flickering lanterns, Gion—to an even greater degree than Pontocho (see p. 208) —is one of the last places to glimpse *maiko* apprentices and full-fledged geisha on their way to

assignments in the evening. Since entry into the kairyukai depends upon both substantial wealth and introduction, the streets of Gion are about as close as most people come to encountering geisha. You'll get a general idea of geisha dancing skills at **Gion Corner,** a small theater offering an eclectic, touristy digest of Japanalia from *bunraku* puppet drama excerpts to the tea ceremony. A more authentic alternative is in the adjoining **Gion Kobu Kaburenjo Theater,** where maiko have traditionally presented glittering Miayko Odori (cherry dance) spectaculars each April for almost 150 years. Standing to the left of Shijo Bridge and on the western edge of Gion, the **Minamiza Theater** is Japan's oldest Kabuki theater; check the city information office for schedules. In particular, the performances staged during December feature some of the country's most famous Kabuki actors.

To the east of Gion is **Yasaka-jinja Shrine,** the main shrine of the Gion Matsuri held in July— Kyoto's greatest Shinto festival. Beyond it lies **Maruyama-koen Park,** a popular public park with a number of landscaped gardens and ponds, as well as food stalls and restaurants.

At the northeastern end of Maruyama-koen is **Chion-in Temple,** one of the largest temples in the country. It is the headquarters of the Jodo school. Founded by the priest Honen in the 1170s, it remains one of Japan's most important Buddhist sects. The original structures, erected in 1234, were lost through fires and war; the current buildings, dating from the 1630s, are rarely rivaled for size and opulence. The temple compound comprises Japan's largest temple gate, the giant two-story **sanmon** in front of the main entrance, standing 79 feet (24 m) tall, and its largest **temple bell.** Devoid of clappers, Japanese temple bells are rung by pushing a suspended beam that strikes the outside. Cast in 1633 and weighing 81.5 tons (74 tonnes), Chion-in's bell traditionally requires 17 monks to handle the beam during Honen's annual memorial service (April 17) and to ring in the New Year. The **Main Hall (Hondo)** accommodates a resplendent golden altar; a statue of Honen, reputedly self-carved, is enshrined in an impressive annex behind the hall. Connected to the main hall via a corridor with a "nightingale" floor—the boards squeak when walked upon—the **Abbot's Residence (Daihojo)** contains fine screen paintings by major exponents of the Kano school. The garden outside was designed by the master 17th-century landscape architect Kobori Enshu. Southeast of the Hondo the **Scripture House (Kyozo),** built in 1616, is noted for a collec-

tion of sutras written in China during the Sung dynasty. On a hill to the northeast of the Hondo is Honen's tomb and the ornate **Chinese gate (karamon)** built in 1633. The temple complex is near the Shionin-mae bus stop, or a ten-minute walk southeast of the Higashiyama-sanjo subway station.

Five minutes' walk north of Chion-in is **Shoren-in.** Until the Meiji Restoration of 1868, the abbot here was customarily the high priest of the Tendai sect, a post held by imperial princes. Set in a grove of large camphor trees, the current buildings date from 1895, but the main hall contains superb sliding screens painted by, among others, Kano Motonobu (1476–1559) and Tosa Mitsunobu (1480–1522). The temple compound possesses one of the finest gardens in Kyoto; it was designed by the great landscape architect Soami (d. 1525) and completed by Kobori Enshu in the 17th century. ■

Minamiza Theater is a Kyoto landmark. Some of Japan's most revered Kabuki actors appear here each December.

Shoren-in

🅼 201 E3

✉ 69–1 Sanjobo-cho, Awataguchi, Higashiyama-ku

☎ 075/561-2345

💲 $

🚇 Subway: Higashiyama City Bus: Jingumichi

Japanese gardens

Gardening, according to a recent government poll, is the seventh most popular leisure activity in Japan; there are 36 million keen gardeners in this densely populated country with little space. Lack of a backyard is no deterrent: The sills and facades of small suburban homes are festooned with pots, while bonsai cultivators tend dwarf trees high on the balconies of urban apartment buildings.

The average garden is small; neither crammed with variegated blooms nor geometrically arranged in lawns and beds, its function is contemplative. Rather than transforming nature, it strives to imitate it and shuns symmetry. The garden path uses stones of irregular shape instead of aligned bricks or flagstones; paths may consist of stepping stones, even over dry land. Fine rocks are considered as important as plants and command high prices. The most important criteria are color and shape. Rocks may be chosen to suggest, for instance, mountains, boats, or animals, especially turtles.

Early gardens

Gardening came to Japan in the sixth century with Chinese culture and Buddhism. Long lost in China, a few early prototypes survive in Japan, where the Japanese used them to develop gardening concepts of their own. Gardens are described in the tenth-century *Tale of Genji* and had become common by then among the clergy and aristocracy—the biggest being stroll gardens laid out around large ponds. A garden abandoned during the 12th century was recently unearthed during archaeological excavations at Motsu-ji Temple in Hiraizumi, Tohoku, and has now been restored; it included an artificial lake, man-made rock formations, and an artificial watercourse. Typically landscaped to represent the Buddhist universe, the ponds and rocks were arranged to evoke oceans and islands.

The garden in Kyoto's Daikaku-ji Temple retains the 215,000-square-foot (20,000 sq m) pond called Osawa-no-Ike, originally designed by the ninth-century emperor Saga. It also once had a dry waterfall, perhaps pioneering the common use of smaller stones that, often striated, are placed in rows to subtly mimic the flow of bodies of water.

Gardening manuals appeared during the 13th century but became more common in the 15th, when gardening trends diversified and spread through the influences of Zen Buddhism and the tea ceremony. Zen introduced a minimalist approach to temple gardens, sometimes landscaping them with expanses of raked sand and rocks alone (as in Ryoan-ji Temple in Kyoto). Exalting naturalism, tea masters favored lush, wooded glades floored with moss and stepping stones to harmonize with the teahouse, as well as the sight and sound of flowing water.

Gardening for all

During the Edo period (1603–1868) commoners took up gardening; most current concepts emerged from practices and manuals proliferating at the time. There are three main styles: *tsukiyama* (artificial mountain or landscape garden), *karesansui* (dry landscape in which watercourses are suggested by using stones), and *chaniwa* (a garden surrounding a teahouse). Gardens may combine them, but strict conventions dictate the positioning of the different kinds of appropriate stone lanterns *(toro)*, bamboo fences, and bridges of wood or stone. Sometimes incorporating all three styles in miniature, *tsuboniwa*—gardens in domestic courtyards—can be exquisite gems showcasing gardening as a master craft. Gardens require careful planning: How will the shadows of the rocks fall? How striking will the elements look from different angles? Consider the climate: With their rocks shining

Left: A dry stone garden with raked gravel and rocks suggesting islands and the sea
Above: Pines are covered in fall to protect them from winter snow at Kenroku-en Garden in Kanazawa.
Below: The grounds of Saiho-ji are revered as Kyoto's most beautiful landscape garden.

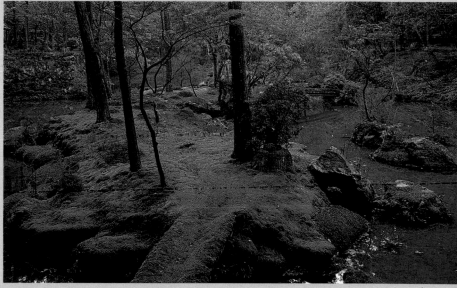

against the intense greens of damp moss and foliage, some gardens look best in the rain.

Although the Japanese appreciate thousands of varieties of flower, some are reserved for ikebana arrangements, while others—potted plants such as chrysanthemums and morning glories—are used exclusively for seasonal displays. The traditional garden excludes all but a few indigenous species: iris, lotus, and flowering shrubs such as camellia, azalea, hydrandgea, and tree peony—an early arrival from China in the sixth century. Large gardens are often wooded, with trees such as cherry and plum, and even tiny ones display pines, maples, and bamboo. Trees and shrubs may be cut, trimmed, twisted, and dwarfed into any traditionally accepted shape—but forget about roses and lawns. ■

Western Kyoto

THOUGH WESTERN KYOTO IS MAINLY RESIDENTIAL, WITH
fewer sights than in the east, some are worth a visit. There are not
always convenient subway stations for the sights, but the visitor information center can supply details of bus routes.

Lying in 27 acres (11 hectares) of
grounds, **Daitoku-ji Temple** is
440 yards (400 m) northwest of
Daitokuji-mae bus stop, or the
same distance northeast of
Funaoka-koen-mae bus stop.
Daitoku-ji is important to the
Rinzai sect of Zen. It was founded
in 1324, but the original buildings
were destroyed during the Onin
War (1467–1477). They were
replaced in 1479, with further additions during the 16th and 17th centuries in accordance with the
practice of moving buildings from
one location to another.

Presented to the temple by the
empress Meisho, the **Imperial
Messengers' Gate (Chokushi-
mon)** was moved here from the
Imperial Palace in 1640; the
Chinese gate (karamon), featuring carvings by the great sculptor Hidari Jingoro, came from the
shogun Toyotomi Hideyoshi's
Fushimi castle. The building of the
sanmon gate was undertaken by
the great tea master Sen-no-Rikyu
(see p. 225) in 1589; the inclusion
of a statue of himself atop it is often
seen as the act of *lèse-majesté* that
prompted Hideyoshi to condemn
him to death. The interior of the
gate has a ceiling and panels painted by Hasegawa Tohaku (1539–
1610). The paintings on the sliding
screens in the **Abbot's Residence (Hojo)** are by Kano Tan'yu
(1602–1674), grandson of the
founder of the Kano school. The
garden outside the Hojo is by
the celebrated landscape architect
Kobori Enshu. The Juko-in holding
Sen-no-Rikyu's tomb lies to the
west of the garden. Once the hermitage of the abbot Ikkyu Soun, the
Shinju-an contains fine screens
painted in the 15th century.

Daitoku-ji's main complex is
surrounded by 23 subtemples,

Daitoku-ji Temple
- ⬛ 201 C5
- ✉ Daitokuji-cho,
  Murasakino, Kita-ku
- ☎ 075/491-0019
- 🕐 Check opening times
  locally. Daitoku-ji is
  partially closed for
  renovation work.
  Several subtemples
  are open all year.
- 💲 $
- 🚌 City Bus: 205 &
  206 to Daitokuji-
  mae

**Painted screen
doors by Kano
school master
Motonobu
(1476–1559) at
Daisen-in
subtemple**

among them **Daisen-in** (northwest of the main hall), featuring screen doors painted by the master Kano Motonobu. The garden is considered to be a masterpiece of the landscape architect Soami. Comprising a teahouse, the garden at **Koto-in** (on the southwestern edge of the complex) is particularly popular when the maples turn red in autumn. Other subtemples with fine gardens are **Hoshun-in** (north of the compound) and **Ryugen-in,** a National Treasure south of the main compound that has five. To the west of the precinct, the **Koho-an** contains seven tea rooms designed by Kobori Enshu, who also designed the garden.

About 1.5 mile (2 km) west of Daitoku-ji, along Kitaoji-dori, is **Kinkaku-ji Temple** (Golden Pavilion). Few sights are more beautiful than Kinkaku-ji mirrored in the pond in front of it, especially when the surrounding trees don their autumn colors. As one of the most famous locations in Japan, it receives crowds by the busload on holiday weekends.

The shogun Ashikaga Yoshimitsu (1358–1408) acquired a nobleman's house and transformed it magnificently into the crowning glory, his retirement villa, the Golden Pavilion (1397). According to his wishes, the villa was converted into a temple after his death. The Golden Pavilion survived the Onin War, but was burned down in an arson attack by a deranged monk in 1950, an incident fictionalized by Yukio Mishima in his famous novel *Kinkakuji*. Erected in 1955, the current structure is said to be an exact copy, although detractors (not without reason) claim that the gold-leaf coating is brighter and more extensive than it was in the original, especially since further restoration during the 1990s.

Ryoan-ji Temple (Peaceful Dragon Temple), 0.5 mile (1 km) southwest of the Golden Pavilion, is an important temple of the Rinzai sect of Zen. Founded in 1473, it is world famous for the stone garden popularly attributed to Soami. The garden, a walled rectangle about the size of a tennis court, is viewed

Though sadly only a copy, the Golden Pavilion at Kinkaku-ji Temple is revered as one of the most famous landmarks in the country.

Kinkaku-ji Temple

🅰 200 B5

✉ 1 Kinkakuji-cho, Kita-ku

☎ 075/461-0013

💲 $

🚌 City Bus: Kinkakujimae or Kinkakujimichi

Ryoan-ji Temple

🅰 201 A5

✉ 13 Goryonoshita-cho, Ryoanji, Ukyo-ku

☎ 075/463-2216

💲 $

🚌 City Bus: 59 from Sanjo-Keihan-mae to Ryoanji-mae

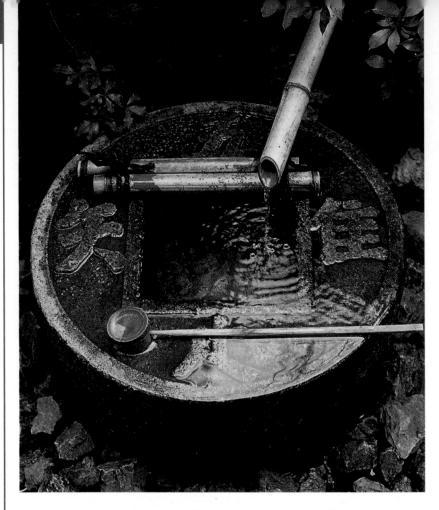

The font at the back of Ryoan-ji Temple provides water for tea ceremonies.

from the veranda of the temple building. It consists of 15 rocks of various sizes standing in a sea of raked white gravel. Minimalism was never as refined as in Japan 500 years ago; thought to represent islands standing in an ocean, the work portends the dawn of modern conceptual art and was devised to induce contemplation. Your meditations can be seriously jeopardized by the volume of both loudspeakers and visiting hordes; this is a temple best approached on weekday mornings during the off-season. The rock garden's fame often eclipses the beauty of the building itself, not to mention the spacious surround-

ing garden with a lovely pond and leafy arbors resplendent in autumn. In the precinct there is also a fine restaurant (itself like an old tea-house in a beautiful garden of its own) specializing in tofu cuisine.

Ninna-ji Temple is ten minutes on foot southwest from Ryoan-ji. Buses stop just outside. Two years after Ninna-ji was founded by his predecessor, the emperor Uda completed it in 888. Initially a residence for retired emperors and known as the Omuro Palace, it now serves as the headquarters of the Omuro chapter of the Shingon sect of Buddhism, as well as of the internationally renowned Omuro

School of Flower Arrangement.

Along with the imposing main gate, the oldest buildings go back to the early 17th century. Among them are two halls, the **Miei-do** and the magnificent main **Kondo,** both brought from the old Kyoto Imperial Palace. The Kondo and the statue of the Buddha Amida Nyorai it contains are National Treasures. North of the precinct is a fine **pagoda** 108 feet (33 m) high, erected by the shogun Tokugawa Iemitsu in 1637. A UNESCO World Cultural Heritage site, Ninna-ji is unusual for possessing a **palace (Goten)** in the precinct (to the west), with a lovely garden. Several of the buildings are exquisitely decorated inside. Lost in a fire in 1887, some were replaced during the 1900s, notably the **Shinden, Kuroshoin,** and **Shiroshoin,** connected by open-sided wooden cloisters framing gardens of rocks, pines, gravel, and meandering watercourses. Open twice a year (*Apr.–May; Oct.–Nov.*), the **Reiho-kan Treasure House** has a wonderful collection of sculptures, paintings, and ceramics. Toward the center of the elegantly landscaped precinct is a celebrated grove of dwarf cherries—a species unique to the region. Splendid in blossom, they attract large crowds in spring.

Myoshin-ji Temple is 15 minutes' walk southeast of Ninna-ji, or you can catch a bus from Ninna-ji's southern gate. Founded in 1337, this Rinzai Zen temple precinct contains many original buildings. Of the 40 subtemples, only four are open to the public. Among the subordinate temples, **Reiun-in** contains so many screens painted by Kano Motonobu that it is sometimes called the Motonobu temple. **Tenkyu-in** has paintings by Sanraku (1559–1635), a pupil of Eitoku, and **Kaifuku-in** showcases screen doors decorated with Tanyu's caricatures. **Taizo-in** has a renowned 15th-century Zen garden. The grounds between the subtemples provide an impressive setting for a stroll. The **Butsuden hall** contains a statue of the Shakyamuni Buddha; a painting of a dragon by Kano Tan'yu (see p. 222) adorns the ceiling of the **Hatto lecture hall** adjacent to the main hall. A National Treasure, the **bell** hanging in Myoshin-ji's belfry was cast during the seventh century. ■

Ninna-ji Temple

- 200 A4
- ✉ 33 Ouchi, Omura, Ukyo-ku
- ☎ 075/461-1155
- $ $; entrance to Reihokan and Goten $$
- 🚌 City Bus: 10 & 26 to Omura-Ninnaji Train: Keifuku Railway, Omura Station

Myoshin-ji Temple

- 200 A4
- ✉ 1 Miyoshinji-cho, Hanazono, Ukyo-ku
- ☎ 075/462-5226
- $ Separate fees for main hall and various temples; generally $
- 🚌 City Bus & Kyoto Bus: Myoshinji-mae Train: Keifuku Railway, Myoshinji Station

Sen-no-Rikyu (1522–1591)

The tea ceremony was developed during the 16th century as an arcane art form by tea masters, notably Sen-no-Rikyu. Spurning ostentatiousness to seek refinement in simplicity, Rikyu became the highest arbiter of Japanese aesthetics.

Courted as such by the shogun Toyotomi Hideyoshi, whose tastes were nothing if not ostentatious, Rikyu walked on thin ice. Inevitably he fell from the jealous shogun's favor, and in 1591 Hideyoshi forced Rikyu to commit *seppuku* (suicide).

The reasons remain unknown. Some conjecture that he was accused of plotting to poison Hideyoshi during a tea ceremony; others have it that Rikyu had slighted the ruler by placing a statue of himself on top of the sanmon gate at Daitoku-ji Temple—it was unthinkable for a shogun to pass beneath the effigy of a vassal. A more plausible explanation is that Hideyoshi had taken a fancy to Rikyu's daughter; when the tyrant demanded her for his harem, the tea master refused. ■

Buddhism

Of the 300 million Buddhists worldwide today, about a third are Japanese. That the function of Buddhism in modern Japan is mainly funereal may seem grim, but death is only the gateway to rebirth; the midsummer Buddhist O-bon festival of the dead involves much merrymaking. At other times many thousands of Japanese join in prayers, ceremonies, and retreats from the stress of day-to-day living in peaceful Buddhist temples.

Buddhism has been vital in shaping Japan. As in Europe at the end of the Dark Ages, monks held the keys to knowledge. Initially Korean and Chinese, they imparted numeracy and literacy, built temples, roads, and cities, and were responsible for laying the foundations of culture, the arts, government, and law.

The philosophy

Buddhism is based upon the discourses of the philosopher Siddhartha Gautama (circa 563–483 B.C.), also known as Sakyamuni, born in what is now southern Nepal. Posthumously known as the Buddha (Enlightened One), his verbal teachings were written down later by his disciples. According to Buddhism, all life is suffering. The cause resides in attachment, desire, and ignorance; the remedy lies in abstinence, righteousness, learning, and meditation—steps along the path to the goal of enlightenment. Then there is karma, the concept whereby your conduct in this life determines the quality of your reincarnation in the next. After death, those who have attained enlightenment break the karmic cycle of suffering and rebirth by entering nirvana, a blissful state of higher consciousness.

There are two main Buddhist doctrines: the original Theravada, practiced today mainly in Sri Lanka and Southeast Asia, and the later Mahayana, or the Great Vehicle, which, after spreading to Tibet and China, was adopted in Mongolia, Korea, and Japan. Mahayana Buddhism teaches that exceptionally enlightened saints become bodhisattvas (*bosatsu* in Japanese)—deified incarnations of aspects of the Buddha-nature. The next step up is Buddhahood, or *Nyorai* in Japanese.

Buddhism in Japan

Mahayana Buddhism, brought by Korean emissaries in either 538 or 552, was decreed the state religion in Japan by Prince Shotoku in 593. The religion progressed substantially during the mid-eighth century under Emperor Shomu, who established temples and monasteries throughout his realm. At first Buddhism appealed only to the ruling class, until the monk Saicho (767–822) founded the Tendai sect. By incorporating Shinto deities into its doctrine, it gained such a popular following that it became the state religion. The monk Kukai (774–835) studied Buddhism in China at about the same time as Saicho and returned to Japan to found the Shingon sect, which advocated esoteric (that is, with complex underlying philosophy) Buddhism. Shingon's influence had overtaken that of Tendai by the end of the Heian era. Today it counts some 12 million followers.

The Jodo and Jodo Shinshu schools, created by Honen (1133–1212) and his disciple

Shinran (1173–1262) respectively, worship the Amida (Pure Land) Buddha and believe that salvation resides in repeatedly chanting *"Namu Amida Butsu"* ("Glory to Amida Buddha"). Both sects have a membership of millions; the Shinshu branch has the largest following of all Japanese sects. The priest Nichiren (1222–1282) based the sect he founded (Nichiren-sho) upon chanting *"Namu-myoho-renge-kyo,"* believed to be the quintessence of the Lotus Sutra. Although his aggressive zeal earned him the displeasure of the shogun and a four-year exile to Sado-ga-shima (see p. 193), his Nichiren-shu school has a colossal following today. Its many sub-sects include the modern Soka Gakkai. With millions of devotees worldwide, it exerts considerable influence on Japanese politics through Komeito—the "clean government party."

Zen (*Ch'an* in Chinese, from the Sanskrit *dhyana*, or meditation), founded in China by the Indian monk Boddhidarma in the sixth century, was introduced in Japan by the

First introduced 14 centuries ago, Buddhism has played a decisive role in defining the culture, aesthetics, and general outlook of Japan.

Japanese monks Eisai (1141–1215) and Dogen (1200–1253), respectively the founders of the Rinzai and Soto sects, which both have a wide following. Devoid of doctrine or scriptures, Zen is imparted verbally from master to disciple and holds that enlightenment is attainable only through meditation *(zazen)*. Focusing on austere self-discipline, frugality, and hard work, Zen also bestowed spiritual concepts upon the martial arts, making it especially appealing to the samurai. Through samurai adherence and patronage, Zen reached its apogee from the 15th through 17th centuries. It brought innovations to calligraphy, poetry, and painting, introduced the tea ceremony, and virtually reinvented flower arrangement as an art in itself. Zen's influence is still much in evidence in Japan today. ■

Outlying Kyoto

ALTHOUGH EASTERN KYOTO PRESERVES MORE OF THE
worldly aspects of the former city, the peaceful west is felt to reflect
Kyoto's aesthetic and spiritual heart. Even the emperors and aristocrats in ancient times liked to get away from the urban bustle, and
when they did, their favorite escape lay in Arashiyama (Storm
Mountain). Today this hilly western edge of the city is both a popular area for strolling and a choice site for luxurious suburban homes.

Koryu-ji Temple

 200 A3

✉ 32 Hachigaoka-cho,
Uzumasa, Ukyo-ku

☎ 075/861-1461

$ $$

🚍 City Bus: 11 to
Uzumasa-Koryuji-
mae
Kyoto Bus: 72, 73,
or 74 to Uzumasa-
Koryuji-mae

Before you reach Arashiyama itself,
stop at Uzumasa Station on the
Keifuku Arashiyama line. Across
the road is **Koryu-ji Temple** (also
called Uzumasa-dera). Founded to
commemorate Prince Shotoku's
death in 622 and belonging to the
Shingon sect, this is one of Japan's
oldest temples. Though none of the
seminal structures remain, the
lecture hall, built in 1165 and
housing a noted statue of the
Buddha Nyorai (an incarnation of
the Buddha), is Kyoto's second oldest building. Erected in 1720, the
Taishi-den behind contains a
statue of Prince Shotoku, believed
to have been carved by himself;
there is another in the octagonal

Keigu-in (or Hakkakudo—Eight-
Sided Hall) to the northwest of the
precinct—built in 1251 and designated a National Treasure. Behind
the Taishi-do is the **treasure hall**
(Reiho-kan) containing more
priceless examples of early
Buddhist art, among them the celebrated **Miroku-Bosatsu**, attributed to Shotoku. Carved during the
Asuka period, this serene and magnificent statue of the Buddhist
Messiah, due to appear 5,000 years
after Buddha's attainment of nirvana, is not only the oldest in Kyoto
but officially listed as No. 1 among
all the National Treasures in Japan.

Just ten minutes' walk northeast
of Koryu-ji is **Toei Uzumasa**

Movie Land (Toei Uzumasa Eigamura), the samurai answer to a tour around Hollywood's Universal Studios. If you need a break from temples, this could be fun, especially if you are traveling with children.

As well as a theme park, this is the Toei movie company's main studio for shooting period dramas. To avoid getting in the way of film crews, tours are guided during shoots. Permanent sets include reconstructions of Edo's Yoshiwara pleasure quarter, old shops, inns, houses, samurai mansions, and a jail. With extras wandering the sets in period garb, the theme park aspect was enhanced with new attractions in 1997; you can even don period costume for pictures or videos to take home.

From Kyoto, the usual way to get to Arashiyama is by train to Saga Station on the JR San-in Honsen line, or you can take the Keifuku Arashiyama line to Arashiyama Station from Shijo-Omiya Station in central Kyoto. A scenic alternative is to take a train 13.5 miles (22 km) west from Kyoto to Kameoka, then return to Arashiyama by river through breathtaking gorges.

Arashiyama abounds in places renowned for springtime cherry blossoms and autumn displays of maple trees, especially northward to the renowned beauty spots Takao, Makino-o, and Togano-o. Although the region's popularity and its proximity to Osaka (only 20 minutes away) draw big crowds in peak periods, it is large enough to offer the weary traveler havens of solitude and quiet. A pleasant way to explore the area is to hire a bicycle from the center (*jitensha sentaa*) just northeast of Togetsukyo Bridge near Arashiyama station, but some paths are too steep and rocky to be navigated on wheels.

When you arrive at Arashiyama Station, walk 550 yards (500 m) northwest and you come to **Tenryu-ji Temple** (Heavenly Dragon Temple). The temple, belonging to the Rinzai Zen sect, was built in 1339 by the first Ashikaga shogun, Takauji, to commemorate the emperor Godaigo. Exiled by Takauji, Godaigo subsequently died. Hearing that his vengeful spirit had appeared to an important priest in the guise of a dragon, Takauji hastily built Tenryu-ji to appease it. All that remains of the original compound

Toei Uzumasa Movie Land

- 200 A4
- ✉ 10 Higashi-hachigaoka-cho, Uzumasa, Ukyo-ku
- ☎ 075/864-7716
- 🕐 Closed Dec. 21–Jan. 1
- 💲 $$$$
- 🚆 Train: JR Sagano line to Hanazono or Uzumasa Stations. Bus: 71, 72, 73 from Kyoto station to Uzumasa-Koryuji; 61, 62, 63 from Sanjo-Keihan to Hachigaokacho-Toei Uzumasa Eigamura

Tenryu-ji Temple

- ✉ 68 Susukinobaba-cho, Tenryuji, Saga, Ukyo-ku
- ☎ 075/881-1235
- 💲 $ (Main Hall $$)
- 🚆 Train: Keifuku Railway to Arashiyama Station

Prince Shotoku Taishi (574–622)

When Empress Suiko acceded to the throne in 593 in Asuka, Japan's first capital, power was assumed by Shotoku, the prince regent. One of Japanese history's most remarkable figures, Shotoku spurred great cultural and architectural advances through the constant ties he fostered with China. Based on Chinese concepts, the Seventeen Articles he devised amounted to Japan's earliest constitution. Government was centralized for the first time, and all people became imperial subjects—making their incomes taxable by local rulers only with the emperor's approval.

A great scholar and devout Buddhist, Shotoku sponsored the building of temples in the Asuka area, including Horyu-ji near Nara. Posthumously deified, Shotoku has since been shrouded in legends about an immaculate birth and a life abounding with miracles. In a more secular vein, the saint's portrait adorns the 10,000-yen note. ∎

Daikaku-ji Temple

☎ 4 Osawa-cho, Saga, Ukyo-ku

☎ 075/871-0071

💲 $

🚌 City Bus: 28, 92 to Daikaku-ji
Kyoto Bus: 61 (from Sanjo-Keihan-mae) or 71 (from Kyoto Station)

Saiho-ji Temple

🅰 231 A2

✉ 56 Kamigatani-cho, Matsuo, Nishikyo-ku,

☎ 075/391-3631

🕐 Send applications for tours at least six weeks prior to your scheduled visit. State name, address, nationality, and occupation, and enclose international postal coupon. If applying from Japan, apply at least one week prior to your visit.

💲 $$$$$ by donation

🚌 City Bus: 63 & 73 to Kokedera
Kyoto Bus: 29 to Kokedera-michi

is its splendid garden, designed by Muso Kokushi in 1340.

More Buddhist temples cluster on the west side of Arashiyama above Tenryu-ji, where the sylvan scenery is particularly pretty. From the north exit of Tenryu-ji, proceed along a narrow lane through a bamboo forest—it's considered Arashiyama's most beautiful. This takes you to **Okochi Sanso Villa.** Once the property of samurai movie star Okochi Denjiro, the villa itself is not the main attraction, but the views over Kyoto and Arashiyama from its lovely grounds and gardens are especially noteworthy.

Past a fishing pond due north from here is **Jojakko-ji Temple** at the top of a flight of weathered stone steps, with a fine view over the thatched gates. North of the precinct, a paved path slopes up through groves of maple and cherry trees to **Nison-in.** With buildings erected in 1521, the temple is most attractive when the trees are at their seasonal best. Temples farther northwest include **Gio-ji** and **Takiguchi-dera,** notable mainly for their setting in a thick bamboo grove, and forlorn **Adashino Nembutsu-ji,** erected in the 1870s. On the grounds of the latter temple are thousands of statuettes of the Buddha, commemorating the unknown dead who for centuries were flung into paupers' graves on this spot.

Between Gio-ji and Nison-in a road leads eastward (past Seiryo-ji) to **Daikaku-ji Temple,** built in the ninth century as a palace by Emperor Saga and later converted into a temple. The complex includes magnificent structures from the 16th century. The buildings and the cloisters connecting them display outstanding paintings by major exponents of the Kano school, including Motonobu, Eikoku, Sankaku, and Tanyu, as well as by Ogata Korin of the 18th-century Rimpa school. East of the precinct and designed by Emperor Saga as a boating pond, **Osawa-no-ike Pond** is surrounded by a beautiful tree-lined path, particularly popular when the cherry trees blossom and the maples turn red.

On the southern foothills of Arashiyama is **Saiho-ji Temple,** of the Rinzai sect of Zen, boasting one of Kyoto's oldest, loveliest, and greenest landscape gardens. Designed by the priest Muso Kokushi (1275–1331), the garden features islets of moss set in a pond surrounded by more moss—small

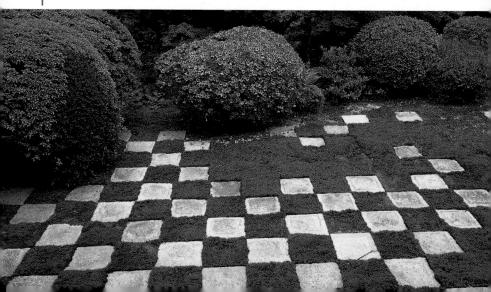

wonder that the temple is better known as Koke-dera (Moss Temple). Unfortunately the volume of visitors proved such a strain on the small precinct that monks were forced into drastic measures to curtail them. Permission to visit must be obtained in advance. Whether as a further deterrent or not, visitors are first treated to a compulsory hour-long lecture about the temple in Japanese, then prevailed upon for a hefty "donation" before leaving.

Generally considered to be a model combination of classical Japanese architecture and landscaping, **Katsura Imperial Villa (Katsura Rikyu)** complex was designed by Kobori Enshu and is widely regarded as the great landscape architect's masterpiece. The villa was commissioned by Toyotomi Hideyoshi for an imperial prince, with work starting in 1590; dying in 1598, Hideyoshi never saw it completed (1624). The screen doors in the main buildings are decorated with fine works of the Kano school of painting, but the overall design concept echoes the stark elegance applied to the teahouses on the grounds. The simplicity is deceptive, however. In the **Imperial Reception Hall**

(Miyukiden), the framework and fittings often employ rare and precious woods; even the *kugi-kakushi* (metal coverings concealing bolts in the structural beams) are decorated with flowers of silver and gold.

On the southeastern edge of Higashiyama, about a mile (2 km) south of Kyomizu-ji, is one of Kyoto's five foremost Zen temples, **Tofuku-ji Temple,** founded in 1236 and belonging to the Rinzai sect. Several of the 24 subtemples have gardens, the finest of which is at the Reiun-in. Built in the 1350s, the **sanmon gate** is notable not only for its imposing size, but also for the 11th-century Buddhist sculptures and early 15th-century paintings on the upper floor. Many of the temple's structures were lost in a fire in 1881 and rebuilt early in the 20th century. Surrounded by maple trees, the spacious grounds between the main hall and the founders' hall feature a stream crossed by an unusual bridge crowned with a tower. The garden behind the founders' hall is renowned for the checkerboard layout of moss and flagstones.

Fushimi Inari Taisha Shrine lies half a mile (1 km) due south of Tofuku-ji. There are about 40,000 Shinto shrines dedicated to

Katsura Imperial Villa

- 200 A1
- Misono, Katsura, Nishikyo-ku
- 075/381-2029
- Visits to the Katsura Rikyu are subject to prior permission from the Imperial Household Agency (see p. 205).
- City Bus: 33 from Kyoto Station to Katsura Rikyu-mae, 5 mins. from villa

Tofuku-ji Temple

- 201 D1
- 778 Hon-machi, 15-chome. Higashiyama-ku
- 075/561-0087
- $
- Train: JR & Keihan Railways, Tofukuji Station
  City Bus: 202 & 208

Fushimi Inari Taisha Shrine

- 231 B1
- 68 Yabunouchi-cho, Fukakusa, Fushimi-ku
- 075/641-7331
- Train: JR Nara line Kyoto Station to Inari on the Keihan line from Keihan-sanjo to Fushimi-Inari Station

Left: Checkerboard design at Tofuku-ji Temple garden

The 11th-century Amithaba trinity at the Sanzen-in Temple in Ohara, which also boasts a fine painted ceiling and particularly beautiful gardens

the deity Inari around the country, and this one, said to have been founded early in the eighth century, is the most important of all. Standing on Mount Inari, the precinct covers a substantial area and incorporates several other shrines dedicated to other deities. As you walk through the wooded hills on the upper reaches, you will pass under thousands of red *torii* gateways straddling the path, all

Daigo-ji Temple

🅰 231 C1

✉ Garan-cho, Daigo, Fushimi-ku

☎ 075/571-0002

🕐 Hoju-in treasure hall was closed for restoration until 2001 at the time of writing.

💲 Sanpo-in $$; Hoju-in $$

🚇 Subway: Tozai line to Daigo Station Bus: City Bus "Higashi-9" from Keihan-Sanjo station terminal stops at Daigo-Sanpoin-mae.

presented to the shrine by devotees; the same applies to the hundreds of stone statues of seated foxes scattered over the landscape. The fox is believed to be the messenger of Inari, a deity concerned with wealth and plentiful harvests. Over New Year hundreds of thousands of people pray here for success in their business enterprises. The shrine's own Sangyo-sai festival on April 8 is a grand affair when prayers are offered for Japan's industrial enterprises. The fox also has a reputation for bewitching people, so the superstitious avoid strolling around Inari shrines after sundown.

About 3 miles (5 km) southeast of Fushimi Inari Shrine is **Daigo-ji Temple** (Temple of Heavenly Milk). Approached via an avenue of cherry trees, this vast temple com-

pound covers much of Mount Daigo. Founded during the mid-ninth century and belonging to the Shingon sect, Daigo-ji is favored by followers of Shugendo, a stringent form of Buddhist asceticism. Comprising more than 70 buildings and subtemples, the precinct is divided into Shimo (Lower) Daigo and Kami (Upper) Daigo, with a steep path some 2 miles (3 km) long dividing them. Visiting both constitutes a pleasant (if substantial) hike taking up a whole afternoon. The structures of Kami Daigo, former Buddhist seminaries, were built between the 12th and 16th centuries. Most of the Shimo Daigo buildings were destroyed during the 15th-century Onin Wars; they were extensively restored and rebuilt by order of the shogun Toyotomi Hideyoshi in the 16th century. The notable exception is the five-story **pagoda,** erected in 951. It is not only the oldest building in Kyoto but the oldest of its kind in Japan. Rebuilt by Hideyoshi, the ornate **Sanpo-in** subtemple is noted for the Kano school paintings gracing its interior and the outstanding landscape garden outside. Nearby is the **Hoju-in treasure hall** (open Apr. 1–May 25 and Oct. 1–Nov. 25). It is renowned for its fabulous collection of scrolls, paintings, sculptures, and miniature shrines.

If you are on your way to Uji (see p. 234), stop off at **Manpuku-ji Temple.** Belonging to the esoteric Obaku branch of the Rinzai sect of Zen, the temple was founded by the priest Ingen in 1659. Ingen, being Chinese, had the entire temple built in the style of the Ming dynasty, which makes it unique in Japan.

In the far northeast of Kyoto, in the western foothills of Mount Hiei-zan, is **Shugaku-in Imperial Villa (Shugaku-in**

Manpuku-ji Temple

📧 Gokasho, Uji-shi

☎ 0774/32-3900

💲 $

🚆 Rail: from Kyoto on either JR Nara line or Keihan Uji line, stopping at Obaku Station (about 30 mins.), then 5-min. walk

Shugakuin Imperial Villa

 201 F6

📧 Yabuzoe, Shugakuin, Sakyo-ku

🕐 Reservations should be made to the Imperial Household Agency (see p. 205). Tours (in Japanese) are at 9, 10, & 11 a.m. and 1:30 and 3 p.m.

🚆 Bus: City Bus No. 5 to Shugakuin-rikyu-michi (about 1 hour), then 15-min. walk

Poets Hermitage

201 E5

📧 Monguchi-cho, Ichioji, Sakyo-ku

☎ 075/781-2954

💲 $

🚆 Bus: City Bus No. 5 from Kyoto station to Ichijoji-Sagarimatsu-cho, then 5-min. walk

Daigo-ji Temple's five-story pagoda is the oldest building in Kyoto.

Rikyu), built by the Tokugawa shogunate for former emperor Gomizuno-o in the early 17th century. The grounds are divided into three large gardens with *chaya* (tea-houses) in each. Like its southwestern counterpart, the Katsura Imperial Villa (see p. 231), this palace is a fine example of landscape architecture, with buildings beautifully complementing their surrounding ponds, pathways, and trees. The uppermost Kami-no-chaya garden contains the celebrated **Rin'un-tei teahouse,** with a fine view over the city and mountains beyond.

Poets Hermitage (Shisendo) is a ten-minute walk south of Shugakuin Rikyu. Ishikawa Jozan, a samurai turned scholar of Chinese classics, had this peaceful retreat built in 1641. The garden is one of Kyoto's most celebrated.

Unspoiled rural areas lie to the north of Kyoto. The valleys of Kurama and Kibune, for example, are favored mountain getaways for Kyotoites; **Kibune** is known for its quiet and scenic riverside *ryokan* (inn).

Surrounded by wooded hills at the foot of Hiei-zan, **Ohara** is a small town renowned for its scenery—especially for its autumnal landscapes and maple trees. The 16th-century **Sanzen-in Temple** here has an exceptionally beautiful garden, tenth-century main hall, and 16th-century buildings. Nearby

Shoren-in Temple, set in an extensive precinct, is noted for its thatched main building dating to 1013. Between the two is the garden temple of **Jikko-in,** reached by a steep flight of stone steps, where one can contemplate the delights of the setting while sipping green tea. The **Jakko-in** nunnery (see below) lies northwest of Ohara. ■

Jakko-in Temple

Jakko-in holds a special place in the hearts of the Japanese as the final haven of one of the country's greatest tragic heroines.

When the Minamoto clan finally defeated the Taira in 1185, the Taira survivors hurled themselves into the water to drown. Among them was the lady Kenreimon-in and her son, seven-year-old Emperor Antoku. To her chagrin, Kenreimon was saved. After renouncing the world, she retired as a nun to Jakko-in, where she spent the last 27 years of her life in melancholy contemplation. ■

Uji

THE TOWNSHIP OF UJI, ABOUT 9 MILES (15 KM) SOUTHEAST of the city center, was one of the first places in Japan to boast a tea plantation. It still enjoys a national reputation for the premium quality of its green tea. It is also known for its historical stone bridge and for cormorant fishing in the Uji-gawa River, which can be viewed by boat from mid-June through August. Above all, Uji is famous for the lovely Byodo-in Temple, one of the most celebrated sights in Japan.

Byodo-in Temple

 116 Uji Renge, Uji-shi

☎ 0774/21-2861

🕐 Treasure Hall is undergoing reconstruction. It will reopen in March 2001 (with separate admission charge).

💲 Byodo-in: $

🚆 Rail: Uji Station on JR Nara line or Uji Station on Keihan line; the Byodo-in is a 10-min. walk from both stations

Built as a villa by Fujiwara-no-Michinaga (966–1024), the most powerful prime minister of Heian times, the **Byodo-in Temple** (Phoenix Temple) was converted into a temple in 1052. The other palatial buildings were all lost to fire in 1336, but the **Phoenix Hall (Hoo-do),** built in 1053, still stands. It is fortunate that one of the only remaining buildings of the period should be this, which represents Heian's architectural zenith. Mirrored in the pond around it, the hall evokes a phoenix *(ho-o)* alighting; the buildings flanking the central body represent extended wings.

Inside, beneath an ornate, intricately carved canopy inlaid with mother-of-pearl, is a beautiful seated statue of the Amithaba Buddha. The surrounding walls are adorned with the 52 charming Cloud Bosatsu, delicate statuettes of Buddhist deities dancing, playing musical instruments, or holding ritual objects. Other walls are decorated with period murals, but the paintings on the doors are reproductions. The originals can be seen in the **Treasure Hall (Homutsukan),** as can the original statues of the male and female phoenixes on the roof, and the old temple bell.

Along the temple approach are several venerable tea merchants' shops that offer a chance to taste the subtleties of different grades of green tea. ■

Hiei-zan

HIEI-ZAN, ABOUT 5 MILES (8 KM) NORTHEAST OF KYOTO city center, has the area's most accessible skiing facilities, but it is special for the place it holds in the city's history. In the ninth century the priest Saicho founded the Tendai sect, an eclectic school of Buddhism that incorporated Shinto deities. Appealing to aristocrats and commoners alike, it became the state religion. According to ancient Chinese geomancy (divination based on geographical directions), the northeast is the most unlucky direction, so Hiei-zan was considered the ideal place for Saicho to build a temple complex to protect the city from evil influences.

Enryaku-ji Temple

✉ Sakamoto-hon-machi, Otsu-shi, Shiga-ken

☎ 0775/78-0001

🚌 Kyoto Bus: 51 or 57 from Kyoto Station
Keihan Bus: 56 from Keihan-sanjo

Enryaku-ji Temple, Saicho's focal temple, spread across the mountain into a temple city of more than 3,000 buildings. During Saicho's lifetime, even emperors studied Buddhism at Enryaku-ji. The monks were so many that they amounted to an army, which is literally what they became. By the 11th century some of these warrior monks were bandits, terrorizing citizens with sporadic raids on Kyoto. Remaining politically and militarily powerful for centuries, the monks were eventually deemed a threat by the shogun Oda Nobunaga, who routed them in 1581 and burned the buildings around Enryaku-ji to the ground. Partially restored by Toyotomi Hideyoshi, the great

monastery was also substantially enlarged during the 17th century.

Among notable buildings of the temple are the central Komponchu-do and Daiko-do (Great Lecture Hall) in the Toto (eastern precinct) and the Shaka-do (Shakyamuni Hall) and Sorinto pagoda in the Saito (western precinct). With its temples set in a forest of soaring cedars, the quieter western side seems the more deeply steeped in peace, piety, and the mystic ambience of Buddhism.

A scenic route to Hiei-zan is to go by Kyoto bus from Kyoto Station to Yase-Yuen. From here it is a short walk east to the station for the **Yase-Yuen cable car** up Mount Hiei-zan (10 minutes). ■

The main hall of Enryaku-ji Temple on Mount Hiei-zan, restored in the 16th century, is all that remains of a 10th-century temple city and stronghold for warrior monks.

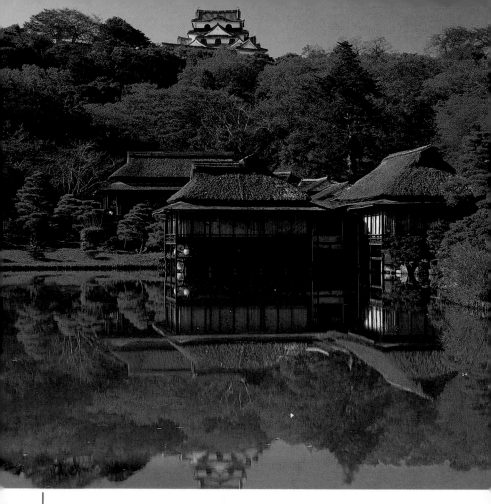

Hikone-jo Castle overlooks delightful gardens.

Biwa-ko & Hikone

BIWA-KO LAKE, IN SHIGA-KEN EAST OF KYOTO, IS NAMED for an ancient Japanese lute whose shape it resembles. At 260 square miles (674 sq km), it is Japan's largest and best known lake. Unfortunately, the scenery is no longer as it was celebrated in 19th-century woodblock prints; many places around the shore have been overdeveloped in terms of both urbanism and tourism.

Hikone

⚑ 199 C3

Visitor information

✉ JR Hikone Station.
40–7 Nanko,
Furusawa-cho

☎ 0749/22-2954

Nevertheless, the town of **Otsu** on the lake's southwestern tip offers sightseeing boat trips around the lake. It is also home to the noted temples of Onjo-ji, Enman-in, and the impressive eighth-century Ishiyama-dera, which preserves the small hall in which

Murasaki Shikibu wrote her monumental *Tale of Genji* more than a thousand years ago.

The other great attraction is **Hikone,** on the lake's eastern shore, famed for its 17th-century castle. The beautiful white main tower-keep still stands intact. ∎

Nara & beyond

Picturesque old shops and houses in Nara's southwest

NARA IS A SMALL TOWN; ITS UNHURRIED AMBIENCE SEEMS designed to avoid disturbing the long sleep of its illustrious ancestors. While Kyoto's grandeur emerges from a comparatively recent past, Nara and its environs contain buildings of such antiquity that their very survival is astonishing. Japanese civilization first appeared in the Nara Basin; ancient burial mounds of the Kofun period (see p. 28) are on view within the modern city confines.

In 710 Empress Gemmei founded the city of Heijo, intended as a permanent capital. About 1 mile (2 km) west of modern Nara, the city was modeled on China's mighty T'ang dynasty city of Chang'an, the cosmopolitan hub of the Silk Road and the most sophisticated metropolis of the ancient world. Profoundly affected by Chang'an, Nara was Japan's window on the world. Its temple treasures include ancient Chinese, Korean, Indian, and even Persian artworks, and experts still wrangle over the influences displayed by its art and architecture.

Though Nara gave its name to an era of great progress, it never realized the permanence to which it aspired. Emperor Kammu built Heian-kyo (Kyoto) in 794, after which Nara slumbered, despite remaining an important center for Buddhism. Natural disasters, fires, and redevelopment obliterated ancient Nara over the centuries, but some of its seventh- and eighth-century temples still stand.

Occupying the northeastern quarter of the city are the 1,235 acres (500 ha) of **Nara-koen Park,** roamed by approximately 1,500 tame deer. Japan's largest city park, it embraces some of Nara's greatest treasures, including the world's largest bronze sculpture (see p. 241).

Nara

▲ 199 C3

Visitor information

✉ Nara City Tourist Center, at intersection of Sanjo-dori and Yasuragi-no-michi

☎ 0742/22-3900

Struck with a stick, this fiercely fishy wooden clapper was once used to assemble the monks at Kofuku-ji Temple.

Kofuku-ji Temple
✉ 48 Noborioji-cho
☎ 0742/22-7755
💲 $
🚉 Train: Kintetsu Nara station, then 5-min. walk east

period. Moved to its present location when Nara became the capital in 710, it comprised 175 buildings at the zenith of the Heian period. As regional conflict increased after the 1150s with the decline of the Fujiwara dynasty, Kofuku-ji raised an army of warrior monks who supported the Minamoto clan engaged by the Fujiwara to protect them against the Taira clan. The warrior monks were defeated in 1180 by a Taira army, which set the temple buildings ablaze. Having vanquished the Taira and moved the capital to Kamakura, the shogun Minamoto Yoritomo set about restoring Kofuku-ji.

A disastrous fire destroyed most of the result in 1717, but the **Northern Octagonal Hall (Hokuen-do)** and **three-story pagoda** survive intact from the Kamakura period. The **five-story pagoda** and **Eastern Golden Hall (Tokon-do)** date from the early 15th century. Reflected in nearby **Sarusawa Pond (Sarusawa-no-ike),** the pagoda is one of Nara's most photographed sights. Various halls of Kofuku-ji

The rest of the city is unremarkable; there are picturesque older neighborhoods in Nara-machi to the southwest, but preservation outside religious contexts is not much of a priority. Though Nara is a small city, the volume of tourists is phenomenal. The major sights can be covered on a day trip from Kyoto. Nara has a good but limited array of accommodations. If you plan to stay, book ahead.

One of the main temples of the Hosso sect of esoteric Buddhism, **Kofuku-ji Temple** was founded in 669 by the wife of Fujiwara Kamatari, an ancestor of the family that ruled Kyoto during the Heian

The Nara deer

Schoolchildren feed greedy Nara deer.

Deer reached Japan before even the Japanese, having crossed continental land bridges during the Ice Age. Divine messen-

gers according to Shinto, they have roamed Nara for centuries. Over generations, the herd in Nara-koen, numbering some 1,500, has perfected the doe-eyed look that guarantees maximum handouts. Stalls trade briskly in deer-feed; *shika sembei* (deer crackers) are allegedly often munched by foreigners who mistake them for local delicacies.

Deer are greedy. They have been accused of overturning trash cans—and even small people. Males can be mildly dangerous during mating season. Whatever their reputation, the deer are mainly docile and delightful. ■

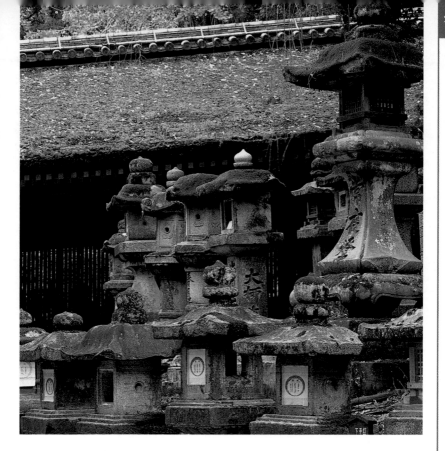

contain a number of outstanding early Buddhist sculptures, as does its **Treasure Hall (Kokuho-kan)** museum.

Nara National Museum (Kokuritsu Hakubutsukan) is 550 yards (500 m) east of Kofuku-ji Temple. Built in 1895, the **West Gallery** contains an impressive collection of Buddhist art, including sculptures, paintings, calligraphy, and decorative arts from the seventh century through the Kamakura and Edo periods. In 1973 the **East Gallery** was added, and this is devoted to archaeological artifacts unearthed in the Nara region. Museum exhibits change on a regular basis; some items in the West Gallery are so precious and fragile that they are exhibited only once a year. The same applies to the trea-

sures formerly kept in the Shoso-in Hall of Todai-ji. These include items of Chinese, Indian, and Persian origin or influence, reflecting Nara's ancient connections to the Silk Road.

Kasuga Taisha Shrine, founded by the erstwhile ruler Fujiwara-no-Michinaga (see p. 234) as a family shrine in 768, is on the southeastern edge of Nara-koen, less than a mile southeast of the National Museum. It comprises four main **Honden** halls—three dedicated to divine warriors and one to the deified ancestors of the Fujiwara line. Epitomizing the Chinese temple style in vogue between the seventh and tenth centuries, Kasuga is an architectural paradigm: Other shrines around Japan with pillars of vermilion

Crowned with moss, stone lanterns have adorned Kasuga Taisha Grand Shrine since the 11th century.

Nara National Museum

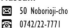 50 Noborioji-cho

☎ 0742/22-7771

🕐 Closed Mon. Special exhibitions in spring and fall

💲 $ (special exhibitions $$)

🚌 Bus: Kukuritsu Hakubutsukan

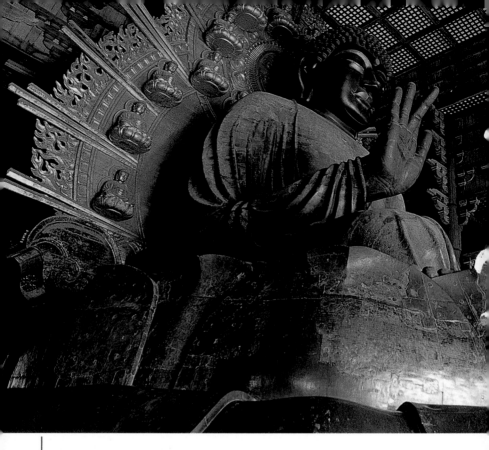

Cast 1,200 years ago, the 53-foot (16 m) Buddha at Todai-ji Temple is the world's largest bronze statue.

Kasuga Taisha Shrine

✉ 160 Kasugano-cho

☎ 0742/22-7788

🕐 Man'yo garden closed Mon.

💲 $

🚌 Bus: Kasuga Taisha-Omotesando stop, then a 650-yd. (600 m) walk east

wood and sweeping Chinese roofs are often described as being in the Kasuga style. Like most major Shinto shrines, the major buildings have been ritually demolished and identically rebuilt every 20 years. With the exception of the old **Oratory (Haiden)** and the **Function Hall (Naoraiden),** the rest of Kasuga was last reerected—for the 56th time—in 1893. The shrine approach, 875 yards (800 m) long, is bordered by some 2,000 **stone lanterns** donated by devotees since the 11th century. A thousand more, made of bronze, hang elegantly from the eaves of the buildings closer to the main precinct. Twice a year, during the Setsubun festival in early February and in August, the lighted lanterns present an enchanting spectacle

enhancing the hallowed atmosphere of the shrine.

A modern building next to the parking lot near the shrine's main entrance, the **Treasure House (Homutsuden)** houses a collection of historical shrine objects including Noh masks and the trappings of Shinto ritual, ceremonies, and festivals. To the left of the shrine approach, the **Man'yo Botanical Garden (Kasuga Taisha Shin-en)** boasts all 300 plant varieties mentioned in the *Man'yoshu,* a celebrated eighth-century anthology of thousands of poems.

Beyond the road flanking Nara Park to the south is **Shin Yakushi-ji Temple.** The temple was founded in 747 by Komyo, consort of Emperor Shomu, as a means

Todai-ji Temple, on the northwestern edge of Nara-koen Park, about 1 mile (2 km) northeast of Nara station, is famous for the mighty bronze Buddha, the Daibutsu. Emperor Shomu (701–758) built the temple (completed in 752) to accommodate a colossal bronze statue of the Vairocana Buddha (the Buddha of which all others are aspects) that he had commissioned. Having renounced the world and retired as a monk, Shomu emerged from seclusion to conduct the grand dedication ceremony for the statue in 749. Like Kofuku-ji Temple, Todai-ji was torched during the conflicts ending the Heian period in 1185.

The finely sculpted octagonal **bronze lantern** in front of the main hall is an eighth-century original. The massive **Great South Gate (Nandaimon)** before the entrance also dates from the eighth century, although it was substantially restored in the 12th century after collapsing in a typhoon. The fierce guardian deities standing in niches on either side—splendid wooden carvings 26 feet (8 m) tall—are attributed to Kamakura-period sculptor Unkei and his school.

Fires and natural disasters mean that most of the precinct's buildings are 16th- and 17th-century reproductions, notably the **Hall of the Great Buddha (Daibutsuden),** rebuilt for the last time in 1708. Although smaller than its predecessor,—it measures 187 feet (57 m) wide by 164 feet (50 m) deep and 157 feet (48 m) high—the hall is still one of the world's largest wooden structures; it had to be to house the **Daibutsu,** the biggest bronze statue in the world. Having been damaged in fires during its 1,200-year history and having lost its head twice during earthquakes, the Daibutsu was last restored in

of praying for the emperor's recovery from an eye infection threatening his sight. The only surviving original structure is the **Main Hall** (formerly the dining hall), renowned for the sculptures (all National Treasures) it contains. The main object of worship is the 14-foot (2.4 m) effigy of the seated **Yakushi Nyorai,** the healing Buddha, flanked by an 11-faced Kannon (Buddhist god of mercy) and the Juni-Shinsho (12 Divine Generals). These tall, exquisitely wrought clay statues of generals in full armor actually number 11: One went AWOL centuries ago. Other notable treasures in the compound are the gilt-bronze **Ko-Yakushi** Buddha and a rare Heian-period painting of Nirvana, the Buddhist paradise.

Todai-ji Temple
- ✉ 406–1 Zoshi-chi
- ☎ 0742/22-5511
- 💲 $
- 🚍 Bus: Daibutsuden

Shin Yakushi-ji Temple
- ✉ 1352 Takabatake, Fukui-cho
- ☎ 0742/22-3736
- 💲 $
- 🚍 Bus: Wariishi

1692. The seated colossus, weighing 550 tons and incorporating 290 pounds of gold, soars 53 feet (16 m) above its pedestal. Sheer scale tends to undermine the artistry its Korean designer intended, but the statue still induces a sense of awe. The main effigy is surrounded by statues of Kannon and two Heavenly Guardians, dating to the 17th and 18th centuries. A huge pillar to the right of the Daibutsu is thought to open the path of enlightenment to those able to crawl through the hole in the base—a privilege reserved for the slim.

East of the Daibutsuden, the **belfry** (12th century) contains a bell dating from 752; damaged during a typhoon, it was recast in 1239. **Nigatsu-do Hall** (Second Month

Hall), rebuilt in 1669, contains effigies of Kannon that only the elite clergy have ever seen. It is celebrated for its view over the city from the veranda, as well as for the Omizu-tori (Water Drawing) festival (March 1–14), whose grand torchlight processions attract thousands of spectators.

Sangatsu-do Hall (Third Month Hall) has stood since the eighth century and is Todai-ji's oldest structure. The marvelous period sculptures it contains are National Treasures, as are some other artworks and buildings in the precinct; they include a tall statue of Kannon attributed to Roben and 14 other major effigies. The two halls are both some 330 yards (300 m) east of the Daibutsuden. Other treasures, including those placed there quarters of the Ritsu school of Buddhism. The temple was built in 759 by the Chinese priest Ganjin (Chien Chen) at the invitation of the emperor Shomu. Opposition from Chinese bureaucrats, five shipwrecks, and bouts of illness that finally left him blind had delayed Ganjin's arrival for ten years. Entirely Chinese in design, Toshodai-ji's main buildings survive as paradigms of Nara-period architecture. Statues inside the **Main Hall (Kondo),** among them the focal Buddha Vairocana carved by Chinese sculptors, are National Treasures. Originally the assembly hall of the Nara court, the **Lecture Hall (Kodo)** was moved here when the temple was built. Although it retains revealing details about Nara-period palace architecture (not least, front pillars that curve slightly to alter their perspective), its overall form has been lost through repairs and alterations over the centuries. The **Founder's Hall (Miei-do)** contains a famous sculpted portrait of Ganjin; more fine works of Buddhist art are exhibited in the **Shin-Hozo Treasure House,** open twice annually *(late March–late May and mid-Sept.–early Nov.).*

Yakushi-ji Temple, less than a mile (800 m) south of Toshodai-ji, was founded in the seventh century. Once one of the Seven Great Temples of Nara, it is the headquarters of the Hosso sect. Yakush-ji's

(continued on p.247)

by Emperor Shomu himself, were once kept in the **Shoso-in,** north of the precinct. This long rectangular building on stilts still stands, but the treasures were moved to the Nara National Museum (see p. 239) in 1963.

BEYOND NARA

About 3 miles (5 km) west of Nara is **Toshodai-ji Temple,** head-

Toshodai-ji Temple

- ✉ 14–46 Gojo-cho
- ☎ 0742/33-7900
- 💲 $
- 🚉 Train: Kintetsu Railway to Nishinokyo Station
  Bus: Toshodaiji

Yakushi-ji Temple

- ✉ 457 Nishinokyo-cho
- ☎ 0742/33-6001
- 💲 $
- 🚉 Bus: 52, 97, or 98 from JR Nara Station or Kintetsu Nara Station to Yakushiji-Higaashiguchi

---

Hokki-ji Temple

Hokki-ji was founded in 638, allegedly according to Prince Shotoku's last wishes. The original stood at Okamoto, where the prince had a palace; moved here later, it is still sometimes known as Okamoto-dera Temple. Its greatest claim to fame is its fine three-story pagoda. Only slightly younger than the pagoda at Horyu-ji Temple but much less visited, it was built in 686 and is widely regarded as one of the finest examples of the architecture of the period. ■

Shinto

Being Shintoist is synonymous with being Japanese. Almost everyone is involved in Shinto rituals at some time: Newborn children are presented at the shrine, and most marriage ceremonies are Shinto.

The Way of the Gods

Meaning "the Way of the Gods," Shinto originated among the tribes of prehistory. It is rooted in an animist folk religion, worshiping *kami*—the gods once believed to inhabit all things under, and including, the sun. Out of many thousands of shrines, Ise-jingu in western Kansai (see p. 259) has been the most sacred for some 1,800 years. Whether inaugurating building sites or factories, or at the shrine itself, Shinto ceremonies suggest extreme antiquity. Waving leafy branches toward cardinal points to ward off evil spirits, the priest is assisted by *miko* (shrine maidens) whose stylized gyrations evoke the movements of a shaman in a trance.

Ancient Chinese influences gradually turned Shinto into an ancestor cult; it was believed that everyone, especially emperors, would become *kami* (spirit gods) after death. Different communities share the basic religion, but believe in variants; tiny hamlets boast a shrine for a protective god, and even homes contain a miniature *kamidana* (god shelf) for statues. With worshipers moved by awe and reverence rather than faith or piety, Shinto is devoid of doctrine or ethics. Its priesthood is a hereditary post serving the community by maintaining the shrine.

The shrine

A Shinto shrine is recognizable by the *torii* (gateway) at its entrance. Shrines are often decorated in red and white, the respective ritual colors of male and female. Being formless, the ancient gods go undepicted, but paired stone *komainu* (lion dogs) often stand at the entrance to guard the shrine against evil. Some shrines contain statues of animals considered divine messengers—especially the fox, the familiar (servant) of Inari, deity of the hearth and harvest. Other shrines embrace an effigy of a horse, an animal once revered for its utility; the small wooden plaques placed before it were called *ema* (horse pictures), a term now referring to votive plaques in general.

State Shinto

The name Shinto came into use only when the vague, heterogeneous beliefs were formalized in 1872 as the nationalistic state religion based on emperor worship. It was repudiated as a state religion after the war. State Shinto exalted the *Kojiki (Record of Ancient Matters)* and *Nihon Shoki (Chronicles of Japan)*. Completed in the early eighth century, both books begin with the Shinto creation myths and chronicle the reigns of emperors from 697 B.C. TO 660, the first 14 being mythical. Seen as politically expedient, the books served to reinforce an emperor's rule by establishing his divinity. Japan, its population, and the gods were all progeny of the female Izanami and the male Izanagi, parents also of the sun goddess Amaterasu, who was the mother of Emperor Jimmu—the first of an unbroken imperial line.

Beliefs and rituals

Many Shinto cults focus on volcanoes and mountains, and a few on phallic variants of human fertility. Above all Shinto is a farmer's religion, bound to crop cycles; the emperor's ritual duties still include the ceremonial planting and harvesting of rice on the palace grounds.

From convivial New Year bonfires in remote country shrines to spectacular annual *matsuri* (festivals) attended by hundreds of thousands, Shinto binds communities. Matsuri feature processions of ornate *mikoshi*

Opposite: Tying fortune paper to a branch for luck
Left: Purification with holy water during a Shinto ceremony
Above: Kyoto's 1,500-year-old Aoi Matsuri
Below: Safety first, Shinto style: A priest blesses a new car.

(palanquins or portable shrines). Some 70 million people visit shrines at New Year to pray for the guardianship of the gods, whose assistance is invoked for a safe journey, success in exams or business, the birth of a healthy child, or protection against illness.

Shinto shuns impurity and the pollution of blood, death, and dirt. When visiting a shrine, use the cisterns standing by the shrine entrance to wash your hands and rinse your mouth before you enter (this is optional).

Next, announce your presence to the god by pulling on the thick bell cord hanging before the altar; toss a few coins into the box in front of you and clap your hands twice, then put them together to pray for some 30 seconds as you bow to the altar. If few believe intrinsically today, everyone likes to play safe. Perhaps it was always so: Moved to tears of reverence before the altar at Ise-jingu, the 13th-century poet-priest Saigyo declared, "I know not at all if anything deigns to be there." ■

Five-story Pagoda
(Goju-no-To)

Sutra Repository
(Kyozo)

Main Hall
(Kondo)

Central Gate
(Chumon)

Important cultural properties

National treasures

KEY TO SITE PLAN

1 South Main Gate (Nandaimon)
2 Central Gate (Chumon)
3 Main Hall (Kondo)
4 Five-story Pagoda (Goju-no-To)
5 Great Lecture Hall (Daikodo)
6 Sutra Repository (Kyozo)
7 Bell House (Shoro)
8 Inner Sanctuary (Kami-no-Mido)
9 West Round Hall (Saiendo)
10 Hall of Prince Shotoku's Soul (Shoryoin)
11 Gallery of Temple Treasures (Daihozoden)
12 Kudara Kannon Hall (Kudara Kannon-do)
13 East Main Gate (Todaimon)
14 Hall of Visions (Yumedono)
15 Reliquary Hall (Shariden)
16 Hall of Buddhist Teachings (Denpodo)
17 Bell House (Toin Shoro)

Great Lecture Hall (Daikodo)

Bell House (Shoro)

Hall of Prince Shotoku's Soul (Shoryoin)

Horyu-ji Temple

✉ 1-1 Horyuji Sannai, Ikuraga-cho, Ikoma-gun

☎ 0745/75-2555

💲 $$

🚉 Train: Kansai main line from JR Nara Station to Koryuji Station
Bus: 52, 60, 97, or 98 from JR Nara Station to Kintetsu Nara Station

(continued from p. 243)

grand buildings are long gone, but the Toto pagoda, 108 feet (33 m) high and dating from 730, is prized both for its elegance and for the unique architectural feat of making its three stories appear as six. The Main Hall (Kondo), rebuilt in 1976, houses a National Treasure; the bronze Yakushi Triad depicting the Yakushi Nyorai Buddha (associated with healing) and attendant bodhisattvas. These once-golden statues, cast in the 720s, have been smoked a glossy black through fires

over the centuries. Another National Treasure is the seventh-century statue of Sho-Kannon in the Eastern Hall (Toin-do), built behind the pagoda in 1285.

Paramount among all Japan's great temples and revered as the fountainhead of national culture, **Horyu-ji Temple**—diagramed at left—was founded in 607 by Prince Shotoku, architect of the first national constitution (see p. 28). The temple complex is said to have been rebuilt after a fire in 670, although some historians doubt the fire ever occurred. Either way, four of the buildings, remaining as they have been for over 1,300 years, are the oldest standing wooden structures on Earth. Counting several buildings from the Heian and Kamakura eras, as well as additions from the 15th to 19th centuries, the complex includes a hall opened in 1998 to house the Kudara Kannon, a masterpiece of wood sculpture and the temple's most famous statue. Horyu-ji, a UNESCO World Heritage Site, holds more than 2,300 items considered of historical importance—190 of them are Important Cultural Assets or National Treasures. The temple is divided into the larger **Western Precinct (Sai-in),** lying beyond the massive 15th-century **Great South Gate (Nandaimon),** and the smaller Eastern Precinct (Toin), which embraces Chugu-ji subtemple.

The seventh-century **Main Hall (Kondo)** houses some of the era's most important bronze and wooden sculptures, visible only through wooden lattices. The hall is also dark, making it hard to see the murals depicting paradise. Badly damaged in a fire in 1949, these have now been beautifully restored. To the left of the Kondo stands the magnificent seventh-century **Pagoda (Goju-no-To),** the oldest in Japan; 110 feet (33 m) high, it contains an elaborate clay sculpture on the first floor, with figures illustrating various Buddhist myths. North of the main compound at the point where the surrounding cloisters meet, the **Great Lecture Hall (Daikodo)** and the statues within date from the tenth century; the original was struck by lightning. Also replacing a damaged predecessor, the 13th-century **West Round Hall (Saiendo)** stands on a hill and contains an eighth-century Yakushi Nyorai image—the oldest dry-lacquer statue in Japan. The two long halls on either side of the central compound were formerly monks' quarters; built during the Kamakura period, the one on the east side is the **Hall of Prince Shotoku's Soul (Shoryoin)** and contains the prince's statue, wrought during the Heian period.

Passing through the ancient East Gate (Todaimon) brings you to the east precinct, with its octagonal seventh-century **Hall of Dreams (Yumedono)** pavilion.

Dominating the statues it contains is a wooden portrait of the deified Prince Shotoku; his likeness retains its original gilding and is in a remarkable state of preservation. Just east of this is **Chugu-in,** a nunnery housing Japan's oldest embroidered picture—and, most notably, the exquisite seventh-century **Miroku Bosatsu,** a Buddha statue of exceptional grace and serenity.

Many of Horyu-ji's treasures are now in Tokyo's National Museum (see pp. 95–97), but about a thousand remain in the **Gallery of Temple Treasures (Daihozoden)** just east of the main precinct. Among them is the Dream-Changing Kannon sculpture, sought out for changing nightmares into auspicious dreams. A small, exquisitely decorated lacquered shrine, the Tamamushi Tabernacle belonged to Empress Suiko. The intricate metalwork on its surface once held thousands of iridescent wings of the *tamamushi* beetle. ∎

Nara crafts

Ink and brushes have been manufactured in Nara for generations.

Nara craftsmen and women still fashion Kogaku-men dance-drama masks and rough-finished wooden *ittobori* dolls. Both were used in ancient religious ceremonies.

Buddhism brought with it many arts from China, especially calligraphy and ink painting. To this day, Nara remains the center for turning out brushes and *sumi* ink tablets. Made of deer, horse, rabbit, squirrel, or badger hair, brushes come in different sizes for different functions. Sumi or *yoboku,* made from the soot of bullrushes, is combined with glue from deer horn and formed into a cake said to improve with age. Depending on the desired intensity of the ink, other ingredients may include *beni* (crimson safflower dye), powdered oyster shell, and even musk; some manufacturers' formulas are secrets handed down for generations. ∎

Nara-ken

TOO OFTEN, VISITORS ARE SO TAKEN WITH NARA THE CITY
that they forget about Nara the prefecture. There is much here that is
worthwhile. Refreshingly rural and mountainous, the countryside
boasts beautiful temples and is said to harbor the legendary heartland
of the cherry tree. Indeed, the hills around the town of Yoshino are
cloaked in the palest pink blossoms each spring.

According to tradition, **Muro-ji Temple** *(78 Muro, Muro-mura, tel 0745/93-2003)*, beautifully situated in a peaceful wooded valley, was founded in 681 (the exact date is not known). Rebuilt in 824 by the priest Kukai, founder of the Shingon sect, it remains an important temple of that sect.

The temple is known as the "women's Koya"; unlike the great temple Kukai founded on Koya-san (see p. 250), this one never barred female visitors. Although the buildings have undergone restorations at various times, they are noted examples of seventh-century architecture; several are National Treasures, as are the statues they contain. The five-storied **pagoda** is among the most photographed buildings in Japan.

Amid forests of tree peonies and cherry trees, **Hase-dera Temple** *(Temple of Flowers, 731–1 Hase, Sakurai-shi, tel 0744-47-7001)* is a popular temple in late spring despite its remote location. Founded in 686 and enlarged by Emperor Shomu, who built the main hall, Hase-dera was once a cherished preserve of Nara-period aristocracy. Containing a celebrated 26-foot (8 m) statue of Kannon, god of mercy, the **Main Hall (Hondo)** is reached by a covered flight of stone steps.

Cherry trees originated in the town of **Yoshino,** legend has it, where they were planted in the seventh century by the priest En-no-Ozuno; he is said to have placed a

curse on anyone cutting them down. Whatever the truth, *yamazakura* (*Prunus cerrulata* or wild cherry), the basis for hundreds of subsequent hybrids, is the favorite variety in Japan; Empress Jito (645–702), for one, practiced blossom viewing here. The cherries cover the hillside after mid-April, blooming higher up the mountainside as the month advances. ∎

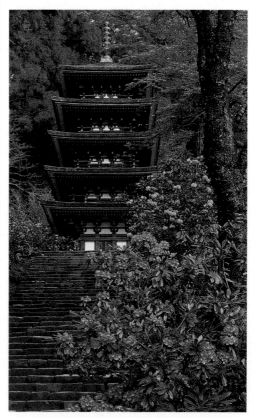

Off the beaten track, ninth-century Muro-ji Temple is cherished for its five-story pagoda and sylvan setting.

Wakayama-ken

KII-HANTO PENINSULA EMBRACES THE SOUTHERN TIP OF Nara-ken, but the bulk of it to the southwest is in mountainous Wakayama-ken. Wooded, agricultural, and almost devoid of industry, this is Kansai's last frontier. With the new Kansai International Airport only 12 miles (20 km) from Wakayama city, this may change; for now, however, even the scenic coastline is relatively unspoiled. The area is served by buses, and a local railroad line runs around the coast, but direct transportation options from major cities are limited, making it a wonderful region to explore by car. Still, you won't need a car to explore the region's principal asset: Koya-san, the mountainous and secluded home of the Shingon Buddhist sect.

Hot springs abound near **Hongu,** along the border between Wakayama-ken and Nara-ken; especially recommended are the more rustic spa villages of **Yunomine Onsen** and **Kawayu Onsen.** Scenic Nachikatsuura, in the south, is famous for **Nachi-no-taki Waterfall,** whose drop of 436 feet (133 m) makes it the highest cascade in Japan.

In the peninsula's northwest, hilly Koya Ryujin Quasi-National Park is the site of **Mount Koya-san,** Japan's best known Buddhist mountain retreat. At about 3,300 feet (1,005 m), Koya-san culminates in a plateau covering 5 square miles (12 sq km). It was here that Kukai (774–835), founder of the Shingon sect of Buddhism, first established a seminary in 816. The exclusive preserve of monks, the Koya-san temple city was forbidden to women until 1873. Frequent fires have left no buildings older than the 12th century; several, in fact, were reconstructed early in the 20th century. **Kongobu-ji Temple,** erected by the shogun Toyotomi Hideyoshi in 1592 and containing fine Kano school screen doors, became the focal temple—and is still the headquarters—of the Shingon sect.

Koya-san is divided into two main areas: the **Danjogoran,** just southwest of Kongobu-ji, and the **Okuno-in** to the east. In the Danjogaran complex is the **Treasure House (Reihokan),** with thousands of wonderful exhibits, many of them registered National Treasures. The latter is essentially a cemetery; more than 100,000 graves and funerary monuments have accumulated here to memorialize the great and the good for over 1,200 years of Japanese history. At the top of the Okuno-in, just south of the great **Kukai's**

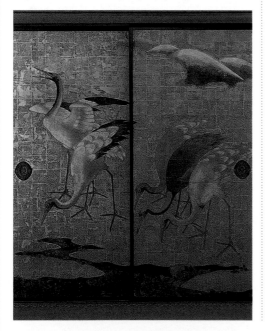

Seventeenth-century painted screen doors in Kongobu-ji Temple, Mount Koya-san

mausoleum, is the **lantern hall.** Among its 11,000 luminaries, two have burned continuously since the tenth century.

The secular part of Koya-san, with all the attributes of an ordinary small town, has no hotels. The majority of the million-odd visitors it receives annually are pilgrims; 50 of the 120 temples in the vicinity provide lodgings known as *shukubo* (see Travelwise, p. 359). Prices and sleeping arrangements are the same as in the average *ryokan* (see p. 358).

Piety is not a prerequisite for appreciating Koya-san, which is much cherished by urbanites as a stress-free retreat. An overnight stay is highly recommended, at the very least as an opportunity to touch the pulse of a unique Buddhist heartland. When the daytrippers have gone home, to stroll in the tranquil early morning or evening is a sublime experience in itself. The temples lie in tall cedar forests where the haze seems scented with incense; the lone passersby are priests and pilgrims, and the sounds of chanting and temple bells only deepen the silence. ■

The rugged coastline of Wakayama-ken

Kukai (774–835)

After studying Buddhism in China, Kukai returned to Japan to found the Shingon sect. Its emphasis on esoteric Buddhism appealed to emperors and noblemen, but Kukai gained converts among the common people, too.

The life of this Buddhist saint is shrouded in myths and miracles. One concerns the rivalry between Kyoto's two main temples, the eastern To-ji Temple (of which Kukai was abbot) and the western Sai-ji Temple. After trapping the celestial rain-dragon in a huge jar, the abbot of Sai-ji apparently caused a serious drought. Kukai's prayers set it free, and rain fell once again. The seminary that Kukai built on Koya-san (see opposite) remains Japan's greatest focus of Buddhism today. ■

Osaka-jo Castle, here lit up at night, is a concrete reproduction of its colossal 16th-century predecessor.

Osaka

"MOKARI MAKKA?"—"MAKING ANY MONEY?" THIS IS WHAT other Japanese claim is the typical greeting between Osakans, who have a reputation as the nation's shrewdest businesspeople. Osaka's 30,000 factories produce about a quarter of Japan's industrial output. If the prefecture were a country, its GNP would make it the tenth most prosperous nation on Earth.

Osaka

⚠ 199 B3

Visitor information

✉ JR Osaka Station, 3-1 Umeda, Kita-ku

☎ 06/6345-2189

Officially, Osaka is Japan's third city. Because Tokyo and Yokohama are close enough to constitute a single megalopolis, however, most people consider Osaka to be the second. Its location on a sweeping bay prompted its use as a port during the reign of Emperor Nintoku, so Osaka has been a primary trading center since the fourth century. While samurai fortunes fell from the late 17th century on, merchants grew ever more wealthy and powerful, especially in Osaka. As the city became the national hub of trade and industry, it saw the foundation of many of today's great Japanese corporations, among them Daiwa, Marubeni, and Sumitomo.

Under the patronage of merchant princes, Osaka flourished as a center for the dramatic arts, particularly when many Kabuki exponents moved here after the devas-

The vast **Umeda Sky Building,** a striking example of modern Japanese architecture, is admired and deplored in equal measure.

tation of Edo in the great fire of 1567. Osaka was renowned for its Bunraku (see p. 48), and today it remains the national center for this unique form of puppetry. A prime target in World War II, the city was flattened, and all of Osaka's historic assets vanished. Osaka-jo castle survived, but it was already a concrete copy (built in 1931) of its predecessor.

Although it caters to special interests with industrial tours, Osaka is no destination for sightseeing. Its monotony is broken by a network of canals, but it is mainly a hideous concrete agglomeration with a reputation for being driven, hectic, polluted, and crowded. This said, Osaka is a boisterous city of sybarites, with some of Japan's best nightlife—and its widest spectrum of fine food. In amusement districts

Marilyn beckons from a building facade in Amerika-mura, Osaka's brash and youthful America village.

The sights rival the sound and the fury of Dotomburi, Osaka's legendary amusement district.

A traditional restaurant in Osaka

and youth fashion hangouts, expect to see building facades adorned with fantastic mechanical signs and doorways surrounded by gigantic fright masks. Ugly but fun, Osaka's appeal lies in its very brashness.

With a JR loop line running around the perimeter and a subway network crisscrossing the city, Osaka is easy to get around. **Kita-ku** (northern sector) encompasses Osaka Station, surrounded by a vast warren of every imaginable kind of restaurant above and below ground. This is the main business district. Its focus is **Umeda,** an area notable for its labyrinthine

shopping mall and soaring modern architecture, especially the sleek **Umeda Sky Building,** a 40-story, twin-towered titan erected in 1993. Dominating the city skyline east of center, **Osaka-jo Castle** is an impressive concrete reproduction set on its massive original walls and girded by the city's largest park. **Minami-ku** (southern sector), a veritable city of covered arcades, is Osaka's most energetic and colorful district. In its northern part, **Shinsaibashi,** you'll find the youthful fashion followers' hangout of Amerika-mura (America village), along with the upscale boutiques of Yoroppa-mura (Europe village). Lying to the south with arcades spreading down to Namba is **Dotomburi,** Osaka's famous amusement district. A rainbow array of signs and lights and a cacophony of screaming sound advertise the area's theaters, bars and pachinko parlors—as well as more risqué entertainments. Also boasting myriad restaurants catering to all budgets, Dotomburi is not surprisingly Osaka's most popular hangout. ∎

Kobe

THE CITY OF KOBE SITS ON THE SOUTHERN SLOPE OF Mount Rokko-san, on the west of Osaka-wan Bay. It embraces the world's sixth largest port, which handles the largest volume of cargo in Japan. A trading post from ancient times, Kobe rose to prominence when the city opened its doors to foreign traders as one of Japan's first treaty ports. In so doing, it acquired a substantial foreign population and a degree of cosmopolitanism—both of which it retains today.

The Port Tower and Maritime Museum sketch some striking geometry against Kobe's night sky.

Along with a mosque, a synagogue, and Christian churches, a small handful of old Western buildings still stand in the northern district of **Kita-ku.** Having been almost totally destroyed during World War II, Kobe is a modern city. It overlooks the sea and is known as a pleasant place to live, but offers few attractions to visitors.

In January 1995, about 6,000 people died when Kobe suffered Japan's worst earthquake since 1923. Some of the most severe damage occurred on the coast. Following extensive repairs, Kobe is now so much back to normal that it is hard to see where the disaster ever took place.

The artificial **Port Island** off-shore is a futuristic complex with a conference center, an exhibition hall, and vast hotels. The city center, **Sannomiya,** includes the main shopping arcades and the lively **Ikuta** amusement district just to the north. East is Flower Road, well known for its foreign bars and restaurants. With its long history of foreign influence, Kobe is a good place for international cuisine, including European, Indian, and Chinese. The best Chinese restaurants are south of Motomachi shopping arcade in Kobe's Chinatown, known locally as **Nankin-machi.** Another famous gastronomic legacy of bygone days is Kobe beef—although you may feel gored by its price. ∎

Kobe
◮ 199 B3
Visitor information
✉ 1-7 Sannomiya-cho, Chuo-ku
☎ 078/322-0220

Himeji

HIMEJI, A MEDIUM-SIZE CITY 34 MILES (55 KM) WEST OF Kobe, was almost obliterated by bombs during World War II, so it is nothing short of miraculous that its magnificent castle still stands. Dubbed Hakuro-jo (White Egret Castle) for its whitened woodwork and plaster walls, Himeji-jo is considered Japan's most beautiful stronghold. It is easily accessible in less than an hour on the Shinkansen line from Kyoto, Osaka, or Kobe, making Himeji a high priority for Kansai visitors.

Built on the site of a 14th-century fortress by local warlords in 1581, **Himeji-jo Castle** was restored and upgraded during the 1600s by Ikeda Terumasa, son-in-law of the shogun Tokugawa Ieyasu. Its ownership passed through various noble samurai families until the Meiji Restoration in 1868. Standing on massive unmortared walls and comprising scores of *yagura* (arrow storehouses), watch-

towers, and other buildings around its magnificent main **donjon,** the castle stands today as it was finished in 1618. Complete with slits in the walls for firing arrows and guns— as well as chutes for pouring

Main keep (Donjon)

Central bailey (Honmaru)

Details of Himeji-jo, known as White Egret Castle

boiling oil on invaders—this formidable fortification remains remarkably preserved because it was never attacked. Of the three moats, the outer one is now buried; it once separated the castle from the town. Parts of the central moat and all of the inner moat survive.

Between the castle buildings stretch many beautifully landscaped areas of greenery with lawns and flowering trees—a good example of the samurai way of melding an unyielding defensive structure with refined living spaces. The main donjon, while displaying the traditional five-story roof structure, actually conceals six stories—and a large cellar beneath. Perfectly echoing the balance between martial might and aesthetic sensibilities, the architectural delicacy of Himeji-jo almost belies its strategic impregnability. ■

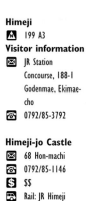

Himeji
🗺 199 A3
Visitor information
✉ JR Station Concourse, 188-1 Godenmae, Ekimae-cho
☎ 0792/85-3792

Himeji-jo Castle
✉ 68 Hon-machi
☎ 0792/85-1146
💲 $$
🚆 Rail: JR Himeji station, then 15-min. walk north

Bizen gate

Rear gate
(Karametemon)

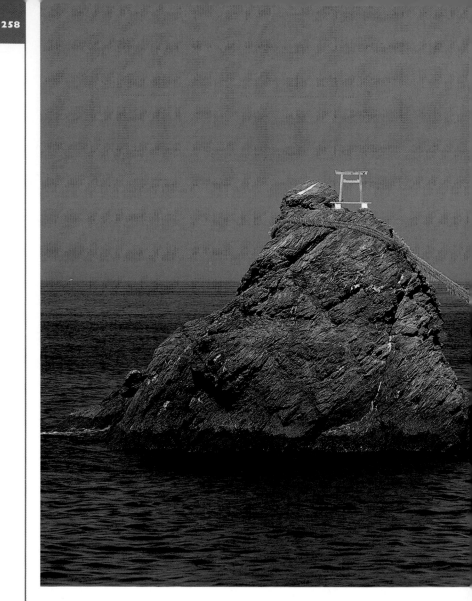

Shima-hanto

THIS SCENIC PENINSULA ON KANSAI'S EASTERN EDGE LIES
within the boundaries of wooded Ise-Shima National Park. Shima-
hanto's principal claim to fame is the Grand Shrine at Ise, Ise-jingu,
the most sacred in all Shinto for some 1,700 years. Of the area's many
resorts, the most popular is Toba, situated on a beautiful bay. The
region makes a good outing from Nagoya in Central Honshu (Chubu) across the Ise-wan Bay. There is an excellent train service (JR
Kintetsu line) that takes about 80 minutes.

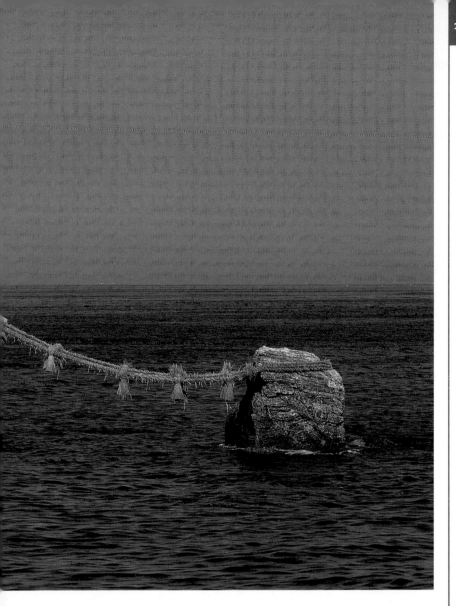

Toba is noted for its aquarium and for **Mikimoto Pearl Island,** a museum complex that focuses on cultured pearls and features demonstrations by female pearl divers (a species saved from extinction by tourism) every half-hour. Six miles (10 km) west is Futamigaura, known for its **Husband-and-Wife Rocks (Meoto-iwa),** two curious outcrops standing in the sea. Connected by a sacred straw rope, they are symbolically wed each year during a Shinto festival on January 5.

With their many sights and recreation facilities, area resorts such as Toba and Futamiguara make a pleasant stopover for those visiting **Ise-jingu Grand Shrine,** the most ancient and holiest center of Shinto. Notoriously

Meoto-iwa (Husband-and-Wife Rocks), sacred to Shinto, are symbolically linked by a straw rope.

Water font at Ise-jingu, the shrine most sacred to Shinto

Ise

🗺 199 D2

Visitor information

✉ Kintetsu Ujiyamada Station, 2-1-43 Iwabuchi

☎ 0596/23-9655

🚉 Rail: Kintetsu Ise line from Nagoya (1 hr. 25 mins.); Kintetsu Yamada line from Osaka or Kyoto (around 2 hrs. each). JR from Nagoya to Ise-shi (2 hrs.)

Ise-jingu

✉ 10-min. walk from Ise-shi or Uji-Yamada Stations to Geku. The Geku & Naiku are 4 miles (6 km) apart but connected by bus service.

crowded, the resorts are best avoided altogether in summer.

Of Japan's thousands of Shinto shrines, Ise-jingu is paramount. The precinct comprises hundreds of subsidiary shrines consecrated to a host of deities, all set amid wooded hills and streams. The chief structures are the **Outer Shrine (Geku),** dedicated to Toyouke-Omikami (goddess of harvests, homes, and food), and the **Inner Shrine (Naiku),** dedicated to the sun goddess Amaterasu-Omikami (mythical ancestor of the emperor and the Japanese race). The two buildings stand 4 miles (6 km) apart, but they are connected by a bus that runs every 15 minutes. Made of fresh *hinoki* (cypress) wood from the Kiso mountains (see pp. 190–92), the main shrine buildings are ritually dismantled and identically reconstructed every 20 years; the process took place for the 61st time in 1993 at a cost of billions of yen.

The shrine buildings—simple, unadorned, and thatched—are architecturally akin to ancient granaries; the design features distinctive ornamental *chigi* (crossed

beams protruding from the gabled ends of the roofs). The main, or inner, halls of both shrines, accessible only to high priests and the emperor, lie behind a series of enclosures fenced in various traditional styles. Although entry to the inner halls is forbidden, the structures are sufficiently visible from the outside to make a visit well worthwhile.

The outside of the main hall of the Geku is reached through three *torii* gateways and along a curving avenue through a cathedral of towering cryptomeria trees. After crossing the bridge over the Isuzu River, the approach to the Naiku is similar; almost palpably enhanced by the worship of countless millions over 1,600 years, the atmosphere is awe-inspiring. The inner sanctum of the main hall of the Naiku contains one of the great imperial treasures: the sacred bronze mirror said to have been presented to the first emperor by the sun goddess Amaterasu herself. Covered by layers of cloth placed over it repeatedly since the third century, the mirror has not been glimpsed by anyone—priests or emperors—since the day it was cast.

This region is divided into San-in—the northern area along the Sea of Japan—and San-yo, the more developed southern coastal region. Basking in a delightful climate, the area is also the gateway to the charming islands of the Inland Sea.

Western Honshu (Chugoku)

Giant wooden *torii* on the shore at Miyajima

Seto Ohashi bridge is one of the world's great feats of engineering.

Western Honshu (Chugoku)

CHUGOKU IS THE WESTERN PART of Honshu, between the island of Kyushu to the west and Hyogo-ken to the east. Coined in the distant past when only the area between Kyushu and Kanto came under any governmental administration, Chugoku literally means the "middle country." The northern coast of Chugoku is known as San-in, while the southern part—a good deal more densely populated and industrialized—is called San-yo.

The remoter **San-in** region, which covers Shimane and Tottori prefectures (the latter with miles of sand dunes) as well as northern Yamaguchi, boasts a unique combination of rural farmland, rugged coasts, and historical towns—an increasingly popular alternative for those seeking the pleasures of an older, quieter Japan.

Following the paths of the great trunk roads of feudal times, the main highways and Shinkansen railroad lines from Tokyo to the island of Kyushu run through **San-yo**. This region includes the gateways to Shikoku and the islands of the Inland Sea, reached both by

0   75 kilometers

0   50 miles

Area of map detail

Tokyo

5▷

OKI GUNTO

Dogo

Nishino-shima

Ama

Nakano-shima

Chiburi-shima   DOZEN

DAISEN-OKI NATIONAL PARK

4▷

J a p a n

Sakaiminato

Izumo Taisha   Hirata   **Matsue**

Izumo Taisha   Shinji-ko

Taisha   Yasugl   **Yonago**   9   Kurayoshi   **Tottori**

Izumo   ▲ 1729m Daisen   TOTTORI-KEN   29

Oda   **SHIMANE-KEN**   s   a   n   c   h   i

o f   Gotsu   Gono-kawa   54   C h u g o k u   Maniwa   Tsuyama   53

Hamada   Shobara   Niimi   **OKAYAMA-KEN**

Miyoshi   Takahashi   53

Masuda   **HIROSHIMA-KEN**   Soja   **Okayama**   Bizen

Kake   Yoshida   Fuchu   **Kurashiki**   Ushimado

54   2

Tsuwano   **Fukuyama**   Tamano

Mihara   **Onomichi**   **Seto Ohashi Bridge**   Washu-zan   30   **F**

2   **HIROSHIMA**   Setoda

Otake   **Kure**   a   k   a   i

Miyajima   **E**

Iwakuni   n

Tokuyama   S e t o   SHIKOKU & SETO-NAIKAI INLAND SEA   p. 291

Hikari   Yanai   **D**

Iyo-nada   S e t o   **C**

KANSAI p. 197

Masuda Residence, a former samurai house in Hagi, Shimane-ken

ferry and by bridge; it also takes in the prefectures of Okayama in the east and Yamaguchi (the southern part) to the west, with Hiroshima in between. Rich in sights of scenic, historic, or cultural interest, the area is much visited and dotted with resorts. ■

San-in

Despite being one of the most attractive regions in the country, the San-in coast of northern Chugoku is often omitted from travelers' itineraries. The oversight is probably due to its location on the shores of the Japan Sea, so notorious for snowy winters and abundant rainfall that people seem to forget it has a summer. Consequently, the San-in coast remains comparatively rural—and little spoiled by development.

The region has justifiably earned an off-the-beaten-track reputation. The main San-in railroad meanders along a coast largely devoted to fishing and farming, where life is more leisurely than in most of Japan. But San-in has more than excellent seascapes and mountain scenery to recommend it. The old coastal town of Hagi preserves picturesque reminders of its feudal past, as does inland Tsuwano. Matsue, adopted home of 19th-century Greek writer Lafcadio Hearn (see p. 272-74), retains a fine castle. Nearby Izumo is famed for Izumo Taisha, the second most sacred Shinto shrine in the country after Ise. Shimane-ken embraces the Oki-shoto Islands with placid scenic resorts and a rich local history. Though San-in is quieter than most places in Japan, don't let

that lull you into forgetting to reserve accommodations ahead. ∎

Yoshida Shoin

In 1854, Commodore Perry's visit convinced the young samurai scholar Yoshida Shoin (1830–1859) that Japan must modernize to resist colonialism. The archaic feudal government had to be overthrown and imperial power restored. Such ideas gained Shoin a following with other Choshu clansmen, among them Ito Hirobumi, who became Japan's first prime minister in 1885. The seminal architect of the 1868 Meiji Restoration, Yoshida never lived to see it; he was executed for inciting rebellion in 1859. Shoin-jinja Shrine, dedicated to him, is in eastern Hagi. ∎

Samurai quarter buildings in Tsuwano

Hagi

HAGI, WITH ITS BEAUTIFULLY PRESERVED SAMURAI QUAR-
ter, evocative castle ruins, pottery kilns, beaches, and attractive
seascapes, is often regarded as the gem of the San-in coast. The town
earned a spot on the map as the domain of the Choshu clan leader
Mori Terumoto, who built a castle there in 1604. While Japan
remained sealed to the outside world for the next 250 years, slum-
bering Hagi produced the Choshu clansmen most instrumental in
overthrowing the old samurai regime and bringing about the Meiji
Restoration of 1868. Hagi-jo Castle was destroyed by anti-feudal
zealots in 1874, after which the town promptly fell back to sleep.

Hagi has long had a reputation for
pottery, particularly tea ceremony
vessels. The ware typically displays
a deceptively rough-hewn quality.
About a hundred kilns are open in
the vicinity.

The main sights congregate in
the west, on the delta of the
Matsumoto-gawa River. The town
is small enough to negotiate on
foot, but there is a lot to see and a
bicycle is invaluable; you can rent
one at Higashi-Hagi Station as well
as in hotels. Arm yourself with the
excellent English-language booklet
from the visitor information center,
then go exploring.

On the eastern confines is the
1691 **Toko-ji Temple.** Built as a
Mori family memorial temple, this
is the graveyard of the first and
odd-numbered members of the
Mori clan; it is the counterpart to
Daisho-in, in the southwest,
which commemorates the even-
numbered Mori. At the back of the
Toko-ji precinct is an avenue
flanked by stone lanterns. ∎

Hagi
◪ 262 B2
Visitor information
✉ Higashi-Hagi Station
☎ 0838/25-3145
🚉 Train: JR San-in line
from Matsue (4
hrs.)

Toko-ji Temple
✉ 1647 Shiibara
💲 $

Daisho-in
✉ 4132 Tsubaki Oumi
💲 $

**Hundreds of
stone lanterns en-
chant the grounds
of Daisho-in Tem-
ple during the
Mantoe festival in
August.**

A hike through Hagi

If you stroll at a leisurely pace, it takes the better part of a day to cover all the sights mentioned in this walk. Omit Teramachi or hire a bicycle, however, and the time can be cut to three hours.

Start in **Jokamachi.** If you are pressed for time, take a cab from either Higashi-Hagi or Hagi Stations to **Edoya Yokocho,** the local name for the street in Jokamachi containing the main sights. Out of several houses preserved in the Jokamachi area, **Kikuya House (Kikuya-ke Jutaku) ❶** is the most elaborate. Representative of a wealthy Edo-period merchant's home, it was built in the mid-17th century and retains many original fixtures and furnishings. There is a museum lodged in a converted *kura* (storehouse), which features samurai memorabilia and antique dolls. Nearby is the **Ishii Tea Bowl Museum (Ishii Chawan Bijutsukan),**

with a fine display of antique Hagi pottery.

After visiting the museum, head northwest toward Horiuchi, the inner moat district, around Hagi's former castle. On the way you will come to the old **Kuchiba House (Kuchiba-ke Jutaku) ❷.** Although the house is closed to the public, the gate in front of it, the largest in Hagi, is listed as an important National Cultural Property. A few minutes northwest is the **Mori clan tenant house (Kyu-Asa Mori-ke) ❸,** the largest of the samurai houses open to the public. Containing rather dusty memorabilia, it gives an impression of austerity; like most samurai in 1868, the Mori, who were instrumental in

Now standing in a park, the ruins of Hagi-jo Ato Castle extend down to the shoreline.

bringing down the shogunate, were anything but rich. From here, walk about 220 yards (200 m) north to reach **Shizuki-koen Park** ④, a spacious bit of greenery extending right down to the beach and the **Ruins of Hagi-jo Ato Castle** ⑤. The castle ruins are a lovely place to wander, at the very least for the views over the sea. More than just moats, ramparts, and scattered foundation stones, these ruins include sections of collapsing outer walls and wooded areas where roof tiles litter the undergrowth. Also in the park, just northwest of the ruins, is the delightful **Hananoe teahouse (Hananoe Chatei)** ⑥, where you can sip green tea in a charming traditional garden.

It's a pleasant walk east around the promontory toward **Kikuga-hama Beach.** Just south of it, along the ocher-colored mud walls of the Horiuchi district, is the Mori Outer Gate and an old **Sufu residence** to its east, featuring beautiful latticed windows. The **Masuda residence** 220 yards (200 m) eastward along the same street is not open to the public, but you can still admire it; the house was once the watchtower next to the main northern gate of Hagi-jo. From here a walk of about 440 yards (400 m) northeast brings you to the **Kumaya Museum (Kumaya Bijutsukan)** ⑦ (*47 Imauo-no-Tana-machi, tel 0838/22-7547*), which houses an impressive collection of Hagi memorabilia, including painted screens, scrolls, and pottery, all

🄰	See area map pp. 262–63
▶	Jokamachi
⇄	2.3 miles (3.6 km)
🕐	3 hours
▶	Teramachi district

NOT TO BE MISSED
- Shizuki-koen Park
- Ruins of Hagi-jo Ato Castle
- Hananoe teahouse
- Kumaya Museum

exhibited in converted 18th-century *kura* (private warehouses). You are now in the **Teramachi** district, home to about 20 temples. Although of relatively minor interest, some are charming enough to make this a rewarding district to wander through if you have the time. Stretching east from the north of Shizuki-koen, Kikugahama beach is not only scenic but very clean, so in summer you can top off your walk with a swim. Otherwise, you might like to go back toward Horiuchi; just south of it is the **Hagi Urakami Museum (Kenritsu-Hagi Bijutsukan,** *586-1 Hiako Hagi, Yamaguchi, tel 0838/24-2400, closed Mon.*), which harbors an outstanding collection of *ukiyo-e* prints and historic Chinese, Korean, and local ceramics. ■

Tsuwano walk

Tsuwano is a pleasant little town with several historical and many charming sights. Try to avoid visiting during weekends when Tsuwano fills with visitors.

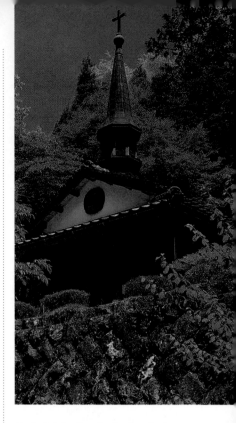

As you exit the station, the visitor information office is to your left. Pick up their excellent bilingual booklet, which exhaustively describes and maps the town. If you like, you can rent a bicycle from Eki Rent-a-Cycle right next door.

Proceed to the intersection and turn right; walk about one third of a mile (500 m) and turn right again into a narrower road that takes you across the railroad track. Take the next right turn and walk about 200 yards (200 m), then take the left fork, which leads to **Maria Sei-do ❶.** This charming wooden Catholic church, set in a sylvan glade, was built in 1951 to commemorate 36 Christian martyrs who died in Tsuwano between 1868 and 1872. It stands on a site along the Otome-Toge Pass. Every May 3 during the Otome-Toge festival, a procession starting from the main Catholic church in town winds toward Maria Sei-do along the Jujika-no-Michi (Road of the Cross), a tree-lined path. Take this path from the southwestern side of the church, following it through the woods.

Turn left into the road as you reach it, then follow it to the next intersection. Turn right into the road leading to a small but stately temple, **Kakuozan Yomei-ji Temple ❷** *(Ushiroda, tel 08567/2-0137).* Built in 1420 as a contemplative retreat, it boasts fine painted interior screen doors and an attractive garden. Go right when you leave the temple compound, following the road downhill before turning right into the main road. Follow the road about half a mile (700 m) and turn sharp right into a secondary road until you see the path leading up the mountain in front of you.

From here it's a winding trek up a concrete stairway to the summit, through a tunnel formed by well over a thousand bright red *torii* gateways. At the top is **Taikodani Inari-jinja Shrine ❸** ; established in 1773, it is one of the most important shrines devoted to Inari, the fox deity. From the south side of

Maria Sei-do chapel, a landmark of Japanese Catholicism, is dedicated to 36 Christians martyred around 1870.

the shrine, a path leads to the chairlift for **Tsuwano-jo Castle ❹;** following a beautifully scenic four-minute ride, this conveyance stops at a point about ten minutes' walk from the castle ruins, which in turn command a breathtaking view over the town and toward Mount Aono-san. Take the chairlift down again and rejoin a narrow road leading to a slightly wider secondary road, where you turn right. Just over 200 yards (270 m) on, turn left and then sharp left again; cross the bridge and on your right you should see the **Mori House and Memorial Museum (Mori Ogai Kyutaku) ❺** *(Machida, tel 08567/2-3210).* Mori was a fascinating man: A military doctor who traveled throughout Europe, he became a pioneer of realism in Japanese literature.

Leaving here and turning to your right will take you onto Tonomachi-dori, the long street

See area map page 224
► Station
↔ 4 miles (6.5 km)
⊕ 4 hours
► Hokusai Museum

NOT TO BE MISSED
• Maria Sei-do chapel
• Kakuozan Yomei-ji Temple
• Taikodani Inari-jinja Shrine
• Tsuwano-jo Castle
• Mori House and Memorial Museum

that goes through the center of town. Tsuwano's main drag, it is preceded by Tonomachi, an avenue flanked by houses dating from the feudal period; their white plaster walls are characteristically patterned with panels of dark gray cross-hatching. Channels of clear water containing thousands of variegated carp run alongside Tonomachi's streets—a sight particularly lovely when the irises bloom in June.

Some of the houses here are open as museums, notably the **Musée de Morijuku (Morijuku Bijutsukan) ❻** (Mori-mura, tel

Straddling the path all the way up to Taikodani Inari-jinja Shrine, thousands of *torii* gateways form a bright red tunnel.

08567/2-3200), which was once a wealthy farmer's house. Endowed with a fine garden, it now exhibits the works of local contemporary artists; on request you can see the camera obscura, a view of the garden projected on a wall through a pinhole aperture.

Over the bridge and a few steps farther on is the Catholic Church, a delightful building dating from 1931 that reproduces Nagasaki's Oura church in candy-color pastels, with its floor covered in tatami matting. From here the avenue narrows somewhat to become Tsuwano's main street, where you will find several interesting shops selling locally made *washi* paper and *genji-maki*—a cake featuring a layer of sponge around a filling of sweet bean jam.

Keep an eye peeled for the sake brewers (look for bottles in the windows or a ball of twigs above the lintel), where you get to taste the brews for free. Finally, stroll through the **Katsushika Hokusai Museum ❼**; it harbors an extensive private collection devoted to Hokusai (1760–1849), Japan's most famous *ukiyo-e* woodblock print artist. ∎

Obake—ghosts & demons

If you travel in Japan in the middle of summer, you will probably find television and theaters airing an annual crop of horror movies, Kabuki programs featuring ghost plays, and haunted rides drawing large crowds in amusement parks. Children will be glued to the comical animated adventures of Ge-Ge-Ge-no-Kitaro, the little boy who battles against ghosts and demons. The Japanese say the perfect antidote to the sultry heat is a nice cool shiver of fear, but the traditions surrounding summertime spirits go back some 1,500 years.

Comprising several species of goblin and demon, as well as the spirits of humans, animals, and even trees or umbrellas, Japan's army of demons is probably second to none in the world. These things are called *bakemono* (*obake* for short), meaning monsters or changelings. Western ghost stories are mainly for wintertime; in Japan they walk abroad mainly during O-bon, a month-long Buddhist festival for the dead starting mid-July—a highlight of the summer holidays. Like the Christian All Saints festival, O-bon is a time for remembrance. Families visit the graves of relatives and pray for them before home altars. During O-bon, the spirits of the dead return for a month-long visit. The celebrations (dancing, feasting, fireworks) are for welcoming them home, but some of the evil dead are said to jump aboard the bandwagon.

Many kinds of bakemono are unrelated to O-bon. The Setsubun festival (Feb. 3 or 4) is for driving out *oni*—horned ogres with an appetite for human flesh. The little clay figurines of froglike imps often seen in gift shops represent *kappa*. Said to inhabit lonely streams and rivers, the cute-looking kappa were nonetheless feared for sucking out the entrails of those venturing into the water—an appetite long emphasized to deter children from dangerous water play.

The winged *tengu*, inhabiting alpine forests, is a demon sometimes depicted with a stubby beak but more usually with a fierce scarlet face and an outsize nose. Originating in ancient masked drama, tengu masks often adorn the walls of Japanese-style bars and restaurants. The kindness of the tengu depends mainly upon the moral character of the beholder. Popular myth has it that the great 12th-century military hero Minamoto Yoshitsune was taught the art of swordsmanship as a child by a wise old tengu he encountered in a forest.

Animal spirits, especially foxes, figure prominently in Japanese folk beliefs. Myths about foxes are of Chinese origin, but they were adopted by the Shinto belief system and adapted. Represented as a statue around shrines dedicated to Inari, god of gain and grain, the fox is believed to be the deity's messenger or familiar. Not always benign, its supposed ability to assume human form inspired many a ghostly tale; in former times the insane were often presumed to be possessed by fox spirits. A mammal unique to Japan, the *tanuki* or raccoon dog is similarly believed to be able to change its shape. Ceramic figures of corpulent tanuki with outsize testicles, often placed in the windows of drinking haunts and sake merchants, are considered lucky.

The appearance of *Kitsune-bi* (fox fire), incandescent marsh gas or will-o-the-wisp in the countryside, is said to augur hauntings by *yurei*—ghosts. As in the West, the ghosts are thought to be transparent, but they drift away into nothing below the waist. Yurei, earthbound spirits regarded as having unfinished business (usually revenge for the wrongdoings that took their lives), were greatly feared.

Tales of ghosts and demons formed the main themes of Noh plays; the tales were compiled in storybooks and celebrated in woodblock prints by, among others, Katsushika Hokusai (1760–1849). Some are well known, as recounted by the 18th-century author Ueda Akinari, but probably the greatest writer of the genre was Lafcadio Hearn (1850–1904), still revered in Japan by his adoptive name of Koizumi Yakumo (see pp. 272–74). He retold the old tales—some hitherto handed down orally—in books such as *Kwaidan*, which have become their definitive form. Many Japanese ghost stories are as chilling as any in the West—eat your heart out, Edgar Allan Poe! ∎

Demon slayers figure prominently in Japanese folktales and ghost stories. In this woodblock print by Yoshitoshi—who began to specialize in ghost pictures during the 1890s—the hero Tametomo drives away the smallpox demon.

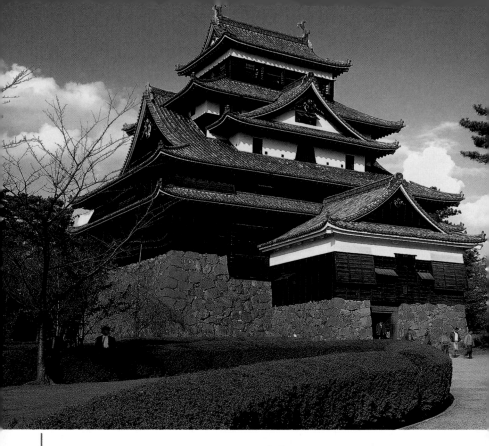

Matsue

SITUATED ON THE NORTHERN SHORE OF LAKE SHINJI-KO, just inland from the coast, Matsue at first seems like another nondescript Japanese city, but its proximity to water blesses it with a number of canals and waterways. And as in many destinations in Japan, bland modern facades hide much of historical and cultural interest, especially in the north of town. You can take in the castle and samurai district in an afternoon; if you want to see other sights in the vicinity, you will need an overnight stop.

Matsue-jo Castle, completed 1611, was built by the lords of the Horio clan. The five-story main keep, which conceals a sixth floor inside, underwent renovations some 30 years later. Matsue-jo changed hands through several feudal families until it was taken from the Matsudaira family during the Meiji Restoration. Spared the destruction wrought on most feudal edifices, the keep and several buildings from the 17th century remain intact, distinguishing Matsue-jo as the only original castle standing in western Japan. Lafcadio Hearn described it as brooding over the city and "fantastically grim." It no

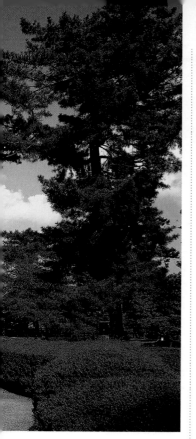

longer quite dominates the skyline as it once did, but this is a fine castle and certainly dark and grim-looking—if only because of the black wood on the facade. Inside is a collection of armor and samurai memorabilia. Just below the castle is a lovely, pale gray, Western-style wooden building, the cultural center, **Matsue Kyodokan;** the town hall in Meiji times, it now houses an excellent museum of local history.

From the castle grounds it is a delightful walk north down a wooded hill to reach the old district of **Shiomi-nawate,** a row of samurai residences beneath the castle along the north side of the moat. Among them is the Meimei-an tea-house and garden, the **Buke-yashiki** samurai residence.

Along the way, stop at the **Jyozan Inari-jinja Shrine,** an enchanting and spooky little shrine devoted to the fox deity. Hundreds of small, moss-covered, often crumbling stone fox effigies litter the precinct. The shrine was one of Hearn's favorites; he liked to stop off here each day on his way to teach at Matsue Middle School.

The **Lafcadio Hearn Residence (Koizumi Yakumo Kyukyo)** is in Shiomi-nawate. You will be handed a pamphlet at the entrance with a passage about the garden that Hearn so loved. He described it in *Glimpses of Unfamiliar Japan,* which he wrote here in 1891. It was here as well that Hearn penned his famous compilation of ghost stories, *Kwaidan* (see p. 270). The garden is somewhat thread-bare, ready now for restoration rather than reverent preservation. Although you are left wondering if it ever had a kitchen or a bathroom, the rest of this small, charming house is intact. By all accounts, the Hearn/Koizumis were happy here, even though they occupied the house a scant seven months.

More poignant still is the adjacent **Lafcadio Hearn Memorial Museum (Koizumi Yakumo**

The entrance to an old house in the Shiomi-nawate samurai quarter of Matsue

Matsue Kyodokan
- ✉ 1-59 Tono-machi
- ☎ 0852/22-3958
- 🚌 Bus: from Matsue Station to Kencho-mae

Lafcadio Hearn Memorial Museum
- ✉ 322 Okutani-machi
- ☎ 0852/21-2147
- 💲 $
- 🚌 Bus: from Matsue Station to Hearn Kyukyo-mae

The house inhabited by Lafcadio Hearn and his wife

Fudoki-no-Oka

🚌 Bus: Matsue to Fudoki-no-oka Irguchi

Kinenkan). On exhibit is Hearn's desk, specially made with disproportionately long legs—his only eye was so shortsighted that he had to work inches from the paper. Here too are his Japanese pipes, the suitcases he carried to Japan from America, and the phrases painted on sheets of newspaper with which he taught his children English.

Farther up in the northeast of the city is the 18th-century **Kanden-an teahouse,** set in a beautiful garden renowned for the inspired graphic effect of its stones and raked sand.

Matsue was part of the region of Izumo, which is regarded as a cradle of Japanese civilization. Six miles (10 km) south of the city is **Fudoki-no-Oka,** where archaeologists have unearthed objects dated from the first century A.D. A museum displays jewels, swords, and pottery from the many grave tumuli in the area. In the vicinity are two very old Shinto shrines; **Kamosu-jinja** with its 17th-century buildings and **Yaegaki-jinja,** whose treasure house exhibits a rare tenth-century fragment of a shrine mural depicting a beautiful mythical princess. ■

Lafcadio Hearn (1850–1904)

Lafcadio Hearn, the son of a Greek mother and an Irish father, left Greece at age six after his parents divorced. Following a lonely childhood with an aunt in England, he emigrated to the U.S. at 19, where he became a successful journalist. Posted to Japan in 1890 as a correspondent for *Harper's,* he remained there. He married Koizumi Setsu, a woman of samurai descent, and became a Japanese citizen, adopting the name Koizumi Yakumo. His compelling and charming period pieces express his enchantment with Japan. He later wrote the more penetrating *Japan—An Attempt at Interpretation,* but is best remembered for his masterly retellings of Japanese ghost stories and folktales. The frail, partially sighted Hearn died at 54 and was buried in Tokyo's Zoshigaya cemetery. Few foreigners have ever been more beloved in Japan, where Koizumi Yakumo is still revered as only a true Japanese writer could be. ■

Izumo Taisha

FOUR MILES (6.5 KM) WEST OF IZUMO IS TAISHA, SITE OF the oldest of all Shinto shrines, Izumo Taisha Grand Shrine. Izumo figures prominently as the backdrop for Shinto creation myths laid down in the *Kojiki* and *Nihon Shoki*—chronicles of history and myth compiled in the late seventh century. One myth concerns the god Okuninushi, a son of Amaterasu, the sun goddess; he is said to have had a palace built for his retirement at Taisha, and this later became Izumo Taisha, the second most sacred Shinto shrine after Ise (see p. 259–60). The origin of Ise is thought to go back some 1,700 years; Izumo Taisha predates even that.

All Shinto shrines deter evil spirits with straw ropes festooned with paper. The one at Izumo Taisha is a colossus commensurate with the shrine's importance.

Rebuilt at intervals—though not on the regular 20-year intervals of Ise—the main shrine buildings at Izumo Taisha are quite recent, dating mainly from 1874. The precinct, surrounded by hills, is pleasantly wooded. It incorporates two long rectangular halls called *juku-sha*, which are specially provided to accommodate all eight million Shinto gods believed to visit annually in October. Legend has it that the Shinto gods take a vacation at that time; the deities pack their bags and head for Izumo, where the month of October is called Kami ari Zuki (the month when the gods are there). October in the rest of Japan , by contrast, is known as Kannazuki (the month without gods). The precinct has a **treasure house** containing historical and religious artifacts connected to the shrine.

Many worshipers come to Izumo Taisha to pray for success in marriage, this being one of the god Okuninushi's spheres of interest (along with medicine, fishing, and silkworm culture). The Izumo Grand Shrine can be comfortably visited on a day trip from Matsue.

Izumo Taisha Shrine

🅰 263 D4

💲 Treasure house: $

🚌 Train & bus: from JR Matsue Station to JR Izumoshi Station, then bus to Izumo Taisha

Daisen-Oki National Park

INVOLVING SOME FOUR HOURS' TRAVEL FROM MATSUE (including the ferry crossing), the Oki-shoto Islands (Daisen-Oki National Park) are sufficiently remote to warrant the description "unspoiled." However, there is now air service to Oki island itself, so it may not be long before this trove of beaches, scenic coves, and fishing villages moves right onto the beaten track for summer vacations.

This group of volcanic islands consists of the larger Dogo island to the east and the westward Dozen Archipelago, with its three main islands and many more islets.

Like Sado off the northwest coast of Honshu, the islands were once used as places of exile, notably for Emperor Godaigo, banished there by the shogun Ashikaga Takauji in the 14th century (see p. 33). Consequently they are rich in history as well as scenery, with several notable temples and shrines—especially on Dogo island and Ama in the Dozen group. The people of Dogo island raise cattle; in a form of bullfighting popular here, two bulls lock horns to push each other, sumo fashion, out of a ring. The Oki-shoto Islands hold many delights for the traveler with plenty of time. Inter-island ferries abound, and most local accommodations are comfortable.

If you are planning a trip to the Daisen-Oki area, arrange your itinerary first with the visitor information center in Matsue; during the high season, make sure you reserve accommodations ahead. ■

Oki island coastlines tend to be delightfully unspoiled—though not always in high summer.

Oyster beds under a sunset on the San-yo coast

San-yo

The San-yo coast lies on the Seto-nakai Inland Sea; it enjoys mild winters and summers less humid than in most of Japan, giving it a reputation as the Far Eastern equivalent of the Mediterranean. The comparison is underscored in some places by the introduction of olive trees as a complement to peach trees, orange trees, and rice; inland the region is predominantly agricultural. Its much-touted "blue waters" are a more recent asset: Until the mid-1970s the densely populated coast suffered from overindustrialization, with severe damage to the marine ecology from chemical pollution. Since then, concerted efforts to clean up the environment have largely restored fish stocks to previous levels and improved the water quality along the beaches.

Japanese vacationers flock to resorts on islands just offshore, but beaches are not really the region's major attractions. Okayama-ken, comparatively little spoiled inland, has some beautiful scenery, while its capital, Okayama, is distinguished by one of Japan's greatest gardens, the Koraku-en. The nearby town of Kurashiki has a delightful old quarter along a canal and is a significant center for the arts.

Highly industrialized Hiroshima-ken is most visited for Hiroshima city, forever associated with the atomic bombing in 1945. But the millions of visitors to Hiroshima's commemorative Peace Memorial Park and museum often bypass the prefecture's other sights.

Just offshore and traditionally hailed as one of Japan's most scenic spots is the island of Miyajima, with the seaside shrine of Itsukushima-jinja, famed for its huge red *torii* emerging from the sea. The picturesque fishing town of Tomo-no-Ura and, above all, the temple town of Onomichi, perched on a hillside with a beautiful view over the Inland Sea, are also worth a look.

Ferry ports in Hiroshima-ken and Okayama-ken serve the islands of Seto-naikai and Shikoku, though Shikoku is now reachable via the gigantic bridges of Naruto-Ohashi (from Hyogo-ken via Awaji-shima Island) and Seto-Ohashi, south of Okayama. ∎

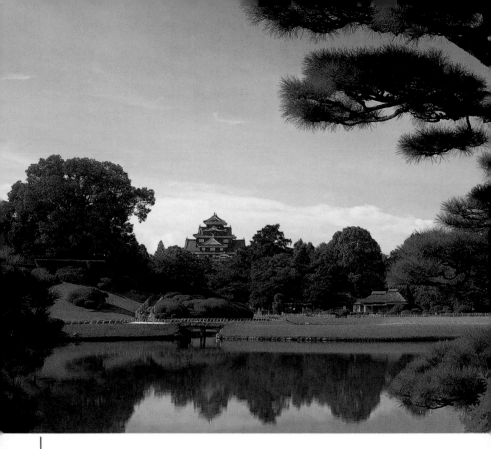

Okayama-ken

OKAYAMA-KEN CONSISTS OF THE PROVINCES OF NORTHERN
and southern Bichu to the west, Mimasaka to the northeast, and
Bizen in the southeast; Bizen includes Okayama city. Though the
coastal areas sometimes suffer from urban-industrial saturation, the
prefecture is rich in scenery, history, crafts, and marine assets—there
is more to Okayama-ken than just the great garden and the museums of Okayama city and the townscape and art of Kurashiki. Blessed
with a mild, Mediterranean-style climate, the region is important
agriculturally, known for peaches and muscat grapes; the town of
Ushimado has the largest olive groves in the Far East.

Local authorities have been concentrating increasingly on tourism
during the past two decades, undertaking conservation and restoration
programs. In northern Bichu, near
Takahashi city, you can see the
fine 17th-century **Bichu**

Matsuyama-jo Castle, preserved samurai houses in **Ishibiya
Furusato village,** and **Raikyu-ji
Temple,** noted for its landscape
garden with raked sand offsetting
stones and azalea bushes shaped to
look like waves. In northern Bichu's

Takahashi
🅰 263 E3
Visitor information
✉ Bus terminal near
   Bichu-Takahashi
   Station
☎ 0866/22-6789
🚉 Train: Hakubi line
   from JR Okayama
   Station (1 hr.)

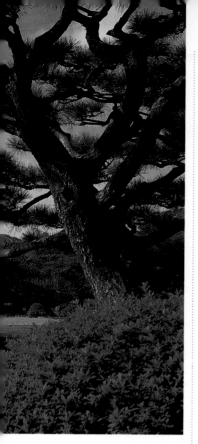

a samurai quarter, the Shuraku-en Garden, and the mid-19th century Tsuyama Archive, one of Japan's first centers of Western learning. There is also **Tanjo-ji Temple,** a National Treasure erected at the birthplace of Honen, founder of the Jodo sect of Buddhism. Tsuyama is known for its *onsen,* but there are several more in nearby **Maniwa,** where the pastoral scenery, complete with grazing cows, could almost be mistaken for Switzerland. In nearby **Shoei** is the eighth-century **Chofuku-ji Temple,** which is noted for a lovely pagoda standing in bold vermilion against a background of green hills.

Southern Bichu is best known for **Kurashiki** (see pp. 282–83), but it also has some pleasant resorts offshore, notably on the islands of Mukuchi, Shiraishi, and Manabe. The area includes **Tamashima** and its Kibi-ji Temple, renowned for its unusual Chinese garden. Looking out over the islands of Seto-naikai Inland Sea, the panorama from **Mount Washu-zan** was legendary—until the completion of the colossal 7.5-mile-long (12.3 km) **Seto Ohashi Bridge** connecting Honshu to Shikoku in 1988. If its six sections now dwarf the islands they span, the bridge is an amazing feat of engineering and a sight in its own right. Enthusiasts can get better acquainted with it at

Fukiya
Visitor information
☎ 0866/42-3211

Bizen city
🅰 263 F3
Visitor Information
🚉 JR Imbe Station
☎ 0869/64-1100
🚆 Train: JR Ako line from Okayama to Inbe Station (40 mins.)

scenic hills is the village of **Fukiya,** which preserves merchant houses from the Edo period, when the local economy thrived on copper mining.

Although its castle is now gone, **Tsuyama** town in Mimasaka has interesting vestiges of feudal days:

Bizen Pottery

Oone of the "big six" ceramic centers from medieval times, Bizen gained a reputation for unglazed stoneware prized for both looks and durability. The popularity of Bizen ware grew during the 15th century, when its rough-hewn quality was sought out by tea masters. The high iron content of the clay gives Bizen ware its typically deep red to dark brown color; it is sometimes used to make roof tiles. Varied firing techniques alter the color and produce a variety of subtle effects. The potteries of Bizen are in Inbe district. The streets around the station abound with workshops; you can learn before buying at Bizen Pottery Traditional & Contemporary Art Museum. ■

Okayama city

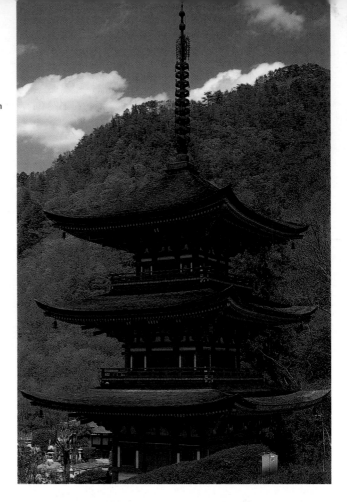

262 E3
**Visitor
information**

JR Okayama Station

086/222-2912

Train: from Tokyo
San-yo Shinkansen
(3 hrs. 15 mins.)

The pagoda at
Chofuku-ji
Temple

the **Seto Ohashi Memorial
Bridge Museum,** or take a boat
cruise around it from Kojima.

Encompassing Okayama city,
the southeastern region of Bizen is
famous for its pottery (see p. 279).
If you are in the vicinity of **Bizen
city,** take time to see the
Shizutani School, built in 1670
as the first public school in Japan
by the Ikeda lord ruling the
province. An abundance of iron
made Bizen a center for sword
making; at the **Bizen Osafune
Museum,** which also contains
local historical artifacts, you can
watch swordsmiths at work. On the
Bizen coast is **Ushimado,** a resort

prized for its olive groves, marine
views, and Mediterranean climate.

Okayama is best known for
the **Koraku-en Garden.** This is
one of Japan's three greatest stroll
gardens, a distinction shared with
the Kenroku-en in Kanazawa (see p.
180) and the Kairaku-en in Mito.
The Koraku-en was commissioned
by feudal lord Ikeda Tsunamasa in
1686 and completed in 1700. This
masterpiece of landscaping, with
ponds, watercourses, and hilly artificial islands, was carefully devised
to use the castle as borrowed
scenery. Here teahouses and elegant
pavilions stand on lawns against
backdrops of maple, cherry, and

apricot trees. Streams are crossed by various kinds of bridges and enhanced in June with displays of iris. Curiously, a rice field lies on the eastern shore of the Sawa-no-ike Pond, with a tea plantation just above it.

With its carefully shaped, rotund azalea bushes providing additional splashes of color against the lawns in early summer, the Koraku-en could have inspired the sets for *The Wizard of Oz*. The walk from the garden to the castle along a leafy path on the riverbank is especially pleasant. There is a small riverside restaurant with a great view over the castle.

Other remnants of Okayama's past were flattened with most of the city during World War II, including **Okayama-jo Castle,** which once stood at the city's heart. The castle was initially built in 1573. Painted black, it was dubbed U-jo—Crow Castle—in contrast to the famous White Egret Castle at Himeji (see pp. 256–57). The current version was built in 1966. Only the moon-viewing turret remains from the original, but the reproduction of the main donjon is realistic enough to provide a magnificent background to the

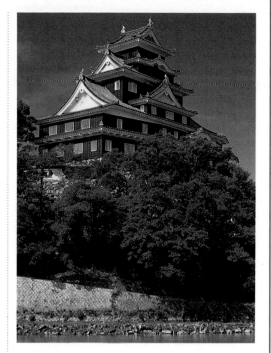

Koraku-en. Inside the stronghold is a museum of samurai memorabilia, including armor, weapons, and lacquerware.

Okayama has several other fine museums, all located in a "cultural zone" near the Koraku-en Garden. In a striking building by architect

Okayama's U-jo Castle was reconstructed in 1966.

Okayama Prefectural Museum of Art
- 8-48 Tenjin-machi
- 086/225-4800
- Closed Mon.
- $

Okayama Orient Museum
- 9-13 Tenjin-machi
- 086/232-3636
- Closed Mon.
- $

Hayashibara Museum of Art
- 2-17-15 Marunouchi
- 086/223-1733
- $

The Kibi Plain cycling path

Just outside the western confines of Okayama is Kibiji, a plain combining scenic beauty with historic temples and shrines. In recent years it has earned plaudits for a marvelous cycling path that takes in its main sights. From Okayama Station, four stops on the Kibi line bring you to Kibitsu, where you can rent a bicycle. Start with the Kibitsu Shrine, renowned for its architecture and long covered walkway. Pedal to Tsukuriyama burial mound (a fifth-century tumulus), then on

to Bichu Kokubun-ji Temple with its beautiful five-story pagoda rising above the rice fields. Near here is Soja, birthplace of the monk Sesshu (1420–1506), the great painter and calligrapher. The 12.5 miles (20 km) of the trip to Soja will have taken you past several more temples, shrines, and burial mounds. Another 2.5 miles (4 km) north of Soja Station is Hofuku-ji Temple, where Sesshu studied as a child. After seeing it, cycle back to Soja to drop off your bike. ■

**Yumeji Art
Museum**
✉ 2-1-32 Hama
☎ 086/271-1000
💲 $$

Okada Shinichi, the **Okayama
Prefectural Museum of Art
(Okayama-kenritsu
Bijutsukan)** displays works by
some of the region's greatest artists,
including the ink painter Sesshu
(1420–1506), the painter/writer/
master swordsman Miyamoto
Musashi (d. 1645), and the wood-
block print master Utagawa
Kuniyoshi (1797–1861). The
**Orient Museum (Oriento
Bijutsukan)** contains Asian
antiquities and is one of the finest
museums of its kind in Japan. The
**Hayashibara Museum of Art
(Hayashibara Bijutsukan)** is
devoted to the many priceless
objects and memorabilia belonging

to the Ikeda clan, which ruled
Okayama until 1868; its exhibits
include furniture, swords, and Noh
costumes, several designated
National Treasures. The **Yumeji
Art Museum (Yumeji
Bijutsukan)** shows many works
by Yumeji Takehisa, a painter and
illustrator beloved in Japan;
the quintessence of the early Taisho
era (1912–1926), this native son of
Okayama depicted willowy beauties
in a style akin to European
Expressionism.

Traveling 9 miles (15 km) west,
you can reach **Kurashiki** by train
from Okayama in roughly 15 min-
utes. The modern part of town near
the station is unremarkable, but

**Ohara Museum of
Art in Kurashiki**

follow the signs for Kurashiki Bikan Chiku to discover one of Japan's most charming townscapes. Mirrored in a still canal crossed by humpbacked stone bridges and bordered by willow trees, sedate and carefully maintained old wooden merchant houses stand alongside the town's quintessential warehouses. Kurashiki means "a spread of warehouses." The warehouses came in handy again from 1889, when an important cotton textile mill was located in Kurashiki.

The warehouse buildings are typically whitewashed, with attractive black-and-white tiled features on the facades. Several have been turned into museums, reflecting Kurashiki's important role as a center for arts and culture—its assurance of preservation during the modern era.

This happy state of affairs is thanks largely to the Ohara family, owners of the Kurashiki Spinning Corporation, which prospered before World War II. A great lover of Western art, Ohara Magosaburo amassed a collection, acquired by connoisseur Kojima Torajiro on his behalf, that warranted the creation of the **Ohara Museum (Ohara Bijutsukan).**

Graced with a Grecian facade, this outstanding museum was opened in 1930; substantially enlarged since then, it is now one of the finest museums in Japan. Don't let the paradox of traveling to Japan to find a museum devoted to Western art deter you from seeing a collection that would be equally impressive in Europe. Indeed, some of the works by Western-style Japanese artists may lead you to conclude they deserve a much wider international reputation. Western art is displayed in the two-story **Main Gallery (Honkan),** featuring a substantial array of works by artists ranging from

El Greco to Jasper Johns, with Gauguin, Monet, and Munch in between. The **Annex (Bunkan)** exhibits 19th-century and contemporary Japanese works in the Western tradition. Featuring rooms devoted to British ceramicist Bernard Leach and modern print master Shiko Munakata, the **Craft Gallery (Kogeikan)** also displays works by notable Japanese craftsmen of the modern era. The **Asiatic Gallery (Toyokan)** displays Kojima's remarkable collection of ancient Oriental art, including Chinese Sung and T'ang dynasty polychrome figurines.

Other notable museums include the **Kurashiki Museum of Folkcraft (Kurashiki Mingeikan),** with some 800 household items from Japan and around the world attractively laid out in a row of storehouses, and the **Japan Rural Toy Museum (Nihon Kyodogangukan),** with a collection of around 40,000 folk toys and dolls, including many from other countries. The **Kurashiki Archaeological Museum (Kurashiki Kokokan)** displays mainly artifacts discovered in Okayama.

The far-reaching Ohara cultural legacy has prevented the indiscriminate redevelopment that has blighted all too many places in Japan; it has transformed Kurashiki into a showcase proving that conservation pays. Although tiny in area, Kurashiki's Bikan district has such a wealth of things to see that it takes up the best part of a day. You could treat yourself to a very pleasant overnight stay, especially in one of the historical *ryokans*. The Ohara's old textile factory still stands, cleverly converted into **Ivy Square,** an attractive complex of exhibition spaces, craft workshops, restaurants, cafés, stores, and a hotel. ■

Kurashiki
🄰 263 E3
Visitor information
✉ JR Kurashiki Station
☎ 086/462-8681
🚆 Train: San-yo Hansen line or Hakubi line from JR Okayama Station (15 mins.)

Ohara Museum of Art
✉ 1-1-15 Chuo
☎ 086/422-0005
$ $$$

Kurashiki Museum of Folkcraft
✉ 1-4-11 Chuo
☎ 086/422-1637
🕐 Closed Mon.
$ $$

Japan Rural Toy Museum
✉ 1-4-16 Chuo
☎ 086/422-8058
$ $$

Kurashiki Archaeological Museum
✉ 1-3-13 Chuo
☎ 086/422-1542
🕐 Closed Mon.
$ $

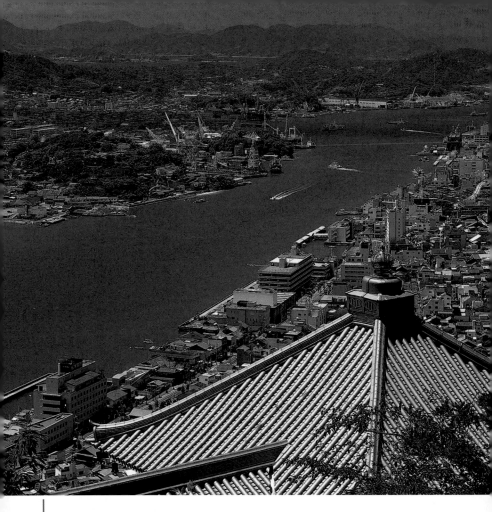

A spectacular view over the city and the Inland Sea unfolds from the peak of Senkoji-koen Park in Onomichi.

Onomichi

ONOMICHI IS ABOUT MIDWAY BETWEEN THE CITIES OF Okayama and Hiroshima, on a hill with a beautiful view over the islands of the Inland Sea. Established as a port during the 13th century, it prospered from trade with Ming China during the 14th. Until the end of the Edo period, it remained important as a center for shipping agents and for ferries to Shikoku.

Onomichi

263 D2

Visitor information

IF Himanami Koryukan

0848/20-0005

Train: Shinkansen from Okayama or Hiroshima to Shin-Omichi Station

Today the town around the foot of the hill is largely industrial, but from higher ground the view over the Onomichi Channel, where ships cross in both directions, has all the charm of an elaborate scale model. Above all, Onomichi is a temple town and a location much favored by Japanese writers and intellectuals since the early 20th century. On the strength of a 1981 hit movie by director Obayashi Nobuhiko that was set in Onomichi, the town acquired even further acclaim.

Onomichi's temples and other sights can be covered in a walking

A cable car climbs to the top of Senkoji-koen Park.

tour, starting in **Senkoji-koen Park.** The path is steep, so it is best to take the cable car near Nagaeguchi bus stop up to the hill-top in Senkoji-koen, which is famed for its cherry trees and azaleas.

On the **Bungaku-no-Komichi** (path of literature) down through the park to **Senkoji Temple,** numerous commemorative stones standing in the pines are carved with the words of famous writers exalting the view, which is probably at its best from outside the temple itself. From here walk about 440 yards (400 m) eastward downhill to **Fukuzen-ji Temple,** built in 1573 and noted for its carved gates. It is quite a climb north from here to **Saikoku-ji Temple,** but well worth the effort. Founded in the ninth century, this Buddhist temple is immediately identifiable by the gigantic *waraji* (straw sandals) at the Nio-mon gate. From here a further trek of a hundred steps takes you up to the main hall and three-story pagoda. As you walk back down, take a look at the antiquarian charm of the small **Josen-ji Temple.** Next, walk five minutes east to **Saigo-ji Temple;** built in 1543, the main hall and gate are fine examples of late Muromachi-period (1341– 1555) architecture.

Just downhill and eastward from Saigo-ji is **Jodo-ji Temple.** Founded in 616, this is a lovely complex of vermilion buildings, including a pagoda and a gate registered as a National Treasure. It also has a garden with a teahouse moved from Fushimi-jo Castle in Kyoto in the early 17th century. If you are up to yet another temple, to the east of Jodo-ji is little **Kairyu-ji Temple** and its statue of the deity Kannon; if you have had enough, at Jodoji-shita bus stop you can catch the bus back to the station. ∎

Hiroshima

Beneath this arch, a cenotaph contains a list of more than 200,000 A-bomb victims.

Hiroshima

📍 263 C2

Visitor information

✉ JR Hiroshima Station

☎ 082/261-1877

Visitor information

✉ Peace Memorial Park

☎ 082/247-6738

🚆 Train: Shinkansen from Tokyo (4 hrs.); from Kyoto (1 hr. 40 mins.)

"HIROSHIMA" IS A SYNONYM FOR THE HORROR OF WAR. It attracts campaigners for peace and nuclear disarmament from Japan and the rest of the world. Yet Hiroshima is also the prefectural capital of an important industrialized coastal region, a thriving new city whose optimistic inhabitants seldom mention the bomb.

Hiroshima's **Peace Memorial Park (Heiwa Kinen-koen)** and Memorial Museum play a useful role in providing future generations with warnings from the past. The image of the shell of a building known as the **A-Bomb Dome (Genbaku Domu)** illustrates history textbooks all over the world. Hiroshima's Industry Promotion Hall until the morning of August 6, 1945, it is now a World Heritage site, preserved much as it was after the explosion. The hypocenter—the point above which the bomb detonated—was about 110 yards (100 m) southeast of this hall. Although the dome stands northeast of the park on the opposite bank of the Motoyasu-gawa River,

Peace Pond, where the **Flame of Peace (Heiwa-no-To)** burns: It will not be extinguished until the last nuclear weapon is destroyed.

South of the cenotaph, the **Peace Memorial Museum (Heiwa Kinen Shiryokan)** completes the picture. The exhibits include detailed "before" and "after" scale models, melted bottles, tiles and metal appliances, burned and tattered school uniforms, a child's twisted tricycle, and disturbing photographs.

Reminders of the prewar city are few. **Hiroshima-jo Castle,** a concrete reproduction of the 16th-century castle obliterated by the bomb, contains a museum. Laid out in 1620, the **Shukkei-en Garden** had to be completely restored. **Fudo-in Temple** (*3-4-9 Ushita Shin-machi*), built on the Ota-gawa River in the mid-14th century, miraculously escaped damage; the main hall is a National Treasure. Crossed by broad rivers, Hiroshima is pleasant without being remarkable; distinctly hedonistic, it offers plenty of good food and a wide gamut of bars and restaurants in the raucous entertainment districts of Nagarekawa and Yagenbori. ■

it is now commonly regarded as one of the main features of the Peace Memorial Park.

Monuments commemorating the tragedy stand approximately in the park's center. The **Children's Peace Monument (Genbaku-no-Ko-no-Zo)** is festooned with garlands of thousands of colored paper cranes, a traditional "get well" symbol still made by schoolchildren all over Japan for the benefit of ailing survivors. At the center is the **Cenotaph (Genbaku Shibotsusha Ireihi)** by Japanese architect Tange Kenzo, underneath which lies a vault containing the names of the victims of the bomb. It stands in front of the rectangular

Peace Memorial Park
- Nakajima-cho, 1-chome, Naka-ku
- Peace Memorial Museum: $
- Tram: from Hiroshima Statin to Genbaku-Domu-mae

Hiroshima-jo Castle
- 21-1 Moto-machi, Naka-ku
- $
- Tram: 1, 2, 6 to Kamiya-cho, then 15-min. walk

Shukkei-en Garden
- 2-11 Kaminobori-cho, Naka-ku
- $
- Tram: 9 to Shukkeien-mae

The A-Bomb Dome stands as a lasting testament to the inhumanity of war.

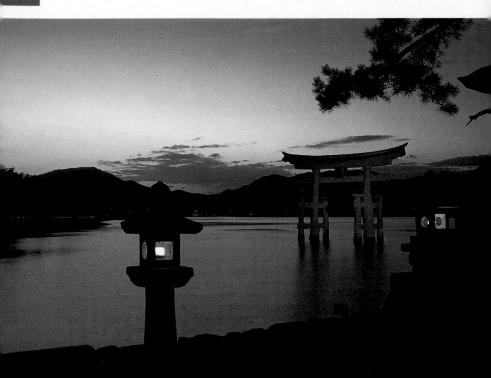

Low tide makes the most of the great _torii_ archway at Miyajima island.

Miyajima

MIYAJIMA (PROPERLY CALLED ITSUKUSHIMA) IS ONE OF Japan's three traditionally designated great scenic spots (the others are Amanohashidate in northern Kyoto-ken and Matsushima near Sendai; see pp. 161–62). Miyajima literally means "shrine island," for the spot has been sacred for around 1,500 years. Itsukushima Shrine, one of the nation's holiest Shinto shrines, complements the island's outstanding natural beauty; seeming to float above the water, its huge red _torii_ gateway is as much a symbol of Japan as Fuji-san.

Miyajima

🅰 263 C2

Visitor information

✉ Inside ferry building

☎ 082/944-2011

🚉 Train: from JR Hiroshima Station to Hiroden-Miyajima (55 mins.)

⛴ Ferry to Miyajima (10 mins.)

Just half an hour by train or streetcar and a ten-minute ferry ride from Hiroshima, Miyajima can be visited quite comfortably in an afternoon, but there is much to see; setting aside a whole day is a good idea. An overnight stop is a very tempting alternative, but not cheap.

Miyajima has scenic attractions year-round, from springtime cherry blossoms to autumn displays of maples in **Momijidani-koen Park,** and from beaches and seascapes to the wooded heights of Mount Misen. The perimeter of the island is almost 19 miles (30 km), making a bicycle the perfect way to get around. You can rent one next to the pier as you arrive; a battery-powered model is a good idea, as some of Miyajima's hills are quite steep. Tame deer roam the island at will, especially in the vicinity of the shrine and Momijidani-koen Park.

All the sights are concentrated on the north side of the island and up on Mount Misen. Extending along the coast between the ferry terminal and Itsukushima-jinja Shrine, Miyajima's little town is charming—if somewhat over-whelmed by souvenir stores. This is hardly surprising; Miyajima is also a center for woodcraft, both turned and carved. The most famous item is the *shakushi*, a wooden rice scoop said to have been invented here by a Buddhist priest during the Edo period and adopted all over Japan.

Itsukushima-jinja Shrine, dedicated to three sea goddesses who were daughters of the Shinto god Susano-o, is said to have been founded during the reign of Empress Suiko in 593. It reached its definitive form in 1168 under the patronage of Taira-no-Kiyomori (1118–1181), the great leader of the Heike (or Taira) clan and penultimate Heian-era ruler. The shrine, flanked by elegant covered corridors, is noted for its sweeping thatched roofs and the intense orange color of its delicate woodwork. Built on pillars right over the sea and appearing to float on the water at high tide, it is a truly outstanding example of Heian-period shrine architecture. Rows of bronze lanterns hang from the eaves; when these are lit on festive occasions along with the many stone lanterns on the shrine's coastal approach, the effect is magical. The famous **torii** is 175 yards (160 m) out from the shrine landing and stands 53 feet (16 m) high; made of camphorwood, it was rebuilt in 1875 for the eighth time.

The shrine precinct includes a nationally revered 16th-century Noh stage, used in sacred Jin-Noh performances (April 16–18). Just southwest of the shrine, the modern **treasure house** contains some 4,000 objects, 130 of which are Important Cultural Properties or National Treasures; these include fans, swords, armor, masks, and a set of famous painted sutra scrolls that once belonged to the Heike clan.

A short climb south of Itsukushima-jinja brings you to the enchanting **Tahoto pagoda,** built in 1523. From here the view over Itsukushima-jinja and the bay is particularly beautiful. On the way you should visit **Daigan-ji Temple,** responsible for the maintenance of Itsukushima-jinja until Shinto-Buddhist unity was outlawed in 1868. Miyajima's most important temple is **Daisho-in,** higher up to the southwest, which once oversaw the shrine's administration.

Itsukushima-jinja Shrine

Ⓢ Shrine: $; Shrine & treasure house $$

Thought to have been introduced by 12th-century warrior Taira Kyomori, ancient Bugaku court dances are still performed at Itsukushima-jinja Shrine on January 2, 3, and 5.

The spectacular hilltop view over Miyajima's charming pagoda

Hokoku Shrine
$ $

The summit of **Mount Misen,** accessible via a cable railway or a 90-minute walk, is well worth visiting. Apart from a breathtaking panorama over the Inland Sea from the summit, this 1,740-foot (530 m) mountain is a **Monkey Park (Misen Yaen-koen).** A sighting of the monkeys is not guaranteed—they often retire to the forest—but be aware that the animals can be fractious if they do appear; they have occasionally been known to attack overly effusive visitors. The rule is twofold: Avoid eye contact, and never try to feed them. Near the summit are a number of small temples, including one said to have been frequented by the priest Kukai (774–835), founder of the Shingon sect of Buddhism.

Up a hill north of Itsukushima-jinja Shrine is evidence of the ancient melding of Shintoism and Buddhism: the main hall of the **Hokoku Shrine (Senjokaku),** famous for its library of Buddhist sutras. Senjokaku means "Hall of a Thousand Mats," though it actually contains only 450.

This impressive open-sided building, reputedly made from the wood of a single camphor tree, was commissioned by Toyotomi Hideyoshi in 1587 to honor the war dead. The original intention was to paint it red to match the magnificent early-15th-century, five-story pagoda next to it, but Hideyoshi died the following year and the building was never completed. The hall contains thousands of *shakushi*—wooden rice scoops—left as votive offerings to the gods. Originating with soldiers about to leave for the front during the Sino-Japanese War of 1894, the custom emerged from a superstitious play on words: *Meshi-toru* means "to take rice," but a homonymous verb means "to conquer." ■

Thousands of islets dot the Seto-naikai, or Inland Sea, which is the channel between mainland Honshu and Shikoku, the smallest of Japan's four main islands.

Shikoku & the Seto-naikai

Women at the Awa-odori festival in Tokushima

Shikoku & the Seto-naikai

THE SMALLEST OF JAPAN'S MAIN ISLANDS, SHIKOKU LIES SOUTH ACROSS the Seto-naikai from Honshu. Despite a very long history of religious and political significance, it has always held the status of a poor relation. Shikoku means "four countries," referring to the feudal provinces of Sanuki, Awa, Iyo, and Tosa, now respectively the four prefectures of Kagawa (in the northeast of the island), Tokushima (south of Kagawa), Ehime (along the Inland Sea and westward), and Kochi (south and east of Ehime).

Although parts of the northern shore are heavily industrialized, Shikoku remains overwhelmingly rural and sparsely populated; the northern factories produce chemicals, but the mainstays of the island's economy are fishing and farming, especially fruits and vegetables. The respective prefectural capitals—Takamatsu, Tokushima, Matsuyama, and Kochi—are the main towns, but even these are comparatively quiet and unhurried. As the castles still standing in the last two imply, they were once the domains of feudal lords; another diminutive and charming castle remains intact in the coastal town of Uwajima in Ehime-ken. A more famous castle stands in Matsuyama, a town known, too, for its historic hot spring suburb of Dogo Onsen. Also in Ehime-ken is the town of Uchiko, unmissable for its unspoiled 19th-century buildings—many connected to a unique local candlewax industry.

Old Japan lives on in Shikoku. Traditional crafts such as ceramics, textile dyeing, weaving, and papermaking still thrive alongside colorful cultural events culminating in the frenzied Awa-odori summer festival in Tokushima (see pp. 299–300).

Between Honshu and its southerly neighbors Shikoku and Kyushu runs the Seto-naikai—literally the Sea within Channels, or Inland Sea. Of the thousands of islands, some are large enough to accommodate a population and, with towns, shrines, and temples, have a long history. Several were used as bases by the many pirates plundering ships around the Inland Sea in medieval times. Others are mere rocks capped with tufts of vegetation. Most share similar features: a rocky shoreline, a beach or two, and a pine forest on a central hill. Some of the larger islands have been inter-bridged for centuries. Nowadays the large islands—and many small ones—are spanned by huge steel bridges stretching from Shikoku. ∎

Area of map detail

Tokyo

0 — 50 kilometers
0 — 30 miles

WESTERN HONSHU (CHUGOKU) *p. 261*

Setoda
Omi-shima
Innoshima
Ikuchi-shima
SHIWAKU SHOTO

Seto Ohashi Bridge
Megi-jima
Shodo-shima

Harima-nada

◁5

◁4

Sakaide
Marugame
Yashima

KANSAI *p. 197*

Zentsuji Temple
Zentsuji
Takamatsu

KAGAWA-KEN

Onarutu Bashi Bridge

Kanonji
Kotohira Shrine
Kotohira
11
Naruto
Naruto-no-Uzishio

n a i k a i

Hiuchi - nada

Imabari
Hojo
32

Yoshino - gawa
Anabuki

Ryozenji Temple

Tokushima

◁3

Dogo Onsen
Matsuyama

Niihama
Saijo
11

Koboke
Oboke
1955m
Tsurugi-san

Iya no Kazurabashi

TOKUSHIMA-KEN

Komatsushima

Kii-suido

1982m
Ishizuchi-san

S h i k o k u - s a n c h i
32

Naka - gawa
Anan

Hiwasa
55

EHIME-KEN

Shikoku Karst
33

Kochi
Tosa
Nankoku

Aki

Ohama Beach
Kaifu

◁2

KOCHI-KEN
Susaki

Tosa - wan

55

△D
△E
△F

Taisho
Kubokawa

Muroto
Muroto-zaki

shimanto - gawa
56

Nakamura

◁I

Tosashimizu
Ashizuri-misaki

△C

An aerial view
of a coastal
town on the
Seto-naikai

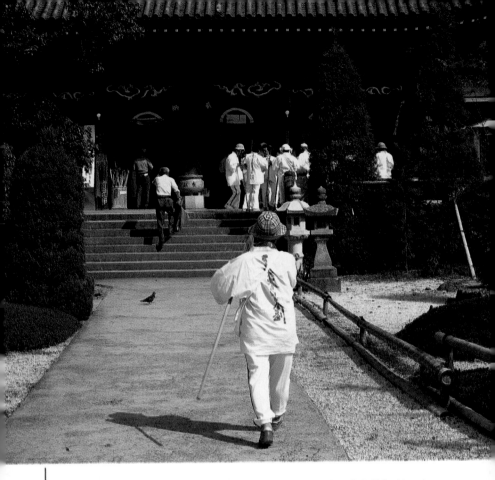

A straggler rushes to join his pilgrim group at Reizan-ji Temple in Tokushima-ken.

Shikoku

With a fairly mountainous topography and peaks reaching nearly 6,500 feet (2,000 m) in the east and center, Shikoku's landscapes are lush and scenic. Farming villages stand against hilly backdrops, fishing villages cling to rugged coastlines, and it is still possible to find deserted beaches on the south coast. Shikoku is endlessly—and justifiably—described as off the beaten track. With new bridges linking locations on the north coast to the mainland, however, and more on the way, all that may change.

Shikoku also has religious resonance. Sanuki province was the birthplace in 774 of Kukai (known posthumously as Kobo Daishi), the founder of the Shingon sect of Buddhism (see p. 226). Eighty-eight temples make up the most important pilgrimage route in Japan, a total of about 870 miles (1,400 km). The *henro*—pilgrims in Shikoku—believe that walking your way around them all is the way to rid yourself of the 88 worldly passions, thereby bringing you closer to salvation. For less pious folks with tight schedules, covering just the main sights and delights of Shikoku is feasible in about four days. ■

Takamatsu

THE ONARUTO BASHI AND SETO OHASHI BRIDGES between Shikoku and the mainland have undermined Takamatsu's status as the island's most important port, but the capital of Kagawa-ken is still the nucleus for ferries serving islands on Seto-naikai Inland Sea. One of the longest bridges in the world, the colossal Seto Ohashi linking Kagawa-ken to Honshu has itself become a tourist site (see p. 279), but the prefecture is better known for its more traditional aspects.

Takamatsu was originally the castle town that headed the feudal realm of Sanuki; **Takamatsu-jo Castle** (*Tamamo-koen Park, 5-min. walk from JR Takamatsu Station*), built in 1588, was later held by the Matsudaira clan until the 1868 Meiji Restoration. Sections of moats, ramparts, and turrets are all that remain, but **Tamamo-koen Park,** containing the castle ruins, is particularly pleasant.

Takamatsu was badly damaged during air raids in World War II, and its surviving sights are precious few; among them, **Ritsurin-koen Park** (*1.20-16 Ritsurin-cho),* one of Japan's most beautiful gardens, is

paramount. Laid out south of the city in the 17th century, this beautiful stroll garden was once the park attached to a villa built by the Matsudaira lords, which was destroyed after the Meiji Restoration. Ritsurin-koen took more than a century to complete and is often compared to the Koraku-en in Okayama (see pp. 280–81), one of Japan's three great gardens. Skillfully incorporating the pine-clad Mount Shiun-zan to the west, this masterpiece of landscaping is graced with ponds, curved bridges spanning meandering watercourses, artificial islands, and elegant teahouses. In one of

Beautiful Ritsurin-koen Park was laid out in the 17th century as a stroll garden for the Matsudaira feudal lords.

Takamatsu
📍 293 E4
Visitor information
✉ Outside JR
Takamatsu Station
✉ 0878/51-2009
🚆 Train: JR Seto-Ohashi
line from Okayama
(1 hr.)

Above: A woman prepares *macha* (powdered green tea whisked with hot water to a froth within the bowl), the refined, bitter beverage prized for the tea ceremony.

Below: A pine tree renowned for its age, outside the Kikugetsu-tei pavilion

the teahouses, **Chrysanthemum -Moon Pavilion (Kikugetsu-tei),** you can enjoy a tea ceremony as you admire the scenery. Your entry ticket to Ritsurin admits you to the Kikugetsu-tei (tea is extra) as well as to the display of local handicrafts at the **Sanuki Folkcraft Museum (Sanuki Mingeikan).**

To the east of the city is the plateau of **Yashima,** as famous to the Japanese for its spectacular panorama over the Inland Sea as for having been the site of one of

the epic battles of the 12th-century Heike Wars (see p. 31). Nearby is **Shikoku Mura** *(91 Yashima-naka-machi, tel 087/843-3111, 10-min. walk from JR Yashima Station),* an open-air museum bringing together several beautiful old farmhouses from all over the island, saved from the wrecker's ball and reerected here in a spacious park.

From Takamatsu you can make a pleasant day excursion to nearby islands, notably Mege-jima and Shodo-shima (see p. 314). ■

Kotohira

SOUTHWEST OF TAKAMATSU IS THE REGION OF KOTOHIRA, wherein lies Kotohira-gu, one of Japan's most sacred Shinto shrines. Just 4 miles (6 km) north of it is Zentsu-ji Temple marking the birthplace of the Buddhist saint Kukai, founder of the Shingon sect. Devotees believe that Shikoku's famous 88-temple pilgrims' route was devised by Kukai himself.

The **Kotohira-gu Shrine,** better known as Kanpira-san, is the most important of Shikoku's Shinto shrines and among the nation's most sacred. Located on the forested slope of Zozu-san, a 1,640-foot (500 m) hill, the shrine is dedicated to Omono-Nushi, god of seafarers and travelers. Particularly inspiring many of its multitudinous visitors with awe is the prospect of an hour's climb up 785 stone steps through the woods to get there. The ascent is not as dire as it sounds, however (except during a heatwave), for the shrine's buildings are so placed as to split the journey into easy stages. It is well worth the effort, and the spectacular views over the Sanuki Plain are a scenic lagniappe.

After passing through the imposing two-story **Main Gate (O-mon)** and along an approach lined with stone lanterns, you reach the **Treasure Hall (Homotsukan),** with Noh theater masks, painted scrolls, ceramics, and armor among the exhibits. The **Shoin** reception hall on the next level dates from 1659 and contains screen doors decorated by 18th-century landscape painter Maruyama Okyo (1733–1795), the greatest of a school of naturalistic painters influenced by Western art. A more arduous walk farther up the hill leads you on to the **Asahi-no-Yashiro** (Shrine of the Rising Sun), dating from the 1830s and famed for its ornate carvings. The next stage leads to the **Honden,**

Pilgrims puff their way up the 785 stone steps to the top of Kotohira-gu Shrine.

Kotohira
⬛ 293 D4

Kotohira-gu Shrine
✉ 892-1 Kotohira-cho, 40-min. walk from either Kotoden-Kotohira Station or JR Kotohira Station
$ Treasure Hall $; Shoin $

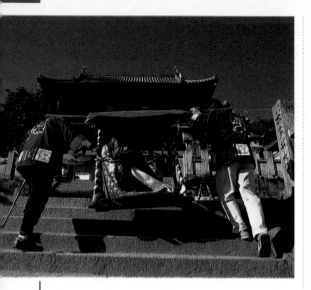

Old-fashioned kago palanquins are on hand if the going gets too tough up the steep steps to the Kotohira-gu Shrine.

and most sacred level, **Okusha,** the inner shrine.

Near the steps leading to the entrance to the shrine compound at the bottom of the hill is the **Kanamaru-za Kabuki Theater;** the oldest Kabuki theater standing in Japan, it was built in 1835 and painstakingly restored in the 1970s. Plays are staged here during the month of April, but you can visit it any other time to see, among other things, the revolving stage from underneath.

Zentsu-ji Temple, 4 miles (6km) to the north of Kotohira Shrine, is one of the most important temples of the Shingon sect and one of the most famous in Japan. Number 75 on the pilgrim route, it is said to have been founded by Kukai in 813 on the spot where he was born, though none of the original buildings survive. With magnificent camphor trees as old as the temple itself, the precinct has a grand five-story **pagoda** and a **Treasure Hall** containing exhibits brought back from China by Kukai himself. ∎

the main hall, built on stilts on a steep incline in a fashion similar to Kiyomizu-dera temple in Kyoto (see p. 213).

On the same level is the **Ema-do,** a hall filled with votive offerings in maritime themes, including model ships. After another half-hour's climb you reach the final

The Sacred 88

The saint Kobo Daishi (born in 774) is popularly attributed with founding the Shikoku pilgrimage route—probably Japan's most famous. The idea is to proceed further upon the path to enlightenment and higher up the karmic cycle of reincarnation by ridding oneself of the 88 worldly passions.

Along the way there are 88 temples, one for each, running clockwise around the island and representing a distance of about 870 miles (1,400 km). Some temples, notably Ishite-ji (No. 51), sell all the proper gear—the kasa or conical sege hat, a white tunic, straw sandals (which need regular

replacement), Buddhist prayer beads, and a wooden staff.

The journey begins at Reizan-ji Temple in Tokushima-ken, winding up at Okubo-ji Temple in Kagawa-ken. The most arduous section is along the mountainous route linking the 16 temples in Kochi-ken (numbers 24–39 of the circuit). A few adepts really do make the trip on foot; it takes roughly two months. Even though attired to look the part, these days most pilgrims bus or drive their way around in about ten days; the majority are retirees. The route is also highly scenic—and thus a great way to discover Shikoku. ∎

Zentsu-ji Temple

✉ 3-3-1 Zentsuji-cho, Zentsuji-shi, 20-min. walk from JR Zentsuji Station

$ Treasure Hall and Founders' Hall $$

Tokushima-ken

A spectacular natural phenomenon, the Naruto Whirlpools have been famed in Japan for centuries.

ON THE EAST OF SHIKOKU, TOKUSHIMA-KEN IS THE starting point for the 88-temple pilgrimage (see sidebar opposite). Pilgrims begin in Ryozan-ji, on the Naruto Peninsula in the north of the prefecture. The coast and mountains here have some particularly exciting natural sights.

Celebrated by Hiroshige in a wood-block print from the 1840s, the most famous seaward sight must be the **Naruto-no-Uzishio Whirlpools.** A curious natural phenomenon caused by the interaction of tidal currents in the straits between Naruto and Awaji-shima, the whirlpools occur four times daily and are best observed from the **Onaruto-bashi Bridge.** Hiwasa, a picturesque fishing town to the south, is known for a phenomenon from the animal world. Sea turtles come onshore on summer nights to lay their eggs, especially on **Ohama Beach,** alongside which is a turtle-related natural history museum. The turtle beaches are protected in summer. Tokushima's southern coast is a paradise for swimming and scuba

diving. Near Shishikui you can take the Blue Marine sightseeing trip under the subtropical waters—the boat is a kind of submarine.

Dominating the central mountain range is **Tsurugi-san** (6,414 feet/1,955 m), the second highest peak on Shikoku. Hiking options are plentiful, but cable cars run up to a point whence the summit is an easy 40-minute walk away.

In the mountains to the west of Tsurugi-san is the **Iya no Kazurabashi**—a dizzying but usable bridge (except for vertigo sufferers) made of intertwined *shirakuchi* vines, which are replaced at regular intervals. This was once the usual way to span gorges in Japan (this bridge has since been reinforced with steel safety cables); the vine bridges in Shikoku are now dyeing (notably for the local *shijira* textiles), and *otani yaki*—local pottery. Plain and unadorned earthenware, otani pottery is devoted mainly to kitchenware and utilitarian items—including huge jars for fermenting soybeans to make miso paste. Some jars are over 6 feet (1.8 m) tall, and potters must work in pairs to turn them.

Open to the public at various locations around the town, some of the workshops offer hands-on opportunities to try out the crafts yourself. To find out what is on offer, visit the new **Tokushima Prefecture International Exchange Association (TOPIA,** *tel 088/656-3303)* or **ASTY Tokushima** *(1 Boji Higashihama, Yamashiro-cho, tel 088/624-5111),* a colossal convention center with an area devoted to exhibitions, demonstrations, and sales of local crafts. Somewhat akin to Gion Corner, the distilled culture spot in Kyoto, ASTY also stages performances of Awa Ningyo Joruri (Awa puppetry), a local equivalent of the Bunraku of Osaka (see p. 48), which originated during the 17th century and was once presented by members of farming communities. The best performances are given at the **Inugai Nosonbutai** in November; amateur groups can be seen each weekend at the puppet theater, **Awa Jurobei Yashiki** *(Tel 088/665-2202).*

Above all, Tokushima is famous for the frenzied **Awa-odori festival** (August 12–15), a popular and boisterous festival. A throng of tens of thousands, most in traditional costumes from all over Japan, winds its way through the town, dancing to the hypnotic carnival music of flute and drums. "We are fools to be dancing and you are a fool to be watching," goes the chant, "So why not join in and dance?" Why not, indeed? ■

The Iya no Kazurabashi vine bridge spans a dizzying drop but is reinforced with steel safety cables.

Tokushima city
🅐 293 E3
Visitor information
✉ In front of Tokushima Station
☎ 088/622-8556
🚆 Train: Limited express from Takamatsu (1 hr. 10 mins.)

among the last. Largely because of the infrequent bus service, the bridge remains fairly remote and the surrounding area unspoiled—overall, a spectacular experience for hikers.

Though more easily accessible, much the same applies to the **Oboke and Koboke Gorges,** where a popular 7.5-mile (12 km) boat trip from the town of Oboke takes you through some equally breathtaking scenery.

The prefectural capital, **Tokushima,** was severely damaged in World War II air raids, and is probably a nicer place to live than to visit. But what it lacks in tourist sights it makes up for with its rich heritage of arts and crafts. Workshops and exhibits are devoted to *washi* papermaking, *aizome* indigo

Matsuyama

MATSUYAMA IS THE CAPITAL OF EHIME-KEN, WHICH stretches along the northern part of Shikoku to the west coast. Presenting the traveler with a perfect balance between the rustic and the historic, this highly scenic prefecture is quintessentially Shikoku. Mount Ishizuchi-san in the south offers fine alpine panoramas, while the subtropical Uwa-kai Sea on the west, facing Kyushu, is renowned for cultured pearls and Uwakai submarine park, where you can admire gardens of coral from a glass-bottom boat.

The shopping arcade in Matsuyama's Dogo Onsen district is replete with restaurants and attractive craft shops.

The city of Matsuyama itself is mainly modern and nondescript, except for the handful of noteworthy sights that survived World War II. Its principal attraction is the well-preserved **Matsuyama-jo Castle** (*1 Marunouchi, tel 089/921-4873*). Built on a hill above the city by feudal lord Kato Yoshiaki between 1602 and 1627, the castle was taken over by Gamo Tadachika when Kato was posted to Northern Honshu. The castle fell into the hands of the Matsudaira family in 1635 and was presented to the city by a descendant in 1923. Damaged by lightning in the 18th century, the main donjon was rebuilt in 1854;

Matsuyama
🅜 293 C3
Visitor information
✉ JR Matsuyama Station
☎ 0899/31-3914
🚆 Train: Limited express on JR Yosan line from Takamatsu (2 hrs. 20 mins.)

The memorial hall for poet Shiki Masaoka (1867–1902); Matsuyama is a national center for haiku poetry.

Matsuyama Municipal Shiki Kinen Museum
- ✉ 1-30 Dogo-koen
- ☎ 089/931-5566
- 💲 $
- 🚋 Tram: Dogo-onsen-eki from JR Matsuyama Station (20 mins.)

Shiki-do
- ✉ 16-3 Suehiro
- 💲 $

Iyo Textile Museum
- ✉ 1165 Kuman-no-dai
- ☎ 089/922-0405
- 💲 $

several turrets were damaged in arson attacks in the 1930s, and other buildings succumbed during World War II. However, the castle compound is intact overall. The harness tower, which contained military equipment and was rebuilt in 1968, is the only building to have been restored with concrete; all the others have been painstakingly put back exactly as they were, using wood and original carpentry techniques. Exhibits inside the castle include paintings, armor, and swords, but none are labeled in English. The castle grounds, reachable by cable car, are pleasant for strolling, especially when the cherry trees blossom out in April.

Matsuyama is where Natsume Soseki (1867–1916), the most celebrated of all early modern Japanese novelists (his portrait graces the 1,000-yen note), taught English as a young man and found inspiration for his novel *Botchan*. Soseki's boarding house has been restored as the **Gudabutsu-an,** now used for tea ceremonies and haiku poetry sessions. As the birthplace of the influential master poet Shiki

Masaoka (1867–1902)—a close friend of Soseki's—Matsuyama is regarded nationally as a center for haiku. **Matsuyama Municipal Shiki Kinen Museum** (of limited interest to foreign visitors) was built to commemorate the poet, along with Matsuyama's literary past. Just southeast of Matsuyama Station is a copy of Shiki's house—the **Shiki-do,** which stands on the precinct of Shoshu-ji Temple.

Eight of the 88 temples on the pilgrim's circuit—all worth visiting for their architecture and setting—are in Matsuyama, but the most revered is **Ishite-ji Temple,** No. 51, in the northeast of the city.

On the northwestern confines of the city is the **Iyo Textile Museum (Mingei Iyo Kasuri Kaikan),** devoted to *Iyo Kasuri*, an intricate local weaving process that uses cloth dyed with natural indigo. Matsuyama is well endowed with stores selling Ehime crafts, notably objects of woven bamboo and ceramics—especially the bold yet simple blue-on-white *Tobe-yaki* ware, made today much as it was 300 years ago. ∎

Dogo Onsen

ABOUT 2.5 MILES (4 KM) NORTHEAST OF MATSUYAMA IS one of Japan's oldest spas. Mentioned in seventh-century historical records, Dogo Onsen is said to date back to the age of the gods. Legend has it that the curative properties of Dogo's water were first noted when a white heron miraculously mended a broken leg by dipping it into the hot jet spouting from a rock; the notion of bathing for sheer pleasure came later.

Whatever the myth, the Dogo area was the administrative and cultural capital of Iyo—now Ehime—until the end of the 16th century. Along with a number of temples and shrines and a delightful streetcar station dating to the 1900s, the area is dotted with resort hotels. These inevitably include monumental kitsch palaces, but the oldest and most famous of the baths is the

Dogo Onsen Main Building (Honkan), an elaborate wooden structure built in Japanese castle style in 1894. Upstairs is the **Yushinden,** a special bath reserved for the Meiji imperial family, and a room said to have been used regularly by writer Natsume Soseki when the building was new. After luxuriating in the Kami-no-Yu (Water of the Gods) bathroom,

Dogo Onsen's ornate main spa remains exactly as it was in the 1890s.

Dogo Onsen
🅰 293 C3
Visitor information
✉ In front of Dogo
Onsen Station
☎ 089/921-3708
🚃 Tram: from
Matsuyama Station
to Dogo Onsen

Dogo Onsen Honkan

- 56 Dogo Yu-no-machi
- 089/921-5141
- Bath only $; bath with tea & sweets $$

Isaniwa-jinja Shrine

- 173 Sakuradani-cho

Ishite-ji Temple

- 2-10-21 Ishite
- Treasure Hall $

The Imperial Lounge at Dogo Onsen main spa building is where the Meiji imperial family would relax after bathing in the 1900s.

you are served tea in a large tatami hall—an experience with a fin-de-siècle appeal.

Just southeast of the Honkan is the imposing **Isaniwa-jinja Shrine.** Built in 1667 with a central tower in the Chinese style and adorned with intricate carvings, it is one of only three in Japan to show the distinctive architecture devoted to Hachiman, a god of war.

Another Dogo landmark, **Ishite-ji Temple** means "stone hand temple" (a local lord is said to have been born with his hand clutching a stone). Founded by Emperor Shomu in 728, this temple is No. 51 on the pilgrim's route and is said to have been rebuilt by Kukai himself (see p. 251)—though if Kukai had really built all the temples ascribed to him, he would have been an architect rather than a priest. The oldest and most noteworthy buildings date from the early 14th century: the beautiful entrance gate (a National Treasure) flanked by statues of fierce Deva

kings, the **Main Hall,** and a specially fine **three-story pagoda.** All three are designated Important Cultural Properties. The **Treasure Hall** contains some 300 exhibits pertaining to the history of the temple and the pilgrimage.

Over and above the cultural and historical, Ishite-ji's main attractions reside in the weird and wonderful. With pond-side statuary on a par with garden gnomes, and a spooky "mantra cave" in which you grope through a dark tunnel toward a cavern illuminated with 1970s-style psychedelic lamps and cosmic mandalas, much of the precinct is like a Buddhist amusement park. Up the hillside are dozens more Buddhist shrines and monuments, notably serried ranks of statuettes of Jizo, the guardian deity of children, travelers, and the unborn. Near the temple entrance is a shop selling proper pilgrim garb: white robe, conical hat, staff, and straw sandals. You can't miss it; look for the 1950s-vintage mannequins modeling the gear outside. ■

Uchiko

IT WOULD BE A SHAME TO VISIT MATSUYAMA WITHOUT traveling a mere 30 miles (50 km) southwest to the lovely rural town of Uchiko. Until the end of the 1920s, Uchiko's main industry was the manufacture of candle wax extracted from the berries of local sumac trees; its output met about one-third of national demand for everything from candles to crayons. Concentrated in the district of Yokaichi-Gokoku, the former workshops and merchant houses still stand.

Homemade candles await customers at Omori Rōsoku, the last candle-maker's shop in Uchiko.

Few Japanese towns can boast quite so many preserved and restored buildings as Uchiko. Painted white and cream and trimmed with black-and-white plaster work, **Yokaichi-Gokoku's** fine buildings are now part of a preservation area. Yokaichi-Gokoku is a single street 650 yards (600 m) long; along the way several buildings have been designated as Important Cultural Properties. Some of the restored buildings are still private houses, such as the **Hon Haga residence (Hon-Haga-tei),** built by the family that launched the Uchiko wax business in 1886; you can admire the house and its garden only from the street. However, the Haga family's 19th-century wax-making factory and attached private residence in the north of Yokaichi district, once the area's largest wax-making concern, is now Uchiko's star attraction, magnificently restored as the enthralling **Japan Wax Museum and Kami Haga Residence (Mokuro Shiryokan-Kami-Haga-tei).** Here you can see all the domestic furnishings and professional tools beautifully arranged in a fascinating display.

Candles have been made for generations by the same family in the workshop called **Omori**

Uchiko
🗺 292 B2
Visitor information
✉ Tourism Section, 3F Uchiko Town Hall
☎ 0893/44-2111
🚃 Train: Limited express from Matsuyama (25 mins.) or Uwajima (50 mins.)

Japan Wax Museum
✉ Yokaichi-Gokoku
☎ 0893/44-2771
💲 $$

Above: The Yokaichi quarter along Uchiko's main street has barely changed since the 1880s. Below: An Uchiko craftsman fashions candles using wax made from local sumac trees.

Rosoku (*Tel 0893/43-0385, closed Mon. and every 2nd and 4th Sat.*) on Yokaichi-Gokoku, where you can watch the process. The workshop is next to the **Machiya Shiryo-kan,** a town house dating from the 1790s and restored as a period museum in 1987.

Unfortunately the government subsidizes restoration only in designated areas, so some equally remarkable houses outside the Yokaichi district are in a sorry state of repair. However, the **Uchiko-za Theater,** a Kabuki theater built in 1916 just south of the Yokaichi area, was splendidly restored in 1985. Also preserved is a former pharmacy converted into the **Business and Livelihood Museum (Akinai to Kurashi Hakubutsukan,** *tel 0893/44-5220),* which uses wax mannequins to show what business was like there in the early 1920s. Exhibits in the rear building reflect the history of Uchiko crafts.

The Uchiko countryside is especially pretty, much of it devoted to farming (rice, shiitake mushrooms, grapes, and persimmons) and forestry. The continuing exodus to large cities, as in most rural areas, is causing some economic decline, but one countermeasure has been the introduction of Sightseeing Farms, where you can pick your own grapes, peaches, apples, or pears. Though often struggling, traditional industries—including candles and Japanese paper products such as lamps and umbrellas—survive in the area too. ■

Uwajima

THE MORE PLEASANT FOR SEEMING UNDERPOPULATED,
Uwajima's wide boulevards and modern buildings merely enhance
the lazy pace of this small port city on Shikoku's west coast. If you
are taking the ferry from Uwajima to Kyushu, the city merits a peek
for two noteworthy sights: its castle and Taga-jinja, a Shinto shrine
with an irresistibly bizarre sex museum.

Uwajima-jo Castle *(1 Maru-nouchi, tel 0895/22-3934)* was
originally built in 1595, then taken
over in 1616 by Masahide, son of
Masamune Date, lord of Sendai. It
remained in the Date family until
the Meiji Restoration of 1868.
Reduced from the original five
stories, the three-story main keep—
one of only 12 survivors nationwide—is virtually all there is. The
keep has been rebuilt several times
and was restored in 1962. It is quite
a trek up the hill to get there; some
say that is why no one took the
trouble to destroy it—the fate of
most other feudal castles during the
Meiji era. Just as likely, it was simply not important enough. Hardly
larger than a sizable mansion—but
elegantly proportioned in white
and perfectly charming—the castle
stands in a beautiful park with a
fine view over the city.

Taga-jinja Shrine is one of
the 40-odd Shinto shrines still

Uwajima

[M] 292 B2

Visitor information

[✉] Across from JR
Uwajima Station

[☎] 0895/22-3934

[🚆] Train: Limited
express on JR Yosan
line from
Matsuyama (1 hr.
30 mins.)

In *togyu*—sumo
for bulls—the
winner pushes
the loser out
of the ring with
his horns.

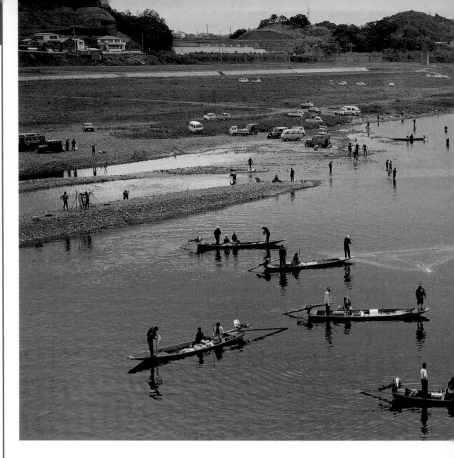

Taga-jinja Shrine

✉ Fujie Niku

☎ 0895/22-3444

💲 Shrine free; sex
museum $$

devoted to fertility deities. It stands in a small garden with miniature ponds and dry water pieces (stones arranged to suggest bodies of water) decked out with stone effigies of phallic gods. Already very small, the main hall is further dwarfed by the monster wooden phallus parked alongside it. To the back of it is a small building crammed with curious votive offerings, such as lengths of women's hair and broken dolls, but what really dominates the whole is the large concrete **sex museum.** Though mainly Japanese, exhibits also hail from India, Tibet, Latin America, and elsewhere; here are three floors of erotic and pornographic prints, paintings, bronze figurines, ceramics, curios, magazine clippings, and photographs.

However tempted you are, don't even think of laughing at anything in front of the high priest who mans the ticket booth. Having amassed this exhaustive and highly eccentric collection himself, he takes a dim view of those failing to take it seriously. "Even the emperor," he admonishes, "has sex."

Uwajima's other claim to fame is *togyu*—a kind of sumo for bulls. Weighing almost a ton each, the animals lock horns; the winner is the one that drives the other out of the ring. The practice is said to have emerged from the late 17th century, when the crew of a foundering Dutch ship presented their rescuers with a pair of bulls. Togyu at **Togyu-jo** (*Tel 0895/25-3511*) is staged only four or five times annually; call for times. ∎

Kochi-ken

EMBRACING THE CENTRAL MOUNTAINS AND THE LION'S share of the island's Pacific coast, Kochi is Shikoku's largest but emptiest prefecture, with one of the lowest population densities in Japan. Devoted to farming and forestry like Ehime-ken Prefecture, its western neighbor, it also boasts areas of genuine wilderness. In recent years its appreciable natural assets have earned it a growing reputation among lovers of the great outdoors.

Though its mild climate and fertile land (yielding two rice crops annually) have made it a choice place of habitation since prehistoric times, Kochi was sufficiently remote for mainland governments to exile renegades there during the medieval period. Kochi remained very poor until the last quarter of the 20th century. Before the Meiji period (1868–1912), it consisted of two fiefdoms, Hata and Tosa; the latter became increasingly dominant during the feudal era. Governing from Kochi-jo, the castle that still stands in the town that is now the prefectural capital (see p. 311), the Tosa lords ultimately emerged as some of the main opponents of the tottering Tokugawa shogunate in the 1860s. Among the dissenting Kochi samurai was Sakamoto

Summary sailors ply Kochi-ken's Shimanto-gawa River, Japan's cleanest and clearest.

Kochi City
🅰 293 D2
Visitor information
✉ JR Kochi Station
☎ 088/882-7777
🚆 Dosan line from Takamatsu (2 hrs.)

Kochi-jo Castle
✉ 10201 Marunouchi
☎ 088/872-2776
💲 $

Ryoma, one of the greatest architects and heroes of the Meiji Restoration, which he instigated by uniting the Satsuma clans (from Kyushu) and the Choshu clans (from the west coast of Chugoku). A statue commemorates Ryoma at Katsura-hama, a famous moon-viewing beach south of Kochi city. Assassinated in 1867 at only 31, he never saw the Restoration occur a year later.

Kochi is a paradise for hikers, campers, canoeists, rafting enthusiasts, swimmers, scuba divers, and even surfers (local connoisseurs have dubbed the stretches of black sand along the remote southeastern **Cape Muroto-misaki** "Little Hawaii"). The unpolluted **Shimanto-gawa River,** the only river in Japan still undammed, is the nation's cleanest. The crystal-clear waters—increasingly attracting visitors, especially kayakers—extend into breathtaking mountain scenery. Farther west, near the border with Ehime-ken, is the popular

and scenic **Shikoku Karst,** featuring alpine grassland with curiously formed outcroppings of limestone.

The western coast of Shikoku used to be much given to whaling, but with the decline of many species and the international ban on hunting the leviathans, **whale watching** tours have given whalers a viable alternative. The seascapes from **Susaki** southward and the landscapes crossing westward toward Uwajima are so lovely that the local train line uses open carriages in summer. Finally the coast narrows down to scenic **Cape Ashizuri-misaki,** noted as a temple stopover on the Shikoku pilgrimage—and as the birthplace of one of Japan's most extraordinary heroes, Nakahama Manjiro or John Manjiro (see below).

The center of **Kochi city,** 6 miles (10 km) from the coast flanked by the rivers Enokuchi-gawa to the north and Kagami-gawa to the south, contains a fine

Nakahama Manjiro or John Manjiro (1827–1898)

One of Japan's most extraordinary heroes, Nakahama Manjiro was born in a poor hamlet near Ashizuri-misaki. Shipwrecked at 14 on an uninhabited island far off the coast of Honshu in 1841, he and his fellows were rescued months later by a U.S. whaling ship. For the next four years, Manjiro traveled the world with the crew. The captain recognized the lad's potential and took Manjiro back to Massachusetts, where he studied English, mathematics, and navigation as John Manjiro. He returned to Japan in 1851 and as interpreter during the negotiations between

Commodore Matthew Perry and the shogunate in Edo played a key role in opening up the country. He pioneered the teaching of English at what would become Tokyo University and traveled abroad as one of Japan's first diplomats after the Meiji Restoration of 1868. ∎

feudal castle. Most other sights are farther out in the suburbs, but that makes little difference, as Kochi—although a prefectural capital—is really a small town, and sights are easily accessible on short bus or streetcar trips.

It was **Kochi-jo Castle,** on a strategic hilltop originally called Kochi-yama, that gave the prefecture its name. Initiated by the Tosa lord Yamanouchi Kazutoyo in 1601, construction lasted a decade. The main keep suffered serious damage in a fire in 1727 and was rebuilt some 20 years later on a smaller scale; with its lovely garden setting, the castle complex became a charming aristocratic residence rather than an awe-inspiring fort.

A century later the main barracks were moved south of the castle to the bank of the Kagami-gawa River as the **Shimoyashiki Nagaya;** still standing, they are open to visitors. After feudal landowners were ousted during the early Meiji period, most of the castle buildings were destroyed, except for the main keep and the main gate. On the path between the gate and the main keep stands a statue of Itagaki Taisuke (1837–1919), a great campaigner for true democracy (as opposed to the mere substitution of authoritarian nationalism for military feudalism) during the Meiji period, and one of Tosa's greatest sons. In addition to samurai memorabilia, the **museum** inside the castle displays a Roman alphabet written by Nakahama Manjiro.

Reflecting Kochi's rural face, a picturesque market held on Sundays runs from the main gate of the castle for half a mile (1 km) along Otesuji-dori—a tradition enduring since the middle of the Edo period.

Kochi city's other main sight is the attractive hilltop **Godaisan-koen Park,** which has a fine city panorama and embraces **Chikurin-ji,** a temple (No. 31 on the pilgrim circuit) founded in the eighth century and noted for its five-story pagoda.

You could also visit **Katsura-hama,** on Urado Bay about 7.5 miles (12 km) south of Kochi city, reputedly the most beautiful of the region's many beaches and a spot cherished since ancient times for moon-viewing. Because of the proliferation of "No Swimming" signs on sand that is more like grit, the appeal to foreign visitors is limited. Katsura-hama's main draws are a statue of Sakamoto Ryoma, Kochi's greatest hero, and the **Sakamoto Ryoma Memorial Museum** just west of it, housed in a striking modern building. The beach is probably better known in connection with Tosa fighting dogs: The hounds are exploited in contests where the first dog to pull down an opponent with its teeth wins. ∎

Shimoyashiki Nagaya
- ✉ 1-3-35 Takajo-cho
- ☎ 088/822-6394

Chikurin-ji Temple
- ✉ Godai-san
- ☎ 088/822-3085
- 💲 Treasure house & garden $$

Sakamoto Ryoma Memorial Museum
- ✉ 830 Shiriyama, Urado
- ☎ 088/841-0001
- 💲 $$

A hybrid between a European mastiff and a bulldog, the Tosa hound is prized for dog-fighting that would make animal lovers squirm.

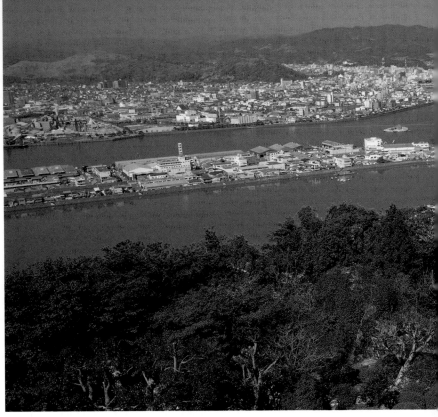

The Seto-naikai is spanned by a series of bridges that link many of the islands.

The Seto-naikai

Few views outside the Aegean equal those on the Seto-naikai—the Inland Sea. At sunset the myriad islands fade back into the horizon or seem to detach themselves against the coastline of Honshu or of Shikoku to the south.

Many of the larger islands are not only interconnected, they are also linked via the bridges and roads crossing from Honshu to Shikoku. Consequently, the islanders find themselves in an era of major change. Lesser-known islands, devoted to fishing and farming, have little to offer except seascapes and tranquillity.

If you're on your way to Shikoku and starting from the eastern end of the Seto-naikai, you can go via the Akashi Bridge near Kobe and cross over to Awaji-shima. Spanning the Inland Sea from south of Kobe to Naruto on Shikoku, Awaji-shima is the Seto-naikai's largest island. A much better gateway for

exploring the Inland Sea is Takamatsu on Shikoku, which provides regular services to Shodo-shima and Oni-ga-shima.

There are many other alternatives as well. Ferries throughout the Seto-naikai start from as far east as Osaka, but the most popular routes are those in the west, notably from Hiroshima and Miyajima by sea or from Onomichi by bridge or boat. Boats on the San-yo coast also offer dozens of richly scenic one-day Seto-naikai tour options. Whatever you choose to do, seek advice first from the visitor information center in your place of departure. ■

The islands

OTHER THAN AWAJI-SHIMA, THE ISLANDS DESCRIBED HERE
are those closest to the San-yo coast of Honshu and those closest
to Shikoku.

Awaji-shima made headlines in
1995, when a spot just beneath the
northern tip of the island was iden-
tified as the epicenter of the Kobe
Earthquake. Mainly flat and scattered with pines, the island is close
enough to Osaka and Kobe to have
become akin to a suburban park.

The Akashi Bridge near Kobe
has made Awaji-shima easily accessible from the mainland, while the
Onaruto-kyo Bridge at the southern tip of the island links the island
with Shikoku. Directly beneath
the bridge are the spectacular
Naruto whirlpools.

Ikuchi-jima, Omi-shima, and
Inno-shima are all main stopping
points on Seto Naikai tour-boat
routes from the San-yo coast,
although the Nishi Seto highway
that connects them means they can
also be visited by car or bus.

The focus of **Ikuchi-jima** is
Setoda, a pleasant little town
embracing all the island's main
sights. You get spectacular panoramas over the Inland Sea from
Kojo-ji Temple, built on the hilltop in 1403 and graced with a fine
three-story pagoda. But the majority of the 500,000 tourists flocking

Awaji-shima
⬛ 293 F4
Visitor information
✉ 2F Highway Oasis-
kan
☎ 0799/72-0168
🚌 Bus: express from JR
Sannnomiya Station
(Kobe) to Iwaji-
Interchange bus
stop (35 mins.)
⛴ Boat: from Kansai
International Airport
to Tsuna, Awaji-
shima (41 mins.)

Ikuchi-jima
[A] 294 C4
Visitor information
☎ 08452/7-0051

Setoda History & Folklore Museum
☎ 08452/7-0280

Omi-shima
[A] 293 C4
Visitor information
✉ Ferry terminal at Miyaura
[FAX] 0897/82-1065

Inno-shima
[A] 293 C4
Visitor information
✉ Inside ferry terminal at Habu
[FAX] 08452/2-333

Oniga-shima
[A] 293 D4
Visitor information
[FAX] 087/873-0211

Shodo-shima
[A] 293 E4
Visitor information
✉ Inside Tonosho ferry terminal
[FAX] 0879/62-6256

Hon-jima
[A] 293 D4
Visitor information
✉ Honjima Park Center
[FAX] 0877/27-3328
🕐 Closed Thurs.

to Ikuchi-jima annually are drawn down Setoda's main street to **Kosan-ji Temple.** Erected in 1936, Kosan-ji is one of Japan's greatest contributions to world kitsch. It is noted for its scaled-down reproductions of famous Japanese religious buildings; made of cheap materials such as plywood and gaudier than the originals by far, they include Nikko's Tosho-gu Shrine and Kyoto's Golden Pavilion. Learn about the island's past at the **Setoda History & Folklore Museum** on the seaward end of the main street.

The pleasant and hilly island of **Omi-shima** was the favored abode of pirates in medieval times. Its **Oyamazumi-jinja Shrine** is as old as any Shinto shrine in Japan, including Ise, though current buildings date from 1427. The shrine is known above all for its **Treasure Hall,** which contains the finest and most extensive collection of samurai swords and armor in Japan.

Inno-shima now depends upon farming, especially flowers and fruit, but this island was once a pirate stronghold, notably for the Murakami clan. Up on a hill is **Konren-ji Temple,** which was the family temple and graveyard; next to it is their castle, known as **Innoshima Suigun-jo Pirate's Castle.** Heavily restored, the three remaining buildings are now a museum. A walk up **Shirataki-yama,** the hill dominating the island, will take you along a path flanked by more than 500 stone effigies of the Buddha and reward you with a superb view over the sea.

Oniga-shima and Shodo-shima, the best known of the islands closer to Shikoku, are usually accessed by ferry from Takamatsu. The small island of **Oni-ga-shima** (also known as Mege-jima), another favorite with pirates, has a network of caves they once used as a hideout.

Legend has it that the caverns were once occupied by demons called Oni—hence Oni-ga-shima (Demon Island). There are few sights on Oni-ga-shima, but there is much to be said for staying in one of the little inns along the beach and, after a fresh seafood dinner, falling asleep to the sound of the surf.

The rocks used to build the ramparts of Osaka-jo Castle in the late 16th century were quarried on the larger island of **Shodo-shima;** the undelivered surpluses at Omi and **Iwagatani** remain as a sight attracting visitors. The quarry, in the island's northeast, is still active. Although Shodo-shima is not short on sights, especially magnificent views, tourists paid more visits to the island after it was used as the setting for *24 Eyes,* a poignant 1954 movie classic about ordinary lives devastated by war and a teacher remembered by her pupils. The fictional teacher and her charges have been immortalized in a monument at the ferry terminal; the village school in **Tanoura,** the one used in the movie, has become a tourist spot. The island's mountain range includes the highly scenic gorges of **Kanka-kei** and **Choshi-kei.** Kanka-kei has a viewing platform accessible by cable car, while Choshi-kei is near a hill where the wild monkey population gathers for handouts. Mainly devoted to farming, the island is known for its olive groves—unusual in Japan. Olives are said to have given the island its name; *shodoshima* literally means "little bean island."

From the port of Marugame, to the west of Takamatsu on Shikoku, you can visit the **Shiwaku-Shoto** group, comprising about a dozen islands in all. The most notable is **Hon-jima,** where there is a street of attractive late-Edo-period houses faced with white plaster ornamented with black and white tiles. ■

The island closest to the Asian mainland, Kyushu has been a gateway to China, Korea, and the rest of the world for centuries. Kyushu is the most volcanic area in Japan—and that makes it one of the most volcanic on Earth.

Kyushu

Detail from ornate Chinese temple roof in Nagasaki

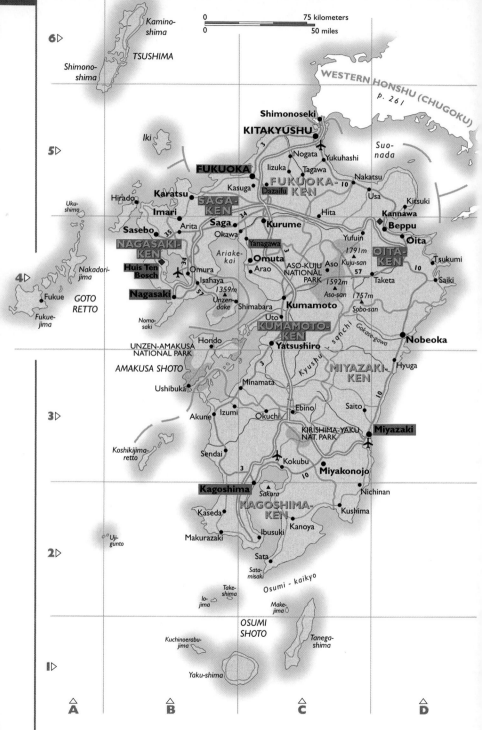

Kyushu

THE JAPANESE ARE FOND OF COMPARING KYUSHU, WITH ITS MILD CLIMATE, vivid blue-green seas, and citrus trees, to the Mediterranean. The character of the residents is also described as Mediterranean, with traditional Japanese reserve taking a backseat to more demonstrative temperaments.

Kyushu means "nine regions," which is what it embraced in ancient times. Today it comprises seven prefectures: Fukuoka-ken, Oita-ken, Kumamoto-ken, Nagasaki-ken, and Saga-ken in the north, and Kagoshima-ken and Miyazaki-ken in the south. The most southerly of Japan's main islands and the third largest, Kyushu is linked to western Honshu by road and rail via an undersea tunnel. The island is heavily industrialized—especially the north—and wealthy: In 1993 its GDP of $411 million equaled one percent of the world total, with most of that from Fukuoka-ken.

The first place you come to when traveling from Honshu is Kitakyushu city, really several townships engulfed in a drab urban-industrial sprawl. Vibrant and hedonistic Fukuoka, the prefectural capital and the island's largest city, offers more historical, architectural, and scenic interest. A host of islands beckons wanderers off the beaten track.

Northern Kyushu is just 125 miles (200 km) from Korea, making Nagasaki closer to Shanghai than to Tokyo. Kyushu was Japan's cradle of civilization, and its history reflects its cosmopolitanism. Archaeological sites in Saga-ken reveal the first evidence of rice farming, introduced to Japan from Korea. The world-class reputation of ceramics from Karatsu and Imari was built upon the skills of Korean craftsmen in the 16th and 17th centuries.

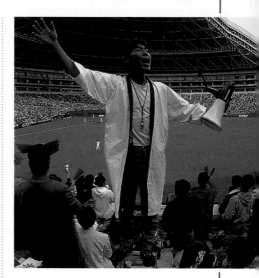

A cheerleader exhorts the fans at Fukuoka Dome baseball stadium.

The first Europeans to come to Japan were Portuguese sailors shipwrecked off the southern Kyushu coast in 1543. They introduced the Japanese to firearms and tobacco and paved the way for traders and missionaries. Vestiges of bygone relations with Europe, both mercantile and religious, survive in Nagasaki city—notwithstanding the horrific destruction wrought by the atomic bomb in 1945.

Kyushu shows even more volcanic activity than the rest of Japan and has a great number of hot springs. Mount Aso-san boasts the largest caldera on Earth; its scenery makes it the most visited of Kyushu's volcanoes despite its temperamental nature. There are also several volcanoes in Miyazaki-ken, renowned for its *onsen* and beach resorts. Sakura, the Japanese equivalent of Vesuvius, stands smoldering just over the bay from Kagoshima, earning the city the designation "the Naples of Japan." ■

Area of map detail

Tokyo

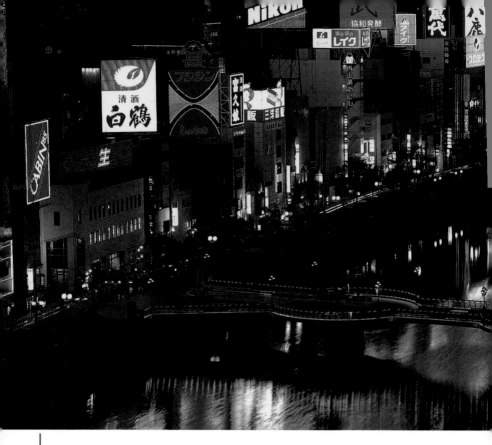

Fukuoka

FUKUOKA IS RAPIDLY BECOMING THE INTERNATIONAL hub of Kyushu, the nation's fourth largest economic zone. Lying on a broad bay, Fukuoka is divided into two: the northeastern sector, Hakata, which embraces the port; and Fukuoka itself, which lies on the western bank of the Naka-gawa River. Mercantile, brash, energetic, and hedonistic, the capital is Kyushu's equivalent to Osaka—and not the place to seek the prefecture's historical sights. However, what Fukuoka city lacks in historical sights is perhaps made up for by its modern architecture, some of which is strikingly innovative—especially in Tenjin, Hakata, and on the west side of the bay.

Fukuoka-Hakata

316 C5

Visitor information

JR Hakata Station

092/431-3003

Train: Shinkansen from Tokyo (4 hrs. 40 mins.)

After building their castle at the outset of the Edo period, the ruling Kuroda clan gave the name Fukuoka to the samurai quarter newly dominating the plebeian and merchant harbor-town of Hakata. It was under this name that the two sections of town were administratively reunited in 1886, but local inhabitants—overwhelmingly descended from commoners rather than samurai—preferred to call it Hakata. They still do, and true native citizens like to be called

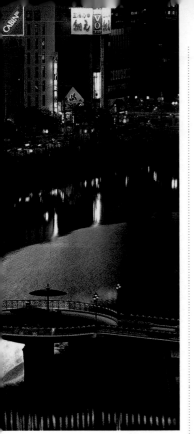

Imazu. Older ruins and archaeological sites surround Fukuoka city; some exhibit evidence of the earliest rice culture in Japan.

The **Fukuoka City Museum (Fukuoka-shi Hakubutsukan)** houses a gold seal unearthed in the 18th century on Shikano-shima, an island in Hakata-wan Bay. It shows just how far back Fukuoka's links with the mainland go; the seal was presented to the ruler of an erstwhile kingdom by the emperor of Han dynasty China in A.D. 57.

Hakata is the more interesting part of the city, and sights tend to concentrate there. To the west of the city center is the business and shopping district of Tenjin, with its futuristic underground mall and the architecturally amazing **IMS (Inter-Media Station) Building,** devoted to fashion and communications.

The city was heavily damaged during World War II air raids, so historical sights are few. Among them is **Hakozaki-gu Shrine.** Founded in 923, it is one of Japan's three great Hachiman shrines, dedicated to the eponymous Shinto god of war. The main buildings date from 1546, and the garden is famous for its year-round display of peonies.

Shofuku-ji Temple, half a mile (1 km) northwest of Hakata station, is celebrated as the first Zen temple in Japan; it was reputedly built by Eisai (1141–1215), founder of the Rinzai sect, but no original structures remain. Said to have been founded in the eighth century, **Kushida-jinja Shrine,** 650 yards (600 m) west of Shofuku-ji toward Naka-gawa River, is Hakata's main shrine. It sees plenty of action as the focus of the Hakata Gion Yamakusa festival (July 1–15), the city's great summer fete.

To the south of the shrine is **Hakata Machiya Folk History**

Hakatakko. If you travel to Fukuoka on the shinkansen, you might be confused: The main station is JR Hakata.

From ancient times, the port of Hakata had been the gateway for exchanges with China and Korea. Not that contacts with the mainland were always peaceful. Hakata twice played a decisive role in fending off Mongol emperor Kublai Khan's attempts to invade Japan. In 1274 the Mongol invaders were strongly resisted, and after that a 12-mile (20 km) anti-Mongol wall was built along the coast. In 1281, the Mongol fleet was destroyed by a spectacular typhoon, a fortuitous intervention venerated ever since as *kamikaze*—the wind of the gods. Parts of the wall still stand at Nishijin, Iki-no-matsubara, and

Hakozaki-gu Shrine
- ✉ 1-22-1 Hakozaki, Higashi-ku
- 💲 Shrine free; Garden $$
- 🚇 Subway: Hakozaki-Miya-mae

Shofuku-ji Temple
- ✉ 6-1 Gokusho-machi, Hakata-ku
- 🚇 Subway: Gion

Kushida-jinja Shrine
- ✉ 1-41 Kami-Kawabata-machi, Hakata-ku
- 🚇 Subway: Kawabata

Hakata Machiya Folk History
- ✉ 6-10 Reisen-machi, Hakata-ku
- ☎ 092/281-7761
- 💲 $
- 🚇 Subway: Gion

(Hakata Machiya Furusato-kan), with exhibits pertaining to the summer festival and the town from the Edo period to the 20th century.

The colorful old-style covered shopping arcade of **Kawabata** lies at the northern end of the shrine, currently part of a preservation-and-reconstruction package for the whole neighborhood.

Fukuoka's other attractions are more contemporary. Most of them center around **Nakasu,** the island amusement district built on what had been a sandbank in the middle of Naka-gawa. Just south of it on the east bank is remarkable new **Canal City,** a hyper-modern shopping and entertainment complex complete with bright red tiers of terraces and fanciful water-pieces providing perpetual sound-and-light shows. Wired with noise and neon, Nakasu island is wall-to-wall restaurants, bars, *pachinko* parlors, strip joints, and questionable cabarets—all vying with Tokyo's Shinjuku as the ultimate amusement district in Japan.

While you're there, don't miss the food stalls along the bank of Nakasu-gawa. Food vendor's carts, or *yatai,* are still trundled into amusement districts each evening. In Hakata, they are permanent—and reputed to serve the best ramen noodles in Japan. ■

Yatai foodstalls along the river pack 'em in with some of the finest noodles in Japan.

Dazaifu

ALMOST A SUBURB OF FUKUOKA AND JUST 40 MINUTES away by train, Dazaifu was Kyushu's seat of government from its establishment in A.D. 664 until it began to decline at the end of the 12th century. It was also important as a center for trade with China.

When you arrive at Dazaifu Station, head straight for the tourist information center just outside to pick up an excellent English-language pamphlet clearly mapping and explaining the area and its sights. Visiting the area by bicycle is a pleasant and convenient alternative; the tourist information center is also the place to rent one.

The ancient government office, called the **Tofuro,** was a vermilion wooden structure with a tiled roof; embedded in an expanse of grassland, the massive foundation stones are all that remain. The same applies to vestiges of earthen walls and embankments to the west and north toward **Ono-jo fortress,** built on a hill to defend Dazaifu. This hill (then called Ono and now Shioji) holds other remnants of the distant past. Despite their rich

background, the old sites are essential viewing only for those with special historical interests.

Just south of the Tofuro, you can find out more about the ancient city at **Dazaifu Exhibition Hall.** At the foot of Shioji is **Chikuzen Kokubun-ji Temple** *(4-14-1 Kokubu, Dazaifu-shi)*. Only foundation stones remain from the huge temple precinct built by Emperor Shomu in 741, but the present temple is attractive and contains a fine eighth-century Buddha statue.

Another of the more famous old historical sites is the **Kaidan-in,** an ordination hall that was one of only three in Japan during the eighth century. Next to it, to the east, is **Kanzeon-ji Temple,** once rivaling even Chikuzen Kokubun-ji in size. Although the old structures vanished long ago, the temple's

Dazaifu Tenmangu Shrine is devoted to Sugawara-no-Michizane.

Dazaifu

🅰 316 C5

Visitor information

✉ Nishitetsu-Dazaifu Station

☎ 092/925-1880

🚉 Train: Nishitetsu line from Fukuoka Station, change at Futsukaichi (35 mins.)

Dazaifu Exhibition Hall

✉ 4-6-1 Kanzeonji, Dazaifu-shi

☎ 092/922-7811

🕐 Closed Mon.

 $

Partly girt by the temple veranda, the landscape garden at Komyozenji Temple has few rivals anywhere in Japan.

Kaidan-in

✉ 5-7-10 Kanzeonji, Dazaifu-shi

Kanzeon-ji Temple

✉ 5-6-1 Kanzeonji, Dazaifu-shi

Dazaifu Tenman-gu Shrine

✉ 4-7-1 Saifu, Dazaifu-shi

Komyo-zen-ji Temple

✉ 2-16-1 Saifu, Dazaifu-shi

💲 $

current buildings date from the 17th century. The bell *(bonsho),* cast around 745, is from the original temple and is reputedly Japan's oldest. Do not miss the **Treasure Hall,** which contains an outstanding collection of Buddhist statues from the 8th to 12th centuries.

The area's greatest draw is the **Dazaifu Tenman-gu Shrine,** dedicated to Sugawara-no-Michizane, a wrongfully exiled tenth-century scholar who was posthumously deified as Tenjin, the Shinto god of literature and learning. Students flock here to pay their respects. The shrine was founded in the tenth century, but the current **Main Hall,** featuring ornate carving beneath its thatched roof, was built in 1591. The precinct encompasses plum and camphor trees, as well as irises; along the approach is a watercourse spanned by a celebrated humpbacked bridge. To the right of the Main Hall is an apricot tree that, according to legend, uprooted itself from Michizane's Kyoto garden and followed him to Dazaifu. It is said to have stood on this spot for a thousand years.

In one of the smallest of the many souvenir shops along the shrine approach sits a craftsman painting ceramic Hakata dolls. A Fukuoka specialty, the dolls represent traditional dancing girls; while the craftsmanship is exquisite, they tend to be aesthetically insipid.

The overwhelming majority of the hordes visiting the Tenman-gu never give a passing thought to **Komyo-zen-ji,** a Zen temple not five minutes' walk to the south. It was founded during the 13th century, though the current buildings date from the Edo period. Refined and simple, they feature expanses of tatami matting surrounded by verandas of polished wood—all intended simply for sitting and contemplating an exquisitely lovely **garden.** A masterpiece of landscaping, it features white gravel "seas" beautifully raked around rocks resembling islands, and green"land" pieces consisting of mosses and trees. You can spend some time here moving from one vantage point to another; the garden has been designed so that the view is perfect from any angle. ■

Yanagawa

THE PICTURESQUE LITTLE TOWN OF YANAGAWA LIES SOME 25 miles (40 km) south of Fukuoka. Like most former castle towns, Yanagawa lost its castle following the Meiji restoration; it was burned to the ground in 1873. The three moats remained, however, forming a canal network that crisscrosses the town. You get the impression that Yanagawa's citizens spent a century wondering what to do with these waterways until someone hit upon a brilliant idea: Take advantage of the town's historical sights and have boat tours shuttle visitors between them. Poled along by famously waggish boatmen past some pretty but mostly unremarkable scenery, the punts have become a major local industry. Still, it's a delightful experience.

Yanagawa
🅰 316 C4
Visitor information
✉ Nishitetsu-Yanagawa Station
☎ 0944/72-3853
🚆 Train: Limited express on Nishitetsu—omuta line from Fukuoka Station (45 mins.)

The main focus is the **Ohana Villa,** built in 1697, but the only true survivor of the era is the villa's **Shoto-en Garden,** laid out with a pond encompassing dwarf pines and rocks to emulate Matsushima Bay in Tohoku (see p. 161). Next to it is the **Seiyokan,** a rambling Western-style mansion built by Yanagawa's feudal lords in the 1880s and currently popular as a wedding hall. The two buildings are virtually joined and contain interesting museums: In the Tachibana house are displays of Meiji-period memorabilia and utensils, while the Ohana Villa showcases a beautiful collection of Edo-period artifacts—including Noh costumes, armor, lacquerware, and miniature painted books.

The town is also pleasant to wander on foot. The north side embraces a number of quaint little temples as well as restaurants and shops. The picturesque streets by the canal have several old traditional houses, notably the birthplace of the celebrated poet Kitahara Hakushu (1885–1942), now open as the **Yanagawa Municipal Folk Museum. ∎**

Ohana Villa, Shoto-en Garden & Seiyokan
☎ 0944/73-2189
💲 Ohana Villa museum $; Seiyokan $$; Seiyokan & Shoto-en $$

Yanagawa Municipal Folk Museum
☎ 0944/73-8940
💲 $$

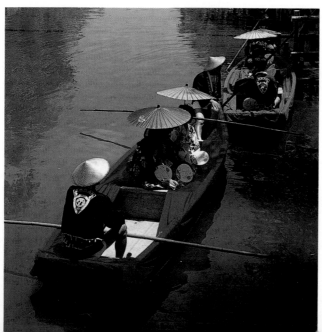

The classic Yanagawa delight: a canal trip along the network of moats remaining from feudal times

Volcanic steam drifts across the cityscape of Beppu, Japan's ultimate *onsen* wonderland.

Beppu

THE TOWN OF BEPPU SITS IN AN AREA OVERFLOWING WITH volcanic hot springs. Sometimes it seems that all you have to do to make a living here is stick a pipe in the ground, turn on a faucet, and build a spa hotel around the outflow.

Beppu
🗺 316 D4
Visitor information
✉ JR Beppu Station
☎ 0977/24-2838
🚆 Train: from Hakata Station, Fukuoka on JR Nippon line (2 hrs. 30 mins.)

The Promised Land for lovers of the long, leisurely soak, Beppu reigns supreme over all *onsen* resorts in Japan. This hardly qualifies it as a paragon of refinement— quite the contrary. Arriving by ferry from Shikoku, you appear to be docking in front of the Tiger Pachinko Parlor, which stands on a palm-flanked seafront boulevard aflame with garish neon signs and uninhibitedly hideous architecture. Arrive by train and you will ponder the source of the music filling the main street before finding out that it is wafting up from the storm drains.

Matched only in the realm of science fiction, Beppu is outlandish and perfectly fascinating. In this contender for the title of the world's most geothermal city, natural hot water cooks food and heats houses in winter. Onsen tourists ply the streets in cotton *yukata* (kimono-dressing gowns) emblazoned with their hotel's crest, even in the town center.

Of the eight onsen areas overall, the most important are **Beppu Onsen** in the center of town, **Kankaiji** on the hill to the north, and **Kannawa** to the northeast. The **Ekimae Koto Onsen** bathhouse in central Beppu, open 24 hours, goes back to the 1930s, but the most venerable is the **Takegawara** (*16-23 Moto-machi, tel 0977/23-1585*), an imposing wooden building dating from 1879 where—apart from the usual mineral-rich hot water—the main attraction is the *suna-yu* (sand bath). Steam filtering up from the boiling water underground heats the sand, which is shoveled over you. Lying buried up to your neck, you sweat away your cares—and possibly, if you stay long enough, your skin. Suna-yu is available at **Shoningahama** beach on the eastern side of the seafront.

If you're after sheer luxury and the latest onsen technology, hilly **Kankaiji Onsen** is for you. The views over Beppu Bay are breathtaking, especially from the **Suginoi Palace** (*1 Kankaiji, tel 0977/24-1141*), a spa and hotel complex offering an astonishing variety of aquatic attractions for families. You need not be a guest to use the facilities.

Beppu is a great city for covered malls. They are halfway down the main street from the station on your right. Festooned with colored paper lanterns and presenting a striking array of restaurants and bars, the main shopping arcades, called **Ginza** and **Yaoyoi,** offer everything from fancy souvenir shops to dingy thrift stores.

Kannawa is celebrated for its eight **Kannawa Jigoku** (Kannawa hells), where you can contemplate geysers, seething expanses of bubbling mud, and pools of steaming hot water dyed strange colors by minerals, the most famous being the red **Chi-no-Ike,** or "pond of blood." Going round them forms an extraordinary half-day excursion.

As if nature's geothermal excesses weren't weird enough, humans have sought to enhance them with grotesque statuary, crocodile farms, greenhouse banana plantations, and stalls selling eggs and vegetables cooked in the boiling pools.

Some might find things equally steamy at the **Hihokan** (*336-5 Shibuyu, tel 0977/66-8790*), a museum devoted to things sexual; it's just opposite the flashy Ashiya spa hotel. An outlandish cross between

a castle and an Indian temple outside, it exhibits phallic statuary, erotic prints, sculptures, and amazing waxwork animations inside.

Kannawa is fascinating to wander. A constant hiss issues from the pipes, chimneys, boilers, and bizarre plumbing fixtures that feed the onsen hotels, *ryokan* (inns), and *minshuku* (small guesthouses) flanking streets and lanes of great charm.

An hour west of Beppu is the genteel resort of **Yufuin.** Featuring outdoor *rotenburo* baths, the hotels here tend to focus on a pleasant but contrived form of rusticity: The town can be toured elegantly by pony and trap. With annual movie and music festivals, Yufuin is one of the cultural hubs of Kyushu—in every way the antithesis of Beppu. ∎

Right: In Beppu you can soak in muddy, mineral-rich hot spa water (as here) or get buried up to your neck in hot sand on the beach.

Ekimae Koto Onsen

✉ 13-14 Eki-mae
☎ 0977/21-0541
$ $
✉ JR Beppu Station
☎ 0977/24-2838

Yufuin

▲ 316 C4
Visitor information
✉ JR Yufuin Station
☎ 0977/84-2446

Kumamoto-ken

ON THE WEST SIDE OF CENTRAL KYUSHU, KUMAMOTO-KEN thrives on its agricultural and marine resources and offers plenty of variety for the visitor. Off the mainland coast, some 120 islands of various sizes form the Amakusa chain, notable for its scenic beauty and historically significant as a bastion of Christianity during the 16th century. Inland is the colossal volcano of Mount Aso-san. It provides plenty of hiking opportunities and a variety of scenery, from alpine meadows and shaded gorges to the grim landscape near the menacing active crater. The prefecture hasn't earned its nickname, Hi-no-Kuni (Land of Fire), for nothing.

Although Kumamoto-ken has markedly fewer factories than Fukuoka-ken, it still suffered indiscriminate postwar industrialization. From an aesthetic viewpoint, development has proved more destructive than war in the prefectural capital, **Kumamoto.** Despite preserving precious few vestiges of the past, it's a pleasant city with a youthful atmosphere (it has two of Kyushu's most important universities) and makes a perfect base for visits to other parts of Kyushu.

Outstandingly well restored, **Kumamoto-jo** is once again one of Japan's finest castles.

Kumamoto
316 C4
Visitor information
JR Kumamoto Station
096/351-3742
Train: JR Kagoshima line from Hakata Station (1 hr. 30 mins.)
Bus: From Fukuoka to Kotsu Center (2 hrs.)

**Lucky *kumade*
rake on sale at
Kato-jinja Shrine
in the grounds of
Kumamoto-jo
Castle**

**Kumamoto-jo
Castle**
✉ 1-1 Honmaru
☎ 096/352-5900
💲 $$

Suizenji-koen Park
✉ 8-1 Suizenji-koen
☎ 096/383-0074
💲 $$

Kumamoto-jo Castle is
one of the city's two major sights
and, though mainly a reproduction,
it is among Japan's finest castles.
Completed in 1607, it was commissioned and designed by feudal lord
Kato Kiyomasa. The walls of the
castle form a perimeter of almost 8
miles (13 km) embracing 49 turrets; the garrison and private quarters took their water supply from
120 wells. Kato's skill as a military
strategist was more than matched
by his brilliance as an architect. The
structural orientation ingeniously
follows the topography of the land;
the architectural feature of Japanese fortresses known as *musha-
gaeshi* (warrior-overturn), referring
to the unclimbable concave shape
of the massive walls supporting
the keep, is regarded as reaching
perfection in Kumamoto-jo, where
some call it *nezumi-gaeshi*—
"mouse-overturn."

Owned by the Kato family for
44 years, the castle passed into the
hands of the Hosokawas, who ruled
the province until 1871. Most of
the castle was burned down when
samurai renegade Saigo Takamori

(see p. 36) was finally routed by
imperial troops during the Satsuma
Rebellion in 1877. Along with the
massive stone foundations, only
the famous **Uto turret (Uto
Yagura),** west of the main keep,
survived undamaged. Beginning
in 1960, restoration work has been
conducted on a spectacular scale
with splendid results. Seventeen
original wells and 13 turrets
have been resurrected. From the
outside, it's hard to imagine that
the new keep hides a concrete
skeleton; inside is a **museum**
containing fascinating exhibits
devoted to the castle and its Kato
and Hosokawa rulers.

Kumamoto's other main sight
is **Suizenji-koen Park,** one of
Japan's most celebrated gardens.
Gentaku, a noted Buddhist monk
from Kyoto, came to Kumamoto
in 1632 at the behest of feudal
lord Hosokawa Tadatoshi to build
Suizen-ji Temple, which included
a magnificent garden. Upon Gentaku's demise the temple was
moved elsewhere, and the Hosokawas built a teahouse on the spot.
Beautifully landscaped to evoke

the sights most characteristic of each of the 53 stations of the old Tokaido trunk road between Edo and Kyoto, the garden features fountains and flowering shrubs, ponds studded with rocks suggesting islands, and miniature hills (one, a cone-shape green hillock, represents Fuji-san).

Minor sights in Kumamoto include the houses of two famous 19th-century writers: Natsume Soseki, whose portrait adorns the 1,000-yen note; and Lafcadio Hearn (see p. 274), who spent a few years here after moving from Matsue. Both houses are now museums. The **Soseki museum** is the more worthwhile; the Hearn residence hardly measures up to its counterpart in Matsue. Kumamoto has several noteworthy craft traditions, and **Kumamoto Prefectural Traditional Crafts Center (Kumamoto-ken Dento Kogeikan),** just east of the castle, presents fine exhibits antique and modern; there is a sales area, and you can watch artisans at work.

Thirty miles (48 km) east of Kumamoto is **Mount Aso-san,** created when the dome of a gigantic volcano collapsed during a cataclysmic eruption some 50,000 years

ago. Aso-san actually embraces five cones, of which Mount Naka-dake (5,223 ft/1,592 m) is the most active. The colossal caldera—it's the largest on Earth—is 11 miles (18 km) wide by 15 miles (24 km) long, covers an area of 98 square miles (255 sq km), and encompasses whole towns and villages with a combined population of about 80,000. The fertile volcanic soil has produced lush green meadows now used as pastureland for cattle and horses. The scenery in the vicinity is superb, even from the road up to Naka-dake from Aso Station.

Perhaps the most famous view along the way is across the lake-dotted **Kusasenri** meadow, with the intense green of **Mount Komezuka** (*komezuke* means "rice mound") rising out of it. The hill, actually a dormant volcano, gets its name from a Shinto myth about a god who scooped a chunk out of the top of a gigantic mound of rice to feed the starving population. Opposite it is the **Aso Volcanic Museum (Aso Kazan Hakubutsukan),** featuring a fascinating array of displays on the volcanology of Kyushu and other parts of the world, as well as video clips of local eruptions. You can

Boat trip on the Kuma-gawa River

watch monitors displaying live pictures broadcast from closed-circuit television cameras mounted inside the Naka-dake crater itself.

From the **cable car station** near the top of Naka-dake, a ten-minute walk brings you to the crater edge. The shelters you see along the rim were erected there in 1960, following a sudden eruption that killed several tourists. That's the nature of Naka-dake, and as you gaze down on clouds of steam billowing up from the pallid, evil-looking, gray-green lake 320 feet (100 m) below, you start to understand it. Naka-dake was closed to visitors during eruptions in 1989 and 1990.

Several hiking trails skirt the rim and run down toward other peaks. To repeat the warning posted on ubiquitous dual-language notices: Stay clear of the crater rim, especially if you suffer from respiratory ailments. The situation is constantly monitored and the area is closed at the first signs of an eruption or poor air quality, but accidents can happen. Vents occasionally open deeper down in the crater, and the sulfurous gases they emit are highly toxic. You can assess the mood of the mountain at the visitor information center before going to Naka-dake. The center also has information on hiking trails.

About 13 miles (20 km) northeast of Naka-dake, accessible by road from Aso Station, is the lovely **Kikuchi Valley,** where the river has carved breathtaking gorges through a wooded landscape. ∎

The colossal Mount Aso-san crater embraces an astonishing variety of scenery: alpine flowers, the grassy Kusasenri cone at the center, and even towns.

Aso Volcanic Museum
✉ Kusasenri, Aso-machi, Aso-gun
☎ 0967/34-2111
💲 $$

The view across
Nagasaki Harbor
from **Glover
Garden**

Nagasaki-ken & Nagasaki

OCCUPYING THE NORTHWESTERN CORNER OF KYUSHU,
Nagasaki-ken contains some of Kyushu's cardinal historical and
scenic sights. To make the most of both aspects in one go, you may
want to begin in the east of the prefecture with a visit to the historical town of Shimabara, then hike around volcanic Unzen-Amakusa
National Park.

Shimabara

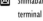 316 B4

Visitor information

✉ Shimabara ferry
   terminal

☎ 0957/62-3986

🚌 Express bus: from
   Nagasaki (2 hrs.);
   from Fukuoka (3
   hrs.)

⛴ Ferry: from
   Kumamoto (1 hr.),
   high-speed ferry
   (30 mins.)

The prefecture's greatest draw is its
capital, with its fascinating history
of contacts with Europe. The long
relationship with Holland is quirki-
ly demonstrated in Huis Ten Bosch
(see p. 338). Nagasaki-ken includes
Goto Retto Archipelago off the west
coast, with more than 200 islands.
In the east of Nagasaki-ken is the
Shimabara Peninsula, noted both
for the town of Shimabara on the
Ariake Sea and for the scenic area

around the Unzen-dake volcano.

Traversed by canals, modern
Shimabara is a small, pleasant
city popular in Japan for its historical connotations. It was here that
Christians made their last stand in
1637 during the Shimabara Rebellion (1637–38). The rebels,
mainly Christians, were defying
harsh oppression by local rulers;
37,000 men, women, and children
were massacred. Their slavery and

of Unzen has such a proliferation of volcanic "hells" and springs that the streets are festooned with pipes and plumbing, feeding the spas and hissing and bubbling with steam. Popular early in the 20th century as a summer haven for Western colonials and "Shanghailanders" from China, the spa resort of Unzen possesses Japan's oldest golf course (founded in 1913) and a hotel dating to the 1930s.

The magma percolating beneath Unzen-dake bubbled upward in a major eruption in 1792, triggering violent earthquakes that killed some 15,000 people; most of them were victims of 50-foot (15 m) tidal waves that thundered in from the sea. Today the most volatile cone of Unzen-dake is **Mount Fugen-dake** (4,580 feet/1,396 m), which lies just 5 miles (8 km) southwest of central Shimabara. Fugen-dake began to erupt again in November 1990. The lava dome collapsed the following month, leading to a lava explosion in June 1991 that killed 43 people, including a group of French and American volcanologists. Intermittent eruptions continued until 1994, damaging or destroying some 2,000 buildings in the process. Some of the buried structures in the **Sembongi** district to the west of Shimabara city and along the **Mizunashi-gawa River** have been preserved as an unusual tourist attraction; only their roofs protruded from the mud and lava. As Japan's youngest mountain, the lava dome that blistered atop Fugen-dake has been called Heisei Shin-zan (Heisei new mountain). The eruption was officially declared over in 1996; depending on the volcano's activity level, however, some hiking trails around Fugen-dake may be closed. Be sure to check with the visitor information centers in Nagasaki or Unzen before heading for the hills.

taxes had built the famous **Shimabara-jo Castle,** demolished during the 1870s, though the walls and impressive main gate remain. Rebuilt in 1964, the keep houses a **museum** featuring ceramics, armor, and exhibits about the rebellion and the Christians in Kyushu. Northwest of the castle is the district of **Teppo-cho,** with its picturesque thatched and white-washed **samurai houses** (two are open to the public). The stone channels that once served as the water supply, like the town's canals, are fed by mountain springs highly prized for their purity.

Other local springs are of the hot variety—the area is volcanically hyperactive, surrounding, as it does, the ferocious **Mount Unzen-dake.** The nearby town

Shimabara-jo Castle
- 1183-1 Jo-nai 1 chome
- 0957/62-4766
- $$

Mount Unzen-dake
- 316 B4

Visitor information
- Unzen Tourist Association (near Post Office)
- 0957/73-3434

Girls stroll past **Nagasaki Peace Park's** commemorative statue.

Nagasaki city
🗺 316 B4
Visitor information
✉ JR Nagasaki Station
☎ 095/823-3631
🚉 Train: from Hakata
   Station, Fukuoka to
   JR Nagasaki Station
   (2 hrs)

Urakami cathedral
✉ Mooto-machi
🕐 Closed Mon.
🚊 Tram: Ohashi or
   Maruyama-machi

Hypocenter Park
🚊 Tram: Matsuyama-
   machi

Peace Park
🚊 Tram: Matsuyama-
   machi

NAGASAKI CITY

The purely practical attributes of modern Nagasaki harmonize so well with its historical and aesthetic character that it is easy to forget the city is also a vital industrial hub. On the peninsula to the west of the bay is the Mitsubishi shipyard, the world's largest corporate shipbuilding facility, although the company now mainly builds heavy machinery. Nagasaki's other great industry is fishing. Its annual catch is the largest in Japan.

As the historical point of entry for both European trade and Christianity in Japan, Nagasaki has a long and fascinating history. Many sights evoke the city's historical links with the rest of the world, despite the devastation of the atomic bombing in 1945. The northern sector, home of the Christian community, was the most extensively destroyed. Some of the old buildings farther south were spared, and others—notably the Urakami Cathedral in the north—were rebuilt. "Restoration of the city has been remarkable," declared a guidebook compiled only five years after the catastrophe, "and it appears to be almost as prosperous as before the war." Today, unless you visit the Atomic Bomb Museum and Peace Park near the hypocenter of the blast, it is hard to imagine that the bombing ever happened.

Surrounded by green, rolling hills and overlooking a deep bay, Nagasaki has recovered its reputation as one of Japan's most beautiful cities. It should be included in any visitor's itinerary in Kyushu.

Sights in the northern sector

Urakami, in the northern sector of the city is where the atomic bomb struck on August 9, 1945. As a predominantly Catholic neighborhood, Urakami was the perfect site for a cathedral. Completed in 1925, the original **Urakami Cathedral (Urakami Tenshudo)** took 30 years to build; it had a seating capacity of 6,000 and was the largest church in East Asia. The district included some 15,000 Christians before World War II, but 10,000 perished in the A-bomb explosion. Standing only 550 yards (500 m) from the hypocenter, the cathedral was vaporized by the blast; the current reproduction was completed on the site in 1959. This is Japan's most important Christian church; a special Mass conducted here by Pope John Paul II in 1981 featured the ordination of priests from around the world.

Heading north from the cathedral, you come to **Hypocenter Park,** where a simple, elegant block of black marble marks the precise spot above which the A-bomb exploded. The park also displays relics assembled from nearby, including all that remains of the original Urakami Cathedral: a section of brick wall and three blackened, eroded statues, one of them headless. To the north of the Hypocenter Park is the **Peace Park (Heiwa-koen),** locus of several memorials donated to the city of Nagasaki by various countries. The **Peace Statue (Heiwa Kinen-zo)** by prominent sculptor Kitamura Seibo dominates the park; massive and clumsily proportioned, it is not to everyone's taste.

South of the Peace Park the new **Atomic Bomb Museum (Nagasaki Genbaku Shiryokan),** which opened in 1996. Burned and twisted debris from the blast, along with horrific video presentations, make this one of the most poignant and terrifying museums anywhere. The wall clock with its hands fused at 11.02 a.m.—the exact moment of the bombing on the 9th of August, 1945—is a Nagasaki emblem.

Nagasaki is renowned for the views afforded by its hilly topography, and they don't get much better than the one from the top of 1,080-foot (330 m) **Inasa-yama,** on the other side of the Urakami-gawa River from the city. The peak is reached via cable car; the panorama over Nagasaki Harbor and the East China Sea from the observation platform is breathtaking, especially when the lights come on around the harbor. Deer and monkeys roam scenic **Inasayama-koen**

Atomic Bomb Museum

- ✉ 7-8 Hirano-machi
- ☎ 095/844-1231
- 💲 $
- 🚃 Tram: Hamaguchi-machi

Mount Inasa Park

- 💲 Park free; cable car access $$$
- 🚌 Bus: Ropeway-mae, then cable car

Grim reminder: clock with hands fused at the time the Nagasaki A-bomb detonated

The monument to the 26 Christian martyrs of Nagasaki, crucified in 1597 and canonized in 1862.

Fukusai-ji Temple

✉ 2-56 Chikugo-machi, 5-min. walk from Nagasaki Station

💲 $

Shofuku-ji Temple

✉ 3-77 Tamazono-machi

🚋 Tram: Sakura-machi

Park, where there is also an open-air concert hall.

Sights in the central and southern sectors

The city's heart and most of its sights lie in the south. Just a short distance north of Nagasaki railway station is **26 Martyrs Memorial (Nihon Niju-roku Seijin Junkyochi).** The bronze bas-relief was erected in 1962, marking the passage of one hundred years since Nagasaki's 26 Christian martyrs were canonized by Pope Pius IX.

Of particular interest is the adjacent museum, with exhibits relating to the history of Christianity in Japan. The country's "Hidden Christians" concealed items such as religious scrolls and prayer books, as well as statuettes of the Virgin Mary disguised as the Bodhisattva Kannon. The fate of the Nagasaki martyrs is thought to be connected to the *San Felipe,* a Spanish galleon wrecked on the Shikoku coast in 1596. After being rescued, its captain boasted about the might of Spain; her many overseas conquests, he claimed, had been

launched by armies marching over ground prepared by Christian missionaries and their converts. When this reached the ears of the shogun Toyotomi Hideyoshi (1536–1598), who was already growing suspicious of Christian designs, he had 26 Christians—including six Jesuit friars and three children—arrested in Kansai and forcibly marched all the way to Nagasaki in midwinter. There they were crucified on Nishi-zaka Hill on February 5, 1597, as a warning to others.

The curious **Fukusai-ji Temple,** some 550 yards (500 m) southwest of the memorial, is one of four that were built by Chinese in the Ming dynasty style in the 1620s; the original temple burned down after the atomic bombing. Although the turtle is a symbol of longevity in Japan as much as it is in China, that hardly justifies rebuilding Fukusai-ji to look like one. This in effect is what happened in 1979; even if the incongruity of shaping a temple like a turtle escapes you, you can hardly miss the 60-foot (18 m) effigy of the Buddhist deity Kannon standing on its back. A bell sounds at 11:02 a.m. daily to commemorate the atomic bombing, and the interior of the temple contains a Foucault pendulum. Fukusai-ji is wildly out of tune with conventional Buddhist temple culture—and worth seeing for that very reason.

Foreign visitors often confuse nearby **Shofuku-ji Temple** with the more celebrated Sofuku-ji, which sounds similar. But Shofuku-ji is noteworthy for its pleasant garden and Chinese-style architecture. Built in 1657, the imposing main gate was moved here from another location in the 19th century, and the main building was reconstructed in 1717.

Continuing east, you come to **Suwa-jinja Shrine,** originally built in 1629 by the feudal government to stem the growing influence of Christianity. Its 277 steps lead up to a grand bronze *torii* gateway in front of the shrine's main buildings, which date from the late 19th century. Nagasaki's most important and popular shrine, Suwa-jinja is the focus of the city's annual O-Kunchi festival in October. Cen-

tering on a Lion Dance, the festival parade reflects strong Chinese influence.

South of Suwa-jinja, walk alongside the picturesque canal of the Nakashima-gawa River. **Meganebashi,** one of several bridges spanning the river, is the most famous. Built by the Chinese abbot of Kofuku-ji in 1634, it is the oldest stone-arch bridge in Japan. The name means "Spectacles Bridge" (you'll understand once you see the twin arches reflected in the water).

The street parallel to the canal on the east is Teramachi-dori. It contains a number of temples (hence the name) and is a pleasant area for strolling. The most famous of Nagasaki's four Chinese temples, **Sofuku-ji** to the southeast, was built by the Chinese monk Chonen in 1629 for the benefit of Nagasaki's large population of Chinese from Fujian. Displaying architecture of the late Ming period now rare in Southern China itself, the Main Hall and Second Gate are National Treasures. The precinct features a giant caldron used to cook food for the starving during

Stone sages seem ready to wax wise in the courtyard of Nagasaki's ornate Koshi-byo, a Chinese temple dedicated to Confucius.

Suwa-jinja Shrine
- ✉ 3 Kaminishiyama-machi
- 🚃 Tram: Suwajinja-mae

Sofuku-ji Temple
- ✉ 5-3 Kajiya-machi
- 💲 $
- 🚃 Tram: Shokakuji Station

The oldest Western-style building still standing in Japan, Nagasaki's Glover Mansion was built in 1863.

Nagasaki Museum of History & Folklore

✉ 3-1 Kamizenza-machi

☎ 095/847-9245

🕐 Closed Mon.

🚃 Tram: Mori-machi

Glover Garden

✉ 8-1 Minami, Yamate-machi

☎ 095/822-8223

💲 $$ (includes all buildings on gardens)

🚃 Tram: Oura-Tenshudo-shita

a famine in 1681. Chinese and Japanese of Chinese ancestry come here from all over Japan to celebrate Obon—the festival of the dead—on the lunar calendar from July 26 to 28.

West from Sofuku-ji toward the harbor is the one-time Dutch trading enclave of **Dejima,** a fan-shaped islet artificially fashioned from land reclaimed in Nagasaki Bay. Only a single building and various salvaged items remain at the **Nagasaki Museum of History and Folklore (Nagasaki-shi Rekishi Minzoku Shiryokan).** In the garden is a one-fifth scale model of the Dejima that was. There are main roads on either side and some new buildings, but aerial photographs reveal Dejima's fan-shaped configuration; recent excavations have unearthed whole sections of the original outer wall. The city of Nagasaki and the Japanese government have ambitious plans to restore Dejima as it was. The old trading post was accurately mapped and depicted by, among others, artist Kawahara Keiga in the early 19th century; displayed in the

museum, such works will form the basis of the project, scheduled for completion in 2010.

On Minami-yamate Hill, in the south of the city and with a spectacular view over the bay, **Glover Garden (Guraba-en)**—actually a sizable park—contains the earliest wooden Western-style buildings (dating from the latter 19th century), still standing in Japan. As such, it is probably Nagasaki's most popular tourist attraction. Originally sited in other parts of the city, most of the houses were dismantled and reassembled here; among them is the **No. 2 Dock House (Kyu-Mitsubishi Dai-ni Dokku Hausu),** moved from the Mitsubishi Shipyard on the bay, and noteworthy **merchants' homes,** including the Walker, Ringer, and Alt houses. The buildings are largely of wood, with verandas and shutters in typical Far Eastern colonial style, betraying the fact that their occupants had mainly been in China before coming to Japan. **Glover Mansion (Kyu-Guraba Jutaku)** is the only one that has always stood on this spot. It was built in 1863 for Thomas Glover (1838–1911), an enterprising Scotsman who arrived in Nagasaki in 1859 and spent the rest of his life in Japan. After running a coal mine, Glover built Japan's first modern shipyard (later operated by Mitsubishi). Also an arms dealer, he supplied weapons to the Satsuma clan, which overthrew the shogunate. Glover defied the ban on travel for Japanese, helping several young men escape to study in London; among them in 1862 was Ito Hirobumi, who later became Japan's first prime minister.

The Japanese like to associate the Glover Mansion with Puccini's tragic opera, *Madam Butterfly,* which is why a marble relief of Puccini graces the house and a statue of Japanese diva Miura Tamaki stands on the hill above it. In those days temporary marriage contracts between foreigners and locals (usually geisha) legitimized relationships far too wittingly carnal to prompt a suicide. Glover's marriage to a local woman—unlike that of Lt. Pinkerton, betrayer of the Nagasaki heroine of the opera—was permanent and produced two children.

In the same area stands **Oura Catholic Church (Oura Tenshu-do).** Built by French priest Bernard Petitjean for the foreign community in 1865, this charming church commemorates Nagasaki's 26 Christian martyrs and was the country's first in the Gothic style. It immediately attracted "Hidden Christians," who came out for the first time in 200 years— albeit with extreme caution, for Japanese were forbidden to practice the religion until 1872. The meeting between the group and Father Petitjean is captured in a bronze bas-relief in the courtyard. Designated a National Treasure, the church is much admired for its

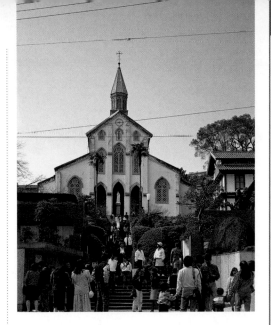

wooden architecture and fine stained-glass windows.

The **Confucian Shrine (Koshi-byo),** renowned for its distinctive bright yellow roof tiles and rich red walls visible from the Dutch slope, was originally built in 1893 by and for Nagasaki's Chinese community to honor the great sage Confucius. Torched in the conflagration that swept the city after the A-bomb, the shrine was rebuilt over an eight-year period and completed in 1967, then extensively refurbished in 1983. Neither this history nor the marble statues of Confucius and his 72 disciples that stand around the courtyard make this shrine unique: Built and maintained by Chinese and kept under the jurisdiction of the Chinese embassy in Tokyo, Koshi-byo is officially a little corner of China.

The adjacent **Historical Museum of China (Chugoku Rekidai Hakubutsukan)** is part of the Koshi-byo complex. It is maintained by its counterpart in Beijing and may contain up to 80 national cultural treasures from China at any given time. ∎

Charming Oura Catholic Church, built by a French priest In 1865, inspired Japan's secret Christians to emerge from centuries in hiding.

Confucian Shrine & Historical Museum of China
✉ 10-36 Oura-machi
☎ 095/824-4022
💲 $$
🚋 Tram: Oura-Tenshudo-shita

Nagasaki's Huis Ten Bosch is a sophisticated re-creation of a classic Dutch town.

More places to visit on Kyushu

HUIS TEN BOSCH

Huis Ten Bosch (pronounced "House Ten Bosh") is probably the ultimate theme park statement in a country obsessed with theme parks. It is on Omura Bay near the town of Sasebo, some 30 miles (50 km) north of Nagasaki. The idea of a small Dutch town complete with gabled house-fronts, windmills, and canals may not sound appealing if you're chasing the Japan experience—but then a concept so outlandish and futuristic could only be Japanese. If you're traveling with kids, this could be a perfect day out. Reproducing famous buildings in Holland (including the eponymous Huis Ten Bosch royal palace and the Domtoren church tower of Utrecht) only a fraction under full size, Huis Ten Bosch is part amusement park, part residential housing.

Huis Ten Bosch is the kind of place you can imagine one day under a bubble in space. Water and sewage systems, climate control, power, even canal and harbor maintenance all derive from cutting-edge, eco-friendly technology: Built on 380 acres (152 ha) of land reclaimed for an industrial park project that was later abandoned, it features 7.5 miles (12 km) of walkways made with brick from

Holland, as well as 400,000 trees and 300,000 color-coordinated tulips.

Just about every kind of quaint, picturesque, and above all Dutch-style conveyance—wheeled or floating—seems to ply Huis Ten Bosch. You can even take a trip around the bay aboard a copy of a vintage tall ship. The park has 11 museums, some devoted to antique Japanese export ceramics, antique glass, or works by Dutch artist M. C. Escher (1898–1972), a master of optical illusion. Fusing futuristic multimedia concepts, the theme park attractions include evocations of Escher's topsy-turvy world, sea travel, and a Dutch fairy tale.

🔺 316 B4 **Visitor information**
✉ 0956/27-0001 💲 $$$$$

POTTERY TOWNS OF SAGA-KEN

Returning from ultimately futile attempts to conquer Korea in the 16th century, Toyotomi Hideyoshi's troops brought back Korean potters to work in Arita in northern Kyushu. Several, including the great Ri Sampei, later took Japanese citizenship. The Nabeshimas, feudal lords of the old province of Hizen, held their potters prisoner, which kept professional

A master potter in Arita puts the finishing touches on a delicate traditional vase.

secrets from rivals; exclusive and reclusive, the Nabeshima potteries dominated the industry until the end of the feudal era. The first Arita ceramics are said to have been created by Ri Sampei in 1616, following his discovery in the local area of kaolin—the exceptionally light clay needed to produce the hardness and whiteness of porcelain.

In 1675 the Korean potters moved from Arita to Okawachiyama, a district of the nearby coastal town of Imari. Whether made in Arita or Okawachiyama, the finished goods were exported from the port of Imari, which gave its name to this kind of pottery. The earliest variety of Imari ware was blue and white, but the Japanese ceramicist Sakaida Kakiemon introduced new polychrome glazing techniques. Applied as an overglaze enamel, the brightly colored designs of Imari were inspired by Japanese screen paintings, textile design, and lacquerware. Imari ware was exported from Dejima (Nagasaki) by the Dutch East India Company and soon caught the attention of the West for its exquisite design and quality. Influenced by Chinese pottery, Imari in turn had an impact on ceramics in Holland (Delft), England, and Germany.

Imari's popularity declined during the 19th century, when the designs became overly ornate and were applied by transfer rather than hand-painting. Kakiemon porcelain, made by Sakaida's descendants and featuring delicate enamel painting on an immaculate white background, was considered the most refined. However, potteries in Okawachiyama and Arita continued to turn out traditional Imari designs, including hand-painted ones—as indeed they still do. Declared Intangible Cultural Assets by the government, the descendants of the Kakiemon and Nabeshima pottery families are still working today.

Arita lies in a valley surrounded by the hills that yield clay. The townscape is characterized by dozens of chimneys rising from its kilns. In addition to these, Arita has a cluster of substantial museums. **Kyushu Ceramic Museum (Saga-kenritsu Kyushu Toji Bunkakan,** *Toshaku, Arita-machi, tel 0955/ 43-3681)* is highly recommended for anyone interested in the history and development of the craft over the island. Many kilns are open to the public; the most prestigious—**Kakiemon, Imaemon** (run by the descendants of the Nabeshima potters), and **Iwao Taizan**—have museums containing fine collections of old Imari ware.

In nearby **Imari,** the site of what were called the "secret kilns" in the early days is now occupied by **Nabeshima Hanyo-koen Park.** This is a kind of theme park, incorporating the ruins of the Nabeshima potteries and focusing on all there is to know about Imari pottery then and now, as well as on the working life of captive Korean potters. The center of Imari's ceramic activities, the Oka-wachiyama vicinity still boasts some 20 kilns. Imari has a number of museums containing not only ceramic collections but also potters working on the premises, notably the **Imari and Arita Ceramic Industry Hall** *(Okawachiyama, Imari-shi, tel 0955/22-6333, closed Mon.)* and the **Imari Ware Hall** *(Shintencho, Imari-shi, tel 0955/23-8121).*

The other great Saga pottery town is **Karatsu,** 15 miles (25 km) due north of Imari. Originally based on Yi ware from Korea, Karatsu ware emerged as the tea ceremony gained popularity during the Momoyama period (1573–1603). Consisting of basic shapes and deliberately (if deceptively) rough-hewn, this type of ware was considered ideal for the tea ceremony. Still much sought after by "tea-ists," Karatsu ware displays brown- and ocher-colored glazes sometimes decorated with geometric shapes, or plants and flowers executed with bold, simple brushstrokes. Kilns are open to the public; check times with the visitor information center.

Like so many former feudal towns, Karatsu rebuilt its vanished stronghold, **Karatsu-jo Castle** *(8-15 Higashi-jonai, tel 0955/72-5697),* during the 1960s. Perched on a hill by the sea, the castle not only looks particularly fine but also contains an interesting museum devoted to local archaeology and pottery.
🅰 316 B4   **Visitor information** Imari
☎ 0955/22-6820; Karatsu ☎ 0955/72-4963

KAGOSHIMA CITY

With a pleasant climate and Mount Sakura-jima, its very own Vesuvius, smoking across the bay, vibrant Kagoshima is known as "the Naples of Japan." Of vital historical importance, Kagoshima saw the arrival of St. Francis Xavier and the Portuguese in the 16th century. It was the domain of the Satsuma—the clan instrumental in overthrowing the shogunate in 1867. The city's most famous hero is Saigo Takamori: Having successfully fought to oust the old regime, he later changed his mind and

met his demise at Kumamoto-jo Castle during the Satsuma Rebellion he instigated in 1877. Badly damaged in World War II, Kagoshima has few vestiges of the past. A couple of notable Western-style buildings from the 1860s, such as Iso Foreigner's Residence, stand in the north of town, and the **Meiji Museum** *(23-1 Kajiya-machi, Kagoshima-shi, tel 099/239-7700)* is reputed for its brilliant evocations of the period.

Kagoshima is popular for its scenic views of Sakura-jima. Ferries run across to it at 15-minute intervals; from the ferry terminal you can board a bus to visit the volcano. As long as the conditions near the summit are safe, Sakura-jima opens hiking trails that approach the crater, notably up to the Yunohira Observation Point.
🅰 316 B2   **Visitor information**   ✉ 1-1 Chuo-cho, Kagoshima ☎ 099/253-2500

MIYAZAKI

Mountainous Miyazaki-ken, 76 percent of which is forested, is refreshingly unspoiled. Attracting Japanese holidaymakers eager for a fix of tropicana with its avenues of palm trees, however, Miyazaki city presents a rather different picture. Its huge Seagaia resort complex is famous for the recent Ocean Dome, the largest artificial beach in the world, featuring white sand and waves beneath a vast retractable roof.

While **Miyazaki-jingu Shrine** is revered for its association with Shinto creation myths, the region itself shows some of the earliest signs of habitation in Japan. Dating as far back as the fourth century, the 311 burial mounds at Saitobaro constitute one of the most important archaeological sites in Japan.

Obi, near Nichinan city, is an old castle town with several old samurai houses and a castle, partially restored as a museum depicting the lifestyle of the last feudal lords.

Among Miyazaki's natural assets is Kirishima-Yaku Parkland, which includes Mount Kirishima, actually consisting of 23 peaks. Here the country's highest *onsen* resort finds adepts even in high summer. Among the prefecture's coastal resorts is Aoshima, known for its fine beaches—some of them the best suited for surfing in the country.
🅰 316 C2   **Visitor information**
✉ JR Miyazaki Station ☎ 0985/22-6469 ∎

S tretching almost to Taiwan, Okinawa-ken consists of the Ryukyu-shoto—a synonym for an exotic getaway. White sands and turquoise seas grace a subtropical archipelago whose culture and atmosphere differ from those of mainland Japan.

Okinawa & the Ryukyu-shoto

**Scuba diving in the waters
of the Ryukyu-shoto**

Okinawa & the Ryukyu-shoto

TOO FAR AWAY TO BE ON THE ITINERARY OF MOST FOREIGNERS VISITING Japan, Okinawa-ken is a destination worthy of consideration in its own right and a firm favorite with mainland Japanese sun-worshippers, water sports enthusiasts, and outdoor fanatics. History and culture make this Japan at its most un-Japanese; to the many mainlanders who increasingly flock there, it is Japan at its most exotic.

Basking in an annual mean temperature of 75°F (24°C) and lying on the same latitude as Miami and the Bahamas, Okinawa-ken is renowned for postcard-perfect coral islands, year-round hibiscus flowers, and turquoise-blue seas. Forty-seven of its 160 or so islands, known as Ryukyu-shoto, are inhabited. The largest is the main island of Okinawa Honto, or simply Okinawa, which includes the prefectural capital of Naha.

Some 200 miles (320 km) southwest, the Miyako group centers on Miyako-jima Island, known for its spectacular beaches and the picturesque old town of Hirara. More fine beaches gird adjacent islets and the Yaeyama Archipelago 60 miles (100 km) southwest. Yaeyama includes Iriomote, the island renowned for possessing Japan's only real jungle, and Yonaguni-jima, popular with t he Japanese as the nation's very last island. It lies little more than 60 miles (100 km) east of Taiwan.

The Okinawans, primarily of Japanese origin, are thought to have migrated from the Japanese mainland rather than from neighboring countries. Virtually incomprehensible to other Japanese, their dialect is believed to be rooted in languages spoken in Japan more than a millennium ago. The Ryukyu islanders were seafarers and traders; an important trading bridge between Japan and Asia from the 14th century on, their kingdom reached its zenith in the 16th century.

The islands present a fascinating cultural mix, influenced by trade with China, Taiwan, and Indonesia. Traditional Okinawan textiles—the beautiful, brightly patterned *bingata* are the best known—show designs strikingly similar to the batik cloth of Java, including flowers, fish, birds, human figures, and festival scenes. The Indonesian connection is evident too in Okinawan music, which is based on a scale closer to the Javanese than the Japanese. Okinawan music spans a range of traditions, including classical, folk, and an interesting, fiercely rhythmic fusion of the latter with rock. Okinawa has several traditional dance forms; *eisa*, the most famous, is performed during the Okinawan equivalent of the Japanese O-bon festival for the dead (see p. 386).

The local architecture blends Japanese with Ming-dynasty Chinese elements. The roofs of Shuri-jo Castle in Naha and the ceramic dragons winding over them testify to this. Even private houses frequently have roofs adorned with *shi-isa*, the fierce ceramic lion-dogs once believed to drive evil spirits from the home. Like the rest of Japan, Okinawa embraces

Shintoism and Buddhism, but the shi-isa is a facet of a different belief system.

With an economy based on sugarcane, pineapples, and fishing, Okinawa has always been Japan's poorest prefecture; tourism has helped the economy. Like industrialization on the mainland, however, the success of tourism has exacted a price. Large Japanese corporations went on an investment spree in Okinawa in the late 1970s, turning pineapple plantations into golf courses and dotting bays and beaches with monster concrete resorts where Muzak is piped in from speakers in the trees. That said, Okinawa is more than just a marshaling point for visiting other, less spoiled islands. It is very much the heart of a cultural heritage separating Ryukyu-shoto from the rest of Japan.

Air and ferry services run between the major islands and the mainland; all islands are interconnected by ferry and the larger ones by air. The islands are at their best from March through May. From June to October, typhoons typically occur six to eight times throughout Okinawa; although they rarely last long enough to ruin a trip, the storms may close airports. In the rainy season *(tsuyu)* from late May to June, expect heavy downpours. ■

Naha

NAHA WAS ALMOST TOTALLY DESTROYED IN 1945. THE town benefited from a layout dictated by the occupying United States Army, which ran bulldozers through the ruins to create a new main drag, Kokusai-dori. Despite subsequent jerry-building and architectural brutalism in the 1960s and 70s, the city is pleasant.

Naha's impressive Shuri-jo Castle was rebuilt using the original 18th-century plans.

Naha

🗺 343 G2

Visitor information

✉ Naha Airport

☎ 098/857-6884

✈ Direct flights to Naha airport from Tokyo (2 hrs. 30 mins.) and other major cities

Since the mid-1980s, legislation has decreed architectural principles for new buildings; the traditional red-tiled roof is de rigueur. Running eastward from the town center, Kokusai-dori is in every way the main artery. Department stores, administrative buildings, plush fashion stores, trendy boutiques, army-surplus stores, souvenir shops (expensive and otherwise), restaurants, bars, *pachinko* parlors, and discos all seem to stand haphazardly and merrily right on or just off it. Eastward along the avenue, the shopping options become more

reminiscent of an Asian bazaar as you turn right at the Mitsukoshi department store and head down the covered arcades. Called Ichiba-dori and Heiwa-dori, these lead to the colorful Dai ichi Kosetsu Ichiba—the city food market. Southeast of it is **Tsuboya,** a traditional Okinawan pottery district since the 17th century, where there are still some narrow lanes and older houses. Visit the potteries and kilns or **Tsuboya Ceramics Museum.** Once purely utilitarian, Okinawan pottery consisted mainly of jars and pots; the repertoire now includes attractive sake flasks and *shi-isa* (lion figurines).

There is certainly no shortage of action after nightfall in Naha. With all the provinces of pleasure from restaurants to raunch, **Makishi** and **Maejima** districts are said to boast the greatest concentration of

the **Kankalmon gate,** were still standing, although heavily damaged. One gate of the former shrine on the compound remains intact, but everything else was reduced to rubble. The ornate Chinese-style **Shureimon** entry gate was reconstructed in 1958

Tsuboya Ceramics Museum

- 1-9-32 Tsuboya
- 098/862-3761
- Closed Mon.
- $$

Shurji-jo Castle

- 1-2 Kinjo-cho, Shuri
- 098/886-2020
- $$$

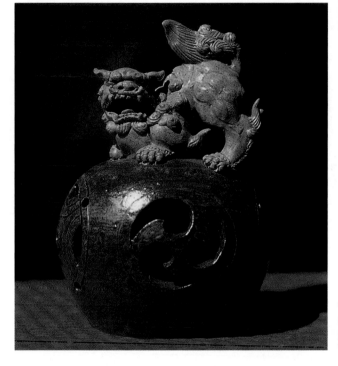

Traditional Okinawan pottery by Kuo Takaesu

bars in Japan. On a more sober note, traditional performing arts are presented weekly at the **Kenritsu Kyodo Theater (Kenritsu Kyodo Gekijo),** near the Asahibashi Bridge.

Some 1.2 miles (2 km) beyond the city's eastern edge is **Shuri,** the old capital of the Ryukyu kingdom, famous for **Shuri-jo Castle,** the region's prime tourist destination. The castle was used as the Japanese Army headquarters during World War II. After the Battle of Okinawa in 1945, only the massive stone walls, including

and is now a symbol of Okinawa. One of the most ambitious and successful restoration projects ever undertaken in Japan, the work was completed in 1992.

By using the surviving 18th-century plans, the restorers were able to leave the main castle buildings looking as they did in the 1700s. The main **Seiden Hall,** originally used for royal state ceremonies, is the most photographed building on Okinawa, but the whole castle compound is an enthralling sight, at the very least as a masterpiece of restoration. ∎

More places to visit in Okinawa & the Ryukyu-shoto

The narrow island of Okinawa is 84 miles (135 km) long. It still has fairly unspoiled areas both inland and on the coast, but most are in the north, beyond the sleepy town of Nago. Some of the best beaches around here have been taken over by plush resort hotels.

Southern Okinawa, known as **Nanbu,** is dotted with monuments and memorials to fallen soldiers and civilians; one of them, the **Konpaku-no-To** on the south coast, is dedicated to the 35,000 war dead buried in a mass grave. About 2.5 miles (4 km) southwest of Naha, the **Underground Naval Headquarters (Kyu Kaigun Shireibugo,** *236 Tomigusuku, Tomigusuku-mura, tel 098/850-4055)* was a stronghold honeycombed with 1,640 yards (1,500 m) of tunnels; 220 yards (200 m) of these are currently open to the public, along with the rooms they connected. Some of the walls are cratered and pock-marked—a gruesome reminder of the 4,000 members of the Japanese Navy who, spurning the disgrace of defeat, committed suicide in here, mainly by hand grenade. More poignant still is **Himeyuri-no-To,** a monument commemorating the mass suicide of 200 Okinawan schoolgirls and their teachers who chose to die by remaining inside a cave in the path of a systematically bombarding U.S. tank regiment. Farther south on the coast is **Mabuni Hill (Mabuni-no-Oka),** site of the Japanese Imperial Army's last stand on June 23, 1945. In addition to the hillside's forest of monuments and memorials contributed from all over Japan, there is an interesting **Peace Memorial Museum (Heiwa Kinen Shiryokan).**

After such grim reminders of the past, you may welcome some lighter entertainment in the form of **Gyokusendo Kingdom Village** *(Bus: 83, 54 from Naha bus terminal to Gyokusendo),* especially if you're traveling with children. This Okinawan cultural theme park has artisans demonstrating crafts such as *bingata* textile making and displays of *eisa* dancing. Underneath it all is the **Gyokusendo limestone cave,** much visited for its hundreds of thousands of stalagmites and stalactites. Nearby is the **Gyokusendo Habu-koen Park.** Be prepared here to see hapless habu vipers (an Okinawan species with a nasty but rarely fatal bite) or cobras being tossed to a voracious mongoose; such shows are one of Okinawa's more dubious tourist attractions.

Urasoe, the first capital of the Ryukyu kingdom, lies about 6 miles (10 km) north of Naha. **Joseki-koen Park** contains the ruins of the first royal castle, and a short walk beyond it is a mausoleum built for kings of the 14th century. The ruins of another feudal castle stand nearby at **Kita Naka-Gusuku,** with fine views from its hilltop site. The area's main attraction is the **Nakamura House (Nakamura-ke),** just over half a mile (1 km) northeast, regarded as the finest example of aristocratic rural domestic architecture still standing in Okinawa. Built during the mid-18th century, it contains many furnishings, implements, and family heirlooms showing how wealthy Okinawans lived until the early 1900s.

As elsewhere in Japan, development has taken its toll on many venerable buildings in Okinawa, so fine farmhouses and other buildings representative of a past way of life were dismantled in other parts of the island and reassembled in an open-air museum.

Okinawan textiles

Depicting flowers, fish, birds, people, festival scenes, and more in vivid colors, *bingata* textile designs rank among the finest in Japan. Bingata are hand-painted using specially prepared stencils, and demand a great deal of skill. The Ryukyus are known for textiles of other kinds, too. *Bashofu* is a lightweight fabric handwoven out of banana fibers in the north of Okinawa island; *kasuri* is a finely woven cloth made in the south. On Miyako-jima, the specialty is lightweight, indigo-dyed *jofu*. The *minsa* fabric of Yaeyama invariably shows a centipede woven in red against a dark background. Women made these for their fiancés as a sign of betrothal; the centipede was a symbol of eternal love. ■

More than half a mile (1 km) of the Gyokusendo limestone cave is open to visitors.

Ryukyu-mura Village is something of a mass-tourism affair, but it has interesting exhibits of Okinawan culture and crafts, including demonstrations on traditional performing arts, music, and textile weaving. Here again you can see regularly staged one-sided combats between mongoose and snake.

🅰 343 F1–H3 **Visitor information**
✉ Okinawa Prefectural Tourism Federation, Naha Airport, 150 Kagamizu
☎ 098/857-6884

RYUKYU-SHOTO

You don't have to go too far from Okinawa to discover an island paradise. The spectacularly beautiful **Kerama Islands** *(Visitor information: ferry terminal on Zamami-jima, tel 098/987-2277)* are only 18 miles (30 km) offshore, placing them smack-dab on the beaten track. Of the three main islands, **Tokashiki-jima** is the largest and most crowded during the holiday season. **Zamami-jima** and **Aka-jima** are both highly prized by divers and snorkelers—the water in the Keramas is so clear that it remains transparent down to quite a depth. Zamami has successfully converted from whaling to whale-watching, a lucrative pursuit that draws pod-people to the island in winter. The inhabited islands are well endowed with hotels and *minshuku,* but they can get crowded; in that case many people without a hotel reservation simply camp on the beaches of the 20 or so uninhabited islands within easy reach. Ferries run regularly between the islands, so getting around is fairly simple. From Zamami or Aka-jima you can visit the remoter island of **Geruma,** notable for the Kerama *shika*—a unique species of deer.

The **Miyako** group *(Visitor information: Miyako-jima Airport, tel 09807/2-0899)*, eight islands boasting spectacular seascapes and coral reefs for diving and snorkeling, has few historical or cultural sights, except in the town of **Hirara** on the main island of **Miyako-jima.** Built low against the ground with thick surrounding walls of coral limestone, the houses here have red-tiled roofs, a style that came to replace the thatch ubiquitous over the Ryukyu-shoto only within the 20th century. Other sights include **Nakasone Toimiya—** the ornate mausoleum of a local 15th-century military hero—and the curious **Jintoze-iseki (Tax Stone).** The stone stands 4.5 feet (1.4 m) high, and only those shorter than this were exempted from the taxes exacted by the ruling Satsuma clan of Kyushu. Taxes were also sometimes paid in a lightweight, indigo cloth called *jofu* (see p. 346), still widely made on the island today—but for the tourist rather than the taxman.

Sports are popular on Miyako-jima: Several serious scuba diving enterprises operate on the island, and each April the isle hosts Japan's infamous Strongman Challenge Triathlon, which involves swimming 1.8 miles (3 km), cycling 87 miles (140 km), then cooling down with a quick marathon run (26 miles/42 km).

Much less visited are Miyako's seven outlying islands, largely to the west, which are accessible by boat and possess beautiful beaches. Notable among them are **Shimoji-jima** and **Irabu-jima,** separated from each other by a narrow channel.

Continuing southwest, you come to the **Yaeyama-Shoto Islands** (*Ishigaki-jima Tourist Association, tel 09808/2-2809*). For many people, **Ishigaki-jima**—the transportation hub (both sea and air) of the Yaeyama group—is simply a stepping-stone to Taketomi-jima and Iriomote (see below). But Ishigaki boasts good beaches, diving options, and a center for black pearl culture on **Kabira-wan Bay** in the northwest. Its noteworthy sights include **Torin-ji Temple** with its 18th-century buildings, the **Yaeyama Minzoku-en village** (*967-1 Montonagura, 09808/2-8798*) devoted to the crafts (mainly textiles and pottery) of the Yaeyama group, and old cobbled streets flanked by typical low Ryukyuan buildings. Among them is the **Miyara Donchi** (*178 Okawa, tel 09808/2-2767, closed Tues.*), a fine aristocratic residence built in the early 19th century and open as a museum. At 1,726 feet (526 m), scenic Mount Omoto-dake at the center of the island is the highest point in Okinawa-ken.

Less than 15 minutes away by boat from Ishigaki-jima, **Taketomi-jima** could be accused of being flat and featureless were it not for the charm of **Taketomi village** with its low, garden-girdled houses and outstanding beaches. The island is also known for textiles. You can see artisans making them at **Taketomi Folk Art Center (Taketomi Mingeikan,** *435 Taketomi, tel 09808/5-2302*). Some beaches, especially those on the west coast, are known as *hoshizunahama,* or starsand beaches; the sand is made up of the star-shaped skeletons of tiny marine creatures.

Iriomote-jima is Japan's great tropical wilderness. An island with a coastline of 80 miles (130 km), it has hills covered in dense, uncharted virgin forest, as well as areas of mangrove swamp. This is the home of the Iriomote wildcat, believed by some zoologists to be a living fossil. Only slightly larger than a domestic cat, the wildcat is speckled rather than striped and has slightly rounder ear tips; otherwise it looks like a pet tabby. Experts reckon that only about 50 of the animals survive, so your chances of sighting an Iriomote wildcat are fairly slim.

Though touted as wild and unexplored, Iriomote is crisscrossed with hiking trails. The best known path traverses the island diagonally from the northwest—an exhilarating prospect if you don't mind leeches. Among spectacular scenic attractions on the island are the waterfalls at **Kampira** and **Pinaisara,** as well as some beautiful boat trips along jungle rivers that have been compared to miniature versions of the Amazon. Otherwise coastal Iriomote offers the usual options for swimming, diving, and resorts. The same goes for other small islands nearby, notably **Kohama-jima** and **Kuro-shima.**

The final stop in the Ryukyu-Shoto is **Yonaguni-jima,** an island 7 miles (11 km) long that lies just 60 miles (100 km) east of Taiwan. Short of clambering up Mount Urabu-dake (755 feet/230 m) in the early morning to glimpse the distant mountains of Taiwan, there isn't a lot to see and do on Yonaguni-jima—which may explain why the island brews the most lethally strong sake in all Japan. If you sample it, don't worry about the size of the moths you might see flitting about—they would look the same if you were sober. Called *yonagunisan,* they are among the world's largest. The island's only other draw is its strange rock formations.

For the Japanese, Yonaguni's real attraction is its role as the last outpost—as though if you went any farther, you would fall off the edge of the world. Much the same applies to the ait of **Hateruma-jima,** south of Iriomote. Japanese daytrippers like to visit this tiny island's **southernmost rock (Sainantan-no-Hi),** a landmark that designates the southernmost point in Japan.■

Travelwise

Festivals are a colorful part of Japanese life.

TRAVELWISE INFORMATION

PLANNING YOUR TRIP

WHEN TO GO

Japan has four distinct seasons, but spring and fall are generally the best times to visit, with the flowering cherries of spring and the autumnal reds of maple leaves constituting favorite postcard images. Rain is no stranger to either season, but fine spring weather really shows the country at its best.

Overall, the archipelago's climate ranges from Siberian (Hokkaido) to subtropical (Okinawa). There is also a mini rainy season known as *tsuyu* lasting from early June to mid-July, when hot winds from the tropical Pacific blow across Honshu, sending summer temperatures up to around 80°F (26°C), with humidity at a debilitating 80 percent plus. Summer temperatures in Kyushu and Okinawa average higher, but with less humidity the climate is more comfortable.

Despite the drawbacks of the Japanese summer, it can also be pleasant, as the frenzy of city life slows down and the country becomes steeped in summer greens. However, peak summer travel is marred by daunting crowds and higher prices; make reservations well ahead. In Northern Honshu (Tohoku) and Hokkaido temperatures rarely go above 70°F (21°C) in late July. With the added attraction of its large wilderness, small wonder that Hokkaido is an increasingly popular summer vacation destination.

Mid-October to mid-November is the time to appreciate Japan's famous autumn colors. In early fall, from the start of September until around the end of October, the Pacific side of the country is prone to typhoons that sweep up from the tropics packing high winds and torrential rain. The oriental equivalent of the hurricane, they can occasionally cause disastrous flooding and mud slides.

Although it can get pretty cold at night, especially on high ground, the winter is consistently fine and sunny on the Pacific coast, but the area of Honshu bordering the Sea of Japan is one of the snowiest places in the world. It is also one of the rainiest: Average annual precipitation stands at 102 inches (265 cm)—about twice as much as Tokyo gets. Winter in northern Japan can be very cold indeed, with ice floes sailing past the coast in Hokkaido's far north, where the sea can freeze over for miles. Far from deterring visitors, such subarctic phenomena are what attracts them; hot springs are plentiful on Hokkaido, which also has some of the finest ski resorts in Japan.

WHAT TO TAKE

It doesn't rain as much in winter, but rainwear is sensible at any other time of year. Inexpensive umbrellas and plastic raincoats light enough to fold up and carry in a pocket or bag are sold everywhere.

Take account of heat and humidity when selecting summer clothing. T-shirts, light cotton shirts, or blouses usually suffice, but air-conditioning is often ferocious. The Japanese are probably the best dressed people in the world; even the clothes of grunge rockers look freshly laundered. Don't wander around urban centers in beachwear, although shorts are acceptable. Coat and tie dress codes operate in some places, especially expensive restaurants.

You will need strong, lightweight footwear. Consider shoes that you can slip out of easily when entering temples, *ryokan,* some restaurants, or private homes. Be warned that the wooden floors of historic buildings such as castles can be bitterly cold in winter, so make sure you wear thick socks.

In summer it can get cold at higher altitudes. On Mount Fuji-san temperatures at the summit can go below freezing in August. Take a lightweight parka or fleece jacket. Winter may be sunny and mild in many places during the daytime, but you will still need warm clothing from December through March.

If you're staying in Japanese-style accommodations or intend to visit *onsen* baths, be warned that the towels issued will be minute—the Japanese *tenugui* is hardly larger than a washcloth. If you feel you cannot get used to this, bring your own towel.

INSURANCE

Japan's medical standards are among the world's highest, but care is priced accordingly and fees are prohibitive. Make sure that medical coverage in your travel insurance is adequate. If your stay in Japan is extended, take out internationally recognized medical insurance (for example, Blue Cross) before going.

ENTRY FORMALITIES

Passports & visas Provided they have a valid passport, U.S. and Canadian citizens may remain in Japan for 90 days without a visa. U.K. citizens are also granted 90 days at time of landing, but can apply for an extension of up to six months. Japan has a bewildering array of visa exemption agreements with different countries. If you are in doubt, it is best to call the Japanese consulate before planning your trip.

The stamp in your passport on arrival grants you temporary

visitor status for the stipulated period. Whatever your allowance, you can get an extension of stay provided that you apply ten days before its expiry date and that your total stay in Japan doesn't exceed six months. You must apply for an alien registration card at a town hall within 90 days regardless of your status. Foreigners are required by law to carry their passports with them at all times; the registration card makes a handy (and mandatory) alternative. Foreigners are sometimes stopped by police (usually at night) and asked to produce their papers.

A maximum of two extensions after the initial visa period is allowed if you have a good enough reason, such as health problems. You will probably have to provide proof that you can afford to remain. If you want to stay in Japan longer than six months and two extensions, the only way is to leave the country and re-enter. Be warned that your passport stamps will make this apparent to the immigration official, and you may find entry difficult. If you wish to leave Japan and come back again within the time allowed on your passport stamp, you have to apply for a re-entry visa at the immigration office.

You are forbidden to work in Japan if your status is temporary visitor or tourist. If you do want to work there, you must come in on a tourist visa and find a potential employer. The employer applies for permission to engage you while you make your application for a work visa at the Japanese consulate in a neighboring country.

Customs The standard allowances into Japan are 57 grams (2 oz) of perfume, gifts (duty-free items other than perfumes, spirits, and tobacco) up to a value of 200,000 yen, and three 760 ml bottles of spirits; to consume, purchase,

or possess alcohol in Japan you must be over age 20. The tobacco allowance is 500 grams (17.5 oz, 400 cigarettes, or 100 cigars).

Immunizations Japan requires no special immunizations, unless you arrive from an area in which diseases such as cholera or yellow fever are endemic, when you should have a World Health Organization certificate of the appropriate vaccinations.

Pets Pets may be brought to Japan provided they have health certificates. They must be examined by quarantine officers at the port of entry. Cats and dogs require certificates of vaccination against rabies. If you bring them from one of the designated rabies-free areas, the detention could be as short as 12 hours, but even with a certificate, they are usually kept in quarantine at the owner's expense for a period of at least two weeks. It can be difficult to find hotels, restaurants, (or stores) that accept pets.

HOW TO GET TO JAPAN

From the U.S. there are several flights daily to Japan both from the East Coast (average time 13 hours via the polar route) and West Coast (average time 10 hours via the Pacific route).

Bound for Tokyo, most people land at Narita airport, but there has been an increase in direct flights to other airports following airport development. The largest is the recently built Kansai International Airport, the most convenient for Osaka, Kyoto, and Kobe. Nagoya airport, best for central Honshu and the Japan Alps, is under refurbishment and enlargement at the time of writing. There are direct flights to Fukuoka on Kyushu from Honolulu and Guam, but not from the U.S. mainland. There are no direct

flights from the U.S. or Guam to Okinawa. The nonstop route from London to Tokyo takes around 12 hours.

GETTING AROUND

FROM THE AIRPORTS

Narita airport, 41 miles (66 km) away from Tokyo, is notoriously inconvenient, but there are several options for reaching the city. A **taxi** journey costs over $200. Much cheaper, and with journeys averaging 70 minutes depending upon traffic, the **Limousine Bus** leaves for Tokyo every 10–15 minutes. You simply purchase your ticket inside the terminal building; the bus stops right outside. Most go to Tokyo City Air Terminal (TCAT), but other, less frequent services stop at major hotels in town and there's another going directly to Yokohama. At TCAT a fleet of taxis wait to take you to your hotel or if you have little luggage and know how to get there, you can take the Hanzomon subway line.

The other way into town is by **train,** though less convenient if you have a lot of luggage. Tickets for the Narita Express (NEX) are between $25 and $30; the train takes 53 minutes to Tokyo Station and 84 minutes to Shinjuku. The service also runs (though less frequently) to Ikebukuro, Shinagawa, and Yokohama.

Leaving around every half hour, the Keisei Skyliner airport express train takes 60 minutes from Narita to Ueno Station in Tokyo. Trains on the Keisei line take about 20 minutes longer, but are substantially cheaper. The Sobu line runs from Narita to Tokyo Station and takes 90 minutes. These lines do not accept JR Rail Passes (see p. 353). There's a similar range of connections from Kansai International airport to either

Osaka or Kyoto; the buses to the former take about an hour and to the latter 90–105 minutes. Trains take about an hour to Osaka and 70–95 minutes to Kyoto. If you have a rail pass coupon and want to take a JR train from Kansai International Airport, you can exchange it for the pass at the JR West information desk in the international arrivals lobby.

When you leave the country, both Kansai International and Narita airports levy a departure tax; Kansai's is around $25, which is payable at the airport, and Narita's is just under $20, which is applicable at the time of ticket issue (prices may vary according to the exchange rate).

TRAVELING IN THE CITIES

Public transport in Japanese cities is fast, efficient, and relatively cheap. With the traffic jams and difficult or expensive parking, the soundest advice is to forget about driving in the city unless you're planning an extended stay.

Subways Tokyo, Fukuoka, Kobe, Kyoto, Nagoya, Osaka, Sapporo, Sendai, and Yokohama all have subway systems. As with local line trains, you generally buy tickets from a machine. Some places have English-language maps inscribed with fare tariffs; most don't. When in doubt, pay the lowest fare and then pay the difference at your destination. This is often the best policy: In Tokyo, for instance, you might change between lines owned by different companies, and the pricing can be complicated. You can always ask the ticket office staff for assistance.

Buses In many cities, public transport is provided solely by buses. Hakodate (Hokkaido), Hiroshima (Honshu), Matsuyama (Shikoku), and Nagasaki and Kumamoto (Kyushu) have streetcar systems. Not all buses

or streetcars have destinations in roman letters, so it's advisable to note the *kanji* characters spelling out your destination on a piece of paper and look for it on the front of the vehicle before boarding.

In Tokyo you pay a flat fare on entering the bus, but in most other places you take a ticket out of the automatic dispenser as you enter the bus or streetcar. The number on your ticket corresponds to the stop from which you boarded. Near the ceiling on the driver's left is an electric sign showing the stop number and the amount you must pay as you leave.

Taxis In Tokyo taxis seem to be everywhere. Although prices vary slightly in different areas, they are expensive. Taking a taxi at rush hour is never a good idea, as traffic jams can be formidable and waste a lot of time; if the cab gets caught in traffic, the extra time will be charged on the meter. There is a 20 percent surcharge for cabs summoned by phone, and the same applies to all taxis after 11 p.m.

Watch for the lights on the taxi roof: Yellow means that the cab is engaged, red that it is free, and green that a surcharge is operative. Whether inside or out of the taxi, don't even think of opening or closing the door—doors are automatically controlled by the driver.

Japanese cabbies are generally polite and helpful, but a Japanese business card, or your destination written in Japanese, is advisable. Remember that most cities are without street names, and that the random numerical address system in suburban and residential areas is decipherable only to postal workers and police; your driver may have to stop and ask the way. Although a small contribution to a helpful driver may be appreciated, tipping is never expected.

TRAVELING AROUND JAPAN

By rail Be it suburban, local, or intercity super express, the train is the most convenient and fastest way to travel in Japan; the standards of punctuality, comfort, and cleanliness throughout Japanese rail services are legendary. But be warned: When changing trains, it can be a long way between platforms, there may be several staircases on the way, and there is no such thing as a porter. The golden rule is to travel light. Tickets can be purchased at all train stations.

The privatized **Japan Railways (JR)**, comprising six companies, runs major routes throughout the country, with other links— both express and local trains— provided by regional firms. It's possible to go virtually anywhere in Japan by train.

JR's most prestigious service is the **shinkansen**—the bullet train. Inaugurated in 1964 for the Olympic Games, the shinkansen remained the world's fastest train until overtaken during the 1980s by France's TGV. Divided into the Tokaido shinkansen (Tokyo–Osaka), Sanyo (Fukuoka), Tohoku (Sendai), and Joetsu (Niigata) lines, the service is impeccable. Depending on the destination, the options are: limited express (*kodama*), express (*hikari*), and super express (*nozomi*). It costs little to reserve a seat, but make sure that you apply at least a month ahead.

Discounts Children under six travel free by rail, and it's half-price for those between 6 and 11; otherwise traveling by train—and by shinkansen especially—can become very expensive. Fortunately there are several different kinds of discount options available, notably the **5-day JR Youth 18 ticket** (*seishun juhachi kippu*), which costs around $100; it's primarily designed for students and is valid only during the college vacation periods, but you can be any age to qualify. Although substantial, savings apply to local trains only—not the shinkansen.

By far the best deal is the **JR Rail Pass,** available for 7 ($260), 14 ($410), or 21 ($520) days (prices are approximate and about one-third more in each category if you want to travel by Green Car, first class). The pass entitles you to unlimited use of transport in the JR system for the duration, including the shinkansen (except for the ultra-fast *nozomi),* other JR trains, JR buses, and JR ferries. If you intend to make more than one intercity journey (e.g. Tokyo–Kyoto return), the rail pass is absolutely essential. Note that it must be purchased outside Japan from an authorized travel agent.

The pass must be validated within three months of the date of purchase, but the actual starting date is determined when you exchange the voucher issued by the travel agent for the actual rail pass in Japan. You can only make seat reservations once you have obtained your pass (obtainable at the JR Travel Service Center in any main line train station—the options are listed on the back of the voucher). The rules governing the passes are strict. You cannot change the date once the pass is issued, and if you lose the pass, it will not be replaced.

JR West Rail Passes or **JR Kyushu Rail Passes** also represent substantial savings; JR East Rail Pass has a discount for those aged between 12 and 25. With the exception of JR West, these passes must also be purchased outside Japan. You are eligible for JR passes only if you are entering Japan with temporary visitor status. You will need your passport bearing the relevant stamps when you exchange the voucher for the pass.

By bus Budget-conscious travelers often opt for the inter-city bus services, a cheaper (though slower) alternative to the train. Fitted with reclining seats, night buses are reasonably comfortable. Tour buses abound in every major tourist center. They can make an excellent alternative to public buses if you are in a hurry but they are costly and, unless stated otherwise, the chances are that the tour will be conducted entirely in Japanese.

By air All of Japan's prefectural capitals are connected by air; there are plenty of options for reaching smaller cities, too. The main carriers are Japan Airlines (JAL), All Nippon Airways (ANA), and Japan Air System (JAS), but since the deregulation of the air transport industry in 1986, the number of local carriers is ever increasing. Domestic flights from Tokyo leave from Haneda airport. The Limousine Bus (see p. 351) shuttles between Haneda and Narita airport.

By ferry With an increasing number of interconnecting tunnels and bridges, it's easy to forget that Japan is an island nation. But if you're fond of older, slower ways of traveling or on a tight budget, the good news is that the inter-island ferry network is extensive. It's the best way to get to Sado Island and the most attractive means of traveling on the Inland Sea. An overnight ferry to Hokkaido costs less than the train. JNTO (Japan National Tourist Office) offices have information about routes, times, and costs (for JNTO centers see p. 356).

Japanese ferries are fun: Passengers simply sprawl over large carpeted (or occasionally still tatami-matted) areas on the lower decks. Having removed your shoes, you select your spot and drop—to eat and drink, play cards, read, gossip, and eventually sleep. Cabins are available at extra cost for those wary of

raucous, bibulous laughter and the excited squeals of children.

By car Unless you are used to driving on the left-hand side of the road and can cope with some road signs in Japanese, you would be advised not to drive in Japan. That said, the car provides an alternative way to travel if you want to venture off the beaten track. The relatively high cost of highway tolls (Tokyo to Kyoto will set you back more than $90) and the price of gas may also deter you. You need a valid international driving permit plus your own license (but if you are staying on after the international driving license expires, you will need a Japanese one). The same pattern applies to motorcycles, although you may be required to take another test in Japan, especially for bikes of 750cc and up.

Car rental operations abound in Japan, with major international firms well represented. In some cases you can reserve your car in Japan through the rental firm at home (try Hertz tel 800/654-3001, or National 800/227-7368). The rental arrangement is often one-way: you must bring the vehicle back to the hiring point or pay an exorbitant fee to have it done for you.

Japan drives on the left. The speed limits are 50 mph (80 kph) on highways, 37.5 mph (60 kph) on secondary roads, and 25 mph (40 kph) in towns. Although bilingual versions are becoming the norm, some signs may still be in Japanese only.

Cycling Bicycle theft is probably the commonest of the few crimes you'll encounter in Japan, so if you cycle, make sure you always leave your bicycle locked. Provided you have a carrying bag *(rinko baggu*—available from cycling shops) and pay a small supplement to your fare, you can take your bicycle on the train. On the whole, this is a cycle-friendly country, provided you stay as much as possible off the main roads. Recommended areas are the foothills of the Japan Alps on Honshu, Kyushu, Shikoku, and the national park areas in Hokkaido. Many places have bicycles for rent, the outlets are typically close to the train station or tourist center.

PRACTICAL ADVICE

COMMUNICATIONS

Post offices You can recognize a post office or mailbox by the sign it carries—a red or white "T" with a bar over the top. Main city and district post offices are open 8 a.m.–7 p.m. on weekdays, 8 a.m.–3 p.m. on Saturdays, and 9 a.m.–12:30 p.m. on Sundays. Branch offices are open 9 a.m.–5 p.m. and close weekends. Only larger post offices have currency exchange and poste restante facilities; uncollected mail is returned to sender after 10 days.

Telephones There are many phone booths in Japan; thanks both to efficient maintenance and the total absence of vandalism, the phones almost always work. There are a few old pink, red, and turquoise pay phones still in operation; if you stumble across one, it will only take ¥10 coins, each buying you a minute's talking time for local calls. These phones don't provide international calls.

Most pay phones use both coins and prepaid telephone cards (terehon kado) available in denominations of ¥500, ¥1,000, and ¥5000. Cards are sold in vending machines, station kiosks, and many other outlets. The ubiquitous lime-green phone, except for those with a gold front plate, is for calls within Japan only; yellow phones are only for local calls. International calls are made most commonly from gray telephones (often located beside the green ones); there are purple, fuchsia, or silver credit card phones in some larger railway stations, which likewise handle international calls. Blue and chrome phones are an even rarer variant, similarly found in stations. Among other American charge cards, AT&T cards are usable on Japanese phones.

NTT (domestic calls only) and KDD (international only) still dominate the market in Japan despite deregulation and the appearance of more competitors since the mid-1980s. Virtually the only ones offering international calls apart from KDD (dialing prefix 001) are IDC (prefix 0061) and ITJ (prefix 0041). When calling the U.S. or Canada dial the prefix, followed by 1 and the number you require. Other useful telephone numbers are: for a collect call, tel 106; NTT's Information for Foreigners, tel 03/5295-1010. Call rates are lower between 7 p.m. and 8 a.m., as well as over the weekend. Pay phones are considerably cheaper than dialing from a hotel room.

Drinking water As you would expect, you can safely drink water straight from the faucet anywhere in Japan, although it does not always taste very good. Bottled water is very popular and both domestic and imported brands are widely available.

ELECTRICITY

Japan's electric current is 100v AC, running at 50 cycles in Tokyo and on the Pacific side, and at 60 cycles in western Japan.

ETIQUETTE & LOCAL CUSTOMS

There are only three absolute no-nos in Japan: soaping yourself in the bath; entering a home, temple, or shrine building without removing your shoes; and blowing your nose in public. Nose-blowing is so frowned upon that you should try to sniff and dab discreetly with a handkerchief until you can retire and blow in private.

The word for foreigner, *gaijin*, a contraction of *gaikoku jin* (outside country-person), was once used offensively, but is now neutral; strangers will politely address you as "*gaijin-san*." Either way the message is the same: If you are not Japanese, then you are an outsider. Japanese also discriminate among themselves and relationships tend to be confined to the circles defining them: mostly kinship, education, or employment.

To most foreigners, Japanese behavior will appear strikingly formal. Harmony, achieved through conformity and consensus, is of the first importance; it dictates masking private cares with public smiles along with the individual's obligation to conform with the group. Outspokenness is bad manners, and conversations find participants doing their utmost to agree with each other. Decisions are reached through consensus; in corporate contexts the process can take quite some time. Nodding means "I understand what you're saying," smiling is just polite, neither means "yes."

The rules of etiquette tend to focus on specific group situations and do not always apply to the street, where men often spit or, late at night, urinate against the nearest wall. The Japanese can sometimes appear churlish. You might not get an apology from someone colliding with you, but, if challenged, the embarrassed offender could well be at a loss for words.

Yet if you address someone, the ice is usually broken immediately. Ask, and most people will go out of their way to help you. The Japanese do not expect foreigners to be familiar with their complex etiquette. If you abide by the universal rules of kindness and consideration, you will get along fine in Japan.

How to behave The proper greeting on meeting or parting is a bow, and its degree (i.e. how low) and repetition are determined by the amount of respect due to the recipient. For a foreigner, a slight inclination will suffice; most Japanese are used to shaking hands with foreigners. Do not embrace anyone; kissing is reserved strictly for babies and lovers.

Introductions entail an exchange of names or business cards, and it is polite to look at them before putting them away. During business meetings, cards are placed on the table. Unless you are instructed otherwise, use of the family name is preferred and carries the suffix *san* (e.g. Yamada-san: Mr. or Ms. Yamada).

In Japan, gifts are less tokens of love or friendship than repayment for favors or a response in kind. If you are entertained in a Japanese home, always bring a present for your hosts, typically a bottle of wine, flowers, or fruit; a small token from your country of origin will also be appreciated. Unless among close friends, avoid anything too extravagant—the recipient may feel obliged to repay you in kind.
(See also tipping, p. 356.)

Table manners As a foreigner, you will often be assumed to be incapable of using chopsticks. Use them if you can—but never stick them in the rice bowl when you have finished. Said to evoke the incense sticks burning in a bowl at a funeral, it's considered very bad manners.

Boiled rice, always served in its own bowl, is sacrosanct and it should remain white. Placing items into it taken from the dishes on the table is acceptable with Chinese food, but

sprinkling the rice with sauce is considered barbaric. The way to eat soup noodles is to raise them with your chop-sticks and suck them up with a loud slurp. This cools them and shows your appreciation.

Women traditionally pour drinks for men first. If your neighbor fills your glass, always return the compliment. There may be a lot of raising or clinking of glasses, invariably accompanied with the word *kampai!*—cheers!

Liquor laws
You must be over 20 years old to consume alcohol.

MEDIA

Newspapers English language publications: *Japan Times, Daily Yomiuri, Mainichi Daily News,* and the *Asahi Evening News*—the first and the last being generally considered the best.

Television Japanese television has a partly justified reputation for being terrible. Still, the game shows, samurai serials, soap operas, quiz programs, and wholly incredible commercials are worth a look for the insights they provide into the country. There are 8 TV channels in Tokyo, two of them being the national network, NHK, which broadcasts news in English at 7 p.m. (receivable only if the set is multiplex or dual language). TV sets in major hotels are generally multiplex or dual language, with films shown in English and Japanese. Cable, satellite, and digital TV are still being developed, with some already in operation. Outside private homes and top-flight hotels you might have to content yourself with NHK.

Radio Radio is generally panned by visitors. English-language programs are largely limited to the U.S. armed forces' Far East Network (FEN). There are four international radio stations nationwide offering programming

in a variety of languages: FM Cocolo in Osaka; Inter FM in Tokyo; Love FM in Fukuoka; RADIOi in Nagoya.

Video The video system is NTSC as in the United States. If you are using recording equipment from the U.K. or countries using other systems, make sure to bring your own video cassettes.

MONEY MATTERS

The Japanese currency is the yen. Bank notes come in denominations of ¥10,000, ¥5,000 and ¥1,000; coins in ¥1 (white metal), ¥5 (brass, hole in center), ¥10 (copper), ¥50 (silver colored, hole in center), ¥100 (silver colored), and ¥500 (silver colored).

NATIONAL HOLIDAYS

January 1 New Year's Day— *Gantan*
January 1–3 New Year— *Oshogatsu*
January, 2nd Mon. Coming of Age Day—*Seijin-no-hi*
February 11 National Foundation Day—*Kenkoku Kinen-no-hi*
March 20 or 21 Vernal Equinox—*Shubun-no-hi*
April 29 Greenery Day— *Midori-no-hi*
May 3 Constitution Memorial Day—*Kenpo Kinenbi*
May 4 People's Holiday— *Kokumin-no-shukujitsu*
May 5 Children's Day— *Kodomo-no-hi*
July 20 Marine Day—*Umi-no-hi*
September 15 Respect for the Aged Day—*Keiro-no-hi*
September 23 Autumn Equinox—*Shubun-no-hi*
October, 2nd Mon. Health Sports Day—*Taiiku-no-hi*
November 3 Culture Day— *Bunka-no-hi*
November 23 Labor Thanksgiving Day—*Kinro kansha-no-hi*
December 23 Emperor's Birthday—*Tenno Tanjobi*

OPENING TIMES

Banks: 9 a.m.–3 p.m. weekdays; closed weekends and holidays. **Post offices:** 9 a.m.–5 p.m. (see also Communications on p. 354). **Department stores:** 10 a.m.–7 p.m. (closed one day a week) **Restaurants:** noon–3; 6–9 p.m (some open all day). **Private offices:** 9 a.m.–5 p.m. weekdays; some are open 9 a.m.–noon on Saturdays. **Public offices:** 9 a.m.–5 p.m. weekdays. Closed weekends.

SMOKING

Smokers still constitute a clear majority in Japan, although the figures are declining yearly. Smoking is prohibited throughout the subway system and on commuter train lines. It is permitted on the shinkansen and other long-distance trains, although the number of no-smoking compartments (kin-en sha) has recently been forced up by public opinion. Only big city restaurants with a large foreign clientele have no-smoking areas. Some international hotels have no-smoking floors or rooms.

TAXES & SURCHARGES

A five percent consumption tax is applicable to all goods and services; it is charged unless you purchase items tax free for export—the tax applies in restaurants and hotels. You can sometimes reduce the tax by asking hotels and ryokan to bill your meals and room separately. Service charges of between 10 and 20 percent are also added to your bill.

TIPPING

In a word: don't; the practice is unknown in Japan. This said, you can give a taxi driver or hotel staff member a token of your appreciation for being especially helpful. Chances are it won't be accepted, but it might if you put it into an envelope first!

TOILETS

Although the Western variety is becoming increasingly common, the most widespread is still the pan-Asian, Middle Eastern squat-toilet; the Japanese variant has a kind of hood at one end and that's the one to face. Toilet technology is a science in Japan, however, where hygiene is an obsession. The computerized Western-style Washlet toilet (increasingly common in upscale hotels) boasts a heated seat and incorporates a cleansing water jet and drier. Technology to take your breath away—especially if you make a mistake over the water-temperature setting! Note that public toilets, especially in stations, do not have toilet paper: Either carry a pack of tissues or purchase paper from the vending machine usually located near the door.

TRAVELERS WITH DISABILITIES

For those with impaired sight, a strip of rubber indicates the edge of station platforms and musical signals give the all-clear at pedestrian crossings. Otherwise, this is not a great country for the disabled. International-class hotels have wheelchair access, but not the majority of ryokan. Access ramps are becoming more widespread, and staff will always offer assistance in train and subway stations, but at all costs avoid rush hour.

Before you set off, get information from the Society for the Advancement of Travel for the Handicapped, 347 5th Ave., Ste. 610, New York, NY 10016, tel 212/447-7284, fax 212/725-8253.

VISITOR INFORMATION

For the Japan National Tourist Office (JNTO) and visitor information centers in Japan, see separate entries in the main gazeteer.

JNTO offices outside Japan

United States
1 Rockefeller Plaza, Ste, 1250, New York, NY 10020 tel 212/757-5640.

401 N. Michigan Ave., Ste. 770, Chicago, IL 60611 tel 312/222-0874.

515 South Figueroa St., Ste 1470, Los Angeles, CA 90071 tel 213/623-1952.

360 Post St., Ste. 601, San Francisco, CA 94108 tel 415/989-7140.

Canada
165 University Ave., Toronto, ON M5H 3B8 tel 416/366-7140.

United Kingdom
Heathcoat House, 20 Savile Row, London W2X 1AE, tel 0171-734-9638.

Websites
Japan Information Network: www.jinjapan.org
Japan Travel Updates (JNTO): www.jnto.go.jp
Asahi News: www.asahi.com/english/
Japan Times Online: www.japantimes.co.jp
Kansai Time Out: www.kto.co.jp/
Tokyo Meltdown: www.bento.com/tleisure

EMERGENCIES

CRIME & POLICE

Japan's streets are among the safest in the world, even at night. Metropolitan neighborhoods have a koban, a police box manned by up to four police officers; this system partly explains the low crime rate. Murder and crimes of violence are reassuringly rare. However, alongside a recent increase in white-collar crime, the incidence of muggings and theft committed by young people is rising. Rape is comparatively rare (though many cases are thought to go unreported). Caution and common sense are advisable around amusement districts when they empty in the wee hours. This said, honesty is one of Japan's greatest virtues, and many are the traveler's tales of lost wallets returned.

EMBASSIES & CONSULATES

United States
1-10-5 Akasaka, Minato-ku, Tokyo, tel 03/3224-5000.

Canada
7-3-38 Akasaka, MInato-ku, Tokyo, tel 03/3408-2101.

United Kingdom
1 Ichiban-cho, Chiyoda-ku, Tokyo, tel 03/3265-5511.

EMERGENCY NUMBERS

Call boxes all have an emergency red button—press this first.
Police: 110
Ambulance/Fire: 119

For credit card loss
Amex: 0120/020-120
Visa: 0120/133-173

EARTHQUAKES

Japan lies in one of the most volcanically and seismically active areas in the world. If there's an earthquake, **don't** just run out of the house (unless you're in open country)—you might be hit by falling debris, power lines, etc. **Do** immediately turn off the gas supply and all cooking and heating appliances, then hide under a table or stand in a doorway.

HEALTH

Travelers needn't be greatly concerned about contracting exotic diseases. The kind that you do have to worry about are much the same as at home. If you need to see a doctor—especially an English-speaking one—the Tokyo Medical and Surgical Clinic (32 Mori Building, 4-30 Shiba Koen 3-chome, Minato-ku, tel 03/3436-3028) is one of several options. It has a 24-hour emergency service.

Carry a sufficient supply of your own prescription drugs to cover your trip (and a letter from your physician for customs). Make sure you know not just the brand name but the generic name, for the former is likely to be wholly different in Japan. You might find some imported drugs in the American Pharmacy in Tokyo, but don't count on it elsewhere. A lot of people complain about not being able to find over-the-counter drugs that are available back home, so bring them with you. You should be able to get equivalents in Japan that give the same results. Herbal remedies (obtained from Chinese-style pharmacies) are widely available.

LANGUAGE GUIDE

airport: *kuukoo*
bank: *ginkoo*
car: *kuruma*
east: *higashi*
left: *hidari*
north: *kita*
plane: *hikoki*
post offIce: *yubIn kyoku*
restaurant: *resutoran*
right: *migi*
south: *minami*
station: *eki*
taxi: *takushi*
temple: *tera/dera* or *-ji/-in*
ticket: *kippu* (plane ticket: *kokuuken*)
visitor (information) office: *kankoo annaisho*
train: *densha*
up: *ue*/down: *shita*
west: *nishi*

this: *kore*/that: *sore*/that (more distant, or not visible): *are*
I want to go to…:…*e ikitai desu*.
What time is it: *nanji desuka?*

Is it near/far? *Tooi/chikai desu-ka*
no (contradiction): *ie* (usually followed with or completely replaced by *chigaimasu*)
won't do/don't do/stop it (including the "no" for women): *dame*
haven't/aren't any…:…*nai desu/…arimasen*
hello (telephone) *moshi-moshi*
how much?: *ikura desuka?*
Do you speak English? *Eigo o hanasemasuka?*
I don't understand: *(Chotto) wakarimasen*
Where is (the tourist information center)?: *(Kankoo annai-shoo wa) doko desuka?*
Do you take credit cards?: *Kurejitto kaado tsukaemasu-ka?*
Do you have a room?: *O heya aitemasu-ka?*
I'd like to make a reservation for …(two people): *(futari bun no)…yoyaku shitai no desu-ga*
Expensive: *takai*
Cheap: *yasui*
Have you anything cheaper?: *Mo chotto yasui no wa arimasen-ka?*
Please show me: *o misete kudasai*
Is there any?: *arimasu-ka?*
I want/would like: *ga hooshi no desu-ga*
Please show me: *o misete kudasai*
Big: *ooki*, little: *chiisai* (little bit: *sukoshi*)
This is too big: *chotto ooki sugimasu*
help!: *tasukete!*
danger: *abunai*
call a doctor/police: *issha/keisatsu o yonde kudasai*
I'm unwell: *chooshi ga warui desu*

(numbers/quantity of things/number of people)
one: *ichi/hitotsu/hitori*
two: *ni/futatsu/futari*
three: *san/mitsu/san nin*
four: *shi* or *yon/yotsu/yon nin*
five: *go/itsutsu/go nin*
six: *roku/muttsu/roku nin*
seven: *nana* or *shichi/nanatsu/shichi nin*
eight: *hachi/yattsu/hachi nin*
nine: *kyu/kokonotsu/kyu nin*
ten: *jyu/to/ jyu nin*

HOTELS & RESTAURANTS

Although it has a broad spectrum of accommodations, Japan (and Tokyo especially) is expensive. That said, the options for tighter budgets seem to be increasing all the time.

As the recent proliferation of Japanese restaurants worldwide suggests, Japan is very much a food country. A bad meal is a rarity in Japan, where the native palate tends to be be discerning and standards of hygiene strict.

ACCOMMODATIONS

The Japan National Tourist Office (JNTO) regularly updates lists of accommodations that include the Welcome Inn Group, the Japanese Ryokan Association, the Japanese Inn Group (JIG), and youth hostels. JIG is particularly recommended. It's a great way to get acquainted with the *ryokan* (traditional inns) system. Reservations can be made over the Internet, as is also the case with many hotels of other kinds. Visit "Japan Travel Updates" on JNTO's website (www.jnto.go.jp), where you can even see what the hotel looks like.

JNTO offices overseas (see p. 356) all have the information you need to make your reservations: Try to make these at least four months ahead. Note that at New Year's (Dec. 28–Jan. 4), many family-run ryokans close for family celebrations.

If you haven't made reservations, the visitor information centers in each locality can help. Staff at visitor information desks in mainline train stations will do the same although they don't always speak English.

Western-style hotels

International chains, such as Holiday Inn, Hilton, Hyatt, and Meridien, are well represented. Japanese chains also operate Western-style hotels, including JAL (Nikko Hotels), Dai-ichi, ANA, Prince, and Tokyu. All Western-style hotels meet the highest international standards although rooms tend to be small. Many hotels also offer Japanese-style rooms, but it will be assumed that you want a Western one. If you choose Japanese style it could be more expensive. All modern hotels and some ryokan offer air-conditioning and elevators. Smaller regional hotels, ryokan, and *minshuku* (see opposite) may not have air-conditioning or elevators; you should check when making your reservations. All hotels, most ryokan, and plenty of minshuku provide TV in the rooms, and some offer English-language pay-movies and cable TV. Hotels typically have a choice of bars and an array of restaurants including Japanese, Western, and Chinese; the standards of cuisine are generally high, but points scored for atmosphere are low.

Business hotels

Bijinesu hoteru are a more economical Western-style option. Targeting business travelers, they usually have small single rooms with adjoining bathroom. Don't expect bellhops, porters, room service, or laundry. You will be given towels and a *yukata* (cotton gown). There is usually a restaurant or coffee shop, but anything else, including canned drinks and beer, comes out of vending machines.

Ryokan

Some ryokan have been operating for more than a century or have been converted from large ancestral residences; others are custom built. If you want a "real Japan" experience and a glimpse of a traditional Japanese home, these are the places to stay. The average ryokan is of modest size; charged mainly on a per-person basis, the prices range from astronomical heights (¥150,000 a head is by no means unknown) to very moderate. The rate normally includes an evening meal (which is often lavish and served in your room) and breakfast—both Japanese style. Some ryokan will reserve the room without meals.

There's usually someone who speaks a little English in JIG's 80 or so ryokans. Their rooms are small, basic, and spotless so it is vital to make reservations in advance. Unless you speak some Japanese, do not wander into a ryokan off the street; you might be turned away.

There are certain rules to bear in mind. When you enter, step out of your shoes, leave them in the entrance hall, and don the plastic slippers provided. Use these in the corridors. You must remove them before stepping onto the tatami matting in your room as well as before entering the toilet, where you use the pairs of plastic or wooden sandals provided. Don't forget to take the sandals off again: Wandering the building in toilet slippers is bad form.

Your room contains no beds; the futon mattresses and bedding (stored in the closets) will be laid out for you by the maid. Although the mattress is placed directly on the floor, the tatami is springy enough to make this a much less spartan sleeping arrangement than it sounds. You will be given a cotton kimono that is both sleepwear and for wandering about the hotel. In winter you'll get a warm gown to wear over it.

Bathrooms tend to be communal and in many ryokan you will find thermal baths. Remember bathing etiquette (see p. 21): You must soap and rinse thoroughly before entering the communal tub.

Dinner is served early; the latest will be about 8 p.m. Smaller, family-run ryokan often impose curfews. There may be no key to lock your door.

Minshuku

Minshuku, literally "people's lodging," are family businesses usually operating in a converted private home—as are many ryokan. There is little difference in price between minshuku and the more modest ryokan, which are run along almost identical lines. Meals in the former may be served in a dining area or family kitchen rather than in the room; some serve no meals at all. Many minshuku provide no towels, though most sell the standard *tenugui* (see p. 350). Some minshuku expect you to take your own bedding from the closets, put the sheets on, and take them off again and put the bedding away in the morning. Minshuku frequently close their doors at a fixed time at night.

Dotted about mountain, *onsen*, or seaside resorts, state-owned *kokumin shukusha* are run along exactly the same lines as ryokan, but without the attentive service. Room rates on average are about $60 a head including two meals.

Pension hotels

Pronounced "pen-shon," this concept derives from the *pension* (full bed and board) formula in France. Usually frequented by young people, these are small Western-style hotels. Some are theme-conceived and specialize in sports and pastimes; many cater to a largely female clientele.

Shukubo

Temples have traditionally offered lodgings to travelers and many still do. The old concept of offering the lodging free in exchange for chores performed (e.g. sweeping, washing dishes, or gardening) sometimes still applies. You don't have to be a Buddhist to qualify. Generally

Shukubo offer inexpensive accommodations, though some of the finer ones can be quite pricey. Some shukubo serve basic vegetarian food and impose a 9 p.m. curfew; others serve gourmet vegetarian cuisine and run their own bars.

Youth hostels

Membership in the International Youth Hostel Association is not essential, though most hostels offer discounts for members. They don't take children under four years, but adults of any age are welcome. Friendly, basic, and very clean, most are run like minshuku and in the Japanese style; the majority also close their doors at night. Dormitory beds cost less than $25, and single and double rooms are about $35 on average (without breakfast). Beware: Some youth hostels also maintain a teetotal-ist sing-around-the-campfire ethic guaranteed to make way-cool *gaijin* (foreigners) squirm.

Love hotels

If it stands on the fringe of an amusement district looking like Cinderella's castle while display-ing garish neon signs, then it has to be a "love hotel." These accommodations are strictly for couples: Single people will be turned away. Expect rotating beds, mirrored walls or ceilings, adult videos, and vending ma-chines containing toys devised to tickle your fancy. Rooms are often larger than hotel rooms in the same price range. Usually on a par with business hotels, prices vary according to the rooms— which are often theme-conceived. The bed might look like a 1950s Cadillac in a Chinese restaurant, or the place could be decked out like a medieval torture chamber (!).

Capsule hotels

The capsule hotel first appeared during the 1980s, and was the inebriated salaryman's dream come true: a cheap (under $40) alternative to the expense formerly incurred by missing the

last suburban train. Reached by a ladder, the capsule is no larger than a ship-board berth, though extremely comfortable and endowed with all kinds of amenities, including TV with hot and cold running porn. The overall design is tellingly like a beehive. Some capsule hotels also feature saunas and public baths with spa pools. The majority are for men only.

RESTAURANTS

Choosing in restaurants doesn't always require Japanese language ability. Many restaurants in big cities have English menus and where they don't, many menus have photographs of the fare served. The windows of almost all Japanese restaurants display disconcertingly realistic plastic models of the dishes served, so all you have to do is point. Unless you're undaunted at the prospect of a hefty check, avoid places that don't display models or menus with prices outside.

In most restaurants, a simple and often cheaper alternative to ordering à la carte is to select *teishoku*—set meals. Served on a tray, these always include a small appetizer, rice, pickles, and a bowl of piping hot *misoshiru* (soup made from miso soybean paste), the basic components of a standard Japanese meal. Low prices for set meals at lunchtime make some of the country's most expensive restaurants an affordable treat.

Sushi & sashimi

Most restaurants specialize in a certain type of cuisine. Sushi restaurants serve nothing else, except perhaps sashimi—slices of raw fish picked up with chopsticks and dipped into a sauce before eating. In sushi parlors, examples of the dishes will be in a glass case behind the counter in front of you; all you have to do is point. In larger places, fish and seafood often swim around in tanks. You can point at those too: Freshness is a golden rule in Japanese cuisine.

HOTELS & RESTAURANTS

For sushi, morsels of raw fish are placed on a bite-size bed of rice. As *norimaki,* sushi delicacies are rolled together with the rice in a sheet of dried seaweed. Like sashimi, sushi is eaten after dipping in soy spiced with *wasabi, a* fierce, bright green variety of horseradish relish.

Vegetarian food

Don't expect many Western-style vegetarian and whole food restaurants outside large cities. The majority of Japanese restaurants serve tofu (soybean curd) and some restaurants specialize in *tofu ryori*—cooking using tofu and other soybean-based products exclusively. *Shojin-ryori,* served in some temple restaurants, is a refined form of vegetarian cuisine.

Sukiyaki & kaiseki ryori

Succulent *sukiyaki* consists of choice slices of beef and vegetables cooked at the table in a sweet, soy-based stock pot. When cooked, the pieces are dipped into a sauce of soy and a raw egg before eating. *Shabu-shabu* is with slices of beef (or pork) with vegetables cooked in bubbling broth.

Kaiseki ryori stands at the summit of Japanese cuisine. It was developed in Kyoto and derived from the delicacies served during the tea ceremony. A succession of small dishes—usually seasonable vegetables, and occasionally fish—made of the finest ingredients, kaiseki is presented with all the elegance of a fine art.

Informal eating

Options include *robatayaki* restaurants, where traditionally garbed attendants cheerfully bellow the orders out to cooks behind the counter. Food here is mainly fish and vegetables broiled over charcoal. Robatayaki are close relatives of yakitori restaurants, which specialize in various cuts and pieces of char-grilled vegetables and chicken on bamboo

skewers. Places serving yakitori are not technically restaurants but are *nomiya*—drinking spots—easily identifiable by the one or more red paper lanterns outside. A nomiya with an extensive menu (fish, yakitori, vegetables, pot stews, and even certain Western dishes) becomes an *izakaya.* They seldom disappoint and are very good value.

Noodles

Noodles are a Japanese staple. The most common are *soba* and *udon,* a thicker variant. Probably most popular of all is *ramen,* a soup-noodle formula of Chinese origin. Fried *(yaki-soba, yaki-udon)* or in hot soup, noodles are served ubiquitously in places ranging from upscale specialists to stand-up noodle joints. Soba restaurants also serve noodles cold *(zaru-soba);* dipped in a sauce of soy with wasabi and spring onions, they make an ideal summer lunch. Noodles are often prepared *teppan-yaki* style, cooked on a hot plate on the table—usually by the customer. The same applies to cheap, delicious *okonomi-yaki.* Often described as "Japanese pizza," it consists of pieces of seafood or pork mixed with a batter consisting of egg, water, flour, and chopped cabbage, and fried like a pancake.

Okonomi-yaki, noodles, and yakitori are served by *yatai* vendors from food carts but the most common and popular dish they serve is *oden,* a variety of items including fish-cakes, seafood, and eggs in a piping hot fish stock.

Tempura & tonkatsu

Tempura consists of shrimp, various kinds of fish, and vegetables, individually deep fried in light, crispy batter. Tempura is dipped into a small bowl of sauce called *tsuyu* mixed with grated ginger and *daikon* (radish).

Tonkatsu consists of pork deep-fried in an egg-and-breadcrumb

batter. This delicious dish finds several variants, including *ebi furai* (fried prawns) and *korokke* (potato croquettes). *Kushi-age,* originating in Osaka, is another delicious variant, consisting of a variety of skewered meat, fish, vegetables, and even cheese-based delicacies, dipped in batter and deep fried.

International cuisine

The Japanese passion for sampling, importing, adopting, and adapting applies very much to food. Coined during the late 19th century, the term *yoshoku-ya* (Western food restaurant) still applies to places serving Euro-Japanese hybrid food. Culinary hybridization remains the order of the day, the most refined recent additions being "nouvelle Japanese" and French food served kaiseki style. The love affair with French and Italian food is a long one; many of the chefs are foreigners, but increasing numbers of Japanese spend years studying in kitchens in France and Italy before opening restaurants serving dishes on a par with the best of its country of origin. French cuisine got there first but Italian currently has the lead; even the remotest rural coffee shops often produce a *spaghetti napolitano*.

Coffee shops are always good for a Western-style snack or *moningu-setto* (morning set)—breakfast. Unlike their big city counterparts, however, coffee shops in smaller towns often don't open until mid-morning. Many will serve lunchtime meals, though be prepared for strange hybrids such as Japanese-style "wafu-pizza" with seaweed—not to mention Chinese-style ginger-pork, Italian spaghetti, noodles, tonkatsu, and potato salad—all on the same plate!

The oldest and most popular forms of non-Japanese oriental cuisine are Chinese and Korean. The past two decades have also seen a remarkable increase in authentic Indian and Thai restaurants in larger towns. Appetites for Indonesian and Malay food are escalating as well.

The hotels and restaurants listed here have been grouped first according to their region, then listed alphabetically by price category. For disabled access, it is recommended that you check with the establishment to verify the extent of their facilities.
L = lunch   D = dinner

TOKYO

GINZA

GINZA TOBU
$$$
6-14-10 GINZA, CHUO-KU
TEL 03/3546-0111
FAX 03/3546-8990
A favorite Western-style hotel known for comfort, good service, and value for money. There are luxury twin rooms on the concierge floor, but others are business hotel size, though better appointed.
🛏 206 🚇 Subway: Higashi Ginza 🅿 💳 All major cards

ALCYONE
$$
4-14-3 GINZA, CHUO-KU
TEL 03/3541-3621
FAX 03/3541-3263
Formerly a ryokan, this turned into a Western-style hotel in 1984, keeping a few Japanese rooms and some with an unusual Western/Japanese mixture. The staff is congenial and some speak English. This is a great location at a great price, especially since you get a ryokan-sized room at a business hotel rate.
🛏 76 🚇 Subway: Higashi Ginza 🅿 💳 All major cards

SUSHIKO
$$$$$
6-3-8 GINZA
TEL 03/3571-1968
The owner-chef of this tiny sushi parlor spurns conventional displays of sectioned fish behind the counter, believing that it would impair freshness. Instead it's kept chilled out of sight, to be sliced when needed. It's widely considered to be the ultimate. Reservations recommended.
🚇 Subway: Ginza 💳 All major cards

OMATSUYA
$$$$
2F EL DORU BLD., 6-5-8 GINZA, CHUO-KU
TEL 03/3571-7053
This is about as refined as noodle cooking gets. In the evening, they grill meat, fish, and vegetables over charcoal at your table.
🕐 Closed Sun. 🚇 Subway: Ginza 💳 All major cards

TEN-ICHI
$$$
6-6-5 GINZA
TEL 03/3571-1949
Flagship restaurant of a prestigious chain launched during the postwar, this is one of the best places to sample tempura. The delicacy of the batter seems the product of both art and science.

Subway: Ginza 💳 All major cards

FARM GRILL
$–$$
GINZA NINE 3, GOKAN, 2ND FLOOR, 8-5 GINZA, CHUO-KU
TEL 03/5568-6156
Serving American fare in the form of excellent broiled meats, pasta, and burgers, this restaurant rapidly acquired its reputation among expats as one of the best of its kind.
🚇 Subway: Shimbashi 💳 All major cards

AKASAKA

AKASAKA PRINCE
$$$$$
1-2 KIYOICHO, CHIYODA-KU
TEL 03/3234-1111
FAX 03/3262-5163
This 40-story hotel, designed by architect Tange Kenzo on a hilltop site, is one of Tokyo's finest. It's at once opulent and minimalist, with expanses of white marble in the lobby and breathtaking cityscapes from the front rooms. Best known of its 12 restaurants is Le Trianon, serving outstanding French cuisine in a 1930s building on the grounds (which also contains the popular Napoleon Bar).
🛏 761 🚇 Subway: Nagata-cho 🚭 Some rooms 🅿 💳 All major cards

IMPERIAL
$$$$$
1-1-1 UCHISAIWAICHO, CHIYODA-KU
TEL 03/3504-1111
FAX 03/3581-9146
Opened in 1890 and still one of the best hotels in Japan; it was rebuilt in 1923 by Frank Lloyd Wright, and again in 1970. Rooms are luxuriously appointed with stunning views from upper stories; impeccable service and tasteful decor throughout.
🛏 1,059 🚇 Subway: Hibiya; JR: Yurakucho 🅿 🚭 Non-smoking floors 💳 All major cards

HOTELS & RESTAURANTS

SOMETHING SPECIAL

🏨 OKURA

Often cited in international business publications as the finest hotel in Asia, the Okura has a reputation for comfort and service. The decor is understated, elegant 1950s modernism, blending with a beautifully landscaped Japanese garden overlooked by the finest rooms.

$$$$$
2-10-4 TORANOMON, MINATO-KU
TEL 03/3582-0111
FAX: 03/3582-3707
🛏 857 🚇 Subway: Kamiya-cho or Torano-mon
🅂 Some rooms 🅿
🅂 All major cards

🏨 FAIRMONT

$$$–$$$$
2-1-17 KUDAN MINAMI, CHIYODA-KU
TEL 03/3262-1151
FAX 03/3264-2476
This venerable postwar relic (built in 1951) sticks resolutely to its dated plush and comfortable obsolescence, despite impressive refurbishment. The front looks out over the park fringing the Imperial Palace grounds; the view over the moat and boating pond is all the lovelier with the flowering cherries in spring.
🛏 207 🚇 Subway: Kudanshita 🅿 🅂 All major cards

🏨 HILLTOP (YAMA-NO-UE)

$$$–$$$$
1-1 KANDA SURUGADAI, CHIYODA-KU
TEL 03/3293-2311
FAX 03/3233-4567
Tokyo's oldest extant Western hotel, built in the 1930s, a firm favorite with writers and academics, matches art deco styling with old-fashioned comforts and charm.
🛏 75 🚇 Subway: Ochanomizu 🅿 🅂 All major cards

🏨 MERIDIEN PACIFIC TOKYO

$$$
3-13-3 TAKANAWA, MINATO-KU
TEL 03/3445-6711
FAX 03/3445-5137
Among the Meridien's assets are a beautiful garden (once owned by the imperial family), and rooms with great views over Tokyo Bay. Panoramic lounge on 30th floor.
🛏 954 🚇 Subway: Shinagawa 🅂 Some rooms
🅿 🅂 All major cards

🍴 LA TOUR D'ARGENT

$$$$$
HOTEL NEW OTANI, 4-1 KIOI-CHO, CHIYODA-KU
TEL 03/3239-3111
The Tokyo branch of this great Parisian temple of gastronomy offers superlative French cuisine; the setting is regarded as one of the most opulent in town. Jacket and tie. Reservations are essential.
🚇 Subway: Akasaka-mitsuke 🕘 Closed Mon. 🅂 All major cards

🍴 INAKAYA

$$$$–$$$$$
7-8-4 ROPPONGI, MINATO-KU
TEL 03/3405-9866
Archetypical robatayaki (see p. 360) restaurant, with cooks working at charcoal braziers behind a counter laden with their raw materials (mainly fish and vegetables). It enjoys a reputation as the best and is priced accordingly.
🚇 Subway: Roppongi 🅂 All major cards

🍴 ZAKURO

$$$$
B1 TBS KAIKAN BLDG, 5-3-3 AKASAKA, MINATO-KU
TEL 03/3582-6841
A great place to sample sukiyaki and shabu-shabu, though not the cheapest; you can also opt to have your meal made from Kobe beef.
🚇 Subway: Akasaka 🅂 All major cards

PRICES

HOTELS

Western-style hotels charge by the room but Japanese-style hotels charge per person. An indication of the cost is given by $ signs.

$$$$$	Over $280
$$$$	$200–$280
$$$	$120–$200
$$	$80–$120
$	Under $80

RESTAURANTS

An indication of the cost of a three-course dinner without drinks is given by $ signs.

$$$$$	Over $80
$$$$	$50–$80
$$$	$35–$50
$$	$20–$35
$	Under $20

🍴 BLUE SKY

$$$
HOTEL NEW OTANI, 4-1 KIOI-CHO, CHIYODA-KU
TEL 03/3238-0028
Mainly Chinese, but also Japanese, not to mention freshly baked Italian pizza. All in a unique setting: the revolving sky lounge atop Hotel New Otani.
🚇 Subway: Akasaka-mitsuke 🅂 All major cards

🍴 MOTI

$$–$$$
3F KIMPA BLDG, 2-14-31 AKASAKA, MINATO-KU
TEL 03/3584-6640
2F AKASAKA FLORAL PLAZA, 3-8-8 AKASAKA, MINATO-KU
TEL 03/3582-3620
This Indian restaurant is one that didn't make compromises to local taste and survived to open several branches. Great tandooris and curries.
🚇 Subway: Akasaka-mitsuke 🅂 All major cards

ROPPONGI-AZABU

🏨 IBIS

$$$
7-14-4 ROPPONGI, MINATO-KU

TEL 03/3403-4411
FAX 03/3479-0609
Rooms, though very small, are comfortable and well appointed. Perfect for party animals, the Ibis is within crawling distance of all the action in Roppongi.
182 Subway: Roppongi
P All major cards

ROPPONGI PRINCE
$$$
3-2-7 ROPPONGI, MINATO-KU
TEL 03/3587-1111
FAX 03/3587-0770
Many would-be users turn pale when they hear about the transparent swimming pool on the patio, designed with only architectural modernism in mind. In Tokyo's hippest neighborhood this targets a mainly young clientele with trendy design and a lively atmosphere. Small rooms are comfortable with a smart minimalist decor.
216 Subway: Roppongi
 All major cards

AJIA KAIKAN (ASIA CENTER OF JAPAN)
$$
8-10-32 AKASAKA, MINATO-KU
TEL 03/3402-6111
FAX 03/3402-0738
Rooms here are basic and clean. Singles are minute, twins and doubles adequate. For the central location and overall quality, rates are outstanding—reservations have to be made six months ahead. Canteen-style restaurant.
160 Subway: Aoyama Ichome All major cards

TAKAMURA
$$$$
3-4-27 ROPPONGI, MINATO-KU
TEL 03/3585-6600
One of the most refined kaiseki (see p. 360) restaurants in Tokyo. You dine in private tatami-mat rooms in a secluded old Japanese-style house, with views over a lovely garden. Reservations essential. Lunch is about half the price of dinner.

Subway: Roppongi
Closed Sun. All major cards

FUKUZUSHI
$$$
5-7-8 ROPPONGI, MINATO-KU
TEL 03/3402-4116
This sushi restaurant, reputed as one of Tokyo's finest, serves exquisite fare in a minimalist modern setting.
Subway: Roppongi
Closed Sun. All major cards (evening only)

KISSO
$$$
AXIS BLDG B1, 5-17-1
ROPPONGI, MINATO-KU
TEL 03/3582-4191
With stores and showrooms devoted to interior design and ceramics, the Axis Building is one of Tokyo's temples of style. This chic restaurant, featuring kaiseki cuisine sometimes with just a soupçon of Europe, perfectly matches the setting.
Subway: Roppongi
Closed Sun. All major cards

GANCHAN
$$
6-8-23 ROPPONGI, MINATO-KU
TEL 03/3478-0092
The yakitori experience at its most relaxed and delicious. Boisterous, colorful, and minute, Ganchan is a popular feeding station for the Roppongi clubbing crowd.
Subway: Roppongi All major cards

KITCHEN FIVE
$$
4-2-15 NISHI-AZABU, MINATO-KU
TEL 03/3409-8835
Everyone loves Kobayashi-san and her tiny counter restaurant, and especially her Mediterranean-ethnic dishes, such as moussaka or lasagne gleaned from her travels around Europe and Latin America. The secret about this place has been out for

some time; you may well have to wait in line.
Subway: Roppongi No credit cards

NANBANTEI
$$
NANBAN BLDG. 1F, 4-5-6 ROPPONGI, MINATO-KU
TEL 03/3402-0606
Essentially yakitori but a cut above the average—one of the specialties is meat dipped in miso sauce and grilled. The difference shows in *nanban yaki*, with succulent pieces of beef instead of chicken.
Subway: Roppongi All major cards

AOYAMA-SHIBUYA-HARAJUKU

NATIONAL CHILDREN'S CASTLE HOTEL (KODOMO NO SHIRO HOTERU)
$$$
5-53-1 JINGUMAE, SHIBUYA-KU
TEL 03/3797-5677
FAX 03/3406-7805
The perfect place for families with small children, the hotel occupies the seventh and eighth floors of the Children's Castle itself—a kiddies' paradise featuring a rooftop playground and supervised facilities for art, music, and computers. Both Western- and Japanese-style rooms—all simple, comfortable, and spotless. Couples without kids can stay too. Its growing popularity makes it advisable to make reservations a long time ahead.
26 Subway: Omotesando   All major cards

PRESIDENT HOTEL
$$$
2-2-3 MINAMI AOYAMA, MINATO-KU
TEL 03/3497-0111
FAX 03/3401-4816
Hard to beat for convenience and value, this hotel stands in fashionable Aoyama, which is in easy reach of just about

everywhere. Although not overlarge, rooms are comfortable and well appointed.
🛏 210 🚇 Subway: Aoyama Itchome 🅿 🃏 All major cards

🏨 SHIBUYA TOBU
$$$
3-1 UDAGAWA-CHO, SHIBUYA-KU, TOKYO
TEL 03/3476-0111
FAX 03/3476-0903
Small, cheery hotel conveniently located near central Shibuya. The comfortable rooms are of business-hotel proportions, but much better appointed. The low-ceilinged, comfortable lobby gives a Parisian atmosphere.
🛏 197 🚇 Subway: Shibuya 🅿 🃏 All major cards

🍴 L'ORANGERIE DE PARIS
$$$–$$$$$
HANAE MORI BLDG, 5TH FLOOR, 3-6-1 KITA-AOYAMA, MINATO-KU
TEL 03/3407-7461
Located in a beautiful building by Tange Kenzo, this elegant French restaurant is both gastronomically and aesthetically a haven of exquisite taste. The Sunday brunch is one of the best-known deals in town.
🚇 Subway: Omotesando 🕐 Closed Sun. D 🃏 All major cards

🍴 EL CASTELLANO
$$$
2-9-12 SHIBUYA, SHIBUYA-KU
TEL 03/3407-7197
As the name suggests, the genial owner of this Spanish restaurant is Castilian. It's informal and high-spirited, with authentic and consistently delectable food. Wonderful paella and one of the only places in Japan serving rabbit. It can get crowded, so reserve a table.
🚇 Subway: Omotesando 🕐 Closed Sun. 🃏 No credit cards

SHINJUKU

🏨 PARK HYATT TOKYO
🍴 $$$$
3-7-1-2 NISHI-SHINJUKU
TEL 03/5322-1234
FAX 03/ 5322-1288
Occupying the 41st to the 52nd floors of Kenzo Tange's Park Tower building, the Park Hyatt was designed as a European-style luxury hotel. The result is plush, intimate, and beautiful. The large rooms have stunning cityscapes from the windows and regal luxury bathrooms. There are four restaurants including the famous New York Grill (see below).
🛏 178 🚇 Subway: Shinjuku 🅿 🛎 Some rooms 🍽 🃏 All major cards

🏨 SHINJUKU PRINCE
$$$
1-30-1 KABUKI-CHO, SHINJUKU-KU
TEL 03/3205-1111
FAX 03/3205-1952
Conveniently located midway between the Shinjuku subway and the boisterous Kabuki-cho amusement district, this streamlined, brown, 25-story building stands out. All but the more expensive rooms are on the small side but sufficiently well appointed to make this very much a cut above the average business hotel; the same applies to the service.
🛏 571 🚇 Subway: Shinjuku 🛎 Some rooms 🃏 All major cards

🍴 NEW YORK GRILL
The Grill is one of Tokyo's prime locales for eating out in style. The food is American including superlative steaks and seafood in a sumptuous modernist art deco setting, with stunning cityscapes from the floor-to-ceiling windows. Reservations advised.
$$$$$
PARK HYATT HOTEL, 3-7-1-2

NISHI-SHINJUKU
TEL 03/5323-3458
🚇 Subway: Shinjuku 🃏 All major cards

🍴 KAKIDEN
$$$$$–$$$$
3-37-11 SHINJUKU
TEL 03/3352-5121
This is the Tokyo branch of a venerable restaurant. Despite the modern building, the interior is highly traditional, with jingling music. There are several set menus of very refined kaiseki cuisine to choose from to suit your taste—and pocket.
🚇 Subway/JR: Shinjuku 🃏 All major cards

🍴 TOKAIEN
$$$
1-6-3 KABUKI-CHO, SHINJUKU-KU
TEL 03/3200-2924
A contender for the largest Korean yakiniku (grilled meat) restaurant in Japan, this covers nine floors run according to different formulas: set meals, à la carte, all-you-can-eat, and sumptuous feasts in private rooms.
🕐 Open every day till late 🚇 Subway/JR: Shinjuku 🃏 All major cards

🍴 TSUKIJI EDOGIN
$$$
4-5-1 TSUKIJI, CHUO-KU
TEL 03/3543-4401
The fish is virtually ocean-fresh at this venerable sushi restaurant close to Tsukiji wholesale fish market. It's packed with the business crowd at lunchtime.
🚇 Subway: Tsukiji 🃏 All major cards

UENO/ASAKUSA

🏨 ASAKUSA VIEW
$$$$
3-17-1 NISHI ASAKUSA, TAITO-KU
TEL 03/3847-1111
FAX 03/3842-2117
This tower didn't please

everyone when it went up in the mid-80s, but most concede it's a very pleasant hotel. Rooms are bright, Western style, with attractive Japanese design motifs and furnishings; some overlook Senso-Ji Temple.
[i] 337 Subway: Tawaramachi All major cards

SOFITEL TOKYO
$$$$
2-1-48 IKENOHATA, TAITO-KU
TEL 03/5685-7111
FAX 03/5685-6171
The outside looks like a Christmas tree made of concrete Lego bricks, but the interior is highly inspired and has superb views over Ueno Park. The same applies to the rooms. Beautifully appointed and close to Ueno's sights.
[i] 71 Subway: Nezu or Yushima All major cards

SADACHIYO
$$$
2-20-1 ASAKUSA, TAITO-KU
TEL 03/3842-6431
FAX 03 3842 6433
This friendly urban ryokan, opened in the late 1980s, has proved a hit with adepts of the "real Japan." Rooms here are beautifully designed in a modern, minimalist Japanese style with bath. The hotel offers a variety of tours and entertainments (geisha-style dinners, sumo, Sumida River boat trips). As with most ryokan, rates do not include meals. Dinner in the ground-floor restaurant is excellent, but costs over $70 per head.
[i] 20 Subway: Tawaramachi All major cards

KUREMUTSU
$$$
2-2-13 ASAKUSA
TEL 03/3842-0906
Charming restaurant located in a small traditional house just below Senso-ji Temple. In a country atmosphere enhanced by genuine antique

fittings, you can dine on kaiseki set meals, sashimi, *fugu* (blowfish), or grilled fish.
 Subway: Asakusa
 Open 4–10 p.m. Closed Thurs. & L daily No credit cards

UENO SEIYOKEN GRILL
$$$
4-58 UENO-KOEN, TAITO-KU
TEL 03/3821-2181
Tokyo's oldest Western-style restaurant first opened its doors in the 1870s. The building replacing the ornate original is nondescript, but big windows look out onto Ueno Park, and the French-style food is of a high standard.
 Subway: Ueno All major cards

DAIKOKUYA
$
1-38-10 ASAKUSA
TEL 03/3844-1111
This has been in business as a tempura restaurant since the late 19th century. It's in a traditional building painted white. What the food lacks in refinement, it makes up for with good, hearty flavor.
 Subway: Asakusa No credit cards

EXCURSIONS FROM TOKYO

YOKOHAMA

Most overseas visitors to Yokohama come on a day trip from Tokyo. Hotels here usually cater for business travelers. Yokohama's international array of restaurants is such that one has the impression that Japanese cuisine takes the back seat.

ROYAL FOOD COURT
$$
LANDMARK TOWER 5F FLOOR, 2-2-1-1 MINATO MIRAI NISHI-KU
TEL 045/222-5566
The deliteria here has a large seating area surrounded by different restaurant counters

with something for everyone: pizza, Chinese, Indian, Japanese—an opportunity to sample all Yokohama's many flavors in one sitting.
 No credit cards

HEICHINRO
$
149 YAMASHITA-CHO, NAKA-KU
TEL 045/681-3001
They do dimsum (*yamucha* in Japanese) at lunchtime here and are recommended for their Cantonese cuisine.
 All major cards

KAMAKURA

RAITEI
$–$$$$
3-1 KAMAKURA-YAMA
TEL 046/732-5656
For many people, this extraordinary restaurant is a highlight of a trip to Kamakura. The location is countrified, with bamboo groves in the garden. You can either choose very cheap and varied noodles or go for the more expensive kaiseki sets, which you need to reserve in advance.
 Closed D All major cards

NAKAMURA-AN
$
1-7-6 KOMACHI
TEL 046/725-3500
Kamakura's most famous noodle place—handmade on the premises. Old favorites include soba soup noodles with tempura shrimp for instance.
 No credit cards

NIKKO

NIKKO KANAYA HOTEL
$$$–$$$$$
1300 KAMI-HATSUISHI, NIKKO-SHI, TOCHIGI
TEL 0288/54-0001
FAX 0288/53-2487
Opened by the Kanaya family in 1873; current buildings and fixtures, including a fireplace

designed by Frank Lloyd Wright, reflect the Western-Japanese hybridization popular in the early 20th century. Amenities include a Japanese garden and a skating rink (winter only). The wonderful columned dining hall of this old hotel provides plenty of atmosphere. Specialties include local rainbow trout. Reservations advisable for weekends and holidays.
🏨 80 🚗 💳 All major cards

🏨 TURTLE INN
$$
2-16 TAKUMI-CHO, NIKKO-SHI CITY, TOCHIGI
TEL 0288/53-3168
FAX 0288/53-3883
A friendly and much-esteemed member of the Japanese Inn Group (JIG), this modern ryokan is conveniently close to the sights. The pleasant, English-speaking owner will give you information about local hiking and sightseeing. Both Japanese- and Western-style (with and without bath) rooms overlook the river. Be sure to order meals (which cost extra) in advance. There is a dining room, but guests can also take their meals in their rooms.
🏨 11 💳 All major cards

🍴 MASUDAYA
$$
439-2 ISHIYA-MACHI, NIKKO-SHI, TOCHIGI
TEL 0288/54-2151
Built during the Taisho era (1912–1926), this venerable restaurant serves very reasonably priced set meals known for incorporating *yuba* (a kind of pasta made from soybean flour, usually served stuffed), a Nikko specialty once reserved exclusively for priests and aristocrats. Reservations advisable, especially for private rooms.
🕐 Closed Thurs. 💳 No credit cards

HAKONE & FUJI FIVE LAKES

🏨 FUJI-VIEW
$$$$–$$$$$
511 KATSUYAMA-MURA, MINAMI TSURU-GUN
TEL 0555/83-2211
FAX 0555/83-2128
A venerable hotel with a lovely lakeside (Kawaguchi-ko) location and handy for climbing Fuji-san. Both Western and Japanese rooms (the most luxurious of the latter are houses in the scenic terrace garden) are full of Old World charm. Staff speaks English, and is always ready to help plan your sight-seeing.
🏨 78 🚕 Taxi from Kawaguchi-ko Station 💳 All major cards

> ### SOMETHING SPECIAL

🏨 🍴 FUJIYA
One of Japan's most famous, old, and charming hotels—a paragon of Japanese-Eurasian style, architecturally, conceptually, and gastronomically. Stroll in beautiful gardens with views (and, hey, John and Yoko used to stay here for months at a time!). English spoken.
Good 1930s Japanese deco style restaurant serving a range of meals from sandwiches to opulent dinners ($–$$$$$).
$$$–$$$$
359 MIYANOSHITA, HAKONE-MACHI, ASHIGARASHIMO-GUN
TEL 0460/2-2211
FAX 0460/2-2210
🏨 146 🚃 JR: Miyanoshita 🚗 💳 All major cards

🏨 ASHIWADA
$$$
395 NAGAHAMA, ASHIWADA-MURA, MINAMI TSURU-GUN, YAMANASHI
TEL 0555/82-2321
FAX 0555/82- 2548
This concrete structure is something of a blight on the lakeside, but the one place you won't see it is inside. Many of its comfortable

rooms—all with bathroom—offer superb views of Kawaguchi-ko. It's a Japanese Inn Group (JIG) member and is convenient for sight-seeing and climbing Fuji-san.
🏨 42 💳 All major cards

🏨 FUJI-HAKONE GUESTHOUSE
$$
912 SENGOKUHARA, HAKONE-MACHI, KANAGAWA
TEL 0460/4-6577
FAX 0460/4-6578
A favorite on the JIG circuit, this lies in a wooded setting with mountain views. The owners speak good English and have a reputation for being very helpful; a great choice if you intend to go hiking. Communal bath only (with natural hot spring water) and breakfast the only meal served.
🏨 12 🚌 Hakone Tozan bus for Togendai from Odawara bus terminal 💳 All major credit cards

HOKKAIDO

SAPPORO & OTARU

🏨 GINRINSO
🍴 **$$$$$**
1-1 SAKURA, OTARU-SHI, HOKKAIDO
TEL 0134/54-7010
FAX 0134/52-2011
Originally built as a herring fishermen's guild hall during the 1930s, and long a local landmark, this is now a *ryotei* (top Japanese restaurant) and one of Japan's most expensive ryokan with beautiful rooms and exquisite service. If you want to sample Hokkaido seafood at its ultimate best, this is the place. Reserving ahead is essential.
🏨 15 🕐 Closed Dec.–April 💳 All major cards

🏨 SAPPORO GRAND
🍴 **HOTEL**
$$$$
KITA 1, NISHA 4, CHUO-KU,

SAPPORO
TEL 011/261-3311
FAX 011/231-0388
The city's longest established and most prestigious hotel (opened in 1934), ten minutes' walk south of the train station, embraces two newer buildings. Rooms are spacious and superbly appointed. Try Le Grand Chef, the hotel's plush French restaurant for wonderful local ingredients (scallops, crab, duck, salmon, lamb, etc.).
🛈 565 💳 All major cards

🏨 **NAKAMURAYA RYOKAN**
$$
KITA 3, NISHI 7, CHUO-KU, SAPPORO
TEL 011/241-2111
FAX 011/241-2118
A long-established JIG ryokan now housed in a modern concrete building, this has good-size tatami rooms, all with bathroom. The cuisine, based on the local seafood, is prepared with pride.
🛈 29 💳 All major cards

🍴 **HYOSETSU-NO-MON**
$$–$$$$
MINAMI 5, NISHI 2, CHUO-KU, SAPPORO
TEL 011/521-3046
King crab—and only king crab—is the stuff of this famous Sapporo institution, serving it in various formats and prices on several floors.
💳 All major cards

🍴 **SAPPORO BIER GARTEN**
$$
KITA 7, HIGASHI 9, HIGASHI-KU, SAPPORO
TEL 011/742-1531
Beer is the favorite tipple in this city, and it goes best with Hokkaido's main regional dish *Jingisukan*—Gengis Khan lamb. It involves broiling thin slices of lamb, vegetables, and onion rings on a cast-iron pan. And the most famous place to sample it is at this cavernous beer hall and

garden adjacent to the Sapporo Beer Museum.
💳 All major cards

HAKODATE

🏨 **HAKODATE KOKUSAI**
$$$$
5-10 OTE-MACHI, HAKODATE
TEL 0138/23-5151
FAX 0138/23-0239
The city's best Western-style hotel. It consists of two adjacent buildings; the sleek new building has the most expensive rooms, with great views over the harbor.
🛈 310 💳 All major cards

🍴 **HAKODATE BEER**
$$–$$$
MEIJIKAN-DORI,5-22 OTE-MACHI, HAKODATE
TEL 013/823-8000.
This popular and crowded restaurant and microbrewery is in a converted warehouse on the waterfront. You dine on Western and Japanese fare in a vast redbrick hall; copper vats behind glass produce the outstanding house brews.
💳 All major cards

SHIKOTSU-TOYA NATIONAL PARK

🏨 **DAI-ICHI TAKIMOTO-KAN**
$$$–$$$$$
55 NOBORIBETSU-ONSEN-MACHI, NOBORIBETSU-SHI HOKKAIDO
TEL 0143/84-2111
FAX 0143/84-2202
Noboribetsu Onsen is the most popular onsen resort in Hokkaido, with an exhaustive array of hot aquatic pleasures. This famous hotel is the most hideous, spectacular, and fun of the spa's many concrete monstrosities. Most rooms are Japanese style.
🛈 400 💳 All major cards

🏨 **SUN PALACE HOTEL**
$$$–$$$$
TOYA-KO ONSEN, HOKKAIDO
TEL 0142/75-4126
FAX 0142/75-2875

This is the largest and most famous of the Toya-ko lakeside resort hotels. In addition to thermal baths, there are swimming pools with water slides for children. Staying at its similarly priced sister hotel, Toya Park Hotel Tensho (Tel 0142/75-2445, fax 0142/75 3918), entitles you to use all the Sun Palace's bathing facilities, and vice versa.
🛈 430 💳 All major cards

🏨 **TAKIMOTO INN**
$$$
76 NORORIBETSU ONSEN-MACHI, NOBORIBETSU-SHI, HOKKAIDO
TEL 0143/84-2205
FAX 0143/84-2645
This Western-style inn is a much more pleasant and moderate alternative to its bigger, brasher relative, Dai-ichi Takimoto-kan. You have the advantage of using the larger hotel's formidable array of spa baths and facilities for free. Rooms are fairly basic; prices include meals. Great value for the money.
🛈 47 💳 All major cards

HOTELS & RESTAURANTS

HOTELS & RESTAURANTS

🏨 RYOKAN HANAYA
$$
134 NOBORIBETSU-ONSEN-
MACHI, NOBORIBETSU-SHI,
HOKKAIDO
TEL 0143/84-2521
FAX 0143/84-2240
A member of the JIG (always
mention the connection when
you book), this is very good
value. Meals are extra, served
in your room. English spoken.
Three Japanese rooms have
bathrooms, otherwise there's
a large public bathroom as
well as outdoor baths—spa
water, of course (see p. 358).
🛏 22 🚌 Bus from
Noboribetsu Station 🏧 All
major cards

DAISETSUZAN SOUNKYO NATIONAL PARK

🏨 MOUNT VIEW
$$$$
SOUNKYO, KAMIKAWA-
MACHI, KAMIKAWA-GUN
TEL 01658/5-3011
FAX 01658/5-3010
This 1980s chalet-style hotel
is a welcome change from
concrete-blockhouse resort
hotel architecture. It lies in a
valley on the outskirts of the
onsen village, the best rooms
being higher up to offer good
views of the gorge.
Communal hot spring bath
(see p. 358). Meals are
included in the price.
🛏 98 🏧 All major cards

AKAN NATIONAL PARK

🏨 HOTEL EMERALD
$$$-$$$$
4-6-5 AKAN-KO-ONSEN,
AKAN-CHO, AKAN-GUN
TEL 0154/67-2011
FAX 0154/67-2864
Considering that the Emerald
is right on the lakeside and
the price includes meals, this is
exceptional value. The
management speaks English
and can help set up various
sports programs including
fishing and hunting (you need

your own gun and license).
🛏 204 🏧 All major cards

🏨 MINSHUKU KIRI
$$
4-3-26 AKAN-KO-ONSEN,
AKAN-CHO, AKAN-GUN
TEL/FAX 0154/67-2755
Right opposite the super
luxury Akan Grand Hotel is
this popular, homey minshuku.
Rooms are basic, clean, and
Japanese style. Includes meals.
Communal bathroom (see p.
358) with spa water.
🛏 9 🏧 No credit cards

NORTHERN HONSHU (TOHOKU)

AOMORI-KEN

🏨 AOMORI GRAND HOTEL
$$$
1-1-23 SHIN-MACHI, AOMORI-
SHI
TEL 0177/23-1011
FAX 0177/34-0505
Though the rooms are
somewhat old-fashioned, this
has good standards of service
and comfort. Some rooms
have views over the sea.
🛏 140 🏧 All major cards

🏨 HOKKE CLUB HIROSAKI
$$$
126 DOTE-MACHI,
HIROSAKI-SHI
TEL 0172/34-3811
FAX 0172/32-0589
This recent addition to a
celebrated business hotel
chain is a cut above most of
the others and is Hirosaki's
top Western-style hotel.
Modern, elegant, and comfortable, though most rooms are
small.
🛏 122 🏧 All major cards

🍴 JINTAKO
$$$$
1-6-16 YASUKATA, AOMORI-SHI
TEL 0177/22-7727
Here you can sample
delicious local specialties, such
as scallops broiled in the shell
and warming codfish stews.

Make a night of it listening to
the *samisen* played live in the
rousing style.
🏧 No credit cards

🍴 YAMAUTA
$$
1-2-7 O-MACHI, HIROSAKI-SHI
TEL 0172/36-1835
The fare is izakaya style (see
p. 360) and the entertainment
is provided by the owner, a
famous samisen virtuoso.
🏧 No credit cards

AKITA-KEN

🏨 AKITA CASTLE
$$$$
1-3-5 NAKA-DORI, AKITA-SHI
TEL 018/834-1141
FAX 018/834-5588
This is a well-established, plush
hotel. Views over the park
and moat surrounding the
ruins of Akita-jo.
🛏 182 🅿 🏧 All major
cards

🏨 KOHAMA RYOKAN
$$
6-19-6 NAKA-DORI, AKITA-SHI
TEL 018/832-5739
The owner of this popular
ryokan is endearingly eccentric and motherly toward her
guests; she claims that the
parrot in the hallway
screeches for her attention
exactly as her son did over 20
years ago. She takes great care
with cooking (meals must be
ordered in the afternoon).
Rooms are well decorated;
communal bath (see p. 358).
🛏 10 🏧 All major cards

SENDAI & MATSUSHIMA

🏨 MATSUSHIMA KANKO
$$$$
155 AZACHONAI,
MATSUSHIMA, MATSUSHIMA-
CHO, MIYAGI-GUN
TEL 022/354-2121
FAX 022/354-2883
Also known as the Ryokan
Matsushima-jo. The rather
lurid samurai castle lying back
from the bay is Matsushima's
oldest Japanese-style inn. The

interiors are decorated with antiques, and some rooms have fine views over the bay. The price includes two meals, which makes this quaint and comfortable surviving example of 1920s seaside Japan a good value.

[i] 28 (Japanese style, 7 with own bath) [S] JCB, Visa

METROPOLITAN SENDAI
$$$$
1-1-1 CHUO, AOBA-KU, SENDAI-SHI
TEL 022/268-2525
FAX 022/268-2521
Conveniently placed next to the station, this is essentially an upscale business hotel, with more amenities, space and greater comfort than usual.
[i] 300 [icon] [icon] [S] All major cards

DONJIKI CHAYA
$
89 AZAMACHIUCHI, MATSUSHIMA, MATSUSHIMA-CHO, MIYAGI-KEN
TEL 022/354-5855
Built in the late 1600s, this remains a charming and venerable noodle stop.
[S] No credit cards

IWATE-KEN

METROPOLITAN MORIOKA
$$$
2-27 MORIOKA-EKIMAE-KITA-DORI (NEW WING), 1-44 MORIOKA-EKIMAE-DORI (OLD WING), MORIOKA-SHI
TEL 019/625-1211
FAX 019/625-1210
The Metropolitan's new wing is slightly more expensive than the nearby old wing. Rooms in the old wing are more basic, but in both places you get comfort and service.
[i] 121 (new wing), 184 (old wing) [S] All major cards

AZUMAYA
$$
1-8-3 NAKA-NO-HASHI-DORI, MORIOKA-SHI

TEL 019/622-2252
This is the most famous place to eat the local specialties. *Wanko soba* consists of soup noodles accompanied by a variety of meat, fish, and vegetable side dishes. The noodles are served in small bowls, and the idea is to stack up as many empty ones as you possibly can, out-eating everyone else (don't worry, competitions are by agreement). *Ramen,* more popular in summer, are thin, translucent noodles served cold with a variety of ingredients.
[S] No credit cards

CENTRAL HONSHU (CHUBU)

NAGOYA

HILTON NAGOYA
$$$$
1-3-3 SAKAE, NAKA-KU, NOGOYA-SHI, AICHI-KEN
TEL 052/212-1111
FAX 052/212-1225
This well-located, 28-story hotel has large rooms with king-size beds, Japanese design motifs, and Western comforts. Great cityscapes from rooms on upper floors. Among the amenities are computer connection and tennis courts. Beds in single rooms are double; during the low season couples can arrange to stay at the basic single rate.
[i] 450 [icon] [icon] [S] All major cards

NAGOYA KANKO
$$$—$$$$
1-19-30 NISHIKI, NAKA-KU, NAGOYA-SHI, AICHI-KEN
TEL 052/231-7711
FAX 052/231-7719
Nagoya's most prestigious hotel was originally founded in the 1930s. Its current concrete-box architecture is unremarkable, but it stands in a pleasant park, and has spacious, beautifully appointed rooms, all Western style. Beds in single rooms are double; during the low season couples

can stay at the basic rate.
[i] 382 [S] All major cards

NAGOYA DAI-ICHI
$$$
3-27-5 MEIEKI, NAKAMURA-KU, NAGOYA-SHI, AICHI-KEN
TEL 052/581-4411
FAX 052/581-4427
Built by the Daichi chain in 1997, this is pretty typical of the best newer business hotels with stylish design, well-appointed, comfortable rooms, and moderate prices.
[i] 314 [S] All major cards

OKURA RESTAURANT
$$$$
25F TOKYO KAIJO BLDG., 2-20-19 MARU-NO-UCHI, NAKA-KU, NAGOYA-SHI, AICHI-KEN
TEL 052/201-3201
Plush, highly reputed French restaurant popular with business executives both foreign and Japanese, serving salmon, veal, and *matsuzaka* beef according to a variety of refined recipes. Coat and tie. Reservations essential.
[S] All major cards

YAEGAKI
$$$$
3-7 NISHIKI, NAKA-KU
TEL 052/951-3250
A rarity in Nagoya, this restaurant is an old wooden building graced with a small garden. It also happens to be the best tempura restaurant in the region. Coat and tie. Reservations essential.
[S] All major cards

YAMAMOTOYA HONTEN
$
B1 DAI-ICHI HORIUCHI BLDG., 3-25-9 MEIEKI, NAKAMURA-KU, NAGOYA-SHI- AICHIKEN
TEL 052/565-0278
Near Nagoya Station, this is the main outlet of the local noodle chain and an excellent choice if you want to try *misonikomi,* Nagoya's favorite dish (there's an English-language menu). Misonikomi is a pot stew containing udon

HOTELS & RESTAURANTS

noodles and flavored with strong-tasting red miso paste (akamiso). The meal is filling and thus popular in winter. It's always made with meat.
All major cards

KANAZAWA

Note that many restaurants in Kanazawa close their doors at 8 and sometimes even 7 p.m.

KANAZAWA NEW GRAND HOTEL
$$$$
1-50 TAKAOKA-MACHI, KANAZAWA-SHI, ISHIKAWA-KEN
TEL 076/233-1311
FAX 076/233-1591
In addition to a convenient location between Kenroku-en Garden and the Nagamachi samurai district, the Grand offers great service, good views, fine cuisine in its four restaurants, and an English-speaking staff. The rooms are plush and well appointed.
108   All major cards

YOGETSU
$$
1-13-22 HIGASHIYAMA, KANAZAWA-SHI, ISHIKAWA-KEN
TEL 076/252-0497
This ryokan in the heart of the old Higashiyama geisha quarter was built in the 1900s as a geisha house. The elderly owner is genial and cooks a good meal (dinner and break-fast must be ordered ahead). If you eat elsewhere, don't even think of overlooking her 9:30 curfew! The tatami rooms are spacious, the front ones with delightful views over the old quarter's picturesque main street. There's a communal bathroom.
5   No credit cards

TSUBAJIN
$$$$$
5-1-8 TERA-MACHI, KANAZAWA-SHI. ISHIKAWA-KEN
TEL 076/241-2181

Belonging to a venerable ryokan, Tsubajin serves the very best of Kaga ryori—the culinary specialty of the region, the local equivalent of kaiseki cuisine. Dishes include crab and duck stew. Kaiseki lunches are around half the price of the dinners. Reservations essential.
All major cards

KOTOBUKIYA
$$–$$$$$
2-4-13 OWARI-CHO, KANAZAWA-SHI, ISHIKAWA-KEN
TEL 076/231-6245
Dine in this merchant house dating from the 1840s, in tatami rooms overlooking a garden. Mountain vegetables are cooked kaga style, and shojin-ryori (vegetarian cuisine) is the specialty; it comes very reasonably priced at lunchtime, with more ex-pensive kaiseki dinners in the evening (last orders 7 p.m.).
No credit cards

MIYOSHIAN
$$–$$$$
1-11 KENROKU-MACHI, KANAZAWA-SHI, ISHIKAWA-KEN
TEL 076/221-0127
Located on the Kenroku-en garden and over 100 years old, this delightful restaurant is the place to sample kaga ryori. In winter they serve jibuni, a duck stew; sashimi and eel on rice is on the menu in other seasons. Lunch sets (mainly bento boxes) are outstanding value; a more expensive option is the kaga ryori dinner, served kaiseki style. Dinner is for a minimum of six persons and requires a reservation.
No credit cards

TAKAYAMA

KAKUSHO
$$$$
2-98 BABA-CHO, TAKAYAMA-SHI, GIFU-KEN
TEL 0577/32-0174

PRICES

HOTELS
Western-style hotels charge by the room but Japanese-style hotels charge per person. An indication of the cost is given by $ signs.

$$$$$	Over $280
$$$$	$200– $280
$$$	$120–$200
$$	$80–$120
$	Under $80

RESTAURANTS
An indication of the cost of a three-course dinner without drinks is given by $ signs.

$$$$$	Over $80
$$$$	$50–$80
$$$	$35–$50
$$	$20–$35
$	Under $20

Takayama's culinary forte is shojin ryori, vegetarian cuisine. Skeptical omnivores should note that the cooking and its ingredients are varied, and come enhanced with hoba miso, sweet and salty soybean paste cooked on a large magnolia leaf over a tiny hibachi on the table. This is best place in town to sample it. An old traditional building with tatami rooms looking out over a tranquil garden. One set menu. Reservation essential.
Closed Wed. or Thurs.
No credit cards

MATSUMOTO

BUENA VISTA
$$$$$
1-2-1 HONJO, MATSUMOTO-SHI, NAGANO-KEN
TEL 0263/37-0111
FAX 0263/37-0666
A business hotel that is the smartest in town. The rooms are small but comfortable. At Hanakirabe, one of the hotel's five restaurants, you can sample most kinds of Japanese cuisine at a variety of counters.
200   All major cards

HOTELS & RESTAURANTS

🍴 KAJIKA
$$–$$$$
1-2-18 FUKASHI, MATSUMOTO-
SHI, NAGANO-KEN
TEL 0263/35-7632
Kajika is a local river fish and
one of the specialties here.
Pleasant traditional decor with
black wood on white plaster.
Different price and prepara-
tion between lunch and
dinner.
🍽 All major cards

🍴 TAIMAN
$$$–$$$$$
4-2-4 OTE, MATSUSHIMA-SHI,
NAGANO-KEN
TEL 0263/32-0882
The Gallic-looking château
facade and high ceilings within
match this ambitious and
successful undertaking in the
field of French haute cuisine.
Reasonably priced for the high
standard of cuisine, the
elaborate lunch sets are
ideal—as long as your
afternoon schedule is
sufficiently leisurely.
🍽 Most major cards

KANSAI

KYOTO

🏨 HIIRAGIYA
$$$$$
ANEKOJI-AGARU, FUYA-CHO,
NAKAGYO-KU
TEL 075/221-1136
FAX 075/221-1139
A superb traditional ryokan
that has accommodated
Japanese royalty. The service is
attentive and the tatami
rooms are beautifully
appointed.
ⓘ 33 🚇 Subway:
Karasuma-oike 🍽 All major
cards

🏨 MIYAKO HOTEL
$$$$$
SANJO-KEAGE, HIGASHIYAMA-
KU
TEL 075/771-7111
FAX 075/751-2490
Set on 15 acres (16 ha) of
woods and manicured

gardens, this is Kyoto's most
famous hotel. Opened in
1890, it's conveniently located
to the sights in east Kyoto.
Expect luxurious comfort and
impeccable service; some
rooms have wonderful views
over the Higashi hills.
ⓘ 528 🚇 Subway: Keage
🏊 summer only 🏋 🍽 All
major cards

🏨 SEIKORO
$$$$$
GOJO-SAGARU, TONYA-
MACHI, HIGASHIYAMA-KU
TEL 075/561-0771
FAX 075/541-5481
This renowned ryokan in east
Kyoto was founded in 1831.
Its current buildings date from
late Meiji (though there's a
recent annex), and the attractive blend of Japanese and
Western antiques throughout
the interior is typical of the
period. Prices include meals
and service, varying according
to choice of room (the best
overlook the garden) and set
meal. English spoken.
ⓘ 23 🚇 Train: Keihan-Gojo
🍽 All major cards

SOMETHING SPECIAL

🏨 TAWARAYA
Founded in the early 1700s,
the Tawaraya has been
patronized throughout its
history by world leaders. Filled
with antiques, it's an oasis of
tranquillity and refinement in
the center of old Kyoto, with
sublime service, the most refined
kaiseki cuisine, and rooms
overlooking a lovely garden.
$$$$$
OIKE-SAGARU, FUYA-CHO,
NAKAGYO-KU
TEL 075/221-5566
FAX 075/221-2204
ⓘ 18 🚇 Subway: Kyoto
Shiyakusho-mae 🍽 All
major cards

🏨 YACHIYO
$$$$
34 FUKUJI-CHO, NANZEN-JI,
SAKYO-KU

TEL 075/771-4148
FAX 075/771-4140
Yachiyo is very much the
luxury historic ryokan, with
the best rooms in the oldest
main building around a
delightful Japanese garden.
Close to Nanzen-ji Temple in
east Kyoto, this ryokan is
popular with foreigners.
ⓘ 20 🚇 Subway: Keage
🍽 All major cards

🏨 GRANVIA KYOTO
$$$–$$$$
657 HIGASHI-SHIOKOJI-CHO,
SHIOKOJI-SAGARU, KARASUMA
DORI, SHIMOGYO-KU
TEL 075/344-8888
FAX 075/344-4400
The hotel's location is hard to
beat for convenience for rail
travelers. And since all the
city's routes lead to and from
here, there's no shortage of
buses and taxis. Rooms are
stylish and there's a sky lounge
with a view over the
mountains.
ⓘ 539 🏊 🍽 All major
cards

🏨 KYOTO GION
$$$
555 MINAMIGAWA, GION-
MACHI, HIGASHIYAMA-KU
TEL 075/551-2111
FAX 075/551-2200
In the geisha district and close
to the sights of east Kyoto, this
is an inexpensive option.
Rooms are cramped but comfortable; ask for one with a
view of the old Gion houses.
ⓘ 135 🚇 Train: Keihan-
Shijo 🍽 All major cards

🏨 HIRAIWA INN
$$
314 HAYAO-CHO,
KAMINOGUCHI-AGARU,
NINOMIYA-CHO-DORI,
SHIMOGYO-KU)
TEL 075/351-6748
FAX 075/351-6969
The Hiraiwa was a founder
member of the Japanese Inn
Group. It's basic, clean, and
very user-friendly to *gaijin*
(foreigners). The main building
is wooden, with a newer

🚭 Non-smoking 🏊 Indoor/🏊 Outdoor swimming pool 🏋 Health club 🍽 Credit cards   **KEY**

concrete annex—both in a quiet neighborhood. It's a short taxi ride from Kyoto train station.
🛏 21 💳 All major cards

🏨 KYOTO TRAVELERS INN
$$
91 ENSHOJI-CHO, OKAZAKI, SAKYO-KU
TEL 075/771-0225
FAX 075/771-0226
Though small, the rooms here are comfortable and clean, and most have bathrooms. This is a pleasant business hotel, popular with travelers for its location in east Kyoto, very close to Okazaki-koen, Heian-jingu, and Nanzen-ji.
🛏 78 🚇 Subway: Higashiyama 💳 All major cards

🏨 RYOKAN OHTO
$
HITOSUJIUME-MINAMI-SAGARU, NANAJO-KAMOGAWA-HIGASHI, HIGASHIYAMA-KU
TEL 075/541-8723
FAX 075-561-9751
This pleasant riverside ryokan in a very recent three-story concrete building is near to the Sanjosangen-do Hall. Breakfast and dinner extra.
🛏 12 🚇 Train: Keihan-Shichijo 💳 All major cards

🍴 MINOKICHI HONTEN TAKESHIGERO
$$$$$
65 TORII-CHO, AWATAGUCHI, SAKYO-KU
TEL 075/771-4185
Founded in the early 18th century, this is the main branch of a well-known kaiseki restaurant chain with branches all over Japan. Commercialization makes it a little slick and contrived, but the setting in east Kyoto is serene and the food is wonderful
🚇 Subway: Higashiyama 💳 All major cards

🍴 IZUMOYA
$$$–$$$$$
SHIJO-AGARU, PONTOCHO-DORI, NAKAGYO-KU
TEL 075/211-2501
On the corner of Pontocho and Shijo-dori in central Kyoto, this is a bit touristy but, spread out over several floors, offers a good choice of different kinds of Japanese cuisine (tempura, shabu-shabu, sukiyaki, sashimi). Choose from models in the window. It also does *kyo-kaiseki* courses—notably out on a riverside veranda in summer. Reservations essential.
🚇 Train: Keihan-Shijo 💳 All major cards

🍴 JUNSEI
$$$–$$$$$
60 KUSAKAWA-CHO, NANZEN-JI, SAKYO-KU
TEL 075/761-2311
Proximity to Nanzen-ji (northeast Kyoto) makes this place a bit touristy, but it's set on a pleasant garden, and some of its several buildings are over 150 years old. Focusing mainly on tofu, but also doing shabu-shabu and sukiyaki, the food is excellent.
🚇 Subway: Keage 💳 All major cards

SOMETHING SPECIAL

🍴 MANKAMERO
The experience in this central Kyoto institution is costly, but quite unique: This is your chance to find out what Japanese emperors used to eat. Manka-mero has been preparing *yusoku ryori* for almost 300 years. It requires special preparation and utensils, and a qualified imperial chef in ceremonial garb. The bento lunchbox version will set you back over $50, but the real feast costs around fourfold. Emperors apparently ate pretty early; the place closes at 8. Jacket and tie; reservations essential.
$$$–$$$$$
DEMIZU-AGARU, INOKUMA-DORI, KAMIGYO-KU

TEL 075/441-5020
🚇 Subway: Marutamachi (then taxi) 💳 All major cards (bento lunch cash only)

🍴 MANYOKEN
$$$–$$$$$
SHIJO-DORI, FUYA-CHO HIGASHI-IRU, SHIMOGYO-KU
TEL 075/221-1022
Manyoken has remained Kyoto's premier temple of French gastronomy since 1915, and crystal chandeliers illuminate the Old World plush. Dine à la carte on such delicacies as lobster, or opt for an elaborate dinner set or more economical lunch set. Reservations recommended.
🕐 Closed Tues. 🚇 Subway: Shijo 💳 All major cards

🍴 MIKAKU
$$$–$$$$$
SHIJO-AGARU, NAWATE-DORI, HIGASHIYAMA-KU
TEL 075/525-1129
This famous old steakhouse in Gion serves meat in a variety of traditional ways, including *teppanyaki* (fried on a hot plate), sukiyaki, and a spicy version of shabu-shabu. Teppanyaki is served at a counter, dishes such as sukiyaki in tatami rooms upstairs.
🕐 Closed Sun. 🚇 Train: Keihan-Shijo 💳 All major cards

🍴 MINOKO
$$$–$$$$$
480 KIYOI-CHO, SHIMOGAWARA, GION, HIGASHIYAMA-KU
TEL 075/561-0328
Owned and managed by the same family since the early 20th century, this restaurant prepares *cha-kaiseki*—the original kaiseki as devised for the tea ceremony. The correlation between delicate flavors and understated aesthetics doesn't get much more refined than this. Choose between a *bento* lunch formula in a tatami

room with a garden view, or a sumptuous kyo-kaiseki dinner in a private room.
Train: Keihan-Shijo   All major cards

HYOTEI
$$–$$$$$
35 KUSAKAWA-CHO, NANZEN-JI, SAKYO-KU
TEL 075/771-4116
In the late 17th century, travelers and pilgrims used to stop here for refreshment on their way to Nanzen-ji in northeast Kyoto. They still do today. You can have a kaiseki meal in one of the small tea-houses in the garden, some of which are as old as Hyotei itself. The bento lunchbox sets come a lot cheaper, though you have to eat those in an ordinary (but very pleasant) dining room. Reservations required for kaiseki.
Closed 2nd & 4th Tues. of month   Subway: Keage   All major cards

NAKAMURARO
$$–$$$$$
509 MINAMIGAWA, GION-MACHI, HIGASHIYAMA-KU
TEL 075/561-0016
Near Yasaka-jinja, this restaurant is said to have been founded in the late 1500s, making it the oldest in Japan. It's a tiny teahouse specializing in tofu dengaku, bean-curd skewered, baked, and covered in miso sauce. The handsome building next door, an addition from the late 19th century, serves kaiseki ryori in tatami rooms looking out over a garden.
Train: Keihan-Shijo   No credit cards

TEMPURA YOSHIKAWA
$$–$$$$$
OIKE-SAGARU, TOMINOKOJI-DORI, NAKAGYO-KU
TEL 075/221-5544
Small restaurant in a delightful old building in central Kyoto, serving excellent tempura and kaiseki. The price range is a bit

extreme, with kyo-kaiseki dinners in the tatami rooms upstairs costing nearly ten times more than a set lunch at the counter. Last orders 8:30 p.m. English spoken.
Counter closed Sun.   All major cards

DIVO-DIVA
$$–$$$$
NISHIKIKOJI-DORI, TAKAKURA NISHI-IRU, NAKAGYO-KU
TEL 075/256-1326
The combination of fine food (including freshly made bread and pasta) prepared by chefs trained in Italy, a trendy decor, and reasonable prices have made this central Kyoto Italian restaurant a favorite with sophisticated young Kyotoites.
Subway: Shijo   Closed Wed.   All major cards

IZUSEN
$$$
4 DAITOKU-JI-CHO, MURASAKINO, KITA-KU
TEL 075/491-6665
Attached to Daitoku-ji Temple (northwest Kyoto), this is ideal for a really good shojin ryori (vegetarian) lunch. Beautifully presented in a lovely setting, the meal focuses on tofu cooked in a variety of ways and is served in tatami rooms, or outside in summer. Reservations recommended.
Subway: Kitaoji   Closed D & Thurs.   No credit cards

YAMATOMI
$–$$$
SHIJO-AGARU, PONTO-CHO, NAKAGYO-KU
TEL 075/221-3268
This is one of Kyoto's few affordable restaurants offering riverside dining on the veranda in summer. Teppan-age is the specialty here—a version of tempura, where you cook meat, fish, and vegetables in batter at the table. In winter they do oden (hardboiled eggs, vegetables, fishcakes, selected from a vat of simmering fish stock).

Train: Keihan-Shijo   Closed Mon.   All major cards

OKUTAN
$$
86-30 FUKUCHI-CHO, NANZEN-JI, SAKYO-KU
TEL 075/771-8709
A perennial and wonderful old standby specializing in tofu. The thatched building is on a garden (sit outside in summer) in the east of the city. They do just one set meal and you'll be surprised at how many ways tofu can be cooked (deep fried, boiled, cut into strips like pasta…).
Subway: Keage   Closed D & Thurs.   No credit cards

MISOKA-AN KAWAMICHIYA
$
SANJO-AGARU, FUYA-CHO, NAKAGYO-KU
TEL 075/221-2525
They've been serving soba in this tiny building in central Kyoto forever. A delightful noodle stop, it even has an English menu. The specialty is hokoro—a satisfying soba pot stew for two containing tofu, chicken, and vegetables.
Subway: Kyoto Shiyakusho-mae   Closed Thurs.   All major cards

OUTLYING KYOTO

NISHIKI
$$$
NAKANOSHIMA KANYUCHI, SAGA, UKYO-KU
TEL 075/881-8888
With a lovely setting on a river island in wooded Arashiyama (west of Kyoto), this restaurant is famous for serving exquisite seven-course kaiseki ryori at an unusually affordable price. The secret is simply that they serve it (beautifully presented) in a layered lacquered bento box. Reservations needed.
Closed Tues.   All major cards

🍴 KITCHO
$$$$$
58 SUSUKI-NO-BABA-CHO,
TENRYU-JI, SAGA, UKYO-KU
TEL 075/881-1101
Kitcho is often said to be the most expensive restaurant in Japan, but a meal here is generally considered the most exquisite kaiseki experience there is: Wonderful food is served on priceless antique tableware in a beautiful sylvan setting in Arashiyama.
🐾 All major cards

🍴 RYOAN-JI YUDOFUYA
$–$$
RYOAN-JI TEMPLE, UKYO-KU
TEL: 075/462-4742
You can't miss this lovely restaurant if you stroll through the grounds surrounding Ryoan-ji. You'll see the roofed gateway and the path beyond leading to traditional buildings alongside a pond and stream. This is where they serve their special "7 herb" *yudofu* (tofu pot stew), either on its own or as part of a reasonably priced vegetarian set meal.
🕐 Closed D 🐾 No credit cards

NARA

🏨 NARA HOTEL
🍴 $$$$$
1096 TAKABATAKE-CHOTEL
0742/26-3300
FAX 0742/23-5252
Built early last century and blending Western and Japanese architecture, the historic building is famed for its lovely main dining hall. Like the high-ceilinged Japanese deco interior, the cuisine is something of a hybrid: The menu typically includes spaghetti and mixed sandwiches, along with more refined meat and seafood dishes, both Western and Japanese. Reservations recommended for dinner.
🛏 132 🐾 All major cards

🏨 RYOKAN SEIKAN-SO
$
29 HIGASHI-KITSUJI-CHO,
TEL 0742/22-2670
FAX 0742/22-2670
This is regarded by many as the jewel in the crown of the Japanese Inn Group. A ryokan made from a former geisha house (built 1916) and set in a lovely garden, it's centrally located near the main sights, including Kasuga-jinga Shrine, Todai-ji and Kofuku-ji Temples. Another bonus is that it's run by a friendly couple who both speak English.
🛏 13 🐾 All major cards

🍴 TSUKIHI-TEI
$$$–$$$$$
158 KASUGANO-CHO
TEL 0742/26-2021
Just behind the Kasuga Grand Shrine, this traditional restaurant offers views over the surrounding woods and some of the finest kaseiki dining in town. Nara has its own version of kaiseki cuisine and its own specialties, which include sushi wrapped in persimmon and a rather tart vegetable pickle called *Nara-zuke*. Reservations required; coat and tie.
🐾 All major cards

🍴 VAN KIO
$$
410 ROKUJO-CHO
TEL 0742/33-8942
Full marks go for both taste and originality here, where the decor comprises purchasable antiques and stone lanterns, and they serve fare steamed, using a hot ceramic plate inside a stewpot. Dishes include duck and, more expensively, Nara venison.
🕐 Closed Mon. 🐾 All major cards

OSAKA

🏨 NIKKO OSAKA
$$$$–$$$$$
1-3-3 NISHI-SHINSAIBASHI,
CHUO-KU

TEL 06/6244-1111
FAX 06/6245-2432
The hotel's tapered, gleaming white tower stands out on the more animated south side of town, near the Dotonburi amusement quarter. Typically Osakan in its rather excessive opulence, it has elegant Japanese design motifs in the rooms (Western style) and an executive floor in which all rooms are decorated by fashion designer Hanae Mori.
🛏 640 🚇 Subway:
Shinsaibashi 🚇 Nearby
🐾 All major cards

🏨 DO SPORTS PLAZA
$$$
3-3-17 MINAMI-SEMBA,
CHUO-KU
TEL 06/6245-3311
FAX 06/6245-5803
At business hotel prices, the rooms are small but light and comfortable. "Do Sports" is really what this place—a favorite with athletes and visiting game pros—is all about. The adjacent sports plaza, with pool, gyms, and fitness facilities, is discounted for guests.
🛏 208 🚇 Subway:

Shinsaibashi 🍴 Nearby
💰 All major cards

🏨 HOTEL CALIFORNIA
$$$
1-9-30 NISHI-SHINSAIBASHI,
CHUO-KU
TEL 06/6243-0333
FAX 06/6243-0148
Near the Amerika-mura
(American village) shopping
precinct, this hotel has earned
a reputation among travelers
for reflecting an America rein-
vented by young(ish) Japan.
Comfortable and reasonably
priced, it also happens to be a
good hotel. If you are amused
by the inadvertent kitsch of its
California tropicana decor,
then this is for you. Pick a
room on the higher floors
(lower ones can be gloomy).
🛏 54 🚇 Subway:
Shinsaibashi 💰 All major
cards

🍴 KANI DORAKU
$$$–$$$$
1-6-18 DOTONBORI, CHUO-KU
TEL 06/6211-8975
Serving crab every which way
Japanese cuisine allows (raw,
stewed, fried, baked, and as an
ingredient in various dishes)
on several floors, this is the
original flagship of a chain with
over 50 branches nationwide.
🚇 Subway: Namba 💰 All
major cards

🍴 TAKOUME
$$
1-1-8 DOTONBORI, CHUO-KU
TEL 06/6211-0321
Reputedly founded during the
18th century and in a quite
venerable building even now,
this is considered Osaka's
premier restaurant for *oden*, a
savory fish stock from which
you select cooked ingredients
such as hardboiled eggs,
various fish cakes, or fried
tofu. The stock is kept on the
boil and the items added in;
this one has reputedly been
kept simmering for decades!
🚇 Subway: Namba 💰 No
credit cards

🍴 KUIDAORE
$–$$$
1-8-25 DOTONBORI,
CHUO-KU
TEL 06/6211-5300
Kuidaore is an Osakan
expression meaning "to ruin
oneself with extravagant
food." A giant mechanical
clown beats a drum outside
this vast restaurant and
innumerable plastic food
displays fill a show window. In
here you can sample almost
any kind of Japanese food,
starting on the ground floor
with many dishes under $10.
Filling eight floors, it gets more
refined and expensive (though
hardly ruinously) as you go up.
🚇 Subway: Namba 💰 All
major cards

WESTERN HONSHU (CHUGOKU)

HAGI

🏨 HOKUMON YASHIKI
🍴 $$$$$
210 HORIUCHI, , HAGI-SHI,
YAMAGUCHI-KEN
TEL 0838/22-7521
FAX 0838/25-8144
Right inside the Horiuchi
samurai quarter near the
castle ruins, this is Hagi's most
prestigious ryokan. The
building is modern, a tasteful
and opulent blend of Western
and Japanese styles—a
curious feature being an
attractive English garden.
Expect large, luxurious rooms
and superlative kaiseki cuisine,
ultrafresh seafood, and *fugu*
(blowfish) delicacies in winter
in the two restaurants.
🛏 44 💰 DC, V

🏨 HAGI GRAND
$$$$
25 FURUHAGI-CHO, HAGI-SHI,
YAMAGUCHI-KEN
TEL 0838/25-1211
FAX 0838/25-4422
Convenient location between
Higashi Hagi Station and the
sights makes this popular with
foreign visitors. It's considered
the town's top Western-style

hotel, although nearly half the
rooms are Japanese. All are
comfortable, and above
average size.
🛏 183 💰 All major cards

🏨 TOMOE RYOKAN
$$$–$$$$
608 HIJIWARA KOBOJI, HAGI-
SHI, YAMAGUCHI-KEN
TEL 0838/22-0150
FAX 0838/22-0152
Built of wood in 1926, the
Tomoe looks far older. The
entire building is filled with
antiques and scrolls. Beautiful
rooms, some looking out over
a peaceful central garden,
contain real antique features.
Indeed, it's as close to the
luxury traditional inn (with
communal bath) as you can
get for its very reasonable
price (which includes two
meals).
🛏 25 💰 All major cards

TSUWANO

🏨 MEIGETSU
🍴 $$$–$$$$
UO-MACHI, TSUWANO-CHO,
KANOASHI-GUN, SHIMANE-
KEN
TEL 08567/2-0685
FAX 08567/2-0637
With plenty of dark polished
wood, spacious rooms, and a
delightful little central garden,
this is probably Tsuwano's
prettiest ryokan. It also has
quite a reputation for local
cuisine—river fish and
mountain vegetable dishes—
served in a large, traditionally
decorated dining room.
Communal bath (see p. 358).
🛏 13 💰 V

🏨 SUNROUTE
$$$
845-1 TERADA, TSUWANO-
CHO, KANOASHI-GUN,
SHIMANEI-KEN
TEL 08567/2-3232
FAX 08567/2-2805
One of a reliable business-
hotel chain, this is Tsuwano's
only Western-style hotel.
Rooms, though very small, are
comfortable, deploying all

modern conveniences including adjoining (micro-) bathrooms.
🛏 50 💳 All major cards

🍴 YUKI
$$$
HON-MACHI, TSUWANO-CHO, SHIMANE-KEN
TEL 08567/2-0162.
The local specialties are mountain vegetables, carp, and *konyaku* (a kind of jelly made with the flour of a variety of potato). The most famous place to sample them is in this traditional restaurant with a carp stream flowing through the dining room.
💳 No credit cards

MATSUE

🏨 MINAMIKAN
🍴 $$$$$
SUETSUGU HON-MACHI, MATSUE-SHI, SHIMANE-KEN
TEL 0852/21-5131
FAX 0852/26-0351
This modern and luxurious ryokan is Matsue's most famous. Renowned for its outstanding cuisine, it's also a restaurant; if the accommodations aren't fully booked (they often are), you could eat here first before deciding to stay. It's very traditional with sublime service, a beautiful garden, natural hot spring baths, and rooms facing Lake Shinji-ko.
🛏 10 💳 All major cards

🏨 RYOKAN TERAZUYA
$$
60-3 TENJIN-MACHI, MATSUE-SHI, SHIMANE-KEN
TEL 0852/21-3480
FAX 0852/21-3422
Owned by the same family for over a century, this ryokan has a high reputation among travelers for convenience, comfort, and exceptional hospitality. You can stay on a with or without meals basis—both are unbeatable value. English is spoken.
🛏 10 💳 No credit cards

OKAYAMA & KURASHIKI

🏨 RYOKAN KURASHIKI
🍴 $$$$–$$$$$
4-1 HON-MACHI, KURASHIKI-SHI, OKAYAMA-KEN
TEL 086/422-0730
FAX 086/422-0990
This is a 250-year-old merchant complex with a lovely inner garden right by the canal. Antiques furnish the dark, polished wood rooms. Renowned for its service and cuisine, it's open also as a restaurant and a tearoom.
🛏 19 💳 All major cards

🏨 KURASHIKI KOKUSAI
$$$
1-1-44 CHUO, KURASHIKI-SHI, OKAYAMA-KEN
TEL 086/422-5141
FAX 086/422-5192
Comfortable and good value, this is by far the area's most respected Western hotel, where the best rooms have great views over old Kurashiki. The lobby exhibits 20th-century print master Munakata Shiko's largest work, and the rooms are tastefully decorated.
🛏 106 💳 All major cards

🏨 OKAYAMA PLAZA
$$$
2-3-12 HAMA, OKAYAMA-SHI, OKAYAMA-KEN
TEL 086/272-1201
FAX 086/273-1557
This is an ideal hotel for both value and location close to the major sights. The comfortable rooms are larger than the norm, the best with fine views over the castle.
🛏 85 💳 All major cards

HIROSHIMA & MIYAJIMA

🏨 IWASO RYOKAN
$$$$$
MOMIJIDANI, MIYAJIMA-CHO, SAEKI-GUN, HIROSHIMA-KEN
TEL 0829/44-2233
FAX 0829/44-2230
This is Miyajima's first, best, and most beautiful ryokan. Prices include two meals and vary according to rooms and dinner menus (both of which must be reserved in advance). The best rooms are in two exquisite old individual cottages on the grounds; the more economical are in the modern annex. Tucked up behind Itsukushima-jinja, it's the perfect complement to the beauty of Miyajima.
🛏 42 💳 All major cards

🏨 SUNROUTE
🍴 $$$
3-3-1 OTE-MACHI, NATA-KU, HIROSHIMA-SHI, HIROSHIMA-KEN
TEL 082/249-3600
FAX 082/249-3677
Sunroute specializes in well-appointed business hotels, and this is one of its best. Located by the river and conveniently close to Peace Park, with some rooms overlooking it, there is a bar, and two fine restaurants, the Kissui (Japanese) and the Viale (Italian)—the latter with a reputation as one of the best Italian restaurants in the city.
🛏 284 💳 Non-smoking rooms 💳 All major cards

🍴 KANAWA
$$–$$$$$
HEIWA-OHASHI HIGASHIZUME, OTE-MACHI 3-CHOME, NAKA-KU, HIROSHIMA-SHI, HIROSHIMA-KEN
TE: 082/241-7416
Hiroshima is famous for oysters farmed on thousands of rafts out in the bay, and this is *the* place to sample them. It's actually a barge moored on the river at Heiwa Bridge (near Peace Park), and owes its distinguished reputation to the quality of its seafood both cooked and raw. Reservations recommended. Coat and tie.
💳 All major cards

OKONOMI MURA BUILDING
$
15-802 SHOWA-MACHI, NAKA-KU, HIROSHIMA-SHI
TEL 082/082/241-8758
In this cherished Hiroshima institution, nothing goes for more than $12. This is where you eat the city's specialty, *okonomi-yaki* (or "Japanese pizza"): patties of flour and egg filled with vegetables, meat, and/or seafood, often taking the place of the soba or udon noodle you might get elsewhere. The building is an entire "village" *(mura)* devoted to nothing else.
No credit cards

SHIKOKU & THE SETO-NAIKAI

TAKAMATSU

LE BON 6
$$-$$$$
HOTEL KAWAROKU, 1-2 HYAKKEN-MACHI, TAKAMATSU-SHI
TEL 087/821-5666
A French restaurant with a nationwide reputation; the Japanese owner-chef is a gold medalist from a prestigious cuisine competition in France. Reservations are essential.
All major cards

TENKATSU
$$-$$$$
NISHIZUME HIROBA, HYOGO-MACHI, TAKAMATSU-SHI
TEL 087/821-5380
The restaurant is centered on a pond containing a live menu. Not surprisingly, it's renowned for its fish dishes, especially sashmi; its other specialties are *nabemono* (stews).
All major cards

MATSUYAMA & UCHIKO

FUNAYA RYOKAN
$$$$$
1-33 DOGOYU-NO-MACHI, MATSUYAMA-SHI, EHIME-KEN
TEL 089/947-0278
FAX 089/943-2139

A luxurious ryokan with a history extending back to the 17th century. The buildings are mainly from the 1930s (with lobby and baths in art deco style), though the latest were built in 1968. Many rooms look onto an exquisite inner garden. With indoor and outdoor public baths, sauna, spa pool, and outstanding food and service, this is the onsen elite.
54 July–Oct. All major cards

RYOKAN MATSUNOYA
$$$$
HON-MACHI 2-CHOME, UCHIKO-CHO, KITA-GUN, EHIME-KEN
TEL 089/344-5000
The rooms are very clean and basic, but the accent here is on food. Reviewed in trendy Japanese travel magazines, this place has earned its reputation thanks to an inspired owner-chef, whose style subtly blends Japanese cuisine with Chinese and European elements. Communal bath.
10 No credit cards

ANA (ZENNIKU) HOTEL
$$$-$$$$
3-2-1 ICHIBAN-CHO, MATSUYAMA-SHI, EHIME-KEN
TEL 089/933-5511
FAX 089/921-6053
South of the castle and within easy reach of shops, Matsuyama's premier Western-style hotel opened in 1980. The rooms are spacious and well furnished.
330 All major cards

MINSHUKU MIYOSHI
$$-$$$
3-7-23 ISHITEI, MATSUYAMA-SHI, EHIME-KEN
TEL 089/977-2581
Although the location behind a parking lot is a tad gloomy, this is excellent value. And it's just over the road from Ishitei-ji, Matsuyama's famous temple. Floored with tatami,

rooms are large, comfortable, and spotless, with their own toilet (there's a communal bath). You can have a room with or without meals. The owners are kindly disposed toward foreigners; if she's there, their daughter (a local tourism official) speaks English.
6 No credit cards

SHIKUMAYA
$$
1030 TOYOAKI, IKAZAKI-CHO, KITA-GUN, EHIME-KEN
TEL 089/344-2754 OR 344-2881
FAX 089/344-3020
This delightful hotel overlooks a river in Ikazaki, just a five-minute taxi ride from Uchiko. It has spacious, comfortable rooms, both Japanese- and Western-style. Price includes two meals (Japanese or Western); dinner must be ordered in advance. Rowena Date, the lady of the house, speaks fluent English.
18 All major cards

AJIKURA
$$-$$$
12-32 DOGOYU-NO-MACHI, MATSUYAMA-SHI, EHIME-KEN
TEL 089/934-7075
This very pleasant restaurant is in the shopping arcade leading from the tram station in the Dogo area (the restaurant has food models in the window). A variety of set meals, notably tempura.
No credit cards

KYUSHU

FUKUOKA-DAZAIFU-YANAGAWA

FUKUOKA GRAND HYATT
$$$$-$$$$$
1-2-82 SUMIYOSHI, HAKATA-KU, FUKUOKA-SHI
TEL 092/282-1234
FAX 092/282-2817
Right in the Canal City shopping-entertainment complex, which is itself an extraordinary architectural

---

Non-smoking Indoor/ Outdoor swimming pool Health club Credit cards **KEY**

HOTELS & RESTAURANTS

achievement, the hotel is futuristic and luxurious with beautiful rooms.

🛏 370 💳 All major cards

🏨 IL PALAZZO
$$$$
3-13-1 HARUYOSHI, CHUO-KU, FUKUOKA-SHI
TEL 092/716-3333
FAX 092/724-3330
Emphasizing European-style elegance, this inspired blend of traditional Milanese urban architecture was designed by Italian architect Aldo Rossi. The hotel is notable for futuristic use of light and space in its beautiful interior, as well as for its comfort, service, and restaurants.

🛏 62 💳 All major cards

🏨 CANAL CITY WASHINGTON
$$$
1-2-20 SUMIYOSHI, HAKATA-KU, FUKUOKA-SHI
TEL 092/282-8800
FAX 092/282-0757
A recent addition to the ubiquitous business-hotel chain, this one is not only well above the usual standard for comfort and amenities, but also has the advantage of a Canal City location.

🛏 423 💳 Non-smoking floor 💳 All major cards

🏨 DAIMARU BESSO
$$$$–$$$$$
1-20-1 YU-MACHI, CHIKUSHINO-SHI, FUKUOKA-KEN
TEL 092/924-3939
FAX 092/924-4126
First built during the 1860s and lying in an elegant stroll garden, this is probably the most prestigious ryokan in Kyushu. All rooms have their own Japanese cypress-wood bath with spa water. Price includes two meals.

🛏 49 💳 All major cards

🏨 OHANA SHOTOKAN
$$$$–$$$$$
1 SHINHOKA-MACHI, YANAGAWA-SHI

TEL 0944/73-2189
The Ohana Villa and Shoto-en Garden are the notable sights in Yanagawa. A good place to appreciate them is right here in this luxury ryokan, which is actually part of the complex. The best rooms look over the garden. The price includes two meals.

🛏 21 💳 All major cards

🍴 GOURMET CITY
$–$$$$
CENTRAZA HOTEL, 4-23 HAKATA-EKI CHUO-GAI, HAKATA-KU, FUKUOKA-SHI
TEL 092/461-0111 (HOTEL)
A couple of smart malls underneath the Hotel Centraza Hakata, just behind Hakata Station, are devoted to restaurants. Chinese, Korean, Italian, French, Indian, and Thai—an international lineup. Watch out for local specialties: *fugu* (blowfish), served here mainly raw and cut into paper-thin slices, and *karashi mentai*, cod roe spiced with chili.

💳 All major cards

BEPPU

🏨 SUGINOI HOTEL
The most famous of Beppu's luxury spa hotels and the Japanese *onsen* enthusiast's idea of paradise (though it's mainly Western style). It adjoins the Suginoi Palace, which provides every imaginable kind of spa bath and sauna as well as karaoke, restaurants and bars, an ice rink, golfing range, shopping malls, amusement park, bowling alley, and more. Despite this, rooms are surprisingly restrained, some with great views over the bay.
$$$–$$$$
1 KANKAIJI, BEPPU-SHI, OITA-KEN
TEL 0974/24-1141
FAX 0974/21-0010
🛏 573 💳 All major cards

KUMAMOTO

🏨 KUMAMOTO HOTEL 🍴 CASTLE
$$$$
4-2 JOTO MACHI, KUMAMOTO-SHI
TEL 096/326-3311
FAX 096/326-3324
This comfortable, rather sedate hotel is close to the castle. The better rooms have fine castle views. Of the three restaurants (the others serve Chinese or Japanese), the Loire is Kumamoto's best for French cuisine.

🛏 185 💳 All major cards

🏨 HOTEL NEW OTANI KUMAMOTO
$$$
1-13-1 KASUGA, KUMAMOTO-SHI
TEL 096/326-1111
FAX 096/326-0800
Everything you'd expect from the chain running one of Tokyo's largest hotels. It's one of the newest and best accommodations options in Kumamoto. Unusually spacious for Japan, rooms feature the latest amenities.

🛏 130 💳 All major cards

🍴 SENRI
$–$$$$
7-17 SUIZENJI-KOEN, KUMAMOTO-SHI
TEL 096/384-1824
A great choice for enjoying Japanese specialties, this restaurant is located in Suizenji-koen Park, with its best tatami rooms overlooking the famous garden itself. Try *karashi renkon*—lotus root stuffed with a savory mixture of miso and mustard, then sliced and deep fried in batter.

💳 No credit cards

NAGASAKI & UNZEN

🏨 NAGASAKI PRINCE
$$$$
2-26 TAKARA-MACHI, NAGASAKI-SHI
TEL 095/821-1111

FAX 095/823-4309
This recent addition to the
Prince chain is regarded by
many as Nagasaki's best hotel.
The ultramodern exterior and
lobby design are almost belied
by the old-fashioned comfort
of the rooms—in which all
amenities are nonetheless on
the cutting edge.
🛈 183 🅢 All major cards

🏨 UNZEN KANKO
$$$–$$$$
320 UNZEN, OBAMA-CHO,
MINAMI-TAKAKIYA-GUN,
NAGASAKI-KEN
TEL 0957/73-3263
FAX 0957/73-3419
Most accommodations in
Unzen are modern, but for
something reflecting the
golden age of Asian travel,
try this famous hotel. It was
built on spacious grounds
early in the 1930s as a hot
spa resort hotel for foreigners
and retains period fixtures.
🛈 59 🅢 All major cards

🏨 HOLIDAY INN
$$$
6-24 DOZA-MACHI,
NAGASAKI-SHI
TEL 095/828-1234
FAX 095/828-0178
In the center of town, this is
Nagasaki's best in the middle
price range. Rooms present a
full range of American-style
comforts and amenities;
tasteful overall Euro-Japanese
decor evoking old Nagasaki is
a bonus.
🛈 87 🅢 All major cards

🍴 KAGETSU
$$$–$$$$
2-1 MARUYAMA-CHO,
NAGASAKI-SHI
TEL 095/822-0191
Set in a tricentennial garden
and a former geisha house,
this is the best place for
shippoku (for two or more
diners only)—a kind of kaiseki
dinner, typically for four or
more persons and presenting
an assortment of delicacies
of Chinese, Japanese, and
even Portuguese origin.

Although prices for dinner are
almost prohibitive, lunch is
merely expensive. You must
be two or more people to
order shippoku. Reservations
advisable.
🅢 All major cards

🍴 SHIKAIRO
$$–$$$$
4-5 MATSUGAE-CHO,
NAGASAKI-SHI
TEL 095/822-1296
Nagasaki's noodle specialties
are champon, a hearty noodle
soup with vegetables and
meat or seafood, cooked
very much in the Chinese
style, and sara udon, udon
noodles stir-fried with similar
ingredients. This restaurant is
said to have invented these
dishes when it opened back
in 1899. Unfortunately it
moved into four floors of a
concrete building during the
1970s, but there's a wealth
of Chinese dishes on an
English menu.
🅢 All major cards

KAGOSHIMA

🏨 SHIROYAMA KANKO HOTEL
$$$$
41-1 SHINSHOIN-CHO,
KAGOSHIMA-SHI
TEL 099/224-2211
FAX 099/224-2222
Atop a wooded 350-foot-high
(105 m) hill, this is
Kagoshima's finest, with well-
appointed, comfortable
rooms, some with superb
views of the city and Mount
Sakurajima. The hotel is
famous for the views from the
top-floor sky lounge.
🛈 398 🈁 🍸 🅢 All
major cards

🏨 KAGOSHIMA TOKYU
$$$
22-1 KAMOIKE-SHIN-MACHI,
KAGOSHIMA-SHI
TEL 099/257-2411
FAX 099/257-6083
The relatively upscale Tokyu
business hotel chain surpasses
itself with this branch, near

the botanical gardens in the
Kamoike waterfront area, and
offers great value for the
quality. Many of the spacious,
luxurious rooms have great
views of the volcano.
🛈 206 🈁 🅢 All major
cards

🍴 KUMASOTEI
$$$–$$$$$
6-10 HIGASHI SENGOKU-CHO,
KAGOSHIMA-SHI
TEL 099/222-6356
Kagoshima's regional cuisine is
Satsuma ryori (the province's
former name was Satsuma),
which enjoys a high reputation
among Japanese gourmets.
This centrally located
restaurant is the best place to
sample Satsuma ryori and its
extensive range of dishes.
🅢 All major cards

OKINAWA & THE RYUKYU-SHOTO

NAHA

🏨 NIKKO NAHA GRAND CASTLE
$$$$
1-132-1 SHURI YAMAKAWA-
CHO, NAHA-SHI, OKINAWA-
KEN
TEL 098/886-5454
FAX 098/887-0070
Located on the hill at Shuri,
near the castle, this towering
white hotel meets all the
standards you would expect
from JAL's Nikko chain.
🛈 340 🅢 All major cards

🏨 SUN PALACE
$$$
2-5-1 KUMOJI, NAHA-SHI,
OKINAWA-KEN
TEL 098/863-4181
FAX 098/861-1313
Behind an inspired facade
featuring tiers of balconies
festooned with tropical plants,
this provides bright, breezy
rooms with a full range of
amenities down to fax
machines. Great value.
🛈 75 🅢 All major cards

SHOPPING

The average Japanese city has a shopping precinct *(shoten gai)*, an arcade *(aakeedo)*—usually simply a street covered with a glass roof—a covered food market, and an underground mall, all around the main train station. In larger cities such as Tokyo this pattern may be repeated in several different districts. Both underground malls *(chikagai)* and shopping arcades are great for bargains particularly photographic equipment, electronics, leather goods, and clothing. In many cities you'll find some interesting junk shops and used clothing stores in arcades, but don't expect any great finds by way of vintage kimono and obi sashes; in recent years prices have gone through the roof even in rural areas.

Some stores offer goods tax free; however, this option applies only to electronic and computer goods, photographic equipment, and jewelry (if it contains precious metals and gems). Many cheap-jack souvenir stores are emblazoned with the term "tax free," when in fact you will be paying regular prices for goods to which the concession doesn't apply. When purchasing tax free, you will need your passport; the store will give you a form to be given to customs when leaving the country.

Antiques
Ceramics and *tansu* chests generally command high prices; although attractive and ubiquitous, *ukiyo-e* prints frequently sell more cheaply overseas. The number of flea markets is growing, although in most cases their prices are only slightly less than in stores. However, they often present a variety of very attractive items made between the 1890s and 1930s that won't put you out of pocket.

Clothing
If you are tall, you may have difficulty with clothing sizes in Japan. Always try on shoes or clothing before purchasing. Some garments carries the "F" (free size) label, but for Americans this is not always the one-size-fits-all guarantee it is for the Japanese.

The less expensive silk kimono you find in large tourist outlets are probably made in China. The real thing, which ranges from

seriously expensive to astronomical, can be made to measure in specialty stores. However, they are heavy and impractical and the large *obi* sash is restrictive. It's preferable to go for the more affordable cotton *yukata;* used either as sleepwear or in high summer, they come ready-made or made-to-order in a range of attractive designs.

Department stores
Wonderful places to buy quality Japanese goods, including ceramics and lacquerware. Many of them have food halls in the basement with a fascinating selection of home grown and imported goods. Stores such as Seibu, Isetan, Marui, and Matsuya operate on a chain basis, often with branches in major cities. The twice yearly sales in these stores offer exceptional discounts. Lasting a week each, sales are held generally from the second Friday in January and July. Prices on designer clothing, for instance, plummet by 50 percent on average.

Discount stores
These appeared around Japan during the 1990s. Every town now has a *hyaku-en kinitsu* (¥100-only) outlet, with an astonishing array of goods (mainly made in China) including stationery, household goods, and novelties each costing exactly ¥100.

Electronics, electrical goods, & computer stores
Goods are at discounted prices. But beware: U.S. and Japanese computer systems are usually incompatible. When it comes

to audio and video, always make sure that the specifications and current match those back home.

Souvenirs
Most of the goods for sale at gift shops and souvenir stalls will be kitsch: hideous calendars, garish sake drinking sets, fluorescent paintings on velvet, key chains, cheap novelties, and so on. The most plentiful souvenirs are the edible kind; every region has its own specialties. In the cake and candy line, there are *sembei* (rice crackers) and *mochi* (a chewy sweet made with rice flour).

Traditional arts & crafts
These make by far the best buys in Japan. They include ceramics, textiles, paper and paperware (umbrellas, fans, hand-painted kites, stationery, etc.), dolls, wood and bamboo products, woodblock prints (antique and modern), cloisonné, and lacquerware. The crafts vary regionally, but craft shops, specialty stores, and department stores in large cities usually offer a range of goods from different parts of the country.

TOKYO

Tokyo has a reputation as a paradise for shopaholics, with something for everyone from platinum card holders to backpackers. The main shopping districts vary because of local consumer trends—Ginza is conservative and upscale, Shibuya a favorite with the young—or by specializing in certain kinds of goods. Akihabara is known for electronics, Harajuku for teen fashion, Kappabashi for catering supplies (including the incredible food models you see in restaurant windows), Jimbocho for books, and Kotto-dori in Aoyama for antiques. Aoyama also has its famous "Killer-dori," named for the prices in its designer outlets.

Markets
The space underneath elevated train tracks has been used for covered markets or filled in with a miscellany of stores since World War II.

Ameyoko Ameya-yoko-cho, Ueno. Tokyo's most exciting street market (see p. 93) is less touristy than the International Arcade.
International Arcade 1-7-23 Uchisaiwai-cho, Chiyoda-ku, tel 03/3591-2764. Presents a huge array of goods and tax-free discounts.

GINZA

Ginza is Tokyo's Fifth Avenue, with a great variety of shops and upscale department stores. More department stores are to be located just west of Ginza in Yurakucho.
Bunkado 5-14-1 Ginza, Chuo-ku, tel 03/3541-8325, closed Sun. Renowned for its array of handicrafts from around Japan, including ceramics and lacquerware.
Kyukyodo 5-7-4 Ginza, Chuo-ku, tel 03/3571-4429, closed Sun. Sells incense, handmade paper, traditional stationery, brushes, and calligraphy requisites. Also stocks a marvelous selection of papercraft, including boxes and miniature chests of drawers.
Mikimoto 4-5-5 Ginza, Chuo-ku, tel 03/3535-4611, closed Wed. Owned by the descendants of Mikimoto Kokichi, who invented the cultured pearl technique, this shop has branches nationwide.
Mitsukoshi 4-6-16 Ginza, Chuo-ku, tel 03/3562-1111, closed Mon. An elegant department store stocking the finest goods both Japanese and imported, with prices to match.
Nihonshu Center 1-1-21 Nishi Shimbashi, Minato-ku, tel 03/3519-2091, closed Thurs. *Nihonshu* is the proper word for sake. You can sample some of 6,000 variations for a nominal fee
Sakai Kokodo Gallery 1-2-14 Yurakucho, Chiyoda-ku,

tel 03/3591-4678. Long-established dealer in woodblock prints, the range here goes from vintage rarities to high-quality modern reproductions.
Seibu 2-5-1 Yurakucho, Chiyoda-ku, tel 03/3286-1111, closed Thurs. The local branch of the department store.
Sony Showroom Sony Bldg., 5-3-1 Ginza, Chuo-ku, tel 03/3573-2371. This corner building at the main intersection is a Ginza landmark; all the latest audio-visual gadgetry and games technology are there for you to try out, as well as a multitude of audio, visual, and digital gizmos.
Tachikichi 5-6-13 Ginza, Chuo-ku, tel 03/3573-1986. Selling quality ceramics from the most famous workshops around Japan, particularly wares from Kyoto, home of its main branch.

ROPPONGI

Aoyama Book Center 6-1-20 Roppongi, Minato-ku, tel 03/3479-0479. Book and magazine store emphasizing art, photography, and design, with a decent-size selection of books in English.
Axis Building 5-17-1 Roppongi, Minato-ku, tel 03/3587-2781, closed Sun. With stores variously devoted to furnishing and crafts (e.g. ceramics and textiles), this sleek building is the ideal place for an overview of the best of contemporary Japanese interior design.
Wave 6-2-27 Roppongi, Minato-ku, tel 03/3408-0111. This gray, minimalist building is a Roppongi landmark; inside, it's one of the best music stores in town with a notable art bookstore on the top floor.
Washikobo 1-8-10 Nishi Azabu, Minato-ku, tel 03/3405-1841, closed Sun. A specialist in papercraft goods including kites, stationery, boxes, handmade *washi* paper, and paper dolls.

SHIBUYA

Seibu 21-1 Udagawa-cho, Shibuya-ku, tel 03/3462-0111,

closed Thurs. The store had a seminal influence on fashion in Japan and remains outstanding for clothing, household goods, and gifts. Basement food hall.
Loft 21-1 Udagawa-cho, Shibuya-ku, tel 03/3464-5111, closed Wed. This "creative store" (a Seibu offshoot), featuring furnishings, fabrics, and endless supplies and materials for hobbies, arts, and crafts, places great emphasis on style.
Parco 15-1 Udagawa-cho, Shibuya-ku, tel 03/3475-0411. Originally an offshoot of Seibu, this store launched the concept of the "fashion building"—meaning several floors devoted solely to clothing, containing boutiques and sections operated by all the world's major designer brands.
Japan Traditional Craft Center 2F Plaza 246, 3-1-1, Minami Aoyama, Minato ku, tel 03/3403-2460, closed Thurs. Though not everything here is expensive, high quality still commands prices. Lacquerware, ceramics, bamboo, papercraft: You'll find the cream of both traditional and contemporary Japanese crafts.
Kiddyland 6-1-9 Jingu-mae, Shibuya-ku, tel 03/3409-3431, closed 3rd Tues. each month. It's the ultimate store for toys, gadgets, gimmicks, models, etc.
Mujirushi Ryohin 2-12-28 Kita Aoyama, Minato-ku, tel 03/3478-5800. Sells high-quality generic goods—everything from noodles to bicycles, with clothes and household items in between.
Oriental Bazaar 5-9-13 Jingumae, Shibuya-ku, tel 03/3400-3933, closed Thurs. Though touristy, this is the best place in town to buy souvenirs —prints, ceramics, lacquerware, paperware, lamps, clothing, as well as a good selection of antiques and vintage kimono at attractive prices.
Ultra Queen 2-6-32 Ebisu, Shibuya-ku, tel 03/3449-9531. Offers an array of clothing including the new and offbeat, the used, and designer dead-stock.

Tokyu Hands 12-18 Udagawa-cho, Shibuya-ku, tel 03/5489-5111, closed on 2nd and 3rd Wed. each month. A great home handyman store, with several floors of tools, materials, and accessories required for arts, crafts, and hobbies.

Tower Records and Books 1-22-4 Jinnan, Shibuya-ku, tel 03/3496-3661. Offering a huge selection of music, the U.S. chain now also has books and magazines in its main Tokyo store. It has the largest stock of English-language publications at the lowest prices in town.

SHINJUKU & IKEBUKURO

Shopping of all kinds at all prices—department stores, high-fashion outlets, general discount stores, and, most famously, discount camera stores west of Shinjuku Station.

Marui 3-30-16 Shinjuku, tel 03/3354-0101, closed 2nd or 3rd Wed. each month. A comprehensive and trendy department store in four sections. All you need to know is that *kan* means building, then choose between Young Kan, Fashion Kan, Men's Kan, and Interior Kan.

Seibu 1-28-1 Minami Ikebukuro, Toshima-ku, tel 03/3981-0111. The original flagship store, and still Seibu's largest branch. (See Shibuya, p. 381)

Sunshine City 3-1-3 Higashi Ikebukuro, Toshima-ku, tel 03/3989-3331. One of Tokyo's tallest and largest buildings contains a branch of Mitsukoshi department store and malls chock-full of boutiques and shops of every description.

Tobu Metropolitan Plaza, 1-1-25 Nishi Ikebukuro, Toshima-ku, tel 03/3981-2211. The rival store to Seibu expanded during the mid-1990s, and here includes not only the colossal store itself, but also the Tobu Museum of Art.

Camera Sakuraya 3-17-2 Shinjuku, Shinjuku-ku, tel 03/3354-3636. This photographic shop is esteemed for new and used equipment and noted for its discounts.

Kinokuniya Bookstore 3-17-7 Shinjuku, tel 03/3354-0131, closed every 3rd Wed. Although rivaled in recent years, this is still one of the city's best places for foreign books, magazines, and paperbacks.

Yodobashi Camera Nishiguchi Honten, 1-11-1 Nishi Shinjuku, Shinjuku-ku, tel 03/3346-1010. Several floors of video, discount cameras and accessories, and general photographic items. There are often great bargains, but don't buy any digital or electronic goods without first checking on system compatibility.

UENO-ASAKUSUA

Great for handmade traditional goods, including hardware and carpenter's tools, kimono and accessories, fans, wooden combs, and paper lanterns.

Adachi-ya 2-22-12 Asakusa, Taito-ku, tel 03/3841-4915, closed Thurs. Traditional working clothes, notably the blue denim *hanten* (or *happi* coat), the Edo-period townsman's garb still worn at festivals.

Hanato 2-25-6 Asakusa, Taito-ku, tel 03/3841-6411, closed Tues. An old-fashioned fireman's lantern bearing your name in *hiragana* characters? No problem: Hanato makes any kind of paper lantern *(chochin)* to order.

Kurodaya 1-2-11 Asakusa, Taito-ku, tel 03/3845-3830, closed Mon. Premier outlet for *washi* paper and papercraft, including kites and festival masks.

Matsuya 1-4-1 Hanakawado, Taito-ku, tel 03/3842-1111, closed Tues. There are often excellent craft exhibitions here, promoting ceramics, woodcraft, and lacquerware, with demonstrations by craftspeople from around Japan.

Sukeroku 2-3-1 Asakusa, Taito-ku, tel 03/3844-0577. This is the last store on the right as you walk up Nakamise to Senso-ji. It sells exquisite miniatures representing period people, houses, and shops, as well as other delightful statuettes.

Yonoya 1-37-10 Asakusa, tel 03/3844-1755, closed Wed. A specialist in handcrafted wooden combs and hair ornaments for the past 150 years; beautiful goods in a beautiful little shop.

AKIHABARA-KANDA

Akihabara's Denki Gai (Electric Town) is famous for sheer spectacle (see p. 105). Good for electronic and electrical goods and bargains (though rare) do turn up for those who really know what they're looking for.

Laox Computer-kan 1-7-6 Soto Kanda, Chiyoda-ku, tel 03/5256-3111. A computer superstore six stories high. If it isn't here, you probably won't find it in Japan.

Rocket Honten 1-14-1 Kanda Sakuma-cho, Chiyoda-ku, tel 03/3257-0606. You can't miss this: It flashes and crackles even more than its neighbors. Within are several floors of electrical and electronic goods.

Oya Shobo 1-1 Kanda Jimbocho, Chiyoda-ku, tel 03/3291-0062. One of the most famous dealers in the used book district, this specialist in period maps and antique books (the illustrated ones are highly attractive) also has a good selection of *ukiyo-e* prints.

CENTRAL HONSHU (CHUBU)

NAGOYA

There are several department stores here starting with **Meitetsu** at the train station, beneath which is a large underground shopping arcade. If you like junk-shops and antiques, you should explore the Osu Arcade and vicinity. There's a weekend flea market at intervals at Osu Kannon Temple; check with the visitor information office or the International Forum Building (see p. 69) for schedules.

Noritake has been famous for Western-style ceramics and chinaware for over a century; you can visit the factory, the **Noritake Craft Center** (Tel 052/561-7114), but an advance reservation is essential.

KANAZAWA

Kanazawa has been a center for ceramics since feudal times, and is known for *Ohi* and *Kutani* pottery. Devised for the tea ceremony, Ohi ware has beautiful warm-colored glazes; Kutani ware has ornate decoration in glowing colors. In the southwest of town is **Kutani Kosengama** (Kosen Kutani Pottery Kiln, 5-3-3 Nomachi, tel 076/241-0902), which has a large sale room.

A major producer of gold leaf since ancient times, Kanazawa is also renowned for Kaga lacquerware *(Kaga maki-e)*, featuring beautiful, intricate designs highlighted with gold and silver dust. The Japanese know the area most of all for *kaga yuzen*—a distinctive dyeing and stenciling technique for silk kimono fabrics. Just north of the Kenroku-en Garden, the **Ishikawa Bussankan** (Ishikawa Prefectural Products Shop, tel 076/222-7788) has all the specialties of the prefecture— arts, crafts, and edibles; it also includes a restaurant. Other specialty craft workshops in Kanazawa can be visited by arrangement through the visitor information center.

TAKAYAMA

There is plenty of local color in Takayama's morning street markets *(asa-ichi)*, which trade daily in produce and flowers grown by local farmers, as well as handicrafts. Both are open from 7 a.m. to noon, one at Jinya-mae near the historic

government building and the other on the eastern bank of the Miya-gawa River, across from Kajibashi bridge.

The old town center of Sanmachi Suji holds an antique market on the 7th of each month from May through October. Good pieces won't come cheap, but will still be priced substantially lower than in Kyoto or Tokyo.

KANSAI

KYOTO

Kyoto's shopping is concentrated in the center of town, especially along Shijo-dori up to the intersection with Kawaramachi-dori. Shopping arcades sprawl from beneath the station and there's also a range of shops in the city's covered arcades: Shinkyogoku and Teramachi.

Kyoto's department stores have large selections of traditional local products and gifts. Among them are **Hankyu** (68 Shin-cho, Shijo-dori, Shimogyu-ku, tel 075/223-2288, closed Thurs.), **Kintetsu** (Karasuma-dori, Shimogyo-ku, tel 075/361-1111, closed Thurs.), and **Daimaru** (Shijo-dori, Shimogyo-ku, tel 075/211-8111, closed Wed.). **Kagoshin** 4-7 Sanjo-dori, Ohashi Higashi, Higashiyama-ku, tel 075/771-0209, closed Sun. In business since the 1860s, this shop specializes in high-quality objects made of bamboo, including ikebana items, woven baskets, and bamboo lacquerware. **Kasagen** 284 Kitagawa, Gion-machi, Higashiyama-ku, tel 075/561-2832. Has sold oiled paper umbrellas for well over a century. **Kyoto Handicraft Center** 21 Shogoin, Entomi-cho, Sakyo-ku, tel 075/761-5080. Artisans and craftspeople not only work on the spot, but also let the public try their hand at some of the techniques.

Kyoto Tojiki Kaikan (Kyoto Ceramics Center) 570-3 Shiraito-cho, Gojo-dori, Higashiyama-ku, tel 075/541-1102. Two floors of works by members of the local potters' cooperative.

Miyawaki Baisen-an Rokkaku-dori, Tominokoji Nishi-Iru, Nakagyo-ku, tel 075/221-0181. This famous shop first started selling fans to geisha, actors, and the general public about 180 years ago and maintains its reputation for the handmade, genuine article today.

Nishijin Orimono Textile Center Imadegawa, Horikawa-dori, Kamigyo-ku, tel 075/451-9231. You can watch designers, dyers, and weavers at work on kimono silk of the highest quality; there's a sales area— though the price for a good piece large enough for a garment could well cost more than your entire trip to Japan.

Tachikichi Shijo-Tominokoji, Shimogyo-ku, tel 075/211-3143, closed Wed. One of the best places for ceramics, with a huge selection of both modern and traditional styles on four floors.

Takashimaya 52 Shin-cho, Shijo-dori, Shimogyo-ku, tel 075/221-8811. Department store reputed to have the best selection of traditional gifts. Some staff at the information counters speak English.

Tanakaya Shijo-dori, Yanaginobanba-higashi, Shimogyo-ku, tel 075/221-1959, closed Wed. A specialist in Japanese dolls, especially the local *kyo-ningyo*. Upstairs is a gallery exhibiting their antique counterparts.

Union Kyoto Craft Center 275 Kitagawa, Gion-machi, Higashiyama-ku, tel 075/561-9660. Here you can see all local arts and crafts together in one place.

Yamato Mingei-ten Takoyakushi-agaru, Kawaramachi-dori, Nakagyo-ku, tel 075/221-2641, closed Tues. Folk craft shop selling a miscellany of quality handmade items both local and from all over Japan.

ENTERTAINMENT & FESTIVALS

ENTERTAINMENT & FESTIVALS

Easy to find for being concentrated in amusement districts, the array of entertainments in large Japanese cities is exhaustive. Even smaller towns have a district with bars, restaurants, discos, movie theaters—and more louche entertainments.

Many visitors to Japan are attracted by the festivals taking place all over the country. You will find information about the different festivals, both countrywide and regional, here.

You'll find English-language listings in magazines such as *Tokyo Journal* and *Kansai Time Out*, as well as on the Internet (e.g. Tokyo Meltdown, see p. 356). You can also check Tokyo and Kansai (Kyoto and Osaka) movie and theater programs in the English-language newspapers (see p. 355). In other areas, you should pick up the newsletters in visitor information centers, which list special events, fairs, exhibitions, and festivals.

Going to the movies is an easy option—more than two-thirds are imports (over-whelmingly from the U.S.) and, with the exception of animated features, are always subtitled and screened in the original language.

Entertainment districts also present a substantial selection of live music venues. Watch the listings: rock, rap, hip-hop, garage, house, techno, thrash, heavy metal, blues, jazz—you name it, someone somewhere is playing it. Discos often bar men unaccompanied by women. Most places charge women lower rates; some have dress codes.

Tokyo, Kyoto, and other large cities feature traditional theater forms including Kabuki and Noh. Elsewhere they are rare; you're more likely to see Western-style performing arts, notably world-class classical music.

TOKYO

When it comes to going out on the town, choose between the entertainment districts of Shinjuku, Roppongi, and Shibuya, with plenty more alternatives in the Aoyama, Ebisu, and Nishi-Azabu neighborhoods.

BARS & CLUBS

The *Tokyo Journal* listings are excellent for bars and clubs. Fashions come and go at an alarming rate in Japan, so be aware that suggestions here may have lost favor or vanished by the time this book goes to press.

Acaraje Tropicana B1 Edge Blvd., 1-1-1 Nishi Azabu, Minato-ku, tel 03/3479-4690. Hippest and most authentic Brazilian dive in town, great samba, lambada, and food. Nearby is **Acaraje,** its smaller parent (Tel 03/3401-0973).

Bar Isn't It? 3F MT Bldg, 3-8-18 Roppongi, Minato-ku, tel 03/3746-1598. Fun, cheap, trendy, and vast, this is the Tokyo chapter of a growing chain.

Blue Note 5-13-3 Minami Aoyama, Minato-ku, tel 03/3407-5781, closed Sun. Like its New York counterpart, this is the place to catch the greatest names in jazz. Two sets nightly at 7 and 9:30.

Gas Panic Togensha Bldg., 2, & 3F, 3-14-13 Roppongi, Minato-ku, tel 03/3405-0633. Actually two bars and a dance club in one, this is cheap, hip, always crowded, and remains popular despite a reputation for occasional brawls.

Hanezawa Garden 3-12-15 Hiro, Shibuya-ku, tel 03 3400 2013, closed Oct.–March. A beer garden that's actually in a real (Japanese) garden. You can dine on barbecued food beneath trees festooned with colored lanterns. Delightful—despite dreadful canned Hawaiian music.

Henry Africa 7-2-17 Ginza, Chuo-ku, tel 03/3573-4563. A relaxed, 1970s-vintage, American-style bar, full of Tiffany lamps. Popular with the non-Japanese business crowd.

Kento's 6F Takiyamacho Bldg., 6-7-12 Ginza, Chuo-ku, tel 03/3572-9161. Another nostalgia fest, with 1950s and '60s hits played by bands sporting box jackets and ducktails. Also at B1 Dai-ni Renu Bldg., 5-3-1 Roppongi, tel 03/3401-5755.

Lexington Queen 3-13-14 Roppongi, Minato-ku, tel 03/3401-1661. Established in 1980, the Lex is where international screen, stage, and rock celebrities visiting Tokyo wind up until the wee small hours—hosted by genial manager Bill Hersey.

Velfarre 17-14-22 Roppongi, Minato-ku, tel 03/3402-8000. The name is Japitalian; a frenzy of os-tentation, noise, color, and high-tech effects. Reputedly the largest disco in Asia.

FOR CHILDREN

Tokyo Disneyland
1-1 Maihama, Urayasu-shi, Chiba-ken, tel 047/354-0001. This is useful if you're traveling with youngsters underwhelmed by museums and temples. A successful clone of its California parent and only a 15-minute train ride to Urayasu (from JR Tokyo Station on the JR Keiyo line to Maihama Station; the park is outside the station). Hours and prices vary seasonally; check with the Tokyo Disney Resort Ticket Center (Hibiya Mitsui Bldg,, 1-1-2 Yuraku-cho, Chiyoda-ku, reachable by the Denki Building exit of Hibiya subway; tel 03/3595-1777, open 10–7).

To reserve tickets for shows, telephone (or get someone to do it for you) the main booking agencies: **Ticket Pia** (Tel 03/5237-9999), **Ticket Saison** (Tel 03/3250-9999), and the largest, **Playguide** (Tel 03/3561-8821). Agencies also sell tickets for sports events.

SUMO

The nation's most important sumo tournaments take place at the **Kokugikan** (National Sumo

Hall, 1-3-28 Yokoami, Sumida-ku, Tokyo, tel 03/3623-5111) from the 1st or 2nd Sunday to the 3rd or 4th Sunday in January and May and from the 2nd to 4th Sunday in September.

THEATER

Tokyo has the largest number of playhouses staging traditional theater such as Kabuki and Noh (see pp 46–49). Programs are seasonal and irregular; check for details in the English-language press or with the Japan National Tourist Office.

Kabuki-za 4-12-15 Ginza, Chuo-ku, tel 03/3541-3131. Two Kabuki programs daily.
Shinbashi Embujo 6-18-2 Ginza, Chuo-ku, tel 03/5565-6000. Mainly traditional fare, including Kabuki and seasonal dance presentations by the dwindling *shimabashi* geisha.
Kokuritsu Gekijo (National Theater) 4-1 Hayabusa-cho, Chiyoda-ku, tel 03/3265-7411. Sometimes presents Bunraku puppet theater; at other times, anything from Kabuki to works by contemporary composers.
Takarazuka Theater 1-1-3 Yurakucho, Chiyoda-ku, tel 03/3591-1711. Tokyo branch of the all-female opera company: lavish revues, operettas, and musicals. Reserve way ahead for a good seat.

HOKKAIDO

SAPPORO

The action in Sapporo is concentrated in Susukino, where side streets present a seemingly unending array of bars and clubs. Depending on the season, you can grab a beer from a vending machine and join in what seems like a party watching a ball game up on the giant TV screen over the area's main intersection.

Gaijin Bar 2F M's Space, Minami 2, Nishi 7, tel 011/272-1033, closed Sun. This is one of the city's top expat hangouts.

King Xmhu Minami 7, Nishi 4, tel 011/531-1388. Pronounced "mu," the hottest dance spot features a colossal Aztec-style effigy of the king dominating the facade with glowing red eyes; a cadaverous interior matches it with glowing laser-eyed demon masks and trendy decor.
Suskino Reien 8F Green Bldg., Minami 4, Nishi 3, tel 011/512-2543. Voodoo lounge where you can sip cocktails in Halloween-inspired surroundings, enhanced with shrunken heads.

CENTRAL HONSHU (CHUBU)

NAGOYA

Has a Noh theater and the Misono-za Kabuki theater, but programs are irregular. Check local listings available from the visitor information center.

There is a concentration of bars and night spots in an energetic amusement district around Sakae 3-Chome.

Sumo is one of the highlights of the summer. Tournaments are held from the 1st to 3rd Sunday in July at the **Aichi-ken Taiiku-kan** (Aichi Prefectural Gymnasium, 1-1 Ninomaru, Naka-ku, Nagoya, tel 052/971-2516).

KANAZAWA

A leading center for Noh drama for centuries. The place to see it is the **Ishikawa Prefectural Noh Theater** (Tel 076/264-2598). Programs run every week during summer but less regularly at other times. Check the visitor information center for schedules.

KANSAI

KYOTO

BARS & CLUBS
Metro Keihan Marutamachi station, tel 075/752-4765. This is Kyoto's most happenin' place. It features star foreign bands and

DJs, art exhibits, fringe theater, and/or weird and wacky theme nights. It's fairly small and gets very crowded on weekends.
Pig & Whistle 2F Shobi Bldg., 115 Ohashi-cho, Sanjo Ohashi, tel 075/761-6022. Lively British-style pub, offering such delights as darts and fish and chips.

THEATER
Noh and Kabuki both originated in Kyoto. The same applies to geisha dance spectaculars; in addition to those mentioned below, others are also presented in the fall. Check for programs at the visitor information center.

Gion Corner 570-2 Minamigawa, Gion-machi, Higashiyama-ku, tel 075/561-1119. A small theater offering an eclectic digest of traditional entertainments from Bunraku puppet drama excerpts to the tea ceremony. It's tacky and touristy, but fun.
Minami-za Kawabata-dori, tel 075/561-1155. This famous Kyoto landmark on the southern bank of the Kamo River is Japan's oldest Kabuki theater.
Gion Shinchi Kobu Kaburenjo 570-2 Minamigawa, Gion-machi, Higashiyama-ku, tel 075/561-1119. The theater where *maiko* (trainee geisha) have been presenting glittering *Miayko Odori* (cherry dance) spectaculars each April for almost 150 years.
Ponto-cho Kaburenjo Theater Ponto-cho, Sanjo Sagaru, Nakagyo-ku, tel 075/221-2025. Ponto-cho maiko and geisha present *Kamo-gawa odori* (Kamo River dance) spectaculars here twice a year—in May and mid-October to mid-November.

OSAKA

Osaka vies with Tokyo as the most hedonistic city in Japan. The reputation is earned from the Dontonbori entertainment district, served by Shinsaibashi and Namba subway stations south of the city center.

ENTERTAINMENT & FESTIVALS

NIGHTLIFE

Murphy's 6F Lead Bldg., 1-6-31 Higashi Shinsaibashi, Chuo-ku, tel 06/6282-0677. Reputedly the best Irish pub and featuring Irish music live on Wednesdays.

Sam & Dave Plaza Umeshin Bldg., 4-15-19 Nishi Tenma, tel 06/6365-1688 and **Amerika Mura,** 2-11-5 Nishi Shinsaibashi, tel 06/213-4107. Ultra-hip bars (Amerika Mura is said to be the wilder of the two), where entertainment ranges from rock bands to fringe performance art.

SUMO

Sumo tournaments are held in Osaka from the 2nd Sunday to 4th Sunday in March at the **Osaka Furitsu Taiiku Kaikan** (3-4-36 Namba-Naka, Naniwa-ku, Osaka, tel 06/6631-0121), near Namba subway station.

THEATER

Check schedules either at the visitor information center or in publications such as *Kansai Time Out* magazine and *Meet Osaka.*

National Bunraku Theater of Japan 1-12-10 Nipponbashi, Chuo-ku, tel 06/6212-2532. Bunraku, the puppet theater form originated in Osaka. It is worth going to see; performances have three-week runs in January, March, April, June to August, and November.

KYUSHU

FUKUOKA

Nakasu amusement district, comprising restaurants, bars, nightclubs, theaters, and discos, is considered one of Japan's best; it is said to rival Tokyo's Shinjuku for raunch. Tenjin, northwest of Nakasu, also has nightspots.

Check the schedule at the **Fukuoka Blue Note** (2-7-6 Tenjin, Chuo-ku, Fukuoka City, tel 092/715-6666), opening late 2000, which hosts international jazz giants when they tour Japan. Fukuoka is also a sumo city, hosting major tournaments from

the 2nd to the 4th Sunday in November at the **Fukuoka Kokusai Center** (2-2 Chikko-Hon-machi, Hakata-ku, Fukuoka-shi, tel 092/272-1111).

FESTIVALS

The *matsuri* (festival) is where the Japanese go to find the "real Japan." Rituals and customs, food and drink, clothing and trappings, music and dance are all redolent of a cultural identity predating Western influence by centuries. A matsuri gives enough local color to constitute the highlight of a trip to Japan. Shinto festival parades always include *mikoshi,* the ornately decorated, gilded palanquins supported on long, thick wooden poles and carried around the streets by scores of chanting bearers. Each mikoshi (some weighing several tons) was thought to be the means of conveyance for a deity; the object of the festival was to show the gods a good time.

Some matsuri are nostalgic pageants with parades of geisha or samurai warriors; others, especially Buddhist festivals such as O-bon, commemorate the dead (which doesn't mean doom and gloom in Japan). Many festivals include markets selling food and sweets, good luck charms, plants, and cheap toys. If you plan to attend a major festival, bear in mind that hotels in the area will be packed solid. There are many hundreds of festivals; those below are merely a few of the more important ones; Confirm actual festival dates at local visitor centers.

COUNTRYWIDE

JANUARY

Seijin-no-hi—Coming of Age Day (2nd Mon.). This national holiday targets all who will reach 20 years of age within the year. Young people often go sight-seeing (at shrines and temples) in formal attire.

FEBRUARY

Setsubun—Parting of the

Seasons (Feb. 3 or 4). Marks the last day of winter. Many shrines and temples host traditional celebrations, often followed by performances with costumed demons and deities.

MARCH

Hina Matsuri—Doll's Festival or Peach Blossom Festival (Feb. 1–4). A girls' festival: Dolls representing an imperial couple of ancient times, with attendant court, are displayed on specially erected shelves in homes.

APRIL

Hanami—Flower Viewing. Colleagues, friends, and families indulge in bibulous picnics beneath flowering cherry trees. **Hana Matsuri**—Flower Festival (April 8). Celebrates Buddha's birthday in temples nationwide.

AUGUST

O-Bon—Festival of the Dead or Lantern Festival (mid Aug.). Opens a season coinciding with the summer vacation. Different events and festivals are held in different places, notably *Bon odori* dancing, spectacular firework displays, and the charming custom of floating candles (each representing a soul) along rivers aboard little paper boats.

NOVEMBER

Shichi-go-san (Nov. 15). Children aged 7 *(shichi),* 5 *(go),* and 3 *(san)* don traditional finery and go to Shinto shrines nationwide for ritual blessing.

TOKYO

JANUARY

Dezome-shiki —New Year Firemen's Parade (Jan. 6). Attired in period garb, firemen parade along Harumi dori on Tokyo Bay, and perform stunning acrobatic feats atop high bamboo ladders.

MAY

Sanja Matsuri (close to May 17). Crowds of people, many in period costume, throng the streets of Asakusa.

JUNE
Sanno Matsuri (June 10–16 annually). Held at Hie-jinja Shrine. Mounted priests lead a lively parade along Akasaka's main avenue every other year.

JULY
Fireworks (last Sat. in July). Held in Asakusa over Sumida-gawa River, this is Japan's greatest fireworks display.

NOVEMBER
Tori-no-Ichi—Rooster Fair (early to mid-Nov., depending on the year). Night markets at Otori-jinja in Asakusa and Hanazono-jinja in Shinjuku. Ornately decorated *kumade* (rakes) are sold (to encourage the gods to help businesses rake in plenty of cash). A marvelous all-night street party, with stalls selling sake, noodles, and yakitori (broiled, skewered chicken).

DECEMBER
Hagoita Ichi (Dec. 17–19). A festive all-night market at Senso-ji Temple. *Hagoita* (battledores), faced with elaborate cloth bas-reliefs inspired from woodblock prints, are still sold here.

EXCURSIONS FROM TOKYO

APRIL
Kamakura Matsuri (2nd to 3rd Sun. in April). Focuses on the Tsurugaoka Hachiman-gu Shrine, and features dances and a parade of historical samurai figures. A *yabusame* (archery on horseback) contest in samurai regalia is an exciting highlight.

MAY
Sennin Gyoretsu (May 17–18). The festival at Tosho-gu Shrine in Nikko culminates with breath-taking pageantry, including a thousand men in samurai armor.

SEPTEMBER
Yabusame (Sept. 16). Tsurugaoka Hachiman-gu Shrine, Kamakura. The most exciting demonstration of yabusame (archery on horseback).

OCTOBER
Toshogu Matsuri (Oct. 17). Autumn Festival at Tosho-gu Shrine, Nikko, featuring a parade of mounted priests and samurai.

NOVEMBER
Daimyo Gyoretsu (Nov. 3). This costumed pageant evokes 17th-century processions of *daimyo* along the Tokaido road in Hakone-Yumoto.

HOKKAIDO

FEBRUARY
Yuki Matsuri—Snow Festival (early Feb.). World-famous Sapporo festival in which intricate and ornate snow sculptures decorate the center of the city.

NORTHERN HONSHU (TOHOKU)

FEBRUARY
Kamakura Matsuri (Feb. 15–16). This children's festival happens in several places, the most famous at Yokote, Akita-ken. It's named after the snow houses *(kamakura)* built for the event; children sit snugly in their candlelit igloos around a brazier for boiling sweet sake, which they offer around.

JUNE
Chaguchagu Umakko—Horse Festival (June 15). In Morioka, dealers and breeders parade their gaily decorated horses to be blessed at the Sozen Shrine.

AUGUST
Nebuta and **Neputa** (Aug. 1–7). These festivals, held at the same time in Aomori and Hirosaki, feature a spectacular parade of huge, beautifully painted, and ornate lanterns.

Kanto Matsuri (Aug. 4–7). Akita City. As the highlight of a rousing parade, men hold huge poles festooned with lanterns, balancing them on their hands, shoulders, chins, and foreheads.

DECEMBER
Namahage (Dec. 31). Held on the Oga-hanto Peninsula in Akita-ken. Groups of bachelors don demon costumes and go from house to house bellowing "Are there any rascals in here?" Residents entertain these *Namahage* with rice cakes and sake.

CENTRAL HONSHU (CHUBU)

MARCH
Tagata Honen Matsuri—Bumper Harvest Festival (March 15). One of Japan's 40-odd remaining phallic shrines, Tagata-jinja, near Inuyama, is renowned for this rousing festival, with a street parade of huge wooden phalli.

APRIL
Takayama Matsuri (April 14–15). This festival centers on Takayama's Hie Shrine. A splendid parade with 12 ornate *yatai*—wheeled juggernauts with performing *karakuri* automatons.

MAY
Cormorant fishing (season opens May 11). This fascinating (if these days purely touristic) activity can be seen on the Nagara River, Gifu-ken, almost nightly until Oct. 15. Birds have been trained to catch fish drawn to the surface by the light of braziers hanging from the boats.

OCTOBER
Takayama Hachimangu Matsuri (Oct. 9–10). Centered on Hachiman-gu Shrine, Takayama, this lively festival dating from the 15th century is renowned for its beautiful floats and *mikoshi*.

KANSAI

JANUARY
Toka Ebisu (Jan. 9–11). At Imamiya Ebisu Shrine in Osaka, thousands pay their respects to Ebisu, a god of plenty, and patron of business workers and fisher-

men. A parade of women in sumptuous kimono is carried aboard ornate palanquins.
Wakakasuyama-yaki (Jan. 15). The grass on Wakakasu-yama Hill (in Nara-koen Park) is burned to commemorate the ending of rivalry between two temples in the 10th century. Rousing celebrations and a spectacular fireworks display.

FEBRUARY
Mantoro—Lantern Lighting Ceremony (Feb. 3 or 4). This magical event takes place in Nara to usher in the spring. All 3,000 bronze and stone lanterns at Kasuga Taisha Shrine are lit.

MARCH
Omizutori—Water-drawing Ceremony (March 1–14). Performed annually at Todai-ji Temple in Nara, since the ninth century. The most exciting day is the 12th, when the water is drawn from the Wakasa Well as bearers swing huge torches producing showers of sparks, while priests blow conch shells.

MAY
Aoi Matsuri—Hollyhock Festival (May 15). Held at Shimo-gamo and Kami-gamo Shrines, Kyoto. With lavish costumes and rich pageantry commemorating visits by courtiers and priests.
Mifune Matsuri (3rd Sun. in May). Poets, musicians, and dancers in period costume perform aboard boats on the Oi River, at Arashiyama.

JUNE
Takigi Noh (June 1 & 2). A torch lit Noh performance, featuring some of the foremost protagonists of the art, in the open air at the Heian Shrine.
Rice Planting Ceremony (June 14). Sumiyoshi Shrine celebrates a rice planting ceremony led by 12 beauties.

JULY
Gion Matsuri (throughout July—parade July17). This famous festival commemorates the sudden end to a ninth-

century plague and centers on the Yasaka Shrine in Kyoto. The climax is a fantastic costumed parade.

AUGUST
Daimonji (Aug. 16). To the accompaniment of festivities and fireworks, the huge character *dai* (meaning "big") is etched in fire on the slope of Nyoiga-dake over the city of Kyoto.

OCTOBER
Jidai Matsuri—Eras Festival (Oct. 22). Heian Shrine, Kyoto. The highlight is a pageant celebrating the foundation of the city in 794, with costumes evoking that and later eras.

DECEMBER
Okera Mairi (Dec. 31). A huge bonfire is lit at midnight in Yasaka-jinja Shrine compound in Kyoto; everyone tries to take home kindling to start the first fire of the new year. Similar festivities are held at the same time at shrines throughout Japan

WESTERN HONSHU (CHUGOKU)

FEBRUARY
Eyo (3rd Sat. in Feb.). The most famous of the *hadaka matsuri* (naked festivals) held at several locations in Japan. In this one, at Saidai-ji Temple, Saidaiji, Okayama-ken, hundreds of youths wearing only loincloths compete within the confined space of a temple tower to catch two wands which, believed to guarantee a lifetime's good luck, are thrown down into the throng by priests. This is not open to the casual participant.

JUNE
Kangensai Music Festival (June 17—lunar calender, so the date changes annually). Displays of ancient court dances and music aboard ornate boats at Itsukushima Shrine, Miyajima.

AUGUST
Peace Ceremony (Aug. 6). Held in Hiroshima. Prayers for

the souls of the victims of the A-bomb.

OCTOBER
Kenka Matsuri—Fighting Festival (Oct. 14–15). At Matsubara-jinja, Himeji, groups of bearers compete to lead the parade and be first at the shrine, each trying to push over their rivals' huge *mikoshi;* fun, but can be dangerous.

SHIKOKU & THE SETO-NAIKAI

JULY
Warei Natsu Matsuri (July 23, 24). Firework displays, torchlit parades, and bullfights on Uwajima.

AUGUST
Awa-odori (Aug. 12–15). Costumed and carousing citizens of Tokushima are joined by thousands of visitors, to become the "dancing fools" partying in the city streets for four days.

KYUSHU

MAY
Hakata Dontaku (May 3–4) A colorful street parade in Fukuoka with costumed revelers attired as gods and demons, some on horseback.

JULY
Hakata Gion Yamakasa (July 1–15). The climax on the last day consists of teams of men racing huge floats representing castles, dolls, warriors, etc. through the streets in Fukuoka.

OCTOBER
O-Kunchi (Oct. 7–9). Focused on Suwa-jinja Shrine, Nagasaki. Highlights show strong Chinese influence (dragon dances), and some floats evoke historical contacts with Europe.

ILLUSTRATIONS CREDITS

Abbreviations for terms appearing below: (t) top; (b) bottom; (l) left; (r) right.

Cover: (tl), Corbis UK Ltd. (tr), Powerstock/Zefa. (bl), Corbis UK Ltd. (br), Pictor International. Spine, Powerstock/Zefa.

1, Ken Straiton. 2/3, Images Colour Library. 4, Chad Elders/Gettyone/ Stone. 9, Asian Art & Archaeology, Inc./Corbis UK Ltd. 11, Images Colour Library. 12/13, Kevin R. Morris/Corbis UK Ltd. 14/15, Kevin R. Morris/Corbis UK Ltd. 16/17, Ken Straiton. 17, Bon Color Photo Agency. 18, Karen Kasmauski/National Geographic Society. 19 Bon Color Photo Agency. 20/21, Images Colour Library. 22, Karen Kasmauski/ National Geographic Society. 23, P Essick/National Geographic Society. 24, Michael S. Yamashita/ Corbis UK Ltd. 24/25, Ken Straiton. 27, Bon Color Photo Agency. 29, Bon Color Photo Agency. 30/31, Michael S. Yamashita/Corbis UK Ltd. 33, Werner Forman Archive. 34/35, Bon Color Photo Agency. 37, Corbis UK Ltd. 38, Corbis UK Ltd. 39, David Samuel Robbins/Corbis UK Ltd. 40, National Geographic Society. 41, National Geographic Society. 43, Bon Color Photo Agency. 44, Ken Straiton. 45, Corbis UK Ltd. 46/47, Michael S. Yamashita/Corbis UK Ltd. 48/49, Farl & Nazima Kowall/Corbis UK Ltd. 50, Hiro Nogami/Q Photo International Inc. 51, Bon Color Photo Agency. 52(l), Tokyo National Museum. 52(r), Ken Straiton. 53, Corbis UK Ltd. 54/55, Sissie Brimberg/National Geographic Society. 56, Bon Color Photo Agency. 56/57, Michael S. Yamashita/Corbis UK Ltd. 59, Michael S. Yamashita/Corbis UK Ltd. 62/63, Ken Straiton. 64, Ken Straiton. 64/65, Bon Color Photo Agency. 67(t), Bon Color Photo Agency. 67(bl), Orion Press. 67(br), Ken Straiton. 68/69, Ken Straiton. 69, Ken Straiton. 70(t), Orion Press. 70(b), Ken Straiton. 71, Bon Color Photo Agency. 72/3, James Stanfield/National Geographic Society. 73, Bon Color Photo Agency. 75(tl), Robert Holmes/ Corbis UK Ltd. 75(tr), M. Glover/ Impact Photos. 75(b), M. Henley/ Impact Photos. 76, Orion Press. 77, Suntory Museum of Art. 78/79, Bon Color Photo Agency.

79, Wolfgang Kaehler/Corbis UK Ltd. 80/81, Ken Straiton. 81, Catherine Karnow/Corbis UK Ltd. 84, Ken Straiton. 85, Ken Straiton. 86, Ken Straiton. 86/87, Bon Color Photo Agency. 87, Ken Straiton. 88/89, Kevin R. Morris/Corbis UK Ltd. 89, Ken Straiton. 90(t), Ken Straiton. 90(b), Hiro Nogami/Q Photo International Inc. 91, Ken Straiton. 92, Jim Holmes/Axiom. 93, Jack Fields/Corbis UK Ltd. 94, Bon Color Photo Agency. 95, Ken Straiton. 97, Tokyo National Museum. 100, Ken Straiton. 101(t), John Dakers/Life File. 101(bl), Ken Straiton. 101(br), Ken Straiton. 102/103, Ken Straiton. 103, Ken Straiton. 104, Ken Straiton. 105, Orion Press. 106, Bon Color Photo Agency. 107, Ken Straiton. 108, Orion Press. 110, Bon Color Photo Agency. 111, Bon Color Photo Agency. 112/113, Ken Straiton. 114/115, Bon Color Photo Agency. 115, Dave Bartruff/Corbis UK Ltd. 116/117, Bon Color Photo Agency. 117, Orion Press. 118, James Davis Travel Photography. 119, Bon Color Photo Agency. 120(t), Bon Color Photo Agency. 120(b), Richard T. Nowitz/Corbis UK Ltd. 121, Gettyone/Stone. 122, Bon Color Photo Agency. 123, Orion Press. 124/125, Karen Kasmauski/ National Geographic Society. 126/127, Bruce Osborn. 129, Bon Color Photo Agency. 131, Orion Press. 132/133, Bon Color Photo Agency. 133, Orion Press. 134, Bon Color Photo Agency. 135, Bon Color Photo Agency. 136, Bon Color Photo Agency. 136/137, Bon Color Photo Agency. 138/139, Bon Color Photo Agency. 139, Bon Color Photo Agency. 140, Bon Color Photo Agency. 142/143, Orion Press. 142, Art Wolfe/ Gettyone/Stone. 143, Bon Color Photo Agency. 144/145, Bon Color Photo Agency. 146, Michael S. Yamashita/Corbis UK Ltd. 146/147, Ryuzo Toytaka/Q Photo International Inc. 148/149, Bon Color Photo Agency. 149, Bon Color Photo Agency. 150, James Nelson/Gettyone/Stone. 151, Image Bank. 152, Bon Color Photo Agency. 155, Ken Straiton. 156, Orion Press. 157, Bon Color Photo Agency. 159, Orion Press. 160/161, Orion Press. 162/163, Orion Press. 164/165, Ken Straiton. 166, Bon Color Photo Agency. 166/167, Michael S. Yamashita/Corbis UK Ltd. 168, Orion Press. 169, Orion Press. 171, Ken Straiton. 172, Mitchell Coster/Axiom. 174, Ken Straiton. 175, Ken Straiton.

176, Bon Color Photo Agency. 177, Ken Straiton. 178, Bon Color Photo Agency. 178/179, Bon Color Photo Agency. 180, Orion Press. 181, Ken Straiton. 182, Orion Press. 183, Bon Color Photo Agency. 184(t), Ken Straiton. 184(b), Ken Straiton. 185, Ken Straiton. 186/187, Bon Color Photo Agency. 187, Ken Straiton. 188, AA Photo Library/Douglas Corrance. 189, Bon Color Photo Agency. 190, Orion Press. 191(t), Ken Straiton. 191(b), Ken Straiton. 192, Ken Straiton. 193, Bon Color Photo Agency. 194, Bon Color Photo Agency. 194/195, Orion Press. 196, Bon Color Photo Agency. 197, Bon Color Photo Agency. 198, Bon Color Photo Agency. 199, Gettyone/Stone. 202/203, Nigel Hicks. 203, Bon Color Photo Agency. 204(l), Robert Holmes/Corbis UK Ltd. 204(r), Francesco Venturi; Kea Publishing Services Ltd./Corbis UK Ltd. 206, Images Colour Library. 207, Gettyone/Stone. 208, Jim Holmes/ Axiom. 209, Orion Press. 210/211, Bon Color Photo Agency. 211, Orion Press. 212, Orion Press. 212/213, Orion Press. 214, Ken Straiton. 214/215, Ken Straiton. 216/217, Ken Straiton. 218, Ken Straiton. 219, Orion Press. 220, Orion Press. 221(tl), Michael S. Yamashita/Corbis UK Ltd. 221(tr), Bon Color Photo Agency. 221(b), Bon Color Photo Agency. 222, Ken Straiton. 222/223, Ken Straiton. 224, Ken Straiton. 226/227, Michael Freeman/Corbis UK Ltd. 228, Bon Color Photo Agency. 230, Orion Press. 232, Ken Straiton. 233, Bon Color Photo Agency. 234/235, Orion Press. 235, Bon Color Photo Agency. 236, Bon Color Photo Agency. 237, Ken Straiton. 238(t), Paul A. Berry/Corbis UK Ltd. 238(b), Nik Wheeler/Corbis UK Ltd. 239, Orion Press. 240/241, Ken Straiton. 242/243, Bon Color Photo Agency. 244, Jim Holmes/Axiom. 245(tl), Nicholas DeVore/Gettyone/ Stone. 245(tr), Bon Color Photo Agency. 245(b), Karen Kasmauski/ National Geographic Society. 248, Ken Straiton. 249, Orion Press. 250, Ken Straiton. 251, Bon Color Photo Agency. 252/253, Bon Color Photo Agency. 253(t), Orion Press. 253(b), Michael S. Yamashita/Corbis UK Ltd. 254(t), Bon Color Photo Agency. 254(b), AA Photo Library/ Douglas Corrance. 255, Ken Straiton. 256(l), Ken Straiton. 256(r), Ken Straiton. 258/259, Bon Color Photo Agency. 260, Pacific Press Service. 261, Bon Color Photo Agency. 262, Bon Color Photo

Agency. 263, Bon Color Photo Agency. 264, Orion Press. 264/265, Bon Color Photo Agency. 266, Bon Color Photo Agency. 268, Bon Color Photo Agency. 269, Bon Color Photo Agency. 271, Steiner & Co./Graphic Communication Ltd. 272/273, Orion Press. 273, Orion Press. 274(t), Bon Color Photo Agency. 274(b), AA Photo Library/ Douglas Corrance. 275, Bon Color Photo Agency. 276, Bon Color Photo Agency. 277, Michael S. Yamashita/ Corbis UK Ltd. 278/279, Bon Color Photo Agency. 280, Bon Color Photo Agency. 281, Bon Color Photo Agency. 282, Orion Press. 284/285, Bon Color Photo Agency. 285, Orion Press. 286/287, Bon Color Photo Agency. 287, Orion Press. 288, Bon Color Photo Agency. 289, Jack Fields/ Corbis UK Ltd. 290, Orion Press. 291, Chad Elhers/Gettyone/ Stone. 293, Bon Color Photo Agency. 294, Bon Color Photo Agency. 295, Orion Press. 296(t), Michael S. Yamashita/ Corbis UK Ltd. 296(b), Bon Color Photo Agency. 297, The Purcell Team/ Corbis UK Ltd. 298, Bon Color Photo Agency. 299, Orion Press. 300, Orion Press. 301, Bruce Osborn/Ozone Inc. 302, Bon Color Photo Agency. 303, Bon Color Photo Agency. 304, AA Photo Library/Jim Holmes. 305, Ken Straiton. 306(t), Bon Color Photo Agency. 306(b), Ken Straiton. 307, Michael S. Yamashita/ Corbis UK Ltd. 308/309 Orion Press. 310, Bon Color Photo Agency. 311, Yann Arthus-Bertrand/Corbis UK Ltd. 312/313, Bon Color Photo Agency. 315, Bon Color Photo Agency. 317, Michael S. Yamashita/National Geographic Society. 318/319, Bon Color Photo Agency. 320, Bon Color Photo Agency. 321, Orion Press. 322, Bon Color Photo Agency. 323, Orion Press. 324/325, Michael S. Yamashita/National Geographic Society. 325, Bruce Osborn/Ozone Inc. 326/327, Q Photo International Inc. 327, AA Photo Library/Jim Holmes. 328/329, Orion Press. 328, Bon Color Photo Agency. 330/331, Bon Color Photo Agency. 332, Demitro Carrasco/Gettyone/Stone. 333, Paul Chesley/Gettyone/Stone. 334, Orion Press. 335, Bon Color Photo Agency. 336, Bon Color Photo Agency. 337, Orion Press. 338, Michael S. Yamashita/Corbis UK Ltd. 339, Bon Color Photo Agency. 341, Orion Press. 344, Pacific Press Service. 345, Ken Straiton. 347, Bon Color Photo Agency. 349, Bon Color Photo Agency.

Published by the National Geographic Society

John M. Fahey, Jr., *President and Chief Executive Officer*
Gilbert M. Grosvenor, *Chairman of the Board*
Nina D. Hoffman, *Executive Vice President*
William R. Gray, *Vice President and Director, Book Division*
Elizabeth L. Newhouse, *Director of Travel Publishing*
Cinda Rose, *Art Director*
Allan Fallow, *Senior Editor*
Barbara Noe, *Assistant Editor*
Caroline Hickey, *Senior Researcher*
Carl Mehler, *Director of Maps*
Joseph F. Ochlak, *Map Coordinator*
Carol B. Lutyk, Lise S. Sajewski, *Editorial Consultants*
Gary Colbert, *Production Director*
Richard S. Wain, *Production Project Manager*
Angela George, *Staff Assistant*

Edited and designed by AA Publishing (a trading name of Automobile Association Developments Limited, whose registered office is Norfolk House, Priestley Road, Basingstoke, Hampshire, England RG24 9NY. Registered number: 1878835).

Rachel Alder, *Project Manager*
David Austin, *Senior Art Editor*
Marilynne Lanng, *Senior Editor*
Phil Barfoot, *Designer*
Inna Nogeste, *Senior Cartographic Editor*
Richard Firth, *Production Director*
Steve Gilchrist, *Prepress Production Controller*
Cartography by AA Cartographic Production
Picture research by Zooid Pictures Ltd.
Cutaway illustrations drawn by Maltings Partnership, Derby, England

Library of Congress Cataloging-in- Publication Data
Bornoff Nicholas.
    National Geographic Traveler: Japan / Nicholas Bornoff
        p   cm
    Includes index.
    ISBN 0-7922-7563-2 (alk. paper)
    1. Japan—Guidebooks. 1. Title
    DC16.N37 1999
    914.404'839—dc21   98-54974
                                  CIP

Printed and bound by R.R. Donnelley & Sons, Willard, Ohio.
Color separations by Leo Reprographics, Hong Kong.
Cover separations by L.C. Repro, Aldermaston, U.K.
Cover printed by Miken Inc., Cheektowage, New York.

Visit the society's Web site at http://www.nationalgeographic.com

The information in this book has been carefully checked and to the best of our knowledge is accurate. However, details are subject to change, and the National Geographic Society cannot be responsible for such changes or for errors or omissions. Assessments of sites, hotels, and restaurants are based on the author's subjective opinions, which do not necessarily reflect the publisher's opinion. The publisher cannot be responsible for any consequences arising from the use of this book.

THE NATIONAL
GEOGRAPHIC TRAVELER

A Century of Travel Expertise
in Every Guide

- **Australia** ISBN: 0-7922-7431-8
- **California** ISBN: 0-7922-7564-0
- **Canada** ISBN: 0-7922-7427-X
- **The Caribbean** ISBN: 0-7922-7434-2
- **Costa Rica** ISBN: 0-7922-7946-8
- **Florida** ISBN: 0-7922-7432-6
- **France** ISBN: 0-7922-7426-1
- **Great Britain** ISBN: 0-7922-7425-3
- **Hawaii** ISBN: 0-7922-7944-1
- **Italy** ISBN: 0-7922-7562-4

- **Japan** ISBN: 0-7922-7563-2
- **London** ISBN: 0-7922-7428-8
- **Los Angeles** ISBN: 0-7922-7947-6
- **Miami and the Keys** ISBN: 0-7922-7433-4
- **New Orleans** ISBN: 0-7922-7948-4
- **New York** ISBN: 0-7922-7430-X
- **Paris** ISBN: 0-7922-7429-6
- **Rome** ISBN: 0-7922-7566-7
- **San Francisco** ISBN: 0-7922-7565-9
- **Sydney** ISBN: 0-7922-7435-0

AVAILABLE WHEREVER BOOKS ARE SOLD